The Other Founders

The Other

Published for the
Omohundro Institute of Early
American History and Culture,
Williamsburg, Virginia, by the
University of North Carolina Press,
Chapel Hill and London

Founders

ANTI-FEDERALISM

AND THE DISSENTING

TRADITION IN AMERICA,

1788–1828

BY SAUL CORNELL

The Omohundro

Institute of Early American

History and Culture is

sponsored jointly by the

College of William and

Mary and the Colonial

Williamsburg Foundation.

On November 15, 1996,

the Institute adopted the

present name in honor of

a bequest from Malvern H.

Omohundro, Jr.

© 1999
The University of North Carolina Press
All rights reserved
Set in Minion type by Keystone Typesetting, Inc.
Manufactured in the United States of America
Library of Congress Cataloging-in-Publication Data
Cornell, Saul.
The other founders : Anti-Federalism and the dissenting
tradition in America, 1788–1828 / Saul Cornell.
    p.   cm.
Includes bibliographical references and index.
ISBN 0-8078-2503-4 (alk. paper). —
ISBN 0-8078-4786-0 (pbk.: alk. paper)
1. United States—Politics and government—1783–1865.
2. Constitutional history—United States.   3. Federal
government—United States—History—18th century.
4. Federal government—United States—History—19th
century.   5. Dissenters—United States—History—18th
century.   6. Dissenters—United States—History—19th
century.   I. Omohundro Institute of Early American
History & Culture.   II. Title.
E310.C79   1999
320.473'049—dc21   99-13685
                            CIP

03   02   01   00   99   5   4   3   2   1

TO SUSAN, EMMA, AND JULIA

for filling the house with the sweet sounds of

laughter

ACKNOWLEDGMENTS

I can still recall the sense of excitement I felt when entering the New York Public Library as a high school student working on a paper for an Advanced Placement history class. The difficulty of becoming a professional historian has been to retain a small measure of that sense of wonder that first drew me to history while gaining some wisdom as a historian. Scholarship is often a solitary process. It is for precisely that reason that one becomes so dependent on family, friends, and colleagues to help one keep things in perspective.

I owe an enormous debt to my teachers in graduate school at the University of Pennsylvania, Richard Dunn, Bruce Kuklick, Jan Radway, and Mike Zuckerman. My dissertation adviser, Rick Beeman, has read many drafts of this project both as a dissertation and as a book manuscript. On many occasions in my professional career I have called upon Rick's sage advice. I have tried to take to heart Rick's injunction that, as graduate teachers, our responsibilities do not end after a dissertation is signed. The earliest phases of my research were helped by grants from the American Antiquarian Society and the John Carter Brown Library. While at those two venerable institutions I was lucky enough to benefit from the advice of John Hench, Norman Fiering, and Gordon Wood. My thinking about this book has profited from the lively discussions first begun while a graduate student at the University of Pennsylvania, and I feel particularly fortunate that the conversation has continued for more than ten years. Many graduate school friends have listened to me talk about this project and have read various incarnations of this study: Amy Bentley, Andy Bell, Alan Clements, Brett

Gary, John Gennari, Rick Halpern, Alan Karras, Alex Lichtenstein, Sybil Lipschultz, Peter Thompson, Barry Shank, and Shirley Wajda.

It is typical for young scholars to turn their dissertation into their first book. Of course, as more than one friend has observed over the years, I have developed a knack for never doing things the easy way. Although my dissertation explored the varieties of Anti-Federalist thought during ratification—a subject worthy of a book—this study considers a different problem: the role that Anti-Federalism played in the evolution of a dissenting tradition of political and constitutional thought over the first four decades of America's history. Much of the material in the dissertation appeared in article form, and individuals curious to see earlier formulations of my argument can easily track down those essays from the citations to them in the notes to this book.

A National Endowment for the Humanities postdoctoral fellowship at the Institute of Early American History and Culture provided the time to both expand and substantially alter my original project on Anti-Federalism. The Institute continues to approach its books like fine Bordeaux wines. I hope that the extra time that this one has spent in the cellar has mellowed the tannins and made the final product smoother and more complex. The staff of the Institute was extremely helpful during my stay in Williamsburg. As a young student at William and Mary, Thomas Jefferson became immersed in a lively intellectual circle in this charming provincial town. I was equally fortunate to have had the chance to share ideas with Kathy Brown, John Brooke, Bob and Ann Gross, Charles Hobson, Nancy Isenberg, Michael Kazin, Michael McGiffert, Ted Pearson, J. R. Pole, David Rabban, John Selby, and Chris Tomlins.

The appointment of Ron Hoffman as Director has brought renewed energy to the Institute, and his support has been crucial to the evolution of this endeavor. The detailed comments on my manuscript by Fredrika Teute, editor of publications, are extensive enough to merit publication as a separate volume. I feel especially fortunate to have completed this project while Jim Horn was visiting editor of publications. Jim's easygoing and supportive editorial guidance helped this project finally come to completion. Any author would be fortunate to have Gil Kelly work his editorial magic on the final text of the manuscript. I consider myself lucky to have been among those to benefit from his talents. A number of scholars read earlier drafts of the entire manuscript and provided detailed critiques, including Lance Banning, Michael Les Benedict, Richard Ellis, Peter Onuf, and Jack Rakove. Thad Tate read the dissertation and was the final reader before the manuscript went into production. His thoughtful suggestions and generous spirit provide a model of scholarly exchange at its best.

The ideas in this work have been refined in dozens of talks and conference presentations. Several of those occasions produced especially valuable insights. An invitation from Steve Conrad to talk at the Indiana University law school produced a lively discussion. On that occasion and on a subsequent visit to Bloomington, political theorist Russell Hanson helped me think about the relevance of the thought of Jürgen Habermas to my project. In the course of revising this manuscript I published several essays exploring the problems and potential of postmodern theory for historical analysis. Ultimately, the ideals of postmodernism proved less useful to this project than did the ideas of postmodernism's most trenchant critic, Habermas. Part of the advantage of publishing article-length think pieces is that they provide an important forum to test out ideas. Bill Nelson's legal history seminar at the New York University law school was another such venue. Over the course of two weeks, Nelson and his seminar read the entire manuscript and provided innumerable useful suggestions. Richard Bernstein, a participant in that seminar, went above and beyond the call of duty to provide a detailed critique of the manuscript. I presented some of the main themes of the book at two conferences at the University of Pennsylvania. On those different occasions I profited from the thoughtful remarks from John Murrin and Jack Greene. The participants in the Philadelphia Early American Seminar and the Columbia Early American Seminar also provided further guidance on how this project might be improved.

The grant of a Thomas Jefferson Chair in American Studies by the Fulbright Commission provided time to think about this project in the cafes of Leyden and Amsterdam. Sadly, I also spent eleven days thinking about the project when I was hospitalized for pneumonia at the end of that stay. The chairman of the Dutch Fulbright commission, Marcel Oomen, was extremely helpful during this unexpected crisis. My hosts at Leyden, Eduard van de Bilt and Joke Kardux, helped raise my spirits during this time and wandered the halls of the hospital with me, patiently listening to me ramble on about how to revise the manuscript.

The College of Humanities at the Ohio State University has provided funding to help complete this project. My colleagues at OSU have listened patiently while I worked through many of the final touches on this manuscript. My chairman, Mike Hogan, offered avuncular advice and helped me navigate through the maze of tenure. Other colleagues in the department of history have helped me on occasions too numerous to count, including

Ken Andrien, Steve Conn, David Hoffman, Margaret Newell, Carla Pestana, Nate Rosenstein, Randy Roth, Leila Rupp, and Birgitte Soland. Helpful suggestions were also offered by the participants in the Ohio Early American seminar: Drew and Mary Cayton, Elizabeth Renker, Grant Rice, and Mitchell Snay.

Graduate student assistance for various aspects of this project was provided by Phillip Adamo, Ray Irwin, and Barbara Terzian. I owe a particular debt to my research assistant, Charlie Finlay, who endured many conversations about the relative importance of Luther Martin and Federal Farmer over countless cups of espresso.

This work has built on the efforts of several ongoing documentary editing projects. For their generous assistance on numerous occasions, I would like to thank, in particular, the editors of the Documentary History of the Ratification of the Constitution, John P. Kaminski, Gaspare J. Saladino, and Richard Leffler.

My family has supported my career choice in too many ways to list, providing everything from chicken soup to state-of-the-art computer equipment. This project would have been impossible without their help. The ideal of the mendicant scholar is deeply rooted in the Jewish tradition, and I am glad to have contributed my small part to this noble ideal. I am sure that my interest in history was in part sparked by the books left lying around my room as a teenager, the tangible product of older brothers' exotic trips beyond the borders of Brooklyn to Strand bookstore and Barnes and Noble. My wife Susan's family has been extremely gracious about listening to me talk about Anti-Federalism at Christmas gatherings for more than a decade. The title for this book emerged out of one such Yuletime discussion. Tania Wilcke and Chris Abouzeid exceeded the bonds of family responsibility and friendship by reading early drafts of the book and providing a host of stylistic suggestions. My father-in-law Link Selleck would often send me clippings from the *Times Literary Supplement* about topics relevant to my project, and I wish that he might have lived to see it sit on his shelf next to so many other fine histories he collected and annotated.

My wife Susan has had to live with the Anti-Federalists longer than I had hoped. Her patience, good cheer, and proofreading skills were indispensable. My daughter Emma made good use of the draft copies of my manuscript for coloring and other important things. Her sister Julia will have to wait for another book to find such a seemingly endless supply of coloring paper.

CONTENTS

Acknowledgments, vii
List of Maps, xiii
List of Abbreviations and a Note on the Notes, xv

Introduction. The Other Founders, 1

PART I. ANTI-FEDERALISM AND THE CONSTITUTION

Chapter 1. Ratification and the Politics of the Public Sphere, 19
  The Dynamics of the Public Debate, 25
  The Anti-Federalist Critique, 26
  The Rhetoric of Ratification, 34
  Reading Politics and the Politics of Reading, 42

Chapter 2. Elite Anti-Federalist Political and Constitutional Thought, 51
  Constitutionalism, 54
  The Problem of Federalism and Localism, 61
  The Theory of the Small Republic, 68
  The Public Sphere, 74

Chapter 3. Popular Anti-Federalist Political and Constitutional Thought, 81
  Middling Constitutionalism, 85
  The Political Sociology of Middling Anti-Federalism, 96
  Centinel and Philadelphiensis: Voices of Radical Democracy, 99

Plebeian Populism, 107
The Carlisle Riot: The Constitutionalism of the Crowd, 109
Plebeian Radicalism and the Public Sphere, 114

Chapter 4. Courts, Conventions, and Constitutionalism:
The Politics of the Public Sphere, 121
The Oswald Libel Case of 1788, 128
The Aborted Second Convention Movement, 136

PART II. ANTI-FEDERALISM TRANSFORMED

Chapter 5. The Emergence of a Loyal Opposition, 147
The Debate over the Meaning of Representation, 147
Rats versus Antirats, 153
Anti-Federalism and the Politics of the First Congress, 157

Chapter 6. Anti-Federalist Voices within Democratic-Republicanism, 172
Hamiltonianism and the Democratic-Republican Opposition, 174
Strict Construction and the Original Understanding, 187

Chapter 7. The Limits of Dissenting Constitutionalism, 195
The Democratic-Republican Societies, 195
The Whiskey Rebellion, 200
Federalism versus Localist Democracy, 213

PART III. THE ANTI-FEDERALIST LEGACY

Chapter 8. The Founding Dialogue and the Politics of
Constitutional Interpretation, 221
The Irony of the Search for an Original Intent, 221
*The Sedition Act and the Transformation of Opposition
Constitutionalism,* 230
The Principles of '98, 237

Chapter 9. Democratic-Republican Constitutionalism and
the Public Sphere, 246
Public Opinion and Dissenting Political Thought, 246
Responses to the Alien and Sedition Crisis, 253
*The Anti-Federalist Blackstone: St. George Tucker and a
Democratic-Republican Jurisprudence,* 263

Chapter 10. The Dissenting Tradition, from the Revolution of 1800
    until Nullification, 274
    Clinton versus Madison, 275
    McCulloch v. Maryland *and the Collapse of the Madisonian
        Synthesis,* 278
    The Revival of Anti-Fedealism: Robert Yates's Secret Proceedings, 288
    Nullification and the Splintering of the Dissenting Tradition, 294
    Van Buren and the Anti-Federalist Mind, 298

Epilogue. Anti-Federalism and the American Political Tradition, 303

Appendix 1. Reprinting of Anti-Federalist Documents, 309
Appendix 2. Pamphlet, Broadside, and Periodical Republication of
    Anti-Federalist Documents, 316

Index, 319

MAP
Map 1. Ratification of the Constitution, 23

LIST OF ABBREVIATIONS AND
A NOTE ON THE NOTES

The primary sources that are the documentary foundation of all work in Anti-Federalism are dispersed in pamphlets, newspapers, and books that are out of print or in manuscript collections. Many of those sources have been collected in both *CA-F* and *DHRC* as well as in other sources listed below and in the notes. Generally in the notes I cite the first publication of such pieces, as of historical and bibliographical importance, and in following parentheses cite the modern source of it, for accessibility and convenience. Items in *CA-F* are grouped by author, items in *DHRC* are grouped chronologically, and there is much duplication from *CA-F* to *DHRC*. Which collection I cite in a specific instance is largely determined by convenience for the reader in consulting.

Annals of Congress: Joseph Gales, ed., *Debates and Proceedings in the First Congress . . .* , I (Washington, D.C., 1834)

CA-F: Herbert J. Storing, ed., *The Complete Anti-Federalist,* 7 vols. (Chicago, 1981).

DHFFC: Linda Grant De Pauw et al., eds., *Documentary History of the First Federal Congress of the United States of America, March 4, 1789–March 3, 1791,* 6 vols. (Baltimore, 1974).

DHFFE: Merrill Jensen et al., eds., *The Documentary History of the First Federal Elections, 1788–1790,* 4 vols. (Madison, Wis., 1976–1989).

DHRC: Merrill Jensen et al., eds., *The Documentary History of the Ratification of the Constitution,* 12 vols. to date (Madison, Wis., 1976–).

FJ: Freeman's Journal: or, the North-American Intelligencer (Philadelphia).
HSP: Historical Society of Pennsylvania, Philadelphia.
IG: Independent Gazetteer; or, the Chronicle of Freedom (Philadelphia).
JAH: Journal of American History.
LC: Library of Congress, Washington, D.C.
NYHS: New-York Historical Society, New York.
WMQ: William and Mary Quarterly.

The Other Founders

INTRODUCTION :

THE OTHER FOUNDERS

Suspicion of centralized authority has deep roots in American history. This distrust has generally been counterbalanced by a remarkable faith in the abilities of state and local governments. One of the great ironies of American history is that the Constitution was framed by the Federalists, the proponents of a stronger central government. Their opponents, the Anti-Federalists, were defeated in one of the greatest political struggles in American history. Ratification of the Constitution did not, however, eliminate Anti-Federalist ideas: localism continues to be a powerful force in American life. If the structure of American government was crafted by the Federalists, the spirit of American politics has more often been inspired by the Anti-Federalists. Indeed, the struggle between the Federalist Founders and the dissenting voices of the Anti-Federalists, the Other Founders of the American constitutional tradition, continues to define the nature of political life.[1]

No Anti-Federalist party emerged after the adoption of the Constitution. Yet, Anti-Federalist texts and rhetoric pervaded the expanding pub-

---

1. The inclusion of Anti-Federalism within the ranks of founders of the American constitutional tradition was greatly facilitated by the work of Herbert J. Storing's *Complete Anti-Federalist*. For other efforts to rehabilitate Anti-Federalist ideas, see Michael Lienesch, "In Defence of the Antifederalists," *History of Political Thought*, IV (1983), 65–87; Paul Finkelman, "Antifederalists: The Loyal Opposition and the American Constitution, *Cornell Law Review*, LXX (1984), 182–207. For a general discussion of the Anti-Federalist revival in contemporary scholarship, see Saul A. Cornell, "The Changing Historical Fortunes of the Anti-Federalists," *Northwestern University Law Review*, LXXXIV (1989), 39–74.

lic sphere of political and constitutional debate in the new Republic, and Anti-Federalism shaped the contours and limits of legitimate dissent within the American constitutional system for generations. Both Jeffersonian and Jacksonian political and constitutional thought owed an enormous debt to Anti-Federalism.[2]

Fortunately, the notion that the opponents of the Constitution were "men of little faith," narrow-minded politicians who lacked either the imagination or intellectual power to challenge their Federalist opponents (a view that once dominated scholarship), has been supplanted by more positive assessments of their contribution to the American political tradition. Diverse historians, political theorists, and legal scholars have come to view the Anti-Federalists as spokesmen for an important alternative constitutional heritage. Many scholars now concede that the Anti-Federalists might well have been more prescient than the victorious Federalists in describing the natural tendency of American constitutionalism to centralize authority.[3]

2. Historians are divided over the relevance of Anti-Federalism to Jeffersonianism. For examples of scholarship that downplays this connection, see Noble E. Cunningham, Jr., *The Jeffersonian Republicans: The Formation of Party Organization, 1789–1801* (Chapel Hill, N.C., 1957); Joseph Charles, *The Origins of the American Party System: Three Essays* (New York, 1961); William Nisbet Chambers, *Political Parties in a New Nation: The American Experience, 1776–1809* (New York, 1963); Mary P. Ryan, "Party Formation in the United States Congress, 1789 to 1796: A Quantitative Analysis," *WMQ*, 3d Ser., XXVIII (1971), 523–542; Stanley Elkins and Eric McKitrick, *The Age of Federalism* (New York, 1993). For scholars who stress the continuities between Anti-Federalism and Jeffersonianism, see John Zvesper, *Political Philosophy and Rhetoric: A Study of the Origins of American Party Politics* (New York, 1977); Lance Banning, *The Jeffersonian Persuasion: Evolution of a Party Ideology* (Ithaca, N.Y., 1978); Richard E. Ellis, "The Persistence of Antifederalism after 1789," in Richard Beeman, Stephen Botein, and Edward C. Carter II, eds., *Beyond Confederation: Origins of the Constitution and American National Identity* (Chapel Hill, N.C., 1987), 295–314; James Roger Sharp, *American Politics in the Early Republic: The New Nation in Crisis* (New Haven, Conn., 1993). On the connections to Jacksonianism, see Richard E. Ellis, *The Union at Risk: Jacksonian Democracy, States' Rights, and the Nullification Crisis* (New York, 1987).

3. Cecelia M. Kenyon, "Men of Little Faith: The Anti-Federalists on the Nature of Representative Government," *WMQ*, 3d Ser., XII (1955), 3–43. On the prescience of Anti-Federalist views of the tendency of the federal system to move toward a more centralized system, see Harry N. Scheiber, "Federalism and the Constitution: The Original Understanding," in Lawrence M. Friedman and Harry N. Scheiber, eds., *American Law and the Constitutional Order: Historical Perspectives* (Cambridge, Mass., 1978), 85–98; for other scholars who argue that the Anti-Federalists might have been more right than wrong, see Akhil Reed Amar, "Anti-Federalists, 'The Federalist' Papers, and the Big Argument," *Harvard Journal of Law and Public Policy*, XVI (1993), 111–118; Charles J. Cooper, "Independent of Heaven Itself:

Interest in Anti-Federalism among modern scholars has exploded. Writers on the political left have applauded its followers for their democratic ideals. The modern political right has praised their hostility to centralized government, particularly their suspicion of a powerful federal judiciary. Libertarians have extolled their defense of individual rights while communitarians have commended their emphasis on civic participation and community.[4]

The revival of interest in the Anti-Federalists has been intensified by the debates in contemporary American jurisprudence about interpreting the Constitution according to the original intent of either the framers or the ratifiers of the Constitution. Judges and lawyers who might have once limited their investigations to *The Federalist* now routinely invoke the authority of Anti-Federalists, particularly with regard to the original understanding of the Bill of Rights.[5]

Different Federalist and Anti-Federalist Perspectives on the Centralizing Tendency of the Federal Judiciary," *Harvard Journal of Law and Public Policy,* XVI (1993), 119–128.

4. On the democratic legacy of Anti-Federalism, see Kenneth M. Dolbeare and John F. Manley, eds., *The Case against the Constitution: From the Antifederalists to the Present* (Armonk, N.Y., 1987); Jennifer Nedelsky, "Confining Democratic Politics: Anti-Federalists, Federalists, and the Constitution," *Harvard Law Review,* XCVI (1982), 340–360. For a modern critique of excessive centralization that invokes the Anti-Federalist legacy, see Gary L. McDowell, "Were the Anti-Federalists Right? Judicial Activism and the Problem of Consolidated Government," *Publius,* XII, no. 3 (Summer 1982), 99–108. Justice William H. Rehnquist's jurisprudence has also been described as essentially Anti-Federalist/Jeffersonian: see Jeff Powell, "The Compleat Jeffersonian: Justice Rehnquist and Federalism," *Yale Law Journal,* XCI (1982), 1317–1370. On privacy, see David A. J. Richards, "Constitutional Legitimacy and Constitutional Privacy," *New York University Law Review,* LXI (1986), 800–862; on communitarianism, see H. N. Hirsch, "The Threnody of Liberalism: Constitutional Liberty and the Renewal of Community," *Political Theory,* XIV (1986), 423–449; Cass R. Sunstein, "The Enduring Legacy of Republicanism," in Stephen L. Elkin and Karol Edward Soltan, eds., *A New Constitutionalism: Designing Political Institutions for a Good Society* (Chicago, 1993), 174–206.

5. On the doctrine of originalism, see Jack N. Rakove, ed., *Interpreting the Constitution: The Debate over Original Intent* (Boston, 1990). The Supreme Court has traditionally favored the perspective of Federalists, not Anti-Federalists: see James G. Wilson, "The Most Sacred Text: The Supreme Court's Use of 'The Federalist' Papers," *Brigham Young University Law Review,* LXV (1985), 65–135. For examples of recent Supreme Court opinions that have invoked the Anti-Federalists, see Lewis Powell, dissent in *Garcia v. San Antonio Metropolitan Transit Authority et al.,* 469 U.S. 569 (1984); and Clarence Thomas, concurrence in *McIntyre v. Ohio Elections Commission,* 514 U.S. 334 (1995). Efforts to strengthen congressional oversight of foreign affairs have been characterized as Anti-Federalist by Lawrence J. Block and David B. Rivkin, Jr., "Legislative Power Grab: The Anti-Federalist Counter-Revolution in the Making," letter, *New York Review of Books,* May 17, 1990, 50–52, and "The Battle

Legal scholars have sought the original intent of Anti-Federalists on a variety of constitutional questions. Anti-Federalist texts have been scoured for clues to the original meaning of nearly every aspect of the Bill of Rights. Even judges and scholars opposed to the philosophy of originalism acknowledge that both sides in the original debate have something to contribute to our understanding of American constitutionalism.[6]

Interest in the Anti-Federalist legacy has not been restricted to the pages of prestigious law reviews and the chambers of Supreme Court justices but has spilled over into popular political culture. References to the Anti-Federalists occur on the Internet. The Anti-Federalists have been invoked by the self-styled citizen militia organizations whose suspicion of government further illustrates the paranoid style of American politics. Just as the fringe elements of the original Anti-Federalist coalition feared that the Constitution might make the pope president, contemporary politics has generated its own political paranoia. In post-Reagan America the analogue of those fears usually takes the form of concern about government conspiracies to repress information about alien contact.[7]

---

to Control the Conduct of Foreign Intelligence and Covert Operations: The Ultra-Whig Counterrevolution Revisited," *Harvard Journal of Law and Public Policy,* XII (1989), 303–355. The movement for term limits has also been characterized as essentially Anti-Federalist; see Garry Wills, "Undemocratic Vistas," *New York Review of Books,* Nov. 19, 1992, 28–34; Troy Andrew Eid and Jim Kolbe, "The New Anti-Federalism: The Constitutionality of State-Imposed Limits on Congressional Terms of Office," *Denver University Law Review,* LXIX (1992), 1–56.

6. Legal scholarship has embraced the perspective of the Anti-Federalists even more enthusiastically. A Lexis search of writing in law reviews revealed 548 references to Anti-Federalists as compared to 674 references to the Federalists in the period 1982–1995. See Gary L. McDowell, "Federalism and Civic Virtue: The Antifederalists and the Constitution," in Robert A. Goldwin and William A. Schambra, eds., *How Federal Is the Constitution?* (Washington, D.C., 1987), 122–144. For a good sample of the effort to explore an alternative Anti-Federalist constitutionalism, see Calvin R. Massey, "Antifederalism and the Ninth Amendment," *Chicago-Kent Law Review,* LXIV (1988), 987–1000, and "The Anti-Federalist Ninth Amendment and Its Implications for State Constitutional Law," *Wisconsin Law Review,* 1990, 1229–1266. For an effort to rethink the meaning of the Bill of Rights in Anti-Federalist terms, see Akhil Reed Amar, "The Bill of Rights as Constitution," *Yale Law Journal,* C (1991), 1131–1210. For a good example of a nonoriginalist who has explored the meaning of Anti-Federalist jurisprudence, see David A. J. Richards, *Foundations of American Constitutionalism* (New York, 1989).

7. Richard Hofstadter, *The Paranoid Style in American Politics* (New York, 1965). A number of right-wing populist movements in the post-Reagan era, including the self-styled militia, have invoked Anti-Federalism. On right-wing populist movements in American history, see Catherine McNicol Stock, *Rural Radicals: Righteous Rage in the American Grain*

Perhaps the most visible manifestation of how the ideas of the Anti-Federalists have moved from the margins of American political discourse to the center is the frequency with which their writings are now reprinted and anthologized. The incorporation of Anti-Federalist texts into the canon of American constitutional history and political thought has given their ideas new legitimacy.[8]

Although there has been a renewal of interest in Anti-Federalist ideas, the prevailing scholarly paradigms that have tried to explain this complex movement have collapsed under the weight of their own contradictions. Neo-Progressive claims that Anti-Federalism represented the voice of an insurgent agrarian democracy have failed to explain why several of the most sophisticated and influential Anti-Federalist writers espoused the views of a rising middling sort whose vision of democracy was tied to commerce. Nor can the Progressive paradigm explain the centrality of the writings of a small but exceedingly important group of elite Anti-Federalists who were neither democratic nor exclusively agrarian. Perhaps the greatest irony associated with the neo-Progressive vision is that it has actually obscured the ideals of the most radical voice within Anti-Federalism, that of plebeian populists.[9]

For many legal scholars, Anti-Federalism provides evidence of a liber-

---

(Ithaca, N.Y., 1996). On contemporary militia movements, see David C. Williams, "The Militia Movement and the Second Amendment Revolution: Conjuring with the People," *Cornell Law Review,* LXXXI (1996), 879–952. The notion of a government conspiracy involving the suppression of alien contact has become a major theme in popular culture during the 1990s; the best example of this is the popular television show *The X-Files:* see David Lavery, Angela Hague, and Marla Cartwright, eds., *Deny All Knowledge: Reading the X-Files* (Syracuse, N.Y., 1996).

8. Some sense of which Federalist and Anti-Federalist texts are considered most important to contemporary scholars can be gleaned from modern anthologies. See J. R. Pole, ed., *The Constitution—for and against: "The Federalist" and Anti-Federalist Papers* (New York, 1987); Michael Kammen, ed., *The Origins of the American Constitution: A Documentary History* (New York, 1986); Ralph Ketcham, *The Anti-Federalist Papers; and, The Constitutional Convention Debates* (New York, 1986); Philip B. Kurland and Ralph Lerner, eds., *The Founders' Constitution,* 5 vols. (Chicago, 1987). The most exhaustive and complete collection of materials is the ongoing editorial project, begun by Merrill Jensen, *The Documentary History of the Ratification of the Constitution.* The best short anthology is Bernard Bailyn's collection, which drew on the material collected in the *DHRC* volumes: Bailyn, ed., *The Debate on the Constitution,* 2 vols. (New York, 1993).

9. The neo-Progressive interpretation was most fully developed in Jackson Turner Main, *The Anti-Federalists: Critics of the Constitution, 1781–1788* (Chapel Hill, N.C., 1961). For another influential example, see Ellis, *The Union at Risk.*

tarian heritage. This view has been challenged by those who cast the Anti-Federalists as conservative proponents of states' rights with little interest in personal freedom. Thus, Anti-Federalist ideas can be marshaled to support the agenda of the American Civil Liberties Union or the Republican party. Neither of those interpretations helps us understand how Anti-Federalists sought to reconcile the contradictions between their concern for liberty and their commitment to the rights of the people to legislate on behalf of the good of the community. When Anti-Federalist ideas are wrenched out of their historical context, it is easy to lose sight of the way in which federalism and individual rights were linked in the minds of the opponents of the Constitution. Cast in modern terms, states' rights and individual rights were not antithetical in Anti-Federalist constitutionalism, but intimately bound together.[10]

For constitutional scholars and political theorists, the debate between Federalists and Anti-Federalists has generally been cast as a founding dialogue. According to this model, the Federalists and Anti-Federalists each represent a single coherent constitutional or political theory. The interpretive assumptions of modern constitutional scholarship and political theory place a strong emphasis on coherence and complexity. Seeking a comparable voice to match the philosophical sophistication of Publius in *The Federalist* has led scholars to focus their attention on the most articulate and intellectually rigorous Anti-Federalist authors.[11]

10. Libertarian readings of Anti-Federalism have been Whiggish; see Richards, *Foundations of American Constitutionalism*. The classic states' rights and decidedly anti-Whig historian is Leonard W. Levy, in *Original Intent and the Framers' Constitution* (New York, 1988). For a discussion of the limits of Whig and anti-Whig constitutional history, see Saul Cornell, "Moving beyond the Canon of Traditional Constitutional History: Anti-Federalists, the Bill of Rights, and the Promise of Post-Modern Historiography," *Law and History Review*, XII (1994), 1–28.

11. The revival of interest in the quality of Anti-Federalist political thought has been greatly facilitated by the publication of Storing's *Complete Anti-Federalist*. The bicentennial of the Constitution produced an explosion of scholarship. For efforts to chart this vast literature, see Peter S. Onuf, "Reflections on the Founding: Constitutional Historiography in Bicentennial Perspective," *WMQ*, 3d Ser., XLVI (1989), 341–375. The impact of the bicentennial on law review literature was even more profound; for an overview, see Richard B. Bernstein, "Charting the Bicentennial," *Columbia Law Review*, LXXXVII (1987), 1565–1624. The dangers of seeking coherence in theorists who might not have been as philosophically consistent are explored by Quentin Skinner, "Meaning and Understanding in the History of Ideas," in James Tully, ed., *Meaning and Context: Quentin Skinner and His Critics* (Princeton, N.J., 1988), 29–67. The contradictions and tensions in political theories are a central concern of "conceptual history"; on this point, see Terence Ball, James Farr, and Russell L.

There are a number of reasons why the debate between Anti-Federalists and Federalists has been cast as a dialogue. During ratification many authors on both sides of this struggle derived considerable advantage from homogenizing and demonizing their opponents. After ratification, Democratic-Republicans deliberately sought to link Anti-Federalist objections with Federalist assurances as a means of restraining the excesses of Hamiltonianism. By casting ratification as a founding dialogue, Jeffersonians were able to keep alive a number of Anti-Federalist concerns. Once we recognize that the idea of a founding dialogue was itself a historical construction, we can move beyond this metaphor and expose the complex realities of ratification and understand the evolution of a distinctive dissenting tradition of constitutional thought.

Historians have been more attuned than either constitutional scholars or political theorists to the diversity of Anti-Federalism. Yet, even when they have noted it, historians have invariably sought an authoritative Anti-Federalist position, focusing on a single strain of Anti-Federalism as an expression of the true voice of the opposition to the Constitution. In most instances historical scholarship has not been driven by the need to establish a coherent political or constitutional theory, but instead has been governed by the need to construct a metanarrative in which the struggle over the Constitution is viewed as a watershed in the development of American political life. Thus, different scholars have linked Anti-Federalism to the rise of democracy, the decline of republicanism, and the emergence of liberalism.[12]

A few scholars have recognized the diversity of Anti-Federalism and acknowledged that those differences were emblematic of the wide range of

---

Hanson, eds., *Political Innovation and Conceptual Change* (Cambridge, 1989); Ball and J. G. A. Pocock, *Conceptual Change and the Constitution* (Lawrence, Kans., 1988). Jack N. Rakove, *Original Meanings: Politics and Ideas in the Making of the Constitution* (New York, 1996), relies primarily on the most systematic thinkers, Federal Farmer and Brutus.

12. On the notion of metanarrative, see Robert F. Berkhofer, Jr., *Beyond the Great Story: History as Text and Discourse* (Cambridge, Mass., 1995). The most important metanarrative in early American history has been aptly characterized by John M. Murrin as "the Great Transition Debate." This metanarrative combines the Progressive historians' search for the roots of American democracy, the new social history's search for the origins of capitalism, and debates about the influence of liberal and republican ideas in American culture; see Murrin, "Self-interest Conquers Patriotism: Republicans, Liberals, and Indians Reshape the Nation," in Jack P. Greene, ed., *The American Revolution: Its Character and Limits* (New York, 1987), 224–229. For one effort to relate Anti-Federalism to the great transition debate, see Gordon S. Wood, "Ideology and the Origins of Liberal America," *WMQ*, 3d Ser., XLIV (1987), 628–640, and more fully in *The Radicalism of the American Revolution* (New York, 1992).

intellectual and political beliefs available to Americans during the Revolutionary generation. This pluralist model represents a significant improvement over monolithic treatments of Anti-Federalism, acknowledging that Americans drew from civic republicanism, liberalism, Protestantism, and the traditions of English common law.[13]

Although appealing in some respects, pluralism does not explain the elasticity of political language: the way the same terms were used in strikingly different ways by various authors. Nor does it make clear the degree to which public debate was not an ideal speech situation in which all ideas competed equally. Certain ideas were more easily articulated in the languages available to authors, whereas others proved more difficult to frame in compelling terms. Most modern commentators have been inclined to the view that the Anti-Federalists lost because they had the weaker argument. Few commentators have recognized that Anti-Federalists might have had the more difficult argument to make.[14]

This study explores the evolution of a dissenting public discourse about politics and constitutionalism. In contrast to the approach of traditional political history or constitutional history, I have concentrated on how this

13. For the best example of the range of views on how to characterize the ideology of Federalists and Anti-Federalists, see the contributions to *"The Creation of the American Republic, 1776–1787:* A Symposium of Views and Reviews," *WMQ,* 3d Ser., XLIV (1987), 549–640. For pluralist accounts, see Isaac Kramnick, "The Discourse of Politics in 1787: The Constitution and Its Critics on Individualism, Community, and the State," in Herman Belz, Ronald Hoffman, and Peter J. Albert, eds., *To Form a More Perfect Union: The Critical Ideas of the Constitution* (Charlottesville, Va., 1992), 166–216. In Kramnick's view, republican, liberal, Protestant, Enlightenment, and jurisprudential idioms were all important to Anti-Federalism. For another important effort to cast the Anti-Federalists in pluralist terms, see Michael Lienesch, *New Order of the Ages: Time, the Constitution, and the Making of Modern American Political Thought* (Princeton, N.J., 1988).

14. Although Herbert J. Storing devoted most of his study of Anti-Federalist thought to identifying what was "fundamental" to Anti-Federalism, he concluded that Anti-Federalists lost the battle over ratification because they were unable to reconcile the contradictions in their constitutional thought (*What the Anti-Federalists Were For* [Chicago, 1981], 6, 71). The notion of an ideal speech situation, in which political thought is free from ideological distortion, is central to the critical theory of Jürgen Habermas. For an application of Habermas's concept to the political thought of the founding era, see Russell L. Hanson, *The Democratic Imagination in America: Conversations with Our Past* (Princeton, N.J., 1985). The problem of distorted communication is also central to the work of scholars influenced by the work of Antonio Gramsci; for a useful introduction to the implications of Gramsci's work for historians, see T. J. Jackson Lears, "The Concept of Cultural Hegemony: Problems and Possibilities" *American Historical Review,* XC (1985), 567–93.

evolving tradition was shaped by a constantly shifting set of texts that defined what Anti-Federalism meant at various moments. Whereas older approaches have tended to homogenize and reify Anti-Federalism, assuming that it was an unchanging construct, I have tried to show the persistence of certain themes while demonstrating how this tradition was evolving and being constantly reshaped. It is a truism in detective fiction that a good sleuth follows the money trail. In analogous fashion, I have chosen to follow the trail of Anti-Federalist texts.[15]

Focusing on the way particular texts circulated within a public sphere that was defined largely by the world of print should not lead to the view that the structure of debate was exclusively discursive. Following the textual trail does not supplant the approach of political and social historians, but supplements their work. It is impossible to understand the distribution and republication of Anti-Federalist texts without some appreciation of the economic and political factors shaping these cultural processes.[16]

15. The methods of French scholars working on the history of the book are discussed by Roger Chartier, "Intellectual History or Sociocultural History? The French Trajectories," in Dominick LaCapra and Steven L. Kaplan, eds., *Modern European Intellectual History: Reappraisals and New Perspectives* (Ithaca, N.Y., 1982), 13–46; and Chartier, "Texts, Printing, Readings," in Lynn Hunt, ed., *The New Cultural History* (Berkeley, Calif., 1989), 154–175; and see also Robert Darnton, "History of Reading," in Peter Burke, ed., *New Perspectives on Historical Writing* (University Park, Pa., 1991), 140–167. On the history of the book in America, see David D. Hall and John B. Hench, eds., *Needs and Opportunities in the History of the Book: America, 1639–1876* (Worcester, Mass., 1987); Cathy N. Davidson, ed., *Reading in America: Literature and Social History* (Baltimore, 1989). For discussions of reader response, see Wolfang Iser, "The Reading Process: A Phenomenological Approach," *New Literary History*, III (1972), 279–299; Hans Robert Jauss, *Toward an Aesthetic of Reception*, trans. Timothy Bahti (Minneapolis, Minn., 1982); Stanley Fish, *Is There a Text in This Class? The Authority of Interpretive Communities* (Cambridge, Mass., 1980). For more general discussions, see Robert C. Holub, *Reception Theory: A Critical Introduction* (London, 1984). On the ethnography of reading, see Janice A. Radway, *Reading the Romance: Women, Patriarchy, and Popular Literature* (Chapel Hill, N.C., 1984); Elizabeth Long, "Women, Reading, and Cultural Authority: Some Implications of the Audience Perspective in Cultural Studies," *American Quarterly*, XXXVIII (1986), 591–612. On the notion of discursive community, see David A. Hollinger, *In the American Province: Studies in the History and Historiography of Ideas* (Bloomington, Ind., 1985).

16. Two useful studies of the dynamics of the various state ratification contests suggest that no single explanatory model can account for the complex dynamics of ratification in particular states: Patrick T. Conley and John P. Kaminski, eds., *The Constitution and the States: The Role of the Original Thirteen in the Framing and Adoption of the Federal Constitution* (Madison, Wis., 1988); Michael Allen Gillespie and Michael Lienesch, eds., *Ratifying the Constitution* (Lawrence, Kans., 1989).

In a sense every Anti-Federalist text was a commentary on the metatext that defined this debate—the Constitution of the United States. In the period between 1788 and 1828, Americans devoted an enormous amount of time and energy to proving that their particular interpretations of that text were correct. Once published, a particular essay might provoke a variety of responses. New readings and misreadings proliferated in direct proportion to the importance of the constitutional topic being investigated. Identifying exactly which texts shaped public debate and exploring the various interpretive strategies different readers used to make sense of those texts has a number of advantages over the approaches that previous scholarship followed.[17]

If all Anti-Federalist texts are weighted equally, the din of different voices does seem cacophonous. Weighting texts according to their influence in their time, however, reveals a clear, consistent Anti-Federalist critique. It seems somewhat ironic that historians and lawyers interested in the original debate over the Constitution have generally relied on the most thoughtful, not the most representative, voices to construct a historical portrait of ratification. The public sphere of print culture was not a democratic town meeting. Some Anti-Federalist texts circulated more widely and were therefore better able to shape public discussion of the Constitution. Except for the common world of print, there was little, if anything, to unite the diverse groups who opposed the Constitution. Planter aristocrats, middling politicians, and backcountry farmers were bound together by the tenuous connection provided by the world of print.[18]

17. For a discussion of a variety of theoretical issues about reader-response theory and intertextuality, see Saul Cornell, "Early American History in a Postmodern Age," *WMQ*, 3d Ser., L (1993), 329–342, and "Splitting the Difference: Textualism, Contextualism, and Post-Modern History," *American Studies*, XXXVI (1995), 57–80.

18. On the notion of the public sphere, see Jürgen Habermas, *The Structural Transformation of the Public Sphere: An Inquiry into a Category of Bourgeois Society,* trans. Thomas Burger and Frederick Lawrence (Cambridge, Mass., 1989). For discussions, elaborations, and critiques of Habermas's original formulation of this concept, see Peter Stallybrass and Allon White, *The Politics and Poetics of Transgression* (Ithaca, N.Y., 1986); Michael Warner, *The Letters of the Republic: Publication and the Public Sphere in Eighteenth-Century America* (Cambridge, Mass., 1990); Craig Calhoun, ed., *Habermas and the Public Sphere* (Cambridge, Mass., 1992). For a sophisticated discussion of the nature of the public sphere in early American history, see John L. Brooke, "Ancient Lodges and Self-Created Societies: Voluntary Association and the Public Sphere in the Early Republic," in Ronald Hoffman and Peter J. Albert, eds., *Launching the "Extended Republic": The Federalist Era* (Charlottesville, Va., 1996), 273–359. My reading of Anti-Federalism and the public sphere has been influenced by Jürgen Habermas, *Between Fact and Norms: Contributions to a Discourse Theory of Law and Democracy,* trans. William Rehg (Cambridge, Mass., 1996).

Although print provided the glue that held the Anti-Federalist coalition together, it is important not to lose sight of the structure of power within the federal system. The nature of federalism created a problematic that all opponents of the Constitution were forced to grapple with: how to preserve the autonomy of the states and localities within a federal system that would command citizen allegiance. The difficulty was how to achieve this goal without endowing a strong central government with considerable coercive authority.

Anti-Federalists agreed on the need to resist greater centralization of authority. Their response included three components: federalism, constitutional textualism, and support for a vigorous public sphere of political debate. In contrast to their Federalist opponents, Anti-Federalists continued to place their faith in a federal system in which the states would be the primary units of political organization and contain the bulk of political authority. Anti-Federalists also insisted that constitutional texts be written in precise terms, including explicit limits on the scope of federal authority. This reverence for constitutional texts written in a plain style was connected to a distinctive approach to constitutional interpretation that construed such texts almost literally. Finally, to cement the nation together and ensure that federalism and textualism would function to protect liberty, Anti-Federalists championed an expanded public sphere of political discourse.

The first part of this study explores the dynamics of the public debate over the Constitution and the range of Anti-Federalist constitutional thought. A relatively small number of texts actually shaped public discussion. They were not, in most cases, the ones that have figured prominently in modern discussions of Anti-Federalism. Interpreting Anti-Federalist texts also requires a new appreciation for the rhetorical context in which authors made particular arguments. Rhetoric not only provides important clues about an author's intent but also reveals much about the intended audience. Although some authors crafted their writing to appeal to republican citizens and consciously avoided appealing to particular classes, many authors addressed their writing to an elite, middling, or plebeian audience. Once their texts entered the public sphere, however, authors no longer controlled how they were read. The response of actual readers often defied the expectations of authors.

Having determined exactly which Anti-Federalist texts set the terms of public debate during ratification, it is important that one consider in greater detail the range of political theories and constitutional philosophies espoused by different Anti-Federalist authors. A common critique of the Constitution did not mean that all Anti-Federalists shared political ideals: the same language might express different political visions. The more decentralized vision of federalism championed by opponents of the Constitution provided a broad canopy under which planter aristocrats and middling politicians might each preserve their own different visions of politics. The one group whose vision was not easily accommodated within this state-centered theory of federalism was plebeian populists, whose radical localism actually threatened the power of state government. Without some appreciation for the way social class shaped the public debate over the Constitution, it is impossible to understand the nature of Anti-Federalism.[19]

Recognizing the different visions of elites and middling Anti-Federalists makes it possible to appreciate the way in which plebeian radicalism actually forced Anti-Federalists into a more moderate stance toward the Constitution. Anti-Federalist writing was not only self-conscious about the problem of social class, but the class dynamics within the Anti-Federalist coalition shaped how opposition evolved after ratification. Instead of developing an anti-constitutional tradition, elite and middling Anti-Federalists chose to work within the system created by the Constitution and create a loyal opposition.[20]

19. Two systematic efforts to explore Anti-Federalist constitutionalism are Storing, ed., *The Complete Anti-Federalist;* and the work of Murray Dry: "The Case against Ratification: Anti-Federalist Constitutional Thought," in Leonard W. Levy and Dennis J. Mahoney, eds., *The Framing and Ratification of the Constitution,* 271–291; "The Anti-Federalists and the Constitution," in Robert L. Utley, Jr., ed., *Principles of the Constitutional Order: The Ratification Debates* (Lanham, Md., 1989), 63–88; "The Debate over Ratification of the Constitution," in Jack P. Greene and J. R. Pole, eds., *The Blackwell Encyclopedia of the American Revolution* (London, 1991), 471–486. Neither Storing nor Dry shows much interest in the role that social class played in shaping Anti-Federalist constitutional thought. In part, this approach reflects their debt to the philosopher Leo Strauss. On the role of Straussians in interpreting the political thought of the founding period, see Gordon S. Wood, "The Fundamentalists and the Constitution," *New York Review of Books,* Feb. 18, 1988, 33–40. The problem of class is central to the work of a number of legal historians associated with Critical Legal Studies and the Law and Society Movement. For a concise overview of these two approaches to law, see William W. Fischer III, "The Development of Modern American Legal Theory and the Judicial Interpretation of the Bill of Rights," in Michael J. Lacey and Knud Haakonssen, eds., *A Culture of Rights: The Bill of Rights in Philosophy, Politics, and Law—1791 and 1991* (Cambridge, 1991), 266–365. On the notion of writing legal history from the bottom up, see William E. Forbath, Hendrik Hartog, and Martha Minow, "Introduction: Legal Histories from Below," *Wisconsin Law Review,* 1985, 759–766. Hartog advises legal historians to look at the legal consciousness of nonelites and focus on the meaning of law as a contested terrain. See also Hartog, "Pigs and Positivism," *Wisconsin Law Review,* 1985, 899–935. For a discussion of the relevance of this approach to constitutional history, see Hartog, "The Constitution of Aspiration and the 'Rights That Belong to Us All,'" *JAH,* LXXIV (1987–1988), 1013–1034.

20. The work of E. P. Thompson is crucial to understanding the nature of Anglo-

Part II charts the role of Anti-Federalist ideas in the emergence of Democratic-Republicanism. Ironically, the demise of Anti-Federalism as a political movement and ideology facilitated a revival of a number of Anti-Federalist constitutional ideas. Although Jefferson and Madison had never been Anti-Federalists, some of the most important dissenting voices in the 1790s had been vehement opponents of the Constitution in 1788. Madison's own evolving constitutional thought drew important lessons from the opponents of the Constitution. He recast those Anti-Federalist ideas and used them as part of his own effort to formulate a coherent alternative to Federalist constitutional theory.[21]

At the end of the decade, opposition theorists faced their most serious threat since ratification. The controversy over the Alien and Sedition Acts was a watershed, further legitimating Anti-Federalist fears about the dangers posed by Federalists and shifting the terms of debate in profound ways. A new set of principles put forth in the Virginia and Kentucky Resolutions focused attention on the constitutional means available to citizens and states to challenge unlawful exercises of federal power. The elaboration of a theory of states' rights transformed the debate over federalism, a central concern of Anti-Federalism, by focusing attention on the nature of union, the proper spheres of state and federal authority, and, most important, the appropriate remedy for disputes over these issues.

Anti-Federalist ideas were not simply floating in the air of the new Republic. Between 1788 and 1828, commentators consciously invoked different Anti-Federalist texts to buttress their arguments: what texts defined Anti-Federalism changed over time. The creation of a dissenting discourse necessitated the development of a canon of dissenting texts and a distinctive approach to interpreting those texts. During ratification a relatively small

---

American class consciousness in this period. See, in particular, "Eighteenth-Century English Society: Class Struggle without Class," *Social History*, III (1978), 133–165; "Patrician Society, Plebeian Culture," *Journal of Social History*, VII (1973–1974), 382–405. For a stimulating discussion of the transplantation of English traditions of popular justice to America in the same period, see Alfred F. Young, "English Plebeian Culture and Eighteenth-Century American Radicalism," in Margaret Jacob and James Jacob, eds., *The Origins of Anglo-American Radicalism* (London, 1984), 185–212.

21. Historians are also divided over the degree to which Madison's later thinking repudiated his earlier ideas about constitutionalism. The strongest case for a shift is Marvin Meyers, ed., *The Mind of the Founder: Sources of the Political Thought of James Madison*, rev. ed. (Hanover, N.H., 1981). For a defense of the continuities in Madison's thinking, see Lance Banning, *The Sacred Fire of Liberty: James Madison and the Founding of the Federal Republic* (Ithaca, N.Y., 1995). A middle position may be found in Jack N. Rakove, "The Madisonian Moment," *University of Chicago Law Review*, LV (1988), 473–505.

number of newspaper essays and pamphlets defined Anti-Federalism. In the 1790s those texts were gradually replaced by the published proceedings of the state ratification conventions. The Alien and Sedition crisis of 1798 generated a new set of texts, which propounded those principles that became the cornerstone of opposition thought. The most important of those texts was James Madison's report to the Virginia legislature, "The Report of 1800." For much of the next two decades Anti-Federalist ideas would be filtered through that lens, which synthesized the various strains of dissenting constitutionalism that had defined opposition thought for the previous decade.

The final section of this study analyzes the evolution of a dissenting tradition of constitutionalism indebted to Anti-Federalist ideas in the period 1800–1828. Although it ceased to be a viable ideology for organizing political action, Anti-Federalism had become an integral part of an evolving jurisprudential and constitutional discourse. The themes of consolidation and constructive interpretation, central concerns of Anti-Federalism, became the cornerstones of opposition constitutionalism. The original opposition to the Constitution gained new legitimacy as various authors attempted to find a solid historical foundation for their critique of the nationalist jurisprudence of the Marshall Court. Determining the original understanding of the Constitution at the time of ratification became even more crucial and led to a reconsideration of Anti-Federalist ideas.

The Madisonian synthesis developed in "The Report of 1800" was exceedingly fragile and collapsed in the wake of the Marshall Court's decision in *McCulloch v. Maryland* in 1819. The publication of Robert Yates's *Secret Proceedings and Debates of the Federal Convention* in 1821 facilitated a revival of interest in Anti-Federalist ideas. This work also republished several Anti-Federalist essays from 1788. Yates's volume became a key text for commentators seeking to formulate an alternative to the Marshall Court's theory of federalism.

Another crisis was spawned in 1828 by the emergence of a radical states' rights philosophy committed to the idea of nullification. This conflict precipitated a split within the dissenting tradition between those who acknowledged a debt to Anti-Federalism, such as Martin Van Buren, and those who sought to reshape the dissenting tradition, such as John C. Calhoun.

The adaptability of Anti-Federalist ideas to a variety of different political and constitutional problems in American history has been impressive. For much of American history, Anti-Federalism has provided a rich legacy for those eager to express their dissatisfaction with the dominant trends in American life. Our renewed interest in Anti-Federalism is itself an important measure of contemporary dissatisfaction with the character of American politics and law.[22]

A reconsideration of the Anti-Federalist's vision of American constitutionalism need not prove that their views were superior to those of their opponents. The American Constitution, after all, is one of the most remarkable success stories in the annals of world history. A reexamination of the Anti-Federalist critique of the Constitution inspires us to continue reinterrogating the basic texts of American constitutionalism. Exploring the complicated nature of Anti-Federalism refreshes us to the insights and limits of the legacy bequeathed to us by the Founders, and the Other Founders, of the American constitutional tradition.

22. For a thoughtful effort to formulate a neo-Federalist response to the rising tide of neo–Anti-Federalism: see Alan Brinkley, Nelson W. Polsby, and Kathleen M. Sullivan, *New Federalist Papers: Essays in Defense of the Constitution* (New York, 1997).

PART ONE :
ANTI-FEDERALISM
AND THE
CONSTITUTION

CHAPTER 1 :

RATIFICATION AND

THE POLITICS OF THE

PUBLIC SPHERE

The publication of the Constitution in September 1787 inaugurated one of the most vigorous political campaigns in American history. In arguing over the merits of the new plan of government, Americans not only engaged in a lively inquiry into the meaning of constitutional government; they helped make constitutionalism a defining characteristic of American political culture. The writings of Anti-Federalists and Federalists not only defined the terms of debate during ratification, but they became the sources that later generations would turn to when seeking to understand the meaning of the Constitution. Although modern commentators have generally presented ratification as a dialogue between discrete Federalist and Anti-Federalist voices, the reality of ratification is far more complex. The debate over the meaning of the Constitution began as a many-sided conversation, a free-for-all. Only after ratification, during the 1790s, did the public debate take shape as a dialogue between distinctive Federalist and Anti-Federalist positions. Thus, it is important to reconstruct the debate over ratification following the dynamics of 1787–1788, not of the 1790s.[1]

Although the Constitution had been drafted in private by a small, select group of statesmen, its meaning was inescapably public. As soon as the results of the Philadelphia Convention became known, Americans began

---

1. The most influential effort to analyze Anti-Federalist ideas as part of a founding dialogue is Herbert J. Storing, *What the Anti-Federalists Were For* (Chicago, 1981).

discussing the new frame of government. A week after the convention adjourned, one Philadelphian reported, "The new plan of government proposed by the Convention has made a bustle in the city and its vicinity." Less than a month later, farther west in Carlisle, Pennsylvania, another observer noted, "The new Constitution for the United States seems now to engross the attention of all ranks." In other parts of America similar observations were made. One Virginia commentator remarked, "The plan of a Government proposed to us by the Convention—affords matter for conversation to every rank of beings from the Governor to the door keeper."[2]

The decision of the Philadelphia Convention to submit the Constitution to state ratification conventions ensured that Americans from all walks of life would be drawn into a wide-ranging public debate about its merits. The Constitution was subjected to unprecedented public scrutiny; every clause of the document was parsed and in some cases literally rewritten by readers who took issue with its phraseology or principles.

The framers of the Constitution were acutely aware of the importance of public opinion to ratification. The Constitution, George Washington confided to a friend, would have to be placed "before the judgment seat." The public nature of ratification meant that the press would play a conspicuously large role in defining the fate of the Constitution. "Much will depend however on literary abilities, and the recommendation of it by good pens." Federalists took Washington's sage advice seriously and worked tirelessly in their campaign to manage public opinion.[3]

Anti-Federalists shared with their Federalist opponents a keen sense of the importance of molding public opinion. Centinel, an influential Anti-Federalist writer, concurred with this view and reminded his readers that the Constitution ought to be given the "fullest discussion, the most thorough investigation and dispassionate consideration." To facilitate such public inquiry, he urged, "Those who are competent to the task of developing the principles of government, ought to be encouraged to come forward."[4]

Washington and Samuel Bryan, the author of the Centinel essays, agreed that the side that was more successful at shaping the public debate would

2. Richard Butler to William Irvine, Oct. 11–12, 1787 (*DHRC*, II, 177); David Redick to William Irvine, Sept. 24, 1787 (II, 135); George Lee Tuberville to Arthur Lee, Oct. 28, 1787 (VIII, 127).

3. George Washington to Henry Knox, Oct. 15, 1787 (*DHRC*, VIII, 56); Washington to David Humphrey, Oct. 10, 1787 (VIII, 48).

4. Centinel [Samuel Bryan?], no. 3, "To the People of Pennsylvania," *IG*, Nov. 8, 1787 (*CA-F*, II, 155, 158–159); no. 1, "To the Freemen of Pennsylvania," *IG*, Oct. 5, 1787 (II, 137).

emerge victorious. The press was crucial. It was both vital to get the message out and necessary to craft that message in such a way that it would be persuasive. The authors who took up the challenge posed by Washington and Centinel were therefore pivotal in the politics of ratification. In arguing over the merits of the Constitution, both sides in the exchange had to grapple with the complex relationship between American constitutionalism and the emergence of a public sphere of political debate.

Authors often invoked the idea of the public. But what exactly was the public? They struggled with the problem of how to understand the cultural arena that modern scholarship has labeled "the public sphere." This term has been used by scholars as a way of conceptualizing the distinctive realm in society in which private citizens shed their personal attachments and participated in the political life of the nation. The public sphere existed as a cultural arena between the state and a private sphere of family and economic production.[5]

Not only was the debate over the Constitution an important phase in the evolution of the public sphere in America, but the contest over it focused unprecedented attention on the politics of the public sphere itself. Federalists and Anti-Federalists accused each other of violating the principles that ought to govern public debate. Even more significant was the argument between these two sides over who could claim to speak with the more authentic public voice. Each side expended enormous energy crafting appeals to persuade citizens that it was better qualified to represent the will of the people.[6]

5. Jürgen Habermas, *The Structural Transformation of the Public Sphere: An Inquiry into a Category of Bourgeois Society,* trans. Thomas Burger and Frederick Lawrence (Cambridge, Mass., 1989). For elaborations and critiques of Habermas that focus on the historical evolution of the public sphere in Europe and America, see Peter Stallybrass and Allon White, *The Politics and Poetics of Transgression* (Ithaca, N.Y., 1986); Michael Warner, *The Letters of the Republic: Publication and the Public Sphere in Eighteenth-Century America* (Cambridge, Mass., 1990); Craig Calhoun, ed., *Habermas and the Public Sphere* (Cambridge, Mass., 1992). On the struggle to define the public sphere in early America, see John L. Brooke, "Ancient Lodges and Self-Created Societies: Voluntary Association and the Public Sphere in the Early Republic," in Ronald Hoffman and Peter J. Albert, eds., *Launching the "Extended Republic": The Federalist Era* (Charlottesville, Va., 1996), 273–359.

6. Two useful studies of the dynamics of the various state ratification contests are Patrick T. Conley and John P. Kaminski, eds., *The Constitution and the States: The Role of the Original Thirteen in the Framing and Adoption of the Federal Constitution* (Madison, Wis., 1988); Michael Allen Gillespie and Michael Lienesch, eds., *Ratifying the Constitution* (Lawrence, Kans., 1989). On the vote, see Charles W. Roll, Jr., "We, Some of the People: Appor-

For Anti-Federalists the task of discerning the will of the people was particularly difficult, given the diversity of the coalition that opposed the Constitution. No group in American political history was more heterogeneous than the Anti-Federalists. Even a cursory glance at the final vote on ratification demonstrates the incredible regional diversity of the Anti-Federalist coalition. Anti-Federalism was strong in northern and western New England, Rhode Island, the Hudson Valley of New York, western Pennsylvania, the Southside of Virginia, North Carolina, and upcountry South Carolina. Although the social history of Anti-Federalism remains somewhat patchy, the opposition to the Constitution brought together rich planters in the South, middling politicians in New York and Pennsylvania, and backcountry farmers from several different regions (Map 1).[7]

Given the range of Anti-Federalist views, it is not surprising that modern commentators would seek a single Anti-Federalist voice and use that as a proxy for the gamut of Anti-Federalist belief. The fact that Anti-Federalists never convened their own constitutional convention and never proposed a concrete alternative to the Constitution only complicates the task of identifying a distinctive Anti-Federalist constitutional philosophy. Ultimately, the only thread tying Anti-Federalism together was print: the circulation of

tionment in the Thirteen State Conventions Ratifying the Constitution," *JAH*, LVI (1969–1970), 21–40. On the Anti-Federalist political campaign, see Robert Allen Rutland, *The Ordeal of the Constitution: The Antifederalists and the Ratification Struggle of 1787–1788* (Norman, Okla., 1966); Steven R. Boyd, *The Politics of Opposition: Antifederalists and the Acceptance of the Constitution* (Millwood, N.Y., 1979). The one systematic effort to analyze the dynamics of the public debate, William H. Riker, *The Strategy of Rhetoric: Campaigning for the American Constitution* (New Haven, Conn., 1996), employs a social scientific rational choice model. He attempts to reduce the meaning of ratification texts to stable units of meaning and then tries to quantify the weighted words each side used to persuade the public. The assumptions underlying his analysis are deeply anachronistic and therefore profoundly flawed.

7. Alexander Hamilton, "Conjectures about the Constitution" (September 1787) (*DHRC*, XIII, 277–278). Studies of ratification by political historians have been shaped by the agenda set by Progressive historians who were primarily interested in the connection between political and economic conflict. For important examples of this tradition, see Forrest McDonald, *We the People: The Economic Origins of the Constitution* (Chicago, 1958); Jackson Turner Main, *The Anti-Federalists: Critics of the Constitution, 1781–1788* (Chapel Hill, N.C., 1961); Main, *Political Parties before the Constitution* (Chapel Hill, N.C., 1973); Orin Grant Libby, *The Geographical Distribution of the Vote of the Thirteen States on the Federal Constitution, 1787–1788* (Madison, Wis., 1894); and, for a thoughtful discussion of Libby's analysis, see Forrest McDonald, "The Anti-Federalists, 1781–1789," in Jack P. Greene, ed., *The Reinterpretation of the American Revolution, 1763–1789* (New York, 1968), 365–378.

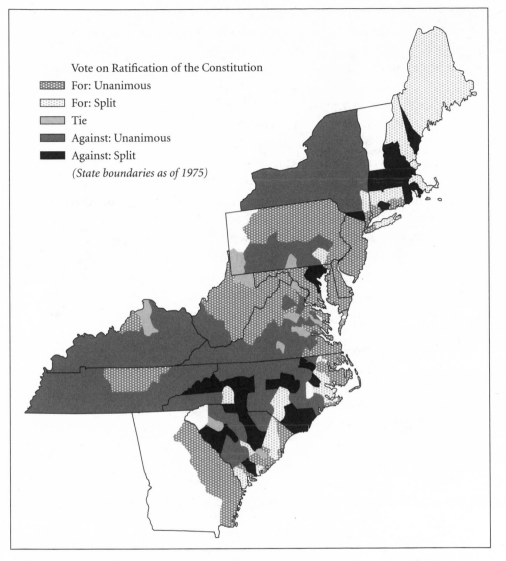

Vote on Ratification of the Constitution

▨ For: Unanimous
▨ For: Split
▨ Tie
▨ Against: Unanimous
■ Against: Split
(State boundaries as of 1975)

MAP 1. The Ratification of the Constitution.
After Lester J. Cappon et al., eds., Atlas of Early American History:
The Revolutionary Era, 1760–1790 *(Princeton, N.J., 1976), 63, 134*

Anti-Federalist texts in the public sphere of print culture provided the one, tenuous connection that united all of those diverse groups. Print, however, proved to be gossamer thread. Once published, an author could not control the way his words were interpreted. Indeed, a few prominent Anti-Federalist authors were sufficiently concerned about this problem to circulate their ideas only in manuscript, hoping that, if their words were distributed among a select group, they might maintain greater control over their texts. This effort to control the reception of their ideas was doomed. Texts circulating in manuscript invariably found their way into print in spite of their authors' efforts to restrict access to their works. Once they were in print, other writers and readers were free to respond to and reinterpret these texts in ways that suited the readers' agenda, not the authors'.[8]

The rereading and in some cases rewriting of Anti-Federalist texts did not end with ratification. The texts written to oppose the Constitution had a life of their own that lasted well beyond the events that first prompted their composition. Long after Anti-Federalism ceased to be an active political movement, Anti-Federalist ideas continued to be invoked, and Anti-Federalist writing to be used to formulate an alternative constitutional discourse. Once published, Anti-Federalist ideas and rhetoric became part of a public sphere of debate that shaped the development of American constitutionalism. Their writings could be quoted, misquoted, cited, or evoked in a variety of direct or oblique ways. For later commentators on the Constitution, Anti-Federalism became an important source for those striving to create a tradition of loyal opposition within American constitutionalism.[9]

---

8. For a discussion of the need to join the study of authorial intent with reader response, see J. G. A. Pocock, *Virtue, Commerce, and History: Essays on Political Thought and History, Chiefly in the Eighteenth Century* (Cambridge, 1985). For a more detailed discussion of these and other methodological issues, see Saul Cornell, "Early American History in a Postmodern Age," *WMQ*, 3d Ser., L (1993), 329–341, and "Splitting the Difference: Textualism, Contextualism, and Post-Modern History," *American Studies*, XXXVI (1995), 57–80. The most important effort to control the dissemination of a text and thereby exercise some control over the response of readers was George Mason's "Objections to the Constitution of Government Formed by the Convention," *Massachusetts Centinel* (Boston), Nov. 21, 1787 (*CA-F*, II, 11–13). (For further discussion of this work, see Chapter 2, below).

9. Perhaps the most blatant case of the rewriting of an Anti-Federalist text was the Edmond Genêt edition of Robert Yates's report of the proceedings of the Philadelphia Convention (*Secret Proceedings and Debates of the Federal Convention . . .* [Albany, N.Y., 1821]); see below, Chapter 10, and James H. Hutson, "The Creation of the Constitution: The Integrity of the Documentary Record," in Jack N. Rakove, ed., *Interpreting the Constitution: The Debate over Original Intent* (Boston, 1990), 151–178.

The Dynamics of the Public Debate

Reconstructing the dynamics of the original debate over ratification requires that texts be weighted according to their influence at the time. Anti-Federalists wrote hundreds of essays and short squibs; the vast majority of these, however, were never republished. Fewer than 150 essays were reprinted at least twice or sustained a print run as a pamphlet large enough to have an impact beyond their immediate point of origin (see Appendixes 1 and 2). Only a small fraction of those essays gained a broad national circulation. Of these items, 90 percent were reprinted fewer than ten times. The Anti-Federalist argument was largely defined by a small core of essays, including "Hon. Mr. Gerry's Objections to Signing the National Constitution," Samuel Bryan's first and second Centinel essays, George Mason's "Objections to the Constitution," Richard Henry Lee's letter to Edmund Randolph, "The Address and Reasons of Dissent of the Minority," and Robert Yates and John Lansing's "Reasons of Dissent."[10]

Modern commentators have generally focused on the most philosophically sophisticated Anti-Federalist authors, essayists such as Federal Farmer or Brutus. Neither of them was widely reprinted in the press. Of the two, the more influential essayist, Federal Farmer, was disseminated in pamphlet. It

10. Elbridge Gerry, "Hon. Mr. Gerry's Objections to Signing the National Constitution," *Massachusetts Centinel*, Nov. 3, 1787 (*DHRC*, XIII, 548–550); Centinel [Samuel Bryan?], no. 1, "To the Freemen of Pennsylvania," *IG*, Oct. 5, 1787 (*CA-F*, II, 136–143); Centinel, no. 2, "To the People of Pennsylvania," *FJ*, Oct. 24, 1787 (*CA-F*, II, 143–154); George Mason, "Objections to the Constitution," *Massachusetts Centinel*, Nov. 21, 1787 (*CA-F*, II, 11–13); "Copy of a Letter from Richard Henry Lee, Esq. . . . [to Edmund Randolph]," *Pennsylvania Packet, and Daily Advertiser* (Philadelphia), Dec. 20, 1787 (*DHRC*, XIV, 366–372); [Samuel Bryan], "The Address and Reasons of Dissent of the Minority of the Convention of Philadelphia to Their Constituents, *Pennsylvania Packet*, Dec. 18, 1787 (*CA-F*, III, 145–147); Robert Yates and John Lansing, "Reasons of Dissent," *New-York Journal, and Weekly Register*, Jan. 14, 1788 (*CA-F*, II, 16–18).

On the importance of various Anti-Federalist authors, see Murray Dry, "The Debate over Ratification of the Constitution," in Jack P. Greene and J. R. Pole, eds., *The Blackwell Encyclopedia of the American Revolution* (London, 1991), 471–486. On the role of pamphlets as supplements to newspapers, see Boyd, *The Politics of Opposition*. Federal Farmer [Melancton Smith?], (*Observations Leading to a Fair Examination of the System of Government Proposed by the Late Convention . . . Letters from the Federal Farmer to the Republican* [(New York, 1787)]), although not widely reprinted in newspapers, was the fourth most reprinted pamphlet: see *DHRC*, XIV, 14–18, XVII, 265–268. For a list of materials reprinted as pamphlets, broadsides, books, or items in the one magazine with national circulation, see Appendix 2, below.

is difficult to assess the relative impact of publication in a newspaper versus distribution as a pamphlet. When compared with essays that were widely reprinted in both newspaper and pamphlet, such as by Centinel, it seems clear that Federal Farmer's impact was more circumscribed. The perspectives of such authors as Federal Farmer and Brutus were certainly not insignificant. Those authors expressed the point of view of middling democrats in New York, who were an important group within the Anti-Federalist coalition. Indeed, Anti-Federalist John Lamb sent copies of Federal Farmer's essays to leading opponents of the Constitution in a number of states. Still, if the measure of influence is taken to be the effect a particular author had on public debate, then Federal Farmer would be counted less influential than other advocates of middling democratic ideology. The more widely reprinted writings of Pennsylvanians, most notably "The Address and Reasons of Dissent of the Minority," were far more effective at shaping public discourse.[11]

That tendency to focus on the most thoughtful and sophisticated voices of middling democrats (such as Federal Farmer and Brutus) has distorted our understanding of ratification in another way. The undue concentration on those authors has effectively truncated the political spectrum of Anti-Federalism—eliminating the more conservative and more radical poles of Anti-Federalist thought. During the original debate over the Constitution, the more extreme voices dominated. At one pole stood elite Anti-Federalists, such as George Mason, Elbridge Gerry, and Richard Henry Lee. At the opposite end, radical authors such as Centinel and Officer of the Late Continental Army courted a more popular audience. Reconstructing the original character of the debate over the Constitution is a necessary first step toward a more complete and subtle account of Anti-Federalism.

The Anti-Federalist Critique

A number of modern commentators have expressed bewilderment at the range of Anti-Federalist ideas, a view shared by Federalists at the time. That reaction makes sense, given the volume of material generated by the oppo-

11. Historical estimates about literacy rates in America at the time of ratification vary considerably. In New England, rates for white males might have exceeded 90 percent, but in the mid-Atlantic they were closer to 60–70 percent. For a useful summary of the literature on literacy, including a discussion of the methodological problems with ascertaining literacy, see Carl F. Kaestle, "Studying the History of Literacy," in Kaestle et al., eds., *Literacy in the United States: Readers and Reading since 1880* (New Haven, Conn., 1991), 3–32.

nents of the Constitution: thousands of columns of text were written during the course of ratification. Federalist Edward Carrington believed that the opponents of the Constitution embraced contradictory arguments against the new government. Carrington felt that the sentiments of Anti-Federalists Richard Henry Lee and Elbridge Gerry demonstrated the incoherence of the opposition to the Constitution. "The disapprobation of Mr. R.H.L and that of Mr. G. are founded on very opposite principles—the former thinks the Constitution too strong, the latter is of the opinion that [it] is too weak." Carrington's confusion was typical of many Federalists, who thought that there was no common agenda uniting Anti-Federalists. For James Madison, the quality of Anti-Federalist leadership and the effectiveness of its campaign varied tremendously from state to state. Yet, taken as a whole, it was their cacophony, not their harmony, that distinguished the opponents of the Constitution. "There was not a single character capable of uniting their wills or directing their measures." The chaotic character of Anti-Federalism was itself a reflection of their failure to present an alternative vision. "They had no plan whatever," Madison wrote; their sole object was "to put a negative on the Constitution and return home."[12]

The opponents of the Constitution were not bewildered by their disagreements—they were actually somewhat shocked by their ability to agree on so many essential points. Anti-Federalists challenged the Federalist claim that their critique of the Constitution was incoherent and that the opposition was disunited. Writing at the end of November, early in the process of ratification, An Old Whig responded directly to the Federalist charge that Anti-Federalism was a jumble of contradictory ideas. It "has too often been suggested" by Federalists that the "objections and amendments" made by the opponents of the Constitution were "irreconcileable." In reality, he argued, the opposite was true. "It appears that from what has been hitherto published in the different states in opposition to the proposed Constitution," the criticisms of the new government "harmonize in a very great degree." At nearly the same time, Centinel claimed that "the opponents to the proposed plan, at the same time in every part of the continent, harmonised in the same objections." Several months later, A Plebeian echoed this judgment: "There is a remarkable uniformity in the objections made to the constitution, on the most important points." Leading Anti-Federalist au-

12. Edward Carrington to William Short, Oct. 25, 1787 (*DHRC*, XIII, 470); James Madison to Thomas Jefferson, Feb. 19, 1788 (XVI, 143). Madison's comments were prompted by the actions of the Massachusetts state convention.

thors were more impressed by the commonalities that united them in their opposition to the Constitution than by the differences that divided them.[13]

Print culture united the Anti-Federalist movement, providing a shared language and common set of criticisms. James Wilson noted that in his "Speech at a Public Meeting in Philadelphia." He attacked the "insidious attempts which are clandestinely and industriously made to pervert and destroy the new plan." He went further: "The impressions of four months constant attention to the subject, have not been so easily effaced as to leave me without an answer to the objections which have been raised." The five most important Anti-Federalist criticisms identified by Wilson were

1. The omission of a bill of rights.
2. The consolidationist/nationalist character of the new government.
3. The charge of aristocracy.
4. Concerns about taxation.
5. Fears about the creation of a standing army.[14]

Wilson's response to Anti-Federalist concerns prompted numerous rebuttals. Attacks on Wilson's ideas became almost as important as the direct criticisms made by Anti-Federalists of the Constitution.[15]

When Elbridge Gerry published his objections to the Constitution on November 3, 1787, in the *Massachusetts Centinel*, he reiterated the same explosive set of issues that Wilson had studiously tried to defuse more than a month earlier. "Hon. Mr. Gerry's Objections" was reprinted forty-six times, more than any other Anti-Federalist essay, including in the *American Museum* of Philadelphia and as a pamphlet in Richmond. It was even reprinted by six of the eight leading Federalist papers. The views of Gerry, in his role as one of the nonsigning delegates to the Philadelphia Convention, were a newsworthy event. Federalist papers provided space to Gerry that few other

13. An Old Whig [George Bryan, John Smilie, and James Hutchinson?], no. 7, *IG*, Nov. 28, 1787 (*DHRC*, XIV, 250); Centinel [Samuel Bryan?], no. 4, "To the People of Pennsylvania," *IG*, Nov. 30, 1787 (*CA-F*, II, 166); A Plebeian [Melancton Smith?], *An Address to the People of the State of New York* . . . (New York, 1788) (*DHRC*, XVII, 156–157).

14. James Wilson, "Speech at a Public Meeting in Philadelphia," Oct. 6, 1787, *Pennsylvania Herald, and General Advertiser* (Philadelphia) (*DHRC*, XIII, 339).

15. A Republican, no. 1, "To James Wilson, Esquire," *New-York Journal*, Oct. 25, 1787 (*DHRC*, XIII, 477); An Old Whig [George Bryan, John Smilie, and James Hutchinson?], no. 2, *IG*, Oct. 17, 1787 (XIII, 399–403), no. 3, *IG*, Oct. 20, 1787 (XIII, 426); Centinel, no. 2, *FJ*, Oct. 24, 1787 (*CA-F*, II, 143–154), no. 10, *IG*, Jan. 12, 1788 (II, 183), no. 13, *IG*, Jan. 30, 1788 (II, 191–192), no. 14, *IG*, Feb. 5, 1788 (II, 194–195).

Anti-Federalists received. Supporters of the Constitution clearly recognized the importance of Gerry's essay, since they devoted considerable effort to rebutting its arguments. Massachusetts Federalist Nathaniel Gorham believed that "Mr. Gerrys Letter has done infinite mischief." Connecticut Federalist Oliver Ellsworth's serialized essays, by A Landholder, devoted the bulk of its energy to attacking Gerry's criticism of the Constitution.[16]

Gerry's essay helped solidify the nature of the Anti-Federalist critique of the Constitution. In a single paragraph he succinctly stated the issues that had come to define Anti-Federalist opposition to the Constitution:

> My principal objections to the plan, are, that there is no adequate provision for a representation of the people—that they have no security for the right of election—that some of the powers of the Legislature are ambiguous, and others indefinite and dangerous—that the Executive is blended with and will have an undue influence over the Legislature—that the judicial department will be oppressive—that treaties of the highest importance may be formed by the President with the advice of two thirds of a *quorum* of the Senate—and that the system is without the security of a bill of rights.

The general flaw in the structure of the new government was its consolidating tendency. "The Constitution proposed has few, if any *federal* features, but is rather a system of *national* government." No other Anti-Federalist essay managed to range as widely and state so concisely the essential Anti-Federalist critique of the Constitution. Gerry's short, synoptic criticisms were appropriated and elaborated by a wide variety of authors.[17]

After Gerry's essay, the most influential public statement of Anti-Federalist principles was George Mason's "Objections to the Constitution of Government Formed by the Convention," published on November 21, 1787, several weeks after "Hon. Mr. Gerry's Objections" and less widely reprinted. Although Mason's essay had a less direct impact on the public debate, it was important in shaping the response of leading Anti-Federalist politicians in several states. Mason's essay had circulated widely in manuscript and been consulted by Gerry as well as by leading Anti-Federalists in Pennsylvania when they formalized their objections in "The Address and Reasons of Dissent of the Minority." Thus, measuring Mason's influence by the number

16. Nathaniel Gorham to Henry Knox, Dec. 24, 1787, Knox Papers, MHS. For more on the republication and reaction to Gerry's essay, see the headnote, *DHRC*, XIII, 546–548.

17. Elbridge Gerry, "Hon. Mr. Gerry's Objections" (*DHRC*, XIII, 548–550).

of times his essay was printed provides only a partial account of the role his ideas played in shaping the Anti-Federalist critique of the Constitution.[18]

There was considerable overlap between Gerry's criticisms and Mason's. In addition to listing the absence of a bill of rights, Mason noted the omission of specific protections for liberty of the press and trial by jury, and of the prohibition of standing armies as particularly egregious. Mason closed his objections with the observation, "This Government will commence in a moderate Aristocracy; it is at present impossible to foresee whether it will, in it's Operation, produce a Monarchy, or a corrupt Aristocracy."[19]

By the time the critiques of Gerry and Mason appeared in print, the main outlines of the Anti-Federalist critique of the Constitution were well established. Nine issues appeared time and again in Anti-Federalist writings.

1. *Consolidation.* The Constitution abolishes the federal character of the Union and creates a single national government acting directly on the people. The states are robbed of important governmental functions. Since republican governments capable of sustaining liberty are possible only in small republics, consolidated government undermines both republicanism and liberty.

2. *Aristocracy.* The Constitution undermines republican principles and promotes the development of an aristocracy. Cabal and corruption are inevitable, given the absence of appropriate checks on the Senate and House. The Constitution lacks important safeguards such as annual elections and forced rotation in office. Without such measures, representatives will cease to be accountable to the people. Control over the manner of election also needs to be returned to the states. The absence of adequate separation of powers may also lead to collusion between the different branches of government, particularly regarding appointments and treaties.

18. The writings of Edmund Randolph, although less important than those of Gerry, Mason, or Martin, were clearly more influential than the objections of Robert Yates and John Lansing.

19. In addition to those concerns, Mason introduced the issue of sectionalism, noting that the Constitution lacked a council to advise the president. Such a council, Mason concluded, would necessarily include "six Members; vizt. two from the Eastern, two from the Middle, and two from the Southern States." Interestingly, a paragraph attacking the power to make commercial regulations that might work against the interests of the South was omitted from newspapers in the North. Mason, "Objections to the Constitution" (*CA-F,* II, 11–14).

3. *Representation.* The Constitution fails to provide for adequate representation of the people in the popular branch of government. The Senate is also too far removed from the popular will.
4. *Separation of Powers.* The Constitution blends the functions of the legislative and executive branches in a dangerous fashion. The provisions covering treaties, appointments, and impeachments are the most notable examples of the blending of functions.
5. *Judicial Tyranny.* The Constitution creates a powerful judicial branch that threatens the integrity of the state courts. The broad jurisdiction of the courts over matters of fact and law is also too extensive.
6. *The Absence of a Bill of Rights.* The Constitution omits a declaration of rights establishing the essential personal liberties retained by the people, particularly the rights of freedom of the press, freedom of conscience, and trial by jury.
7. *Taxes.* The Constitution grants extensive powers to tax, which may be used to oppress the people and further threaten the autonomy of the states by depriving them of the revenue necessary to govern.
8. *Standing Army.* The Constitution neglects to prohibit standing armies during times of peace and threatens the integrity of the state militia.
9. *Executive.* The extensive powers given to the president risk creating an elective monarchy.

What is remarkable about the ratification debates is the consistency with which these arguments recur. Although the mix of these different arguments and the particular emphasis on various ones might vary from author to author, the persistence of these themes over the course of the debate on ratification is remarkable. In general, the overall logic of Anti-Federalist attack remained fairly consistent for the duration of ratification.[20]

Anti-Federalists showed a greater range of responses over *what to do* about the defects in the Constitution. Some authors suggested a second convention to revise the Constitution. Others preferred the idea of prior amendment. The subject of amendments received greater attention in the press after the Massachusetts state convention's list of recommended amendments was reported in early February 1788. The actions of Massachusetts led a number of authors to consider the question of revisions in greater detail. The various lists of recommended amendments proposed by individ-

---

20. For a different view, see Riker, *The Strategy of Rhetoric.* His combination of synoptic content analysis and rational choice theory renders his conclusions highly dubious.

ual state conventions were among the most widely reprinted items in the press.[21]

Amendments were proposed by the state conventions in Massachusetts, Maryland, South Carolina, New Hampshire, Virginia, New York, and North Carolina. The demand for amendments was complicated by the political conditions of ratification in each of the states. Many of the provisions recommended by those state conventions reflected the local concerns of Anti-Federalists, but the suggested amendments were also shaped by the perspective of moderate Federalists who sided with Anti-Federalists in many instances. A total of 124 amendments to the Constitution were suggested. In a few cases, specific amendments proposed by different states contradicted one another, and many of the same demands were made by more than one state. Determining what, if any, commonalities united Anti-Federalist calls for amendments seems almost as daunting as identifying the nature of the Anti-Federalist critique. Indeed, in one sense the subject of amendments is even more complicated, since it produced a concrete political result that had to be approved by the individual state conventions.[22]

One of the earliest and most widely distributed proposals for amendments was framed by the Pennsylvania Anti-Federalists in their influential "Address and Reasons of Dissent of the Minority," which drew on the proposal for amendments suggested by Robert Whitehill in the Pennsylvania state convention. "The Dissent" suggested the following amendments:

1. Affirmation of the right of conscience.
2. Provision for the right of trial by jury.
3. The right of defendants to confront their accuser and a prohibition of self-incrimination.
4. A prohibition of excessive bail and fines and of cruel and unusual punishment.
5. A prohibition of general warrants.
6. Protections for freedom of speech, publishing, and the press.
7. Protection for the right to bear arms, a prohibition of standing armies

---

21. On the need for a second convention to revise the Constitution, see An Old Whig, no. 4, *IG*, Oct. 27, 1787 (*DHRC*, XIII, 497). The Massachusetts convention's proposal for amendments was published on Feb. 6, 1788 (*DHRC*, XVI, 60–69). For Anti-Federalist reactions, see Philadelphienesis, no. 10, *FJ*, Feb. 20, 1788 (*DHRC*, XVI, 158–161); A Plebeian [Melancton Smith?], *An Address to the People of the State of New York . . .* (New York, 1788) (*DHRC*, XVII, 137).

22. Riker, *The Strategy of Rhetoric*, 243.

in times of peace, and a guarantee that the military be placed under civilian control.

8. Protection for hunting and fowling rights.
9. Affirmation of state power to levy internal taxes.
10. An increase in the size of the lower house and a return to state control over the election of senators and representatives.
11. Return of control of the militia to the states, an affirmation of the sovereignty of the states, and limits on the powers of the federal government to those expressly delegated.
12. Affirmation of the need to keep the legislative, executive, and judicial functions of the new government distinct; creation of a council to advise the president.
13. Affirmation that all treaties must conform to the laws of the United States and the several states.
14. Limits on the powers of the federal judiciary to decide cases affecting ambassadors; admiralty and maritime controversies in which the United States is a party; controversies between two or more states; controversies between a state and a citizen of a different state; disputed land grants affecting different states; and controversies between a state or inhabitant and foreign states.[23]

The amendments thus proposed included explicit protections for basic rights and echoed the language used by most state bills of rights. Although modern scholars have tried to distinguish Anti-Federalists' commitment to civil rights from their concern for states' rights, the two conceptions of rights were closely connected in the minds of most Anti-Federalists. Thus, the limits on the federal judiciary reflected a desire to protect individual liberty and ensure that the federal government did not expand the scope of its authority via judicial fiat. But attempts to categorize particular provisions for amendments as republican or liberal seem anachronistic. Some Anti-Federalists embraced a more liberal conception of rights while others framed these problems in more republican terms.

One of the most important forms of liberty Anti-Federalists sought to guard was the right to participate in political life and communicate freely. "The Dissent" did call for a number of structural changes in the Constitution that would shift the balance of power within the federal system. The affirmation of the states' power to tax, control of the militia, restriction of

23. [Bryan], "The Address and Reasons of Dissent of the Minority" (*CA-F*, III, 150–152).

the new government's powers to those expressly delegated, limits on the scope of the judiciary, and federal powers to make treaties all sought to undo the consolidating tendencies of the new government. The expansion of the size of the lower house and the creation of a presidential council were designed to eliminate the aristocratic tendency of the new government. Increasing the size of the lower house would also make it more responsive to the people. "The Dissent" also demonstrated the fear that the separation of powers was not effectively implemented by the structure of power within the new federal government. The senate's advise-and-consent function regarding treaties and appointments seemed to invite collusion. To remedy this defect, "The Dissent" called for a council of advisers to the executive as a means of reducing the chances of a conspiracy between the executive and legislative branches.

With the notable exception of the right of hunting and fowling, the list of amendments in "The Dissent" anticipated most of the proposed amendments recommended by the individual state ratification conventions. Interestingly, the amendments that were most widely proposed were, not those that sought explicit safeguards for individual rights, but those that attempted to shift the balance of power within the federal system: prohibitions of federal oversight of elections and direct taxation and explicit restriction of the power of the federal government to those powers expressly delegated by the Constitution. Those provisions were suggested by five state conventions.[24]

The Rhetoric of Ratification

Simply identifying the substantive critiques made by Anti-Federalist authors provides only a partial understanding of how those critiques were interpreted by the readers of them. Many of the key terms associated with the Anti-Federalist critique of the Constitution, such as "aristocracy," "democracy," or "virtue," were interpreted in radically different ways by various groups within the Anti-Federalist coalition. A commonly voiced criticism, such as the aristocratic character of the Constitution, took on one meaning

24. Kenneth R. Bowling, " 'A Tub to the Whale': The Founding Fathers and Adoption of the Federal Bill of Rights," *Journal of the Early Republic*, VIII (1988), 223–251. Originally, the idea of amendments proposed by Anti-Federalists did not distinguish between protections of individual rights and structural changes in the Constitution. On the commonalities among the amendments proposed by the state ratification conventions, see Donald S. Lutz, *A Preface to American Political Theory* (Lawrence, Kans., 1992), 49–88; Riker, *The Strategy of Rhetoric*, 242–249.

in a plebeian satire lambasting the wellborn but carried an entirely different set of connotations if embedded in an erudite essay filled with Latin quotations. Authors could adopt a variety of voices in print. The rhetorical persona, or mask, of an author was one of the most important ideological tools available to persuade an audience. One might choose to speak as a gentleman, a member of the sturdy yeomanry, or a plebeian artisan or farmer. The language of a text and everything from its diction to the choice of metaphors were all designed to reinforce the writer's message. Rhetoric was, therefore, tied to the particular ideological vision of an author.[25]

An ideological analysis of Anti-Federalist rhetoric also offers important clues about the intended audiences for particular essays. Particular rhetorical strategies were calculated to appeal to the taste and assumptions of various types of readers. Although authors could not control how their essays would be interpreted once in print, some appreciation for how they conceived their readership is crucial to interpreting them.

Once published, the meaning of texts was shaped as much by the response of Anti-Federalist readers as by the decisions of authors, editors, or others responsible for disseminating Anti-Federalist materials. Still, by combining literary evidence about how authors imagined their audiences with the surviving documentary evidence about the way actual readers interpreted particular texts, it is possible to gain some appreciation for the different patterns of Anti-Federalist reading. An analysis of different rhetorical strategies and,

25. For a discussion of the dominant approach to rhetoric favored by historians, see Gordon S. Wood, "Rhetoric and Reality in the American Revolution," *WMQ*, 3d Ser., XXIII (1966), 3–32. Wood's pioneering study focused attention on the content, not the form, of Revolutionary rhetoric. A different, less satisfying approach to content analysis informs William H. Riker, "Why Negative Campaigning Is Rational: The Rhetoric of the Ratification Campaign of 1787–1788," *Studies in American Political Development*, V (1991), 224–283. Riker takes the public nature of rhetoric as proof that meaning must be stable and objective. For a forceful critique of his approach, see Jeffrey K. Tulis, "Comment: Riker's Rhetoric of Ratification," *Studies in American Political Development*, V (1991), 284–292. For a more general critique of Riker's assumptions about the nature of political language, see Terence Ball and J. G. A. Pocock, *Conceptual Change and the Constitution* (Lawrence, Kans., 1988). On the problem with synoptic content analysis, see Dominick LaCapra, *Rethinking Intellectual History: Texts, Contexts, Language* (Ithaca, N.Y., 1983), and *History and Criticism* (Ithaca, N.Y., 1985). For two suggestive studies of the rhetorical structure of early American literary and political writing, see Jay Fliegelman, *Declaring Independence: Jefferson, Natural Language, and the Culture of Performance* (Stanford, Calif., 1993); Albert Furtwangler, *American Silhouettes: Rhetorical Identities of the Founders* (New Haven, Conn., 1987). On the democratization of rhetoric in this period, see Andrew W. Robertson, *The Language of Democracy: Political Rhetoric in the United States and Britain, 1790–1900* (Ithaca, N.Y., 1995).

where possible, different reader responses illuminates how elite Anti-Federalists like George Mason could work side by side with spokesmen for an emerging middling sort like Melancton Smith. Similarly, it is possible to see how a skilled pamphleteer like Samuel Bryan could simultaneously craft essays designed to sway the middling sort in Philadelphia and plebeian rioters in Carlisle, Pennsylvania. A shared conceptual vocabulary allowed wealthy southern planters, affluent New England merchants, newly empowered middle-class politicians in the Middle Atlantic, and plebeian farmers and artisans in the backcountry to unite in opposition to the Constitution.

The distribution and reception of Mercy Otis Warren's *Observations on the New Constitution* aptly illustrates the complexity of the problems of understanding the relationship between authorial intent, rhetoric, and reader response. Writing as A Columbian Patriot, Warren clearly intended her essay to express the views of "the most distinguished of her patriots." Others within the Anti-Federalist coalition clearly believed that the argument of the pamphlet was worth reprinting. The New York City Anti-Federal Committee obtained seventeen hundred copies of it in early April 1788, several weeks before the election of delegates to the New York ratification convention. The pamphlet met with a cool reaction outside New York City. The response of the members of the ratifying committee in Albany demonstrates the importance of rhetorical style to the reception of an essay. Albany Anti-Federalists confided to their counterparts in New York that they thought the pamphlet was "a well composed piece." It was, however, written "in a stile too sublime and for us common people in this Part of the Country." To the members of the Albany committee the arguments of A Columbian Patriot, while significant, were not easily detached from the author's rhetoric. While many of the substantive issues raised by the author were deemed important, its effectiveness was compromised by the author's style. The failure of Warren's essay to elicit a more favorable response from the common people was not simply stylistic. The tone and voice Warren *chose* for this essay reflected her own patrician values, which were integral to her republicanism. For middling and plebeian Anti-Federalists, the issues of style merely reinforced the ideological content of the essay. The common people of Albany recognized that A Columbian Patriot was not a spokesman for the more democratic ethos that defined their political sensibility.[26]

26. A Columbian Patriot [Mercy Otis Warren], *Observations on the New Constitution, and on the Federal and State Conventions* (Boston, 1788) (*CA-F*, IV, 270–286); Warren to Catherine Macaulay Graham, May 16, 1788 (*DHRC*, XVIII, 20–22); "Albany Anti-Federal

Although the most widely reprinted Anti-Federalist essays were all signed by actual persons, the typical Anti-Federalist essay was written pseudonymously. The participants in the public debate over ratification, printers as well as authors, were extremely self-conscious about the rhetorical identities they constructed when adopting pseudonyms. Anti-Federalist Thomas Greenleaf, the editor of the *New-York Journal*, believed that this practice was sufficiently important for him to declare that his paper would always provide a "spacious ground for the rencounter of a CATO and a CAESAR—for a REPUBLICAN and ANONIMOUS—for a SIDNEY."[27]

Greenleaf's description of the editorial policy of his paper listed several different categories of pen names. Classical republican figures such as "Brutus" or "Cato" were popular, as were modern Whig republican names, such as "Sidney" or "Hampden." Rather than pluck names from antiquity, some authors fashioned names to sound as though they were classical in origin, such as "Aristocrotis." Pseudonyms that affirmed an allegiance to a particular abstract ideal were also common. Thus, some Anti-Federalists sought to claim the mantle of traditional Whig ideals, federalism, or simple patriotism and adopted names such as "An Old Whig," or "A Federal Farmer," or "A Columbian Patriot." Names meant to trade on the positive associations of the pastoral also appeared with some regularity, including "A Farmer" or "A Yeoman." Finally, a few authors invoked democratic ideals, calling themselves "One of the Common People," "A Plebeian," or "A Democratic Federalist."[28]

In the case of the more vituperative Anti-Federalist essays, anonymity protected the author from possible libel charges. Under the cloak of anonymity authors were free to savage individuals and ideas they found objectionable. In the pamphlet edition of his *Genuine Information*, Luther Martin informed his audience that "few, very few, even of the *anonymous* publications have *insinuated* the information to be in any respect uncandid." The

---

Committee," Apr. 12, 1788, Lamb Papers, NYHS. For a general discussion of reactions to Warren's pamphlet, see the discussion in the headnote, *DHRC*, XVI, 274.

27. *New-York Journal*, Oct. 4, 1787 (*DHRC*, XIII, 315). The practice of publishing under pseudonyms has created problems for historians interested in identifying the authors of particular Anti-Federalist essays. Although the authors of a number of the major essays have been identified, the vast majority of essays, particularly those not widely reprinted, cannot be identified.

28. A good sense of the range of names adopted by Anti-Federalists can be obtained from the table of contents in *CA-F*. The most radical popular voices, it is important to note, are underrepresented there.

absence of blistering attacks was, in Martin's view, itself proof of the truth of his claims.[29]

Arthur Lee's Cincinnatus essays employed a distinctly elite variant of rhetoric, his rhetorical identity drawing on a patrician Roman ideal of virtue. The essays were written as a rebuttal to James Wilson's "Speech at a Public Meeting," and Cincinnatus addressed Wilson as one gentleman to another. He peppered his essays with references to Blackstone and Coke and other English jurists, Roman history, Latin quotations, and excerpts in French borrowed from Montesquieu and Jean Louis Delolme. Cincinnatus's intended audience was clearly other members of the gentry, men schooled in ancient and modern languages who were comfortable with such displays of learning. The rhetorical power of this essay depended on the author's ability to demonstrate that he was a man of learning and reason.

Cincinnatus framed his response to Wilson's speech following the conventions governing exchanges among gentlemen. "I am not without hope," he wrote, "that candor, of which no gentleman talks more, will render you a convert to the opinion, that some material parts of the proposed Constitution are so constructed" that they would destroy *"the liberties of the people."*[30]

A very similar rhetorical strategy was employed by the Virginian Cato Uticensis, who was careful to stress that his critique of the Constitution implied no insult of its framers. Cato expressed his own hesitancy to challenge the wisdom of so distinguished a body of gentlemen, expressing his "reverential awe" for the framers. Only "impious arrogance" and "vain presumption" would prompt an individual to question their intentions. Such insolence would serve only to discredit an author, earning him "the most deserved infamy and contempt." Having made clear his respect for the gentlemen who composed the "General Convention," Cato reminded his readers of their duty as freemen and citizens to consider "measures," not "men."[31]

The middling sort favored a different rhetorical style. Federal Farmer captured the essence of middling rhetoric when he declared that his opinion was "only the opinion of an individual, and so far only as it corresponds with the opinions of the honest and substantial part of the community, is it entitled to consideration." The author of these essays (Melancton Smith)

29. Luther Martin, *The Genuine Information Delivered to the Legislature of the State of Maryland* . . . (Philadelphia, 1788) (*CA-F,* II, 26 [pamphlet edition]).

30. Cincinnatus [Arthur Lee], no. 1, "To James Wilson, Esq.," *New-York Journal,* Nov. 1, 1787 (*DHRC,* XIII, 530), no. 2, "To James Wilson, Esq.," *New-York Journal,* Nov. 8, 1787 (XIV, 11–14), no. 4, "To James Wilson, Esq.," *New-York Journal,* Nov. 22, 1787 (XIV, 188–191).

31. Cato Uticensis, "To the Freemen of Virginia," *Virginia Independent Chronicle* (Richmond), Oct. 17, 1787 (*DHRC,* VIII, 70–72).

evoked the values of the sturdy yeomanry. The tone of the essays was also moderate, stressing that the author was "open to conviction, and always disposed to adopt that which, all things considered, shall appear to me to be most for the happiness of the community." Although Federal Farmer appealed to the notion of the commonweal, the notion of community he defended was quite different from the one championed by elite Anti-Federalist authors such as Cincinnatus: his audience was the middling sort. This perspective reflected the views of middling politicians such as New York's John Lamb, who informed Richard Henry Lee: "It would far exceed the Bounds of a Letter to detail to you our Objections to the proposed Constitution. And it is the less necessary that we should do it, as they are well stated in a Publication, which we take the Liberty of transmitting you in a series of Letters from the Federal Farmer to the Republican."[32]

A similar style was employed by A Plebeian (also Melancton Smith?), who claimed to be a spokesman for "the common people, the yeomanry of the country." It was that group who had the most to fear from the new Constitution: "When a tyranny is established, there are always masters as well as slaves; the great and the well-born are generally the former, and the middling class the latter." In contrast to appeals to learned authorities, this middling author appealed to common sense and the virtues likely to be possessed by any solid citizen. The solutions to America's economic problems, for example, required only an application of the simple values of industry and frugality: "Common sense dictates, that if a man buys more than he sells, he will remain in debt; the same is true of a country." America's problems required the application of the kind of wisdom that men of the middling sort were best able to provide. This appeal was couched in a simple style that invoked the values and ideals of the broad class of yeomen and artisans who defined the middling classes. Common sense, not displays of erudition, was the value that made this author trustworthy. The rhetoric of middling Anti-Federalists asserted the superiority of those values most closely associated with the yeoman class.[33]

If some Anti-Federalists were eager to claim the mantle of middling respectability, others were not afraid to fan the flames of class antagonism.

32. [Smith?], *Letters from the Federal Farmer*, nos. 1, 5 (*CA-F*, II, 224, 252–253); John Lamb to Richard Henry Lee, May 18, 1788 (*DHRC*, IX, 814). For a detailed discussion of Federal Farmer's identity, see Chapter 4, below.

33. A Plebeian [Melancton Smith?], *Address* (*CA-F*, VI, 146–166). The term "plebeian" carried two rather different senses. It could either refer to the lowest stratum of society or could describe a broad range of society below the rank of patrician. This Anti-Federalist author followed the latter sense, equating the plebeians with the middling sort.

The use of class-conscious rhetoric defined the writings of authors who sought to appeal to a more popular audience. Authors such as Centinel, An Officer of the Late Continental Army, and Philadelphiensis employed a more inflammatory style, with blistering and acerbic attacks on aristocracy. The content of the essays and their literary style differentiated them from the more moderate appeals found in the essays of middling democrats such as An Old Whig, Federal Farmer, Cato, or Brutus, which were more suited to middling tastes.

Although radical polemicists portrayed the struggle over the Constitution in stark terms, plebeians versus patricians, they did not cast themselves as plebeians. Instead of seeking to speak by virtue of their social status, they claimed the right to speak by virtue of their close connection to the people. As Centinel noted, "Those who are competent to the task of developing the principles of government, ought to be encouraged to come forward, and thereby the better enable the people to make a proper judgment." His choice of signature underscored his effort to portray himself as a guardian of the people's liberties. This set of essays employed some of the most scathing, class-conscious rhetoric found in any Anti-Federalist writing. Centinel rejected the traditional idea that wealth and leisure were essential to cultivate the disinterestedness necessary for republican virtue. For Centinel, quite the opposite was true. Wealth actually made one less likely to be virtuous: "The love of domination is generally in proportion to talents, abilities, and superior acquirements." He warned, or reminded, his readers, that "the wealthy and ambitious" were not the disinterested paragons of virtue they claimed to be, but were intent on domination. The better sort had to be watched closely: "In every community they think [they] have a right to lord over their fellow creatures." The struggle between the many and few was eternal, and Centinel attacked the wellborn aristocrats who were engaged in a deliberate conspiracy to subvert liberty and republicanism.[34]

In contrast to the mild and respectful tone that characterized elite responses to James Wilson's "Speech at a Public Meeting," radical polemicists were more likely to excoriate Wilson for his aristocratic leanings. The Pennsylvanian who styled himself An Officer of the Late Continental Army not only challenged Wilson's arguments; he scorned Wilson's aristocratic temperament: "The whole tenor of his political conduct has always been strongly tainted with the spirit of *high aristocracy;* he has never been known to join in a truly popular measure, and his talents have ever been devoted to the patrician interest." Wilson's affection for the upper classes was balanced

34. Centinel, no. 1, *IG*, Oct. 5, 1787 (*CA-F*, II, 136–137).

by his contempt for the people. An Officer went on to denounce Wilson for "despising what he calls the inferior order of people." "Popular liberty and popular assemblies offer to his exalted imagination an idea of meanness and contemptibility which he hardly seeks to conceal." Much like Centinel, who spoke to the people but did not seek to portray himself as one of the people, An Officer followed the same rhetorical strategy. He adopted, not the identity of a common soldier, but the rhetorical posture of an officer. He sought to convey his ties to the people while simultaneously demonstrating that he himself was not one of the common people.[35]

Some Anti-Federalist authors went even further than radical polemicists, choosing not merely to express sympathy with but actually to identify themselves as plebeians. These authors did not follow the model of Centinel or An Officer of the Late Continental Army in differentiating themselves from the common people. In contrast to radical polemicists, plebeian authors asserted that their voices expressed the true will of the people because they were themselves common folk. A Customer, worried that "the lower class" might "fall in with the views of some of the better sort who reprebate the old-fashioned ideas of 1775, viz. that the common people were good judges in the affairs of government; and that their time was well spent when it was devoted to the study of politicks." Satire was especially effective for this style of plebeian assault: it afforded a potent means of humiliating Federalist aristocratic pretensions. The author of a spurious letter from James Bowdoin to James de Caledonia (that is, James Wilson) adopted this approach. He mocked Wilson's Scottish background, conferring on Wilson the mock title "de Caledonia." The letter parodied Federalists, informing readers that, after the Constitution was adopted, Federalists "shall never again be troubled with the people, never dread the event of elections." The better sort would, with the help of the new government, "be able to keep the people at a proper distance."[36]

Plebeian texts could be enacted as well as written, employing a rhetoric of gesture and ritual, not metaphor and syllogism. In Carlisle, Pennsylvania, an Anti-Federalist crowd drew upon plebeian traditions of protest to express its

35. An Officer of the Late Continental Army, *IG*, Nov. 6, 1787 (*DHRC*, II, 211, 213). Paul Leicester Ford identified William Findley as the author of this essay. There is, however, some reason to doubt this attribution. The tone of the essay does not resemble Findley's "Hampden" essay, *Pittsburgh Gazette*, Feb. 16, 1788 (II, 663–669). Findley expressed some concern that the use of overly biting language might be counterproductive; see William Findley to William Irvine, Mar. 12, 1788 (XVI, 373–375).

36. A Customer, *Cumberland Gazette* (Portland, Maine), Mar. 13, 1788 (*CA-F*, IV, 202); James Bowdoin to James de Caledonia, *IG*, Feb. 27, 1788 (*DHRC*, XVI, 240).

view of James Wilson's "Speech at a Public Meeting." Plebeian Anti-Federalists did more than simply denounce James de Caledonia for betraying the liberties of the people; they prepared an effigy bearing the name "James Wilson the Caledonian" for a ritual trial and execution. Wilson was treated as a traitor, paraded around town, repeatedly whipped, then hanged, and his symbolic remains were committed to a funeral pyre. The ritual humiliation and execution of Wilson were an especially dramatic means of attacking aristocracy.[37]

Diverse literary techniques, including the tone of an essay, the patterns of citation, and the choice of signature helped Anti-Federalist authors project their arguments. These rhetorical strategies and their different tropes were each shaped by a different ideological agenda. Some authors wrote as if America were a homogeneous society of independent yeomen. Others chose to appeal to different audiences that were composed of three inchoate social classes: the better, middling, and lower sorts. Other authors preferred simply to view their audiences and categorize society in a sharp dichotomy between an elite and the people. The rhetoric of Anti-Federalist writing reflected all of those conceptions of audience. Thus, an analysis of the various imagined communities that Anti-Federalist texts were written for is an important first step to reconstructing the actual audiences that specific essays were intended to reach.[38]

Reading Politics and the Politics of Reading

Rhetoric, while deeply revealing about how authors understand their audience, does not tell us how actual readers responded to the texts they read. Although the surviving historical record does not provide enough information to create a detailed ethnography of reading, it does suggest clear patterns. Glimpses of how Anti-Federalist essays were actually read can be gleaned from the letters of participants in this struggle and the surviving marginalia on the actual texts of Anti-Federalist essays. Intertextual patterns of reading and citation also provide important clues to the way Anti-Federalist texts were read. The relationship between reading and authorship was close: authors were invariably readers of other Anti-Federalist texts.

37. For a discussion of the Carlisle riot, see Saul Cornell, "Aristocracy Assailed: The Ideology of Backcountry Anti-Federalism," *JAH*, LXXVI (1989–1990), 1148–1172.

38. On the notion of an implied reader, see the discussion in Robert C. Holoub, *Reception Theory: A Critical Introduction* (London, 1984), 84–85, 100–101; and Jonathan Culler, *On Deconstruction: Theory and Criticism after Structuralism* (Ithaca, N.Y., 1982).

Evidence about how particular essays could be read can, therefore, be obtained by carefully studying how different texts, in effect, read each other's arguments.[39]

The reading habits of Richard Henry Lee and Arthur Lee seem typical of the Anti-Federalist elite. When queried about James Wilson's widely reprinted "Speech at a Public Meeting," Richard Henry Lee wrote, "The Press has produced such Manly and well reasoned refutations of him and his System, that both have lost ground amazingly in the public estimation." Lee read broadly and was familiar with a diversity of Federalist and Anti-Federalist essays. He was not limited to Anti-Federalist materials published in local papers. Lee corresponded with leading politicians throughout the nation, many of whom sought out his advice. This extended network of correspondents allowed him to procure additional printed materials easily. Many influences shaped Lee's broad, cosmopolitan reading habits, which were at least as important to his thought as any of the items published by other Anti-Federalist authors. Lee, a model republican statesman, supplemented published materials with information he gathered from his wide circle of contacts, which included men on both sides of the question of ratification.[40]

Although Lee expressed great confidence in the quality of Anti-Federalist material published in the press, he felt compelled to publish his own views of the defects of the Constitution. It was fitting that Lee's major contribution to the public debate would take the form of a published letter. The world of print represented by newspapers and the gentry world of letters were not easily separated for a man of Lee's social prominence. In this published letter to Governor Edmund Randolph, Lee acknowledged, "The establishment of the new plan of government, in its present form, is a question that involves

39. For a discussion of the historical application of reader-response techniques, see Cathy N. Davidson, *Revolution and the Word: The Rise of the Novel in America* (New York, 1986); James L. Machor, *Readers in History: Nineteenth-Century American Literature and the Contexts of Response* (Baltimore, 1993); Robert Darnton, *The Great Cat Massacre and Other Episodes in French Cultural History* (New York, 1984). One of the most important insights of modern literary theory is the notion of intertextuality. Every text can be approached as a reading or response to other texts. When we locate information about the actual authors of particular texts, we can then use their writings as proxies for broader patterns of reading. For a discussion of this approach, see Cornell, "Early American History in a Postmodern Age," *WMQ*, 3d Ser., L (1993), 329–341.

40. Richard Henry Lee to Samuel Adams, Oct. 27, 1787 (*DHRC*, XIII, 484); Harry Innes to John Brown, Dec. 7, 1787 (VIII, 223); Richard Henry Lee to William Shippen, Jr., Oct. 2, 1787 (XIII, 289).

such immense consequences to the present times and to posterity, that it calls for the deepest attention of the best and wisest friends of their country." Lee cited Blackstone and invoked the authority of Montesquieu. His brother Arthur Lee was even more self-conscious in his pattern of citation. His wide reading in philosophy and jurisprudence was ultimately at least as important as any Federalist or Anti-Federalist texts.[41]

Members of the gentry were expected to be well read but independent-minded. Their status as gentlemen required that they not be too reliant on the ideas of newspaper writers. This approach to reading, shaped by the traditional Whig republican notion of disinterested virtue, shaped the way they processed their reading.[42]

A somewhat different pattern of reading shaped the perspective of Maryland's Samuel Chase, a politician who exploited the rising tide of democratic sentiment created by Independence. Chase's popularity and ability to manipulate the democratic rhetoric of the Revolution made him one of the most effective politicians in Maryland in the post-Revolutionary period.

In the notes for his speech to the Maryland ratification convention, Chase listed citations to the materials that supported his arguments. Although Chase made passing reference to Montesquieu and a compendium of famous English legal cases, the most important influence on his speech was the writings of other Anti-Federalist authors. He showed a clear preference for writers from the Middle Atlantic, especially Brutus, Cato, An Old Whig, and Federal Farmer. The range of materials suggests that he had access to Anti-Federalist printers in Philadelphia and New York. Although he did not enjoy the national reputation of Lee, Chase was an established state politician, whose circle of contacts included important Anti-Federalist leaders in Maryland and other neighboring states. In contrast to patrician politicians like Richard Henry Lee, Chase did not include prominent Federalists among his immediate correspondents. His political network was more circumscribed, providing him with access to other middling politicians and a wider range of Anti-Federalist writings than was available in the local press.[43]

41. Richard Henry Lee, "Copy of a Letter from Richard Henry Lee [to Edmund Randolph]," *Pennsylvania Packet*, Dec. 20, 1787 (*DHRC*, XIV, 364–372); Cincinnatus [Arthur Lee], no. 1, "To James Wilson, Esq.," *New-York Journal*, Nov. 1, 1787 (XIII, 530), no. 2, "To James Wilson, Esq.," *New-York Journal*, Nov. 8, 1787 (XIV, 11–14), no. 4, "To James Wilson, Esq.," *New-York Journal*, Nov. 22, 1787 (XIV, 188–191).

42. Richard Henry Lee, "Copy of a Letter from Richard Henry Lee [to Edmund Pendleton]," *Pennsylvania Packet*, Dec. 20, 1787 (*DHRC*, XIV, 364–372). See also William Fleming to Thomas Madison, Feb. 19, 1788 (XVI, 141).

43. The original copy of Chase's speech has been lost. A transcript made by George

Chase's clear preference for the writings of Anti-Federalists from the Middle Atlantic is striking. He was most influenced by those who presented a moderate democratic critique of the Constitution. Authors such as Brutus, Cato, Federal Farmer, and An Old Whig captured the animus that inspired the many middling democrats who dominated political life of the Middle Atlantic region. Cato's critique of the new Constitution encapsulated those concerns. "The small number of representatives," Cato warned, would undermine the democratic character of the new government. "But few of you will have the chance of sharing even in this branch of the legislature," and the consequences of such inadequate representation would work against the interests of the middling sort. Cato conceded, "In every civilized community, even those of the most democratic kind, there are principles which lead to an aristocracy." Under the new system "natural and artificial eminence" would be "assisted by principles interwoven in this government." In choosing to identify the interests of society with those of the middling sort, Cato was not espousing a traditional republican vision of the commonweal, but a new, middle-class ideal. The good of society was identical to the good of the numerical majority, which was drawn from the broad ranks of the middling sort. Chase attacked the new Constitution in similar terms: "A few men cannot possibly represent the *opinions*, wishes and *interests* of great numbers. It is impossible for a few men to be acquainted with the sentiments and interests of the United States, which contains many different classes or orders of people—Merchants, farmers, planters, mechanics and gentry." In particular, Chase feared that the House of Representatives would become a domain of "the rich and wealthy," who would be "ignorant of the sentiments of the middling class of citizens." Chase's reading habits typified those of middling politicians. He showed a clear preference for the more moderate democratic voices within Anti-Federalism.[44]

The town of Carlisle, Pennsylvania, provides another interesting venue to examine a different pattern of consumption among Anti-Federalists, one typical of more popular reading habits. The local newspaper, the *Carlisle Gazette*, printed moderate amounts of Anti-Federalist materials, including

---

Bancroft, however, survives in New York Public Library; see James A. Haw, "Samuel Chase's 'Objections to the Federal Government,'" *Maryland Historical Magazine*, LXXVI (1981), 272–285. On Maryland politics, see Norman K. Risjord, *Chesapeake Politics, 1781–1800* (New York, 1978). On Chase, see Stephen Presser, *The Original Misunderstanding: The English, the Americans, and the Dialectic of Federalist Jurisprudence* (Durham, N.C., 1991).

44. Cato, no. 5, "To the Citizens of the State of New York," *New-York Journal*, Nov. 22, 1787 (*DHRC*, XIV, 185); no. 6, "To the People of the State of New York," *New-York Journal*, Dec. 13, 1787 (XIV, 431); Haw, "Samuel Chase's 'Objections,'" *MHM*, LXXVI (1981), 275.

installments of Centinel, Old Whig, Philadelphiensis, and such essays as Gerry's "Objections to Signing the National Constitution" and "The Address and Reasons of Dissent of the Minority." Essays written by Pennsylvania Anti-Federalists dominated the list of materials published in the *Carlisle Gazette*. Despite the publication of several important Anti-Federalist essays, local opponents of the Constitution were not satisfied with the amount of material published. They sought out local Anti-Federalist politicians to help them obtain additional writings of Centinel, the essayist they found most compelling.

William Petrikin, one of the most outspoken Anti-Federalists in Carlisle, captured the frustrations of many in the backcountry when he wrote, "We are at a great loss here for Intelegence." Anti-Federalists were especially upset by their inability to gain access to a broader range of newspapers. This isolation stood in contrast to the ease with which local Federalists seemed to be able to procure Federalist materials. As Petrikin noted, "Our advarsary carrys on a constant intercourse with their confederates every where." Petrikin did not enjoy a wide circle of correspondents either in Pennsylvania or elsewhere who could provide him with additional information or Anti-Federalist materials. His understanding of the Constitution was largely shaped by information he could obtain from the local press and information disseminated by word of mouth.[45]

Although he did not have a large Anti-Federalist network of political connections, he did on his own initiative contact John Nicholson, a key Anti-Federalist organizer in his own state of Pennsylvania. Petrikin requested that he be sent "afew of the Centinals," noting that "they are much admired here." Centinel stood out among Anti-Federalist authors as one of the most adept at reaching a broad popular audience. It was not just Petrikin who recognized Centinel's popular appeal. Local Federalists echoed him, viewing Centinel as a rabble-rouser. One Federalist lamented, "It is amazing to see how blindly they follow those guides below, and terrify themselves with imaginary evils."[46]

Federalists were sufficiently impressed with Centinel's popular influence to work hard at discrediting him by publishing counterfeit editions of him. Petrikin, worried that such efforts might undermine the local Anti-Federal-

---

45. William Petrikin to John Nicholson, Feb. 24, 1788 (*DHRC*, II, 694); Petrikin to Nicholson, May 8, 1788 (II [microfiche], 675). For a discussion of the Carlisle riot, see Cornell, "Aristocracy Assailed," *JAH*, LXXVI (1989–1990), 1148–1172.

46. Petrikin to Nicholson, Feb. 24, 1788 (*DHRC*, II, 695); John King to Benjamin Rush, Nov. 5–6, 1787 (II, 208).

ist cause, forwarded to John Nicholson a forged "Centinel" written by a local Federalist and requested that the real author of "Centinel" be notified and a suitable rebuttal composed. Petrikin informed Nicholson, "We would have answered it here," but local Anti-Federalists "were of opinion it would come best from the Centinal himself." The esteem in which Carlisle Anti-Federalists held Centinel seems to have been typical of a more radical constituency within the ranks of Anti-Federalists. The clear egalitarian and democratic tone and style of Centinel set him apart from the more erudite and dispassionate writings of some Anti-Federalists. Centinel's critique of aristocracy was directed at a specific social class that he described as the "well-born." His writing exposed the efforts of the "aristocratic . . . *well-born few,* who had been zealously endeavoring since the establishment of their constitutions, to humble that offensive *upstart, equal liberty.*" He went on to cast the battle over the Constitution in clear class terms, a battle between "well-born" and "low-born." Centinel's vision of the underlying dynamic at work in the struggle over ratification appealed to a more radical plebeian populist core within the ranks of the Anti-Federalist coalition. It was this radicalism that led Carlisle Anti-Federalists into the streets to protest the ratification of the Constitution by Pennsylvania. Wellborn Federalists versus lowborn Anti-Federalists was precisely how William Petrikin and the other Anti-Federalists who participated in the Carlisle riots viewed ratification.[47]

Since a reply by the real Centinel was not forthcoming, Petrikin took up his pen under the name Aristocrotis and mounted his own attack on local Federalists, a biting satirical pamphlet, *The Government of Nature Delineated.* The most important influence on this essay was Centinel. Petrikin had recycled ideas from other Anti-Federalist authors available in the Pennsylvania press and recast them to reflect the perspective of plebeian populists. Local reaction to the essay appears to have been extremely positive. Petrikin was convinced that his efforts might actually be helpful to the larger cause of Anti-Federalism, and he sought funds to publish the pamphlet and have it distributed elsewhere.[48]

Richard Henry Lee, Samuel Chase, and William Petrikin all read the rhetoric of ratification in ways that reflected their different positions in

47. Petrikin to Nicholson, Feb. 24, 1788 (*DHRC,* II, 695); Centinel, no. 3, "To the People of Pennsylvania," *IG,* Nov. 8, 1787 (*CA-F,* II, 156).

48. Aristocrotis [William Petrikin], *The Government of Nature Delineated . . .* (Carlisle, Pa., 1788) (*CA-F,* III, 196–212); Petrikin to Nicholson, Feb. 24, 1788 (*DHRC,* II, 694–696). A comparison of the pamphlet and Petrikin's letters suggests that his published writing had been edited by someone with some education.

society. Social class not only determined what sort of access to print these men would have, but it shaped how they read the materials available to them. Lee's reading habits reflected the cosmopolitan tastes of the Anti-Federalist elite, going well beyond what was available in the press. The grand tradition of Western thought shaped his worldview, and information obtained directly from leading political figures influenced how he read the rhetoric of ratification. Ultimately, a gentleman was supposed to demonstrate his independence and act in a manner consistent with the ideals of republican virtue.

Samuel Chase's tastes reflected the perspective of middling democrats who dominated Anti-Federalism in Pennsylvania and New York and parts of Maryland. Chase's ideas were much more strongly influenced by those essayists and pamphleteers whose ideas filled the pages of newspapers, and he turned to them to supplement his own knowledge and the information he obtained from political contacts in other states.

William Petrikin depended more heavily on the local press, both for news and for the ideas that would shape his critique of the Constitution. His clear preference was the most radical Anti-Federalist authors, essayists who framed the struggle over the Constitution in the most stridently class-conscious terms. Largely lacking newspapers from elsewhere and a wide circle of political contacts, he relied primarily on local information. Petrikin's efforts to contact Pennsylvania Anti-Federalist John Nicholson were unusual: had local Federalists not overplayed their hand and published a spurious edition of Centinel, Petrikin might never even have sought Nicholson's help. Yet, even with Nicholson's assistance, Anti-Federalists in Carlisle continued to be frustrated in their efforts to procure outside materials or the political intelligence readily available to politicians of national stature such as Lee or even to state politicians such as Chase.

Anti-Federalist support depended on three crucial groups in American society: backcountry farmers and artisans, the middling sort who dominated politics in the Middle Atlantic, and a small but highly influential group of elite politicians. Despite the social and political diversity of the movement, a relatively small number of Anti-Federalist essays defined the terms of political debate. Contrary to the suggestions of Federalists and modern scholars, the Anti-Federalist critique of the Constitution, if not unanimous, was certainly not incoherent. The dynamics of the public debate over the Constitution worked to focus, not fragment, their argument. Their main outlines, in fact, emerged early in the ratification debate and were repeated frequently over the course of that debate.

This common critique did not mean that there were not important tensions within the opposition to the Constitution. While public discourse worked to unify the nature of the Anti-Federalist argument, it did not diminish the important differences that separated Anti-Federalists from one another. A common language did not mean that opponents of the Constitution were united behind a common political vision. Virtually all of the key terms of Anti-Federalist discourse were essentially contested concepts whose meaning could differ markedly for different members of the Anti-Federalist coalition.[49]

The most important divisions within Anti-Federalist writing reflected the inchoate class divisions in America. Although some authors sought to address their audience as citizens, without particular attachments, the vast majority of Anti-Federalist writers acknowledged that American society was divided into three amorphous classes: the better sort, the middling sort, and the lower sort. Authors adopted techniques focused on reaching each of those audiences. The tone of an essay, quotations from other authors, and the choice of pen name were all selected to help an author get a particular message across. Style and content were therefore inextricably linked.

Once printed, however, those messages could be interpreted in different ways by particular audiences and readers. Readers could take from texts whatever they needed and ignore arguments or ideologies that failed to persuade them. The evidence about the behavior of actual readers confirms the textual evidence about the existence of different interpretive communities. Members of the gentry, middling democrats, and plebeians often favored different Anti-Federalist authors. Their distinctive ideologies also led them to read and react differently to many of the same texts. The range of responses to James Wilson's "Speech at a Public Meeting" is perhaps the most dramatic example of the distinct interpretive communities within the Anti-Federalist coalition—elite authors respectfully disagreed with Wilson while plebeians burned him in effigy.

To be persuasive in the struggle over the Constitution, authors had to do more than attack the Constitution: they had to put forward an alternative constitutional vision. Although individual Anti-Federalists did not always advocate a clear institutional framework or blueprint for government, their writings did embody a variety of different conceptions of constitutionalism. The vast outpouring of materials during ratification makes it possible to

---

49. On the notion of essentially contested concepts, see Terence Ball, James Farr, and Russell L. Hanson, eds., *Political Innovation and Conceptual Change* (Cambridge, 1988); Ball and Pocock, *Conceptual Change and the Constitution*.

explore in considerable detail the constitutional ideas of individuals from across a broad social spectrum, running from backcountry farmers to planter aristocrats, and the range of those ideas discussed by both elite and more popular spokesmen is astonishing. Although united by a common critique, Anti-Federalist constitutionalism was as variegated as the coalition of groups that opposed the Constitution. Anti-Federalist ideology made it possible for planter aristocrats and middling democrats each to champion a system reposing the bulk of authority in the states; Anti-Federalist federalism allowed Virginians to defend a decidedly hierarchical vision of republicanism, even as it accommodated the more democratic vision of New Yorkers and Pennsylvanians. Anti-Federalist constitutionalism provided a broad tent under which many different political visions could rest. The one group that could not easily be accommodated was plebeian populists, whose extreme vision of localism and radical democratic ideas set them apart from elites and the middling sort.

CHAPTER 2 :

ELITE ANTI-FEDERALIST

POLITICAL AND CONSTITUTIONAL

THOUGHT

A small group of highly articulate and influential Anti-Federalists was vital in shaping opposition to the Constitution. These elite Anti-Federalists were not typical of the grass-roots opposition to the Constitution. Yet, their social status, political influence, and intellectual energy allowed them to have a profound impact on the debate over ratification.[1]

Many of the most widely reprinted Anti-Federalist essays were written by members of this elite. Perhaps the most important of these were the objections of the participants in the Philadelphia Convention who refused to sign the Constitution, the three most influential being Elbridge Gerry, George Mason, and Luther Martin. Their opposition to the Constitution was invoked as warning, demonstrating the need for prudence and caution. If men like those had concerns, then surely the Constitution merited further scrutiny to ensure that their fears were unfounded.

1. Relatively few studies of Anti-Federalism have taken note of the importance of a small elite in shaping the terms of public debate. On elite Anti-Federalism, see Robert H. Wiebe, *The Opening of American Society: From the Adoption of the Constitution to the Eve of Disunion* (New York, 1984), 27–30. Wiebe argues that elite Anti-Federalists were nationalists. It would be more apt to describe them as committed cosmopolitan localists. Jackson Turner Main, *Political Parties before the Constitution* (Chapel Hill, N.C., 1973), categorized Anti-Federalism as a form of agrarian localism. Main's focus on the most democratic Anti-Federalists obscures the vital role of elites in shaping public discourse. On the importance of their writings, see William H. Riker, *The Strategy of Ratification: Campaigning for the American Constitution* (New Haven, Conn., 1996).

Gerry's and Mason's synoptic explanations of their reasons for opposition circulated widely among an influential group of elite Anti-Federalists (see Chapter 1). The short, concise recapitulations of the Anti-Federalist critique of the Constitution also benefited from the personal prestige of its authors. Luther Martin's widely reprinted series of essays, *The Genuine Information*, served a different function for most Anti-Federalist readers. It became the primary and, for many, the only source of information about the proceedings of the Philadelphia Convention. Few, if any, details about the convention had been leaked to the press during its deliberations. Indeed, its decision to impose a rule of secrecy itself became an issue that Anti-Federalists used to question the intent of that body. Martin's essays detailed the convention's activities, and his account lent credence to the frequently voiced Anti-Federalist charge that the Constitution had intended to create a consolidated government based on the principles of aristocracy.[2]

Although elite Anti-Federalists spoke the same language as other groups who opposed the Constitution, the underlying constitutional and political philosophy animating their opposition was distinctive. The perspective of the Anti-Federalist elite reflected their social position in American society. Indeed, their opposition to the Constitution was motivated by their belief that the new government would undermine their influence and leave America open to the dangers of aristocratic subversion or mobocracy.

An exceedingly cosmopolitan group, the wealth, social status, and education of leading Anti-Federalists were in many cases similar to the trappings of prominent Federalists. Members of the Anti-Federalist elite were active in state politics, and a number of them served in prominent positions in the Confederation government. Elite Anti-Federalists enjoyed a wide circle of political contacts, which allowed them to forge effective alliances with Anti-Federalists in both their own and other states. The breadth of political

2. Elbridge Gerry, "Hon. Mr. Gerry's Objections to Signing the National Constitution," *Massachusetts Centinel* (Boston), Nov. 3, 1787 (*DHRC*, XIII, 548–550); Luther Martin, *The Genuine Information Delivered to the Legislature of the State of Maryland* . . . (Philadelphia, 1788) (*CA-F*, II, 19–82); George Mason, "Objections to the Constitution of Government Formed by the Convention," *Massachusetts Centinel*, Nov. 21, 1787 (*CA-F*, II, 11–13). For biographical information on Martin, see Paul S. Clarkson and R. Samuel Jett, *Luther Martin of Maryland* (Baltimore, 1970). Anti-Federalist authors as different as Columbian Patriot and Centinel each referred to Martin's *Genuine Information* when discussing the Philadelphia Convention. For a general discussion of reactions to it, see the headnote in *DHRC*, XV, 146–150. For a thoughtful discussion of Martin's federalism, see Peter S. Onuf, "Maryland: The Small Republic in the New Nation," in Michael Allen Gillespie and Michael Lienesch, eds., *Ratifying the Constitution* (Lawrence, Kans., 1989), 171–200.

experience they could draw upon was impressive. Luther Martin was one of the most distinguished lawyers in the new nation and had served as Maryland's attorney general. Elbridge Gerry was a respected politician and prosperous New England merchant. Arthur Lee had been a diplomat, a delegate to the Confederation Congress, and a member of the Board of Treasury. No state produced a more distinguished roster of opponents than Virginia, many of whose most influential politicians and jurists were arrayed against the Constitution. In addition to Arthur Lee, the Old Dominion boasted such eminent figures as George Mason, Richard Henry Lee, James Monroe, William Grayson, and Spencer Roane.[3]

One important group within the Anti-Federalist elite was the Old Republicans, men like James Warren and Richard Henry Lee who had been leading figures in the Revolutionary cause. The voices of the Old Patriot leaders dominated elite Anti-Federalist thought and epitomized the traditional Whig republican ideal of virtue. Contemporaries even compared men such as Richard Henry Lee to "one of Plutarch's Men." George Mason was often compared to Cato. While the traditional Whig republican ideas of the Old Patriots dominated elite Anti-Federalist thought, they were not the only elite voices that challenged the Constitution. A number of new voices, such as Massachusetts Anti-Federalist James Winthrop, added their objections. Descended from a distinguished New England family, Winthrop held a number of minor local political offices and even volunteered to help put down Shays's Rebellion. He served as the librarian of Harvard College and was twice passed over for his father's professorship in mathematics. Although not the most influential member of the Anti-Federalist elite, Winthrop was one of the most original and sophisticated Anti-Federalist writers. In contrast to the Old Republican elite, Winthrop propounded a forward-looking liberal critique of the Constitution that was among the most theoretically sophisticated of any Anti-Federalist author.[4]

Although there was considerable diversity among the Anti-Federalist elite on such vital matters as political economy, their political and constitutional ideals, particularly the Old Republicans', followed a number of common themes.

3. For biographical information on Lee, consult Louis W. Potts, *Arthur Lee: A Virtuous Revolutionary* (Baton Rouge, La., 1981).

4. Pauline Maier, *The Old Revolutionaries: Political Lives in the Age of Samuel Adams* (New York, 1980). Winthrop was clearly not an influential figure and received 82 votes of 1,867 votes cast in the Middlesex County congressional election in 1789. On this point, see *DHFFE,* I, 654–655. For a brief biographical sketch of Winthrop, see *Dictionary of American Biography,* s.v. "Winthrop, James."

Constitutionalism

Liberty was central in elite Anti-Federalist constitutionalism. Anti-Federalists pondered the classic problem of Whig constitutional thought: how to create an effective government without threatening liberty. It is important to stress that, for most Anti-Federalists, liberty was understood in Whig republican terms. Although the sphere of government authority was restricted, it need not be narrowly defined in those areas in which it exercised legitimate authority. Constitutions existed to curb the threat of arbitrary power, not the actions of representative governments. The rights of the individual were important, but government enjoyed tremendous latitude to legislate on a broad range of issues that could restrict individual liberty. As long as government's actions were a product of the people's own representatives, government was entitled to limit the actions of its citizens in a manner consistent with the public good. A few of the more libertarian Anti-Federalists embraced more genuinely liberal constitutional principles. For them, the sphere of government authority was extremely limited, and the rights of individuals were conceptualized in more expansive terms. The vast majority of Anti-Federalists fell somewhere between those two poles of constitutional thought. To complicate matters even further, particular individuals did not always present an intellectually consistent approach to the problem of rights. It was possible for an individual to frame his discussion of freedom of the press in traditional Whig republican terms while conceptualizing religious freedom in a more liberal pluralist fashion.[5]

Elite Anti-Federalist thought reflected the uneven development of American constitutionalism. Individual strains of American constitutional thought evolved at different rates, producing theories that were neither uniformly republican nor uniformly liberal. Whereas some authors self-consciously

5. On constitutionalism in this period, see Gordon S. Wood, *The Creation of the American Republic, 1776–1787* (Chapel Hill, N.C., 1969); Donald S. Lutz, *Popular Consent and Popular Control: Whig Political Theory in the Early State Constitutions* (Baton Rouge, La., 1980); Willi Paul Adams, *The First American Constitutions: Republican Ideology and the Making of the State Constitutions in the Revolutionary Era* (Chapel Hill, N.C., 1980); Marc W. Kruman, *Between Authority and Liberty: State Constitution Making in Revolutionary America* (Chapel Hill, N.C., 1997). On liberty and its relation to republicanism, see Lance Banning, "Some Second Thoughts on Virtue and the Course of Revolutionary Thinking," in J. G. A. Pocock and Terence Ball, eds., *Conceptual Change and the Constitution* (Lawrence, Kans., 1988), 194–212; Michael Kammen, *Spheres of Liberty: Changing Perceptions of Liberty in American Culture* (Madison, Wis., 1986); John Phillip Reid, *The Concept of Liberty in the Age of the American Revolution* (Chicago, 1988).

sought to reconcile the potential contradictions between republican and liberal ideals, others were satisfied with an eclectic mix of different and sometimes contradictory approaches. In many instances individual thinkers were not aware of any contradiction between the goals of promoting the public good and of protecting liberty.[6]

The view of the "the old Patriots" was captured by Mercy Otis Warren, who cast the struggle over the Constitution as a battle between those who wished "to see a form established on the secure principles of republicanism," and "an influential party in all the states" who "secretly wish for aristocracy."

Her argument demonstrates one effort to synthesize Whig republican and liberal ideas in elite Anti-Federalist constitutionalism. Warren quoted approvingly from liberal theorists such as Locke, at the same time citing the French republican theorist Gabriel Bonnet de Mably's *Observations sur les romains*. Warren saw no contradiction between these two traditions and sought to unite them into a coherent statement of constitutional principles.[7]

Writing as A Columbian Patriot, Warren accepted Blackstone's dictum, "The principal aim of society is to protect individuals in the absolute rights

6. The relevance of classical republican ideas to both Federalists and Anti-Federalists has been hotly debated by scholars. On republicanism, see J. G. A. Pocock, *The Machiavellian Moment: Florentine Republican Thought and the Atlantic Republican Tradition* (Princeton, N.J., 1975); Robert E. Shalhope, "Toward a Republican Synthesis: The Emergence of an Understanding of Republicanism in American Historiography," *WMQ*, 3d Ser., XXIX (1972), 49–80, and "Republicanism and Early American Historiography," *WMQ*, 3d Ser., XXXIX (1982), 334–356; on "country republicanism," James H. Hutson, "Country, Court, and Constitution: Antifederalism and the Historians," *WMQ*, 3d Ser., XXXVIII (1981), 337–368. On the historiography, Daniel T. Rodgers, "Republicanism: The Career of a Concept," *JAH*, LXXIX (1992–1993), 11–38. For works stressing the liberal character of thought in the founding era, see Gary J. Schmitt and Robert H. Webking, "Revolutionaries, Anti-Federalists, and Federalists: Comments on Gordon Wood's Understanding of the American Founding," *Political Science Reviewer*, IX (1979), 195–229; Thomas L. Pangle, *The Spirit of Modern Republicanism: The Moral Vision of the American Founders and the Philosophy of Locke* (Chicago, 1988); Joyce Appleby, *Liberalism and Republicanism in the Historical Imagination* (Cambridge, Mass., 1992). For efforts to chart a middle ground, see Forrest McDonald, *Novus Ordo Seclorum: The Intellectual Origins of the Constitution* (Lawrence, Kans., 1985); Linda K. Kerber, "The Republican Ideology of the Revolutionary Generation," *American Quarterly*, XXXVII (1985), 474–495; James T. Kloppenberg, "The Virtues of Liberalism: Christianity, Republicanism, and Ethics in Early American Political Discourse," *JAH*, LXXIV (1987–1988), 9–33; Paul Rahe, *Republics Ancient and Modern: Classical Republicanism and the American Revolution* (Chapel Hill, N.C., 1992).

7. Mercy Otis Warren to Catherine Macaulay Graham, Aug. 2, 1787, Mercy Otis Warren Letter-Book, MHS. (The date on the letter is probably mistaken, since the text of the Constitution was not published until September.)

which were vested in them by the immediate laws of nature." Warren was comfortable with the central tenets of liberal constitutionalism, that "the rights of individuals ought to be the primary object of all government" and that "government is instituted for the protection, safety, and happiness of the people." The Constitution imperiled those ideals by failing to make explicit the basic rights retained by the people and by failing to provide the mechanisms to check the power of government.[8]

Although Warren owed a profound debt to liberal theory, she also drew on civic republican ideas about the necessity of virtue in a republic. A Columbian Patriot quoted Mably's observation that "an heroic love for the publick good" formed the "only foundations of a free government." Although Warren invoked classical ideals of virtue, reminding her readers that "every age has its Bruti" and "its Caesars," she believed that the lessons of antiquity could provide only limited insight, since America's experience was not comparable to that of the ancient world. The "brave sons of America" had displayed a "heroism scarcely paralleled even in ancient republicks." Civic republican ideas were recast to reflect the unique character of the Revolutionary experience. American history was exceptional and promised to surpass the achievements of both Greece and Rome. Warren's constitutional vision did not require the creation of a Christian Sparta: her republicanism was decidedly Whig, not classical, in conception. As long as men of wisdom guided the ship of state and representative institutions functioned to refine the public will, republicanism would thrive.[9]

Warren's effort to synthesize aspects of Whig republicanism with natural rights theory is evident in her discussion of Blackstone. After quoting the influential jurist's discussion of liberty, Warren reminded her readers, "Society has thus deputed a certain number of their equals to take care of their personal rights, and the interests of the whole community." Apart from a limited number of inalienable rights, all political rights were subject to regulation by the legislature, which would be composed of the most virtuous members of society, who would act on behalf of the good of the community. Whig republican theory emphasized disinterested leadership, public participation by an informed citizenry, and a commitment to place the good of

8. A Columbian Patriot [Mercy Otis Warren], *Observations on the New Constitution . . .* (Boston, 1788) (*CA-F,* IV, 274, 275, 279).

9. Ibid.(IV, 272, 273, 285). For a more detailed discussion of Warren's views on ancient and modern republicanism, see Mercy Otis Warren, *History of the Rise, Progress, and Termination of the American Revolution . . .* (1809), ed. Lester Cohen, 2 vols. (Indianapolis, 1988), II, 678–679. For a perceptive analysis of these differences, see Rahe, *Republics Ancient and Modern.*

the community above individual interests when the legislature deemed such action necessary.[10]

Another example of the way liberty was conceptualized in Whig republican terms can be found in the frequent calls by elite Anti-Federalists for religious tests for public office. Thus, Luther Martin, the influential Anti-Federalist lawyer from Maryland, forcefully argued that some sort of generic Protestant religion was necessary to nurture virtue and hence essential for the survival of republicanism. Martin accepted this reasoning and attacked the Constitutional Convention for failing to acknowledge "A *belief of the existence of a Deity,* and of a *state of future rewards and punishments,*" a provision that would have offered additional "security for the good conduct of our rulers." And Martin went further, affirming that in "a Christian country it would be at *least decent* to hold out some distinction between the professors of Christianity and downright infidelity or paganism." The rights of the people to legislate on matters of public morality took precedence over the right of conscience, at least with regard to public officeholding. Tolerance, although compatible with republicanism, fell far short of a truly liberal pluralist vision of society. Many Anti-Federalists would have accepted Luther Martin's justification for instituting a religious test for public officeholders.[11]

One Anti-Federalist author who rejected the idea of religious tests was Arthur Lee. Writing as Cincinnatus, Lee applauded the Constitution's prohibition of them, thus parting company with many other elite Anti-Federalists. This prohibition did, however, trouble Lee on different grounds. Why prohibit religious tests unless the new government had the power to impose them? This prohibition would be necessary only if the new government had the authority to impose religious tests. The ban served only to legitimize the fear the new government would operate directly on individuals, posing a serious threat to personal liberty. Lee endorsed the common Anti-Federalist demand for an explicit bill of rights to guard basic liberties, including the right of conscience.[12]

10. Columbian Patriot [Warren], *Observations on the New Constitution* (*CA-F,* IV, 275).

11. Martin, *Genuine Information* (*CA-F,* II, 75). Elite Anti-Federalists were divided on the subject of government support for religion at the state level. In the controversy over religious assessment in Virginia, future Anti-Federalists were on both sides of the issue. Richard Henry Lee favored nonpreferential support for religion while George Mason opposed government support; on this point, see Merrill D. Peterson and Robert C. Vaughan, eds., *The Virginia Statute for Religious Freedom: Its Evolution and Consequences in American History* (Cambridge, 1988).

12. For discussions of Anti-Federalist views of religious freedom, see Morton Borden,

A few Anti-Federalist authors championed a genuinely liberal variant of constitutionalism. No one within the ranks of the opposition to the Constitution was more committed to a distinctly libertarian outlook than was James Winthrop. In his Agrippa essays, Winthrop defended the *"extreme liberty"* that characterized American society against the many critics who suggested that America's commitment to freedom bordered on licentiousness. "Happiness," Agrippa wrote, "arises from the freedom of our institutions and the limited nature of our government." Winthrop's commitment to a more liberal vision was also evident in his reading of Montesquieu, the theorist most frequently cited by opponents of the Constitution. For most Anti-Federalists, Montesquieu's writings were invoked because they furnished irrefutable evidence that republicanism could survive only in a small, homogeneous republic. Anti-Federalist authors generally took this injunction to mean that the vast majority of people had to be engaged in agricultural pursuits and landownership. Only those material conditions would sustain virtue and ensure that people's interests would harmonize. Agrippa dispensed with appeals to a homogeneous yeoman myth. Commercial republicanism did not, in his view, require a society in which everyone had the same interests: commercial society was ultimately the only type of society that could sustain the freedom essential for republican government.[13]

Elite Anti-Federalist constitutionalism embraced a profound reverence for written constitutions, and many authors embraced a form of constitutional literalism and a commitment to a constitutional plain style. Writing under the name John DeWitt, one Anti-Federalist reminded readers, "Language is so easy of explanation, and so difficult is it by words to convey exact ideas, that the party to be governed cannot be too explicit." Regarding the division between those powers retained by the people and those ceded to government, DeWitt wrote, "The line cannot be drawn with too much precision and accuracy." DeWitt was not satisfied with the argument, frequently employed by Federalists, that the Constitution was a limited grant of authority and hence did not require a bill of rights. Bills of rights functioned as an additional check on those who might try to manipulate the language of

---

"Federalists, Anti-Federalists, and Religious Freedom," *Journal of Church and State,* XXI (1979), 469–482; Thomas J. Curry, *The First Freedoms: Church and State in America to the Passage of the First Amendment* (New York, 1986). For other examples of Anti-Federalists who supported the concept of religious tests, see Martin, *Genuine Information* (*CA-F,* II, 75); "The Society of Western Gentlemen Revise the Constitution," *Virginia Independent Chronicle* (Richmond), Apr. 30, May 7, 1787 (*DHRC,* IX, 779).

13. Agrippa [James Winthrop], no. 12, "To the Massachusetts Convention," *Massachusetts Gazette* (Boston), Jan. 14, 1788 (*CA-F,* IV, 95–96).

constitutions for nefarious purposes. Americans were aware "that the words made use of, to express those rights so granted might convey more than they originally intended." The proper remedy for such a danger was to "express in different language those rights which the agreement did not include." Judged by DeWitt's standards, the new constitution was flawed in two profound ways. It lacked a formal bill of rights and contained too many ambiguous grants of power.[14]

The ambiguity of the language of the document was frequently commented on by Anti-Federalists. A Columbian Patriot charged that the entire document lacked precise language specifying the limits of the new government's authority. "The undefined meaning of some parts, and the ambiguities of expression in others, is dangerously adapted to the purposes of an immediate *aristocratic tyranny*." The extensive and vague powers of the executive and legislature were also "couched in such ambiguous terms—in such vague and indefinite expression, as is a sufficient ground without any other objection, for the reprobation of the system." The construction of the judiciary only compounded this problem, since there were "no well defined limits" to its power. The framers of the Constitution had set judges on a "boundless ocean." The solution was to frame constitutional texts in a clear and precise language and insist that judges and legislators not attempt to manipulate constitutional texts by interpretive construction.[15]

Textual mechanisms were not the only means by which Anti-Federalists hoped to protect liberty. The question of rights was inextricably linked to their notion of federalism. As Luther Martin observed, "It is the *State governments* which are to watch over and protect the *rights* of the *individual*." Martin's emphasis on the role of the states as the proper guardians of liberty was evident in his discussion of trial by jury and his defense of state control of the militia. Jury trial provided an important means of checking a potentially tyrannical government: it forced government to bring its case before an impartial body of citizens before it could enforce unjust laws.[16]

In Martin's view the broad appellate jurisdiction accorded federal courts by the Constitution would undermine the right to trial by jury. Federal judges would have a right to review both the law and the facts of a case. Martin argued that, as the framers of the Constitution did "not trust *State*

14. John DeWitt, no. 2, "To the Free Citizens of the Commonwealth of Massachusetts," *American Herald* (Boston), Oct. 27, 1787 (*CA-F*, IV, 21, 22).

15. Columbian Patriot [Warren], *Observations on the New Constitution* (*CA-F*, IV, 274, 276).

16. Martin, *Genuine Information* (*CA-F*, II, 44).

Judges, so would they not confide in *State juries."* Martin believed that the Constitution deliberately sought to prevent state courts and juries from protecting the interests of their citizens.[17]

Arthur Lee, as Cincinnatus, also challenged the broad appellate jurisdiction accorded the Supreme Court and the supremacy clause in Article 6 of the Constitution. Taken together, these threatened the autonomy of the states. Cincinnatus feared that this "one sweeping clause, bears down" on "every constitution in the union, and establishes its arbitrary doctrines, supreme and paramount to all the bills and declarations of rights, in which we vainly put our trust." Only by restoring some measure of authority to the states could these dangers be remedied. The simplest means of accomplishing this end would be to include language comparable to Article 2 of the Articles of Confederation, which restricted the powers of the new government to those "expressly given."[18]

It would be difficult to overstate the importance of trial by jury in the minds of Anti-Federalists like Cincinnatus or Martin. For Martin, the right of trial by jury was an indispensable safeguard. The absence of explicit protection for this right meant that Americans might again be driven to reassert the *"principles* of the American revolution," which recognized that *"arbitrary power may* and *ought* to be resisted even by *arms* if necessary." Recognizing the potential for tyranny under the new government, Martin devoted considerable attention to the ultimate check on despotism, the right of armed resistance. Martin did not advocate a permanent right of revolution or an individual right of resistance. The appropriate remedy to incursions on the rights of people was to rally state government to their cause. State control of the militia and a prohibition of a standing army would prevent the use of military force against the people by a tyrannical government. "When a government *wishes* to deprive their citizens of freedom, and reduce them to slavery, it *generally makes use of a standing army* for that purpose, and *leaves the militia in a situation as contemptible as possible, least they might oppose its arbitrary designs."* State control of the militia was necessary to guarantee that the federal system functioned as an effective guardian of individual rights.[19]

From Martin's point of view, individual rights were inextricably linked to

17. Ibid. (II, 71).

18. Cincinnatus [Arthur Lee], no. 1, "To James Wilson, Esq.," *New-York Journal,* Nov. 1, 1787 (*DHRC,* XIII, 531–533), no. 2, "To James Wilson, Esq.," *New-York Journal,* Nov. 8, 1787 (*DHRC,* XIV, 14).

19. Martin, *Genuine Information* (*CA-F,* II, 58, 59, 71).

the nature of federalism. "If the general government should attempt to oppress and enslave" the people, "they could not have any possible means of self defence; because the proposed system" robbed them of their control over the militia. State control of the militia was the proper check on the arbitrary authority of the central government. Martin's defense of the militia was, not a libertarian defense of an individual's right to take up arms to defend his liberty, but an affirmation of the state's responsibility to defend those rights.[20]

Martin conjured up an image of federal excise officers bleeding citizens "at *every vein* as long as they have a *drop* of blood." The danger lay, not in the power of taxation, but in the absence of checks on that power. For Martin the great danger was that those taxes would be enacted by a distant government and collected by officials of "the *general government*" and would not be "accountable to the *States*." The danger posed by the new government's power to tax stemmed from its inability truly to represent the people. "The *States* were much *better judges* of the circumstances of their citizens." It followed that, as far as taxation was concerned, "the manner in which it could be raised, with the *greatest ease* and *convenience* to their citizens," was best left to the states to decide. Only in cases of delinquency should the "general government" have the power of direct taxation.[21]

The Problem of Federalism and Localism

The most sophisticated elite discussion of the problem of federalism was formulated by Luther Martin, who came closer than any other Anti-Federalist to developing a distinctive theory of states' rights. According to Martin, the Revolution had placed the individual colonies into a state of nature. The Confederation was a compact among those sovereign and independent states. In effect, Martin rendered the states, not the people, as the original parties to the compact that created the Union. By acting directly on individuals and bypassing the states, the new government undermined the sovereignty of the states. Martin recast the critique of consolidation that was central to Anti-Federalism to focus attention explicitly on the question of sovereignty. "The favourers of monarchy, and those who wished the total abolition of State Governments" opposed the federal principle, which was founded on the recognition that the *"Thirteen State governments"* were to be *"preserved in full force and energy."* Martin went further than most Anti-

20. Ibid. (II, 59).
21. Ibid. (II, 55).

Federalists in tenaciously defending the sovereignty and authority of the states. He also took a more radical stance on the appropriate remedy for the defects of the Constitution, insisting that the conception of sovereignty in the Articles of Confederation was the only legal and prudent basis on which to construct a revised federal system.[22]

Martin denied that the opponents of the Constitution were "*unwilling to form a strong* and *energetic federal government.*" The frame of government proposed by the Philadelphia Convention, however, was not, in Martin's estimation, "in reality a *federal* but a *national* government" that would effect a "*consolidation* of all *State governments.*"[23]

Martin moved beyond Montesquieu's dictum that republican government was possible only in a small republic. His interpretation of federalism was based on his own understanding of "the genius and habits of the people" as reflected in the unique pattern of settlement and history of America. The distinguishing characteristic of American life, Martin argued, was its pervasive localism: "If a *county* is *rather large* the people complain of the inconvenience, and clamour for a division of their county, or for a removal of the place where their courts are held, so as to render it more central and convenient." The most extreme examples of this impulse were the many moves to create new states. Martin cited the examples of the "western parts of Virginia and North-Carolina, of Vermont and the province of Main" and "the inhabitants of the western parts of Pennsylvania." When states ceased to function as effective units to organize local sentiment, then it was necessary to form new states. The fact that a state might become too large or populous did not undermine this principle, but merely suggested that it might be necessary to create new states from time to time. Although framed in general terms, Martin's theory of federalism was especially appealing to the small states, since the division of larger states into smaller states served only to enhance the power and prestige of states such as Maryland.[24]

Federalism had evolved in America as a response to the nature of American society and culture. Americans were "accustomed," he noted, "to have their seats of government near them, to which they might have access, without much inconvenience." If Americans protested the inconvenience of

22. Ibid. (II, 33, 34).
23. Ibid. (II, 40, 45).
24. Ibid. (II, 48). For two useful discussions of the politics that deal with these issues, see Peter S. Onuf, *The Origins of the Federal Republic: Jurisdictional Controversies in the United States, 1775–1787* (Philadelphia, 1983); Rosemarie Zagarri, *The Politics of Size: Representation in the United States, 1776–1850* (Ithaca, N.Y., 1987).

not having local institutions of government like county courts closer, how would they respond to a much more powerful and distant government? Martin endorsed the common Anti-Federalist argument that when a government lacked the confidence of the people—something he predicted of the new government created by the Constitution—it would have to rely on force to carry out its dictates. Such a government was destined to become a despotism.[25]

The states were the cornerstones of the federal system. Echoing a common Anti-Federalist argument, Martin attacked the new Constitution for eroding the authority of the states and bypassing their role as the governments closest to the people. It is easy to see why Anti-Federalists objected to the language of the Constitution's Preamble, which invoked the people and ignored the states. Martin argued that the authority of the new government ought to proceed from the sovereign states. He denied that a single American people existed; apart from the existing structures of government created by the various states, there was no means of discerning the will of the people. Abstract appeals to the people were merely a pleasing fiction, designed to make political authority appear legitimate when, in reality, the Federalists sought to bypass the true expression of the people's political will—the states. Martin's defense of federalism, cast in terms that self-consciously invoked states' rights, was the most systematic in the corpus of Anti-Federalist writings.

Few other elite Anti-Federalists framed their discussions of federalism in the aggressive states' rights terms chosen by Martin. Indeed, the idea of sovereignty defended by most opponents of the Constitution made it especially difficult to formulate such a theory. As part of their indictment of the Constitution, a number of Anti-Federalists raised the troubling question about how two sovereign governments could exist in the same polity. Few, however, were willing to pursue this issue in much depth: to have done so would have demonstrated a basic flaw in Anti-Federalist constitutional theory. Relatively few Anti-Federalists were willing to return to the Confederation as a model for federalism, and few of the Anti-Federalist elite were willing to challenge the Federalist claim that the Articles of Confederation were inadequate and that some central authority ought to be created with sufficient power to force compliance from the states. Most Anti-Federalists conceded that some limited degree of coercive authority had to be ceded to the federal government. That concession effectively validated the Federalist argument, most cogently expressed by Madison, that the new government was partly federal and partly national. The most thoughtful Anti-Federalist

25. Martin, *Genuine Information* (*CA-F,* II, 48).

theorists recognized that Madison was correct. Admitting this point, however, would have undermined the claim that the new government aimed at consolidation, but few elite Anti-Federalist theorists grasped it. In reality their quarrel with Federalists was, not over consolidation, but the degree to which the new government would be nationalized.[26]

Rather than elaborate a theory of states' rights, most Anti-Federalists fell back on a general indictment of the Constitution's consolidating tendencies. The solution favored by most Anti-Federalists was to restrict the sphere of federal authority by calling for something like Article 2 of the Articles of Confederation, which restricted the national government's authority to those powers expressly delegated.[27]

Localism prompted commentary by a number of the most lucid Anti-Federalist theorists. No Anti-Federalist author was more aware of the localistic character of American society than James Winthrop, as Agrippa.

> It is necessary that there should be local laws and institutions; for a people inhabiting various climates will unavoidably have local habits and different modes of life, and these must be consulted in making the laws. It is much easier to adapt the laws to the manners of the people, than to make manners conform to laws.

Since local customs had been sanctified by more than a century and a half of history, Americans were unlikely to submit to a distant authority. "To attempt to reduce all to one standard," Agrippa argued, was "absurd in itself, and cannot be done but upon the principle of power, which debases people." It was precisely this state of affairs that had precipitated the rupture with Britain. Agrippa viewed the Revolution as a necessity that had resulted from the inability of the British government to support a system of representation

26. The only theorist to grapple effectively with this issue was Federal Farmer.

27. Impartial Examiner, "To the Free People of Virginia," *Virginia Independent Chronicle*, Feb. 20, 1788 (*CA-F*, V, 178). There has also been considerable confusion over Anti-Federalist ideas of federalism. Daniel J. Elazar, *The American Constitutional Tradition* (Lincoln, Nebr., 1988), argues that Anti-Federalists were confederalists, not federalists. Moreover, he argues that true federalism involved noncentralization as opposed to either centralization or decentralization (29, 145–150). Martin Diamond, *As Far as Republican Principles Will Admit: Essays*, ed. William A. Schambra (Washington, D.C., 1992), characterizes Anti-Federalist thought as small-republic federalism. Elazar's's notion of confederalism and Diamond's notion of small-republic federalism each treat Anti-Federalists as continuing supporters of a style of government similar to that of the Articles of Confederation. Yet, apart from a few Anti-Federalists such as Luther Martin, most opponents of the Constitution abandoned this as untenable and conceded that, within its limited sphere, the central government had to be supreme and had to be able to force the states to comply with its decisions.

that could adequately address the rights or needs of local communities. During the Revolution, Americans had resolutely declared that "one legislature could not represent so many different interests for the purposes of legislation and taxation." Rather than appeal to disinterested virtue, the cornerstone of so much Revolutionary republicanism, Agrippa resolutely defended interest.

It is vain to tell us that we ought to overlook local interests. It is only by protecting local concerns, that the interest of the whole is preserved. No man when he enters into society, does it from a view to promote the good of others, but he does it for his own good.[28]

He even went so far as to claim that to disregard local interest required individuals to act in a manner inconsistent with common sense.

In most cases leading opponents of the Constitution viewed localism and federalism (often used interchangeably) as complementary goals. Anti-Federalists were not only concerned about state authority, but they were also eager to protect local authority. Although federalism and localism were often melded in Anti-Federalist thought, a few authors recognized that those spheres of authority were not identical, most noticeably in the case of the right of trial by jury. Discussion of jury power pushed the distinctive character of localism to the fore.[29]

28. Agrippa [Winthrop], no. 12, "To the Massachusetts Convention," *Massachusets Gazette,* Jan. 14, 1788 (*CA-F,* IV, 93), no. 5, "To the People," Dec. 11, 1787 (II, 77), no. 7, "To the People," Dec. 18, 1787 (II, 82).

29. On the importance of localism to constitutionalism in this period, see Jack P. Greene, "The Colonial Origins of American Constitutionalism," in Greene, *Negotiated Authorities: Essays in Colonial, Political, and Constitutional History* (Charlottesville, Va., 1994), 25–42; Greene, *Peripheries and Center: Constitutional Development in the Extended Polities of the British Empire and the United States, 1607–1788* (Athens, Ga., 1986). In both of these accounts Greene conflates localism and federalism, blurring an important distinction within Anti-Federalist thought. Most discussions of localism have linked it to a democratic or egalitarian political culture; see Robert E. Shalhope, "Republicanism, Liberalism, and Democracy: Political Culture in the New Nation," in Milton M. Klein et al., eds., *The Republican Synthesis Revisited: Essays in Honor of George Athan Billias* (Worcester, Mass., 1992), 37–90. A number of political theorists have also equated localism with democracy. See Joshua Miller, *The Rise and Fall of Democracy in Early America, 1630–1789: The Legacy for Contemporary Politics* (University Park, Pa., 1991); Christopher M. Duncan, *The Anti-Federalists and Early American Political Thought* (DeKalb, Ill., 1995). Two useful correctives to this view that explore the way localism could function to support hierarchy are Kenneth A. Lockridge, *Settlement and Unsettlement in Early America* (Cambridge, 1981), and Michael Zuckerman, *Peaceable Kingdoms: New England Towns in the Eighteenth Century* (New York, 1970). Local-

In Richard Henry Lee's view, "The impartial administration of justice, which secures both our persons and our properties, is the great end of civil society." The Constitution threatened to undermine that impartial administration of justice. Lee was both a strong supporter of an independent judiciary and an advocate for strong juries and devoted considerable time to analyzing the defects of the federal judiciary, whose broad appellate jurisdiction threatened the state judiciaries. In his opinion the structure of judicial authority became another mechanism of consolidation. The proper remedy was to restrict the authority of federal courts. The absence of specific protections for jury trial in civil cases also seemed ominous. Remedying that problem required not only providing for jury trials but necessitated that jurors be drawn from the same communities as defendants. Lee wondered, "What then becomes of the jury of the vicinage?"[30]

Virginians were particularly worried that debt cases might not be tried in the locality in which the debt was incurred. The underlying fears animating that concern were captured by William Grayson, who forcefully reminded Virginians of the danger posed by the Constitution's failure to protect a general, localist conception of the jury. Grayson did not wish to give the impression that he sought unfair advantage for those in debt: "I have ever been an advocate for paying the British creditors." Yet, Grayson went on to remind members of the Convention, "it is a maxim in law, that debts should be on the same original foundation they were on when contracted." Contracts in Virginia were drawn with an understanding that they would be adjudicated by "State Judiciaries only." Debtors and creditors were familiar with "the procrastination and delays of our Courts." Grayson believed, "Trial by jury must have been in the contemplation of both parties, and the *venue* was in favour of the defendant." Removing debt cases from local courts would have disastrous results for Virginians. He was emphatic that local courts empaneling local juries were necessary to protect the interests of Virginians, stressing that, when Virginians spoke about local juries, they meant "the idea which I call the true vicinage," a notion that required "that a man shall be tried by his neighbours." Grayson's conception of the jury went beyond a defense of federalism and was a true expression of localism. He not only feared the threat to the state judiciaries but also worried that under the

---

ism was also closely related to the notion of community; for a general discussion, see Thomas Bender, *Community and Social Change in America* (New Brunswick, N.J., 1978).

30. Richard Henry Lee, "Copy of a Letter from Richard Henry Lee, Esq. . . . [to Edmund Randolph]," *Pennsylvania Packet, and Daily Advertiser* (Philadelphia), Dec. 20, 1787 (*DHRC*, XIV, 368).

Constitution individuals "may be tried in any part of the State." Grayson provides one important example of the importance of distinguishing between federalism and localism. In contrast to some elite opponents of the Constitution, he went to great efforts to assert that jury trial was an expression of the will of the *local* community. Merely securing trial by jury within the same state was not sufficient; it had to be a jury of vicinage.[31]

Leading Virginians were not unaware of the danger of "juries running riot" and "acting wildly at particular seasons." The solution, however, was not to lessen the powers of the jury. Other, more subtle means existed that could compel juries to act responsibly. Confidence in the jury depended on a number of implicit assumptions. Jury service would be limited to persons with a permanent stake in society; individuals serving on the jury would also be enmeshed in a complex web of social relationships defined by deference. The participation of attorneys and judges would act as a moderating influence on juries. The jury system facilitated the participation of the gentry and the substantial yeomanry while still allowing men of wisdom and rank to exert their stabilizing influence.[32]

In the view of Richard Henry Lee, the structure of the judiciary captured this sort of balance by giving an appropriate role to judges and juries. In fact, he argued strenuously that "the Independency of the Judges, seem to be so capital and essential." The ability of judges to serve this vital function was tied to a written bill of rights which served "to regulate the discretion of Rulers in a legal way, restraining the progress of Ambition and Avarice within just bounds." While Lee placed tremendous faith in an independent judiciary, he believed that jury trials were equally essential to safeguard liberty. Judges and juries were the natural analogues of natural aristocracy and democracy. Liberty could be secure and government function to pro-

31. *Debates and Other Proceedings of the Convention of Virginia* . . . , 3 vols. (Petersburg, Va., 1788–1789): William Grayson, Speech in the Virginia State Convention, June 21, 1788 (*DHRC*, X, 1447, 1449); Patrick Henry, Speech, June 16, 1788 (X, 1330); George Mason, Speech, June 19, 1788 (X, 1402, 1404, 1406–1407); Patrick Henry, Speech, June 20, 1788 (X, 1424–1425). Similar concerns were expressed by Richard Henry Lee: Richard Henry Lee to James Gordon, Jr., Feb. 26, 1788 (VII, 418–419). On the culture of debt in Revolutionary Virginia and its contribution to the mentality of the gentry, see T. H. Breen, *Tobacco Culture: The Mentality of the Great Tidewater Planters on the Eve of the Revolution* (Princeton, N.J., 1985). Another problem that prompted some comment by Anti-Federalists was the concern that trials in federal courts would place an especially heavy burden on individuals of more modest financial resources: see George Mason, "Objections to the Constitution," *Massachusetts Centinel*, Nov. 21, 1787 (*CA-F*, II, 12).

32. Cincinnatus [Arthur Lee], no. 2, "To James Wilson, Esq.," *New-York Journal*, Nov. 8, 1787 (*DHRC*, XIV, 13).

mote the common good only when it combined the advantages of aristocracy and democracy. Although he placed considerable faith in judges to uphold the law, he recognized, quoting Blackstone, that it was dangerous to allow this task to "be entirely entrusted to the magistracy." It was inevitable, "in spite of their own natural integrity," that judges would have "an involuntary bias towards those of their own rank and dignity." "It is not to be expected from human nature, that the few should always be attentive to the good of the many." No figure within the Anti-Federalist elite was more sensitive to the need for a republic to have virtuous leaders. Lee's commitment to virtue was, however, tempered by his realization that government would not always be guided by virtuous men. It was necessary to restrain the actions of government by explicit protections for liberty, and only then would government attend to the concerns of the many and the few.[33]

The Theory of the Small Republic

Elite Anti-Federalists conceptualized politics as a perennial struggle between the many and the few, and republican government was in their view best suited to protect the rights of both. In a letter to a friend, Richard Henry Lee captured this essentially pessimistic view of human nature:

33. Richard Henry Lee, "Copy of a Letter from Richard Henry Lee [to Edmund Randolph]," *Pennsylvania Packet*, Dec. 20, 1787 (*DHRC*, XIV, 368); Lee to Edmund Pendleton, May 26, 1788 (*DHRC*, IX, 878–879). A number of scholars have focused on the jury as a quasi-representative body. See Shannon C. Stimson, *The American Revolution in the Law: Anglo-American Jurisprudence before John Marshall* (Princeton, N.J., 1990); J. R. Pole, "Reflections on American Law and the American Revolution," *WMQ*, 3d Ser., L (1993), 123–159. This argument has been challenged by a number of scholars, in *WMQ*, 3d Ser., L (1993), including Peter Charles Hoffer, "Custom as Law: A Comment on J. R. Pole's 'Reflections,'" 160–167; Bruce H. Mann, "The Evolutionary Revolution in American Law: A Comment on J. R. Pole's 'Reflections,'" 168–175; James A. Henretta and James D. Rice, "Law as Litigation: An Agenda for Research," 176–180. Qualifications for jury service and methods of jury selection could drastically alter the representative character of juries. Juries in Lee's Virginia are a good case in point. The jury functioned in the context of the hierarchical nature of southern society. Grand juries were composed of men of considerable wealth and social standing, whereas petit juries were drawn from the ranks of the propertied. Judges, justices of the peace, grand jurors, and petit jurors were enmeshed in a complex social web of deference. This particular system was especially effective at protecting landowners against actions by creditors. For an illuminating discussion of legal culture in Virginia and its connection to Anti-Federalism and Jeffersonianism, see F. Thornton Miller, *Juries and Judges versus the Law: Virginia's Provincial Legal Perspective, 1783–1828* (Charlottesville, Va., 1994).

If all men were wise and good there would be no necessity of government or law—But the folly and the vice of human nature renders government and laws necessary for the Many, and restraints indispensable to prevent oppression from those who are entrusted with the administration of the one and the dispensation of the other.[34]

In Lee's understanding, republican government, ideally, blended the wisdom that natural aristocracy offered with the strength and knowledge of a well-ordered democracy.

This aspect of elite thought is evident in Arthur Lee's critique of the Constitution's provision for the legislative branch. The structure of Congress failed to provide the lower house with numbers sufficient to represent the diverse interests of society. As Cincinnatus, Lee believed that the lower house ought to be the "true representative of the democratic part of the system; the shield and defence of the people." In place of a well-ordered democracy, the Constitution promised "an Oligarchy . . . in the persons of the President and Vice President, who, if they understand one another, will easily govern the two Houses to their will." Like so many elite Anti-Federalists, Lee sought to balance the virtues of democracy with those of natural aristocracy, but he felt that the structure of the lower house was inadequate to achieve its end. "All this," he wrote, "is calculated to ensure a feeble Representative and a powerful Senate—that is to sacrifise the Democracy to the Aristocracy." "I wish," he wrote, "to see the Aristocracy have its due weight . . . and I am persuaded, that a due balance is the best guard to the Aristocracy itself, otherwise it will soon run riot and lose itself in a despotism." Lee's attack on aristocracy drew on well-established Whig ideals about the dangers of corruption and the need for a popular check on society's rulers. Without such checks, all elected officials, no matter how virtuous, would inevitably become corrupt. Checks on natural aristocracy did not, however, mean that Lee rejected its importance. His goal was to ensure that natural aristocracy would not degenerate into the oppressive aristocracy predicted by George Mason and other members of the Anti-Federalist elite.[35]

Recognizing the need for a lower house to function as the democratic voice of the people did not signal a commitment to egalitarian ideals. A proper measure of democracy was necessary for rulers to enjoy the confi-

34. Richard Henry Lee to William Shippen, Jr., in James Curtis Ballagh, ed., *The Letters of Richard Henry Lee*, 2 vols. (New York, 1911–1914), II, 441–444.

35. Cincinnatus [Arthur Lee], no. 4, "To James Wilson, Esq.," *New-York Journal*, Nov. 22, 1787 (*DHRC*, XIV, 189); Arthur Lee to John Adams, Oct. 3, 1787 (XIII, 307–308); Lee to Edward Rutledge, Oct. 29, 1787 (VIII, 131).

dence of the people. Scrutiny by the lower house provided an indispensable check on society's rulers. Adequate representation was also important to provide legislative bodies with information to function effectively. Bicameralism, in this scheme, reflected the existence of a clear division between patricians and plebeians and embodied the virtues of both social classes. The goal of constitutionalism was to secure each group its rights and draw upon the particular political strengths of each group so that legislative bodies could better discern the common good. Elite Anti-Federalists did not conceptualize this tension in modern class terms, but in terms of a society of different ranks, where relations between men of different rank were characterized by mutualism, not class hostility. Obligation and duty in a ranked society were counterpoised in a complex balance. The body politic, much like the human body, could be healthy only when each part performed its appropriate function.[36]

Writing as a patrician Roman figure, Arthur Lee attacked the Senate and charged it with creating "a baneful aristocracy." The structure of that body was "removed from the people" and "exactly in the ratio of their removal from the people, do aristocratic principles constantly infect the minds of man." The long term for senators only compounded this problem: "In proportion to the duration of power, the aristocratic exercise of it, and attempts to extend it, are invariably observed to increase." Part of the problem with the scheme of representation under the Constitution was that it removed representatives from localities. When representation was rooted in the locality, the ideals of deference and democracy could be harmonized. The structure of representation under the Constitution threatened this delicate balance.[37]

No Anti-Federalist author was more concerned with the decline of deference and dangers of popular democratic politics than Mercy Otis Warren. In the voice of Columbian Patriot, she cast her diagnosis of the drift of post-Revolutionary American society as a jeremiad. Instead of following the wise counsel of Old Patriot leaders, America behaved like a dissipated youth: "restless, vigorous, luxurious youth, prematurely emancipated from the authority of a parent, but without the experience necessary to direct him to act with dignity or discretion." What recent history had demonstrated was the continuing need for virtuous leadership to guide the young nation.

36. For a discussion of the notion of rank, see Harold Perkin, *The Origins of Modern English Society, 1780–1880* (London, 1969).

37. Cincinnatus [Arthur Lee], no. 4, "To James Wilson, Esq.," *New-York Journal*, Nov. 22, 1787 (*DHRC*, XIV, 187–188).

Warren blamed the common people and those designing politicians who misled them.[38]

The common people had forgotten the ideal of deference, preferring the flattery of demagogues to the wisdom of virtuous leaders. Warren denounced the "supple multitude" who were "paying a blind and idolatrous homage to the opinions of those" false leaders who deceived the people. In private, Warren expressed her hope that a few virtuous men might rise and stand above the "absurd enthusiasm that often spreads itself over the lower classes of life." Without some measure of popular virtue, republicanism could not survive. If the people could not distinguish between true patriots and demagogues, then America would emulate the republics of the past and slip into a period of slow decline.[39]

In place of disinterested virtue, the postwar period was dominated by demagogues who pandered to the people. Warren observed that, "when patriotism is discountenanced and publick virtue becomes the ridicule of the sycophant," the path toward despotism and slavery is inevitable. She excoriated the courtiers, speculators, and demagogues who lusted after aristocracy and monarchy. The behavior of the people allowed unscrupulous politicians to displace those disinterested patriots who continued to espouse the values of traditional Whig republicanism. Although somewhat disillusioned, Warren placed great hope in the ability of enlightened leadership to restore virtue to its proper place in American life. Warren hoped that America's leaders would once again "find a firmness of mind that renders us independent of popular opinion." Disinterestedness defined this elite conception of virtue: leaders had to have the ability and character to take a principled stand even if that involved challenging popular opinion. Unfortunately, corruption and ambition had taken the place of disinterested virtue. Unscrupulous politicians exploited the vanity of the people and manipulated public opinion to further their own interests.

38. Columbian Patriot [Warren], *Observations on the New Constitution* (*CA-F*, IV, 285). On the role of the jeremiad in New England literary culture, see Sacvan Bercovitch, *The American Jeremiad* (Madison, Wis., 1978).

39. Columbian Patriot [Warren], *Observations on the New Constitution* (*CA-F*, IV, 274); Mercy Otis Warren to Catherine Macaulay, July 1789, Mercy Otis Warren Letter-Book, 27–29, MHS. On Anti-Federalist views of human nature, see Cecelia M. Kenyon, "Men of Little Faith: The Anti-Federalists on the Nature of Representative Government," *WMQ*, 3d Ser., XII (1955), 3–43. On the notion of Anti-Federalists as men who kept faith with the Revolution's ideals, see Bernard Bailyn, *The Ideological Origins of the American Revolution*, rev. ed. (Cambridge, Mass., 1992), 331.

Warren remained cautiously optimistic, continuing to place her faith in the regenerative ability of a few good men, virtuous leaders, like Moses or Brutus, who would lead the people in the direction of virtue. "America," she wrote, "may yet produce characters who have genius and capacity sufficient to form the manners and correct the morals of the people, and virtue enough to lead their country to freedom."[40]

The conception of representation favored by elite Anti-Federalists was distinctly localistic, for only within localities could deference survive. In a letter to Samuel Adams, Richard Henry Lee clearly stated the underlying assumptions at the heart of this vision of politics.

> Both reason and experience prove, that so extensive a territory as that of the United States, including such a variety of climates, productions, interests; and so great difference of manners, habits, and customs; cannot be governed in freedom—until formed into states, sovereign, *sub modo*, and confederated for the common good.[41]

In a federal republic it would be possible for government to reflect both the virtues of natural aristocracy and the vitality of democracy. In a small republic citizens could have confidence in their representatives and elect men drawn from the ranks of the wise and virtuous. Such men could share in the cosmopolitan vision possessed by members of the natural aristocracy while maintaining their ties to the community that elected them. It would thus be possible to represent the interests of democracy in a more refined fashion.

Elite Anti-Federalist localism was tied to a distinctive approach to political sociology. The key to this ideology was the belief that virtue and liberty could survive only in a small republic. The more distant government was from the people, the more likely it was that interested and designing politicians would displace men of wisdom and discernment. Ultimately, demagogues would persuade the people to betray their own liberties, and republicanism itself would be replaced by tyranny. The weakening of state government would erode the patterns of deference essential to the survival of this vision of politics. Elite constitutionalism was therefore inescapably concerned about class consciousness. That conception of class was framed in a distinctly classical vocabulary, one in which the tensions between patricians and plebeians were an eternal fixture of politics.[42]

40. Columbian Patriot [Warren], *Observations on the New Constitution* (*CA-F*, IV, 272, 285, 286).

41. Richard Henry Lee to Samuel Adams, Apr. 28, 1788 (*DHRC*, IX, 765).

42. Most studies of Anti-Federalist constitutional thought have dismissed the relevance

The analysis of society at the heart of elite Anti-Federalist constitutional theory was a mirror image of Federalist thought. For Federalists, the closer government was to the people, the greater the danger of corruption and demagoguery. Elite Anti-Federalists, by contrast, believed that it was vital to preserve the integrity of state and local government so that republican institutions could thrive. For these Anti-Federalists, the states provided models of the small republics in which liberty and virtue could both flourish. In a properly constructed federal system, each state would function as a small republic in which men of wisdom and virtue would naturally rise to positions of leadership while maintaining their ties to local communities. The theory of the small republic allowed elite Anti-Federalists to reconcile their commitment to a deferential conception of politics with their recognition that government had to have effective representation to possess the confidence of the people. In fact, elites feared that further centralization would only hasten democratization. The end result would be greater demagoguery and, ultimately, mobocracy.[43]

This theory assumed that within particular localities there was a homogeneity of interests. Luther Martin stated this assumption explicitly when he observed that, when districts were not very large, representatives would have a *"common interest"* with those they represented. Under such circumstances, Martin argued, "laws can scarcely be made by *one* part *oppressive* to the *others,* without *their suffering in common."* Like other members of the Anti-Federalist elite, Martin believed that there was a basic division between the many and the few. Government had to protect the interests and rights of both groups. Distinctions regarding "rank and fortune" required an upper

of class-conscious constitutionalism. Herbert Storing and Murray Dry each misread Gordon Wood's suggestion that the debate between Federalists and Anti-Federalists turned "on an essential point of political sociology" (Wood, *Creation of the American Republic,* 485). For the most systematic efforts to explore Anti-Federalist constitutionalism, see Introduction, n. 19, above. For Wood, these sociological perceptions were not separate from the constitutional vision of Anti-Federalists, but the central animating impulse behind it. What Wood's analysis does not explore is the degree to which a different type of class-conscious constitutionalism inspired the Anti-Federalist elite. On the role of class in ancient political theory, see G. E. M. de Ste. Croix, *The Class Struggle in the Ancient Greek World: From the Archaic Age to the Arab Conquests* (Ithaca, N.Y., 1981).

43. For a discussion of Madison's diagnosis of the problems with localism, see Wood, *Creation of the American Republic;* Lance Banning, *The Sacred Fire of Liberty: James Madison and the Founding of the Federal Republic* (Ithaca, N.Y., 1995). On the importance of the idea of the small republic to Anti-Federalist thought, see Kenyon, "Men of Little Faith," *WMQ,* 3d Ser., XII (1955), 3–43; Herbert J. Storing, *What the Anti-Federalists Were For* (Chicago, 1981).

house composed of men "respectable for their wealth and dignity" to check "the hasty and rash measures of a representation more popular." State government provided an appropriate arena in which the diverse interests of different localities could be reconciled, whereas shifting authority to a more distant government and weakening the states would destroy the representative character of American institutions.[44]

The Public Sphere

Implicit in elite Anti-Federalist views of society was a conception of the way that the public sphere functioned. The version of the public sphere defended by elite Anti-Federalists was far more localist than that of the Federalists. The faith of men like Richard Henry Lee in the small republic was based upon their recognition of the role of public opinion in securing consent without force. When the people's judgments were "founded on the knowledge of those who govern," the faith in their leaders' virtue "procures obedience without force." "But remove the opinion, which must fall with a knowledge of characters in so widely extended a country, and force then becomes necessary to secure the purpose of civil government." Only a federal system could adequately represent the diversity of American society. In a letter to Samuel Adams, Lee contrasted the "obedience resulting from fear" with the "obedience flowing from esteem and confidence, the legitimate offspring of the knowledge that men have of wisdom and virtue" were guiding government.[45]

The public sphere as embraced by Lee and other elite Anti-Federalists was shaped by a more traditional aristocratic conception of the role that elites ought to play in politics. The conception of the public at the heart of this understanding was not embodied in an anonymous world of print.

The case of George Mason's "Objections to the Constitution" illustrates the way the emerging idea about the anonymous public sphere of print could conflict with a more traditional understanding of the appropriate manner for gentlemen to act in matters of public concern. Mason took advantage of his broad network of political correspondents and distributed

44. Martin, *Genuine Information* (*CA-F,* II, 37–44). My reading of Federalist political thought and the concept of a "political fiction" draws on Edmund S. Morgan's analysis in *Inventing the People: The Rise of Popular Sovereignty in England and America* (New York, 1988).

45. Richard Henry Lee to Samuel Adams, Apr. 28, 1788 (*DHRC,* IX, 765).

copies of his "Objections" in manuscript to influential politicians in Virginia, Pennsylvania, New York, and New Hampshire. Disseminating his thoughts in this fashion, he believed, would allow him to maintain some measure of control over how his ideas would be interpreted. Any ambiguities or confusions arising from his essay could be discussed in a private exchange of letters. To Mason the decision to rely on his social position and wide circle of personal contacts made perfect sense. Mason did not view his actions as partisan. He sought to engage in a principled discussion with men of influence on both sides of the debate, Federalists and Anti-Federalists. Despite his effort to limit access to his text, he was drawn into the debate in print. Once in print, it was no longer possible for a gentleman to control the way his texts were interpreted.[46]

Mason's actions were viciously attacked by Tobias Lear, a Virginia Federalist. Lear accused Mason of trying to avoid public scrutiny by distributing his thoughts among a select body of citizens. Lear procured a copy of Mason's manuscript and arranged for it to be printed in a Federalist paper with an appropriate rebuttal. Adopting the pen name Brutus, Lear questioned Mason's actions by invoking the ideal of a depersonalized public sphere in which citizens acting under the cloak of anonymity engaged in rational discussion about matters of general concern. "When a man of acknowledged abilities and great influence," Lear wrote, "*hands forth* his opinion, upon a matter of general concern, among those upon whom he has reason, to think it will make the most favorable impression, without submitting it to the test of public investigation, he may be truly said to take an undue advantage of his influence." He denounced such actions and implied that Mason's behavior implied that he "could not accomplish" his object "by an open and candid application to the public." True patriots did not take advantage of their status, but rather submitted their ideas to public scrutiny under the cloak of anonymity so that the public would not be swayed by their personal reputation.[47]

Richard Henry Lee, another prominent member of the Anti-Federalist elite, faced a situation analogous to Mason's. An active correspondent with leading politicians in Virginia and elsewhere, Lee decided to publish a letter to Virginia's governor Edmund Randolph detailing his objections to the

46. On the circulation of Mason's "Objections," see the discussion in the headnote, *DHRC*, XIII, 346–348.

47. Brutus [Tobias Lear], *Virginia Journal and Alexandria Advertiser*, Nov. 22, 1787 (*DHRC*, XIV, 152).

Constitution. Lee expressed his confidence that the governor would "make such use of this letter" as would further the "public good."[48]

Lee's letter prompted a scathing attack by a Federalist author, Valerius, who excoriated Lee for taking advantage of his social position in print. He chided Lee for his presumption that "the supposed weight which your name, might perhaps, carry" ought to influence the debate over the Constitution. Only anonymous publication was compatible with republican ideals: Lee's signed letter implicitly traded on its author's personal prestige. Participation in the public sphere, Valerius argued, demanded that one renounce any privilege based on social position. Valerius defended the use of pseudonyms, as the only appropriate choice for republican statesmen. "To such as make a fictitious signature an objection to belief, I reply, that it matters very little, who is the author of sentiments, which are intended for public consider-ations." Lee's actions were an abuse of his position and evidence of the inferiority of his critique of the Constitution.[49]

In Virginia, Federalists attacked leading Anti-Federalists for violating the republican belief that the public sphere ought to be defined by a deper-sonalized world of print. Mason and Lee embraced a more traditional con-ception of the public sphere shaped by an older aristocratic conception of the role that elites ought to play in politics. The anonymity of print under-mined the ability of men such as Lee and Mason to carry out their patrician conception of political leadership.[50]

The anonymity of print posed another problem of leading Anti-Federal-ists, particularly in the South. In places like Virginia, political spectacle, not the anonymity of print, allowed members of the gentry to demonstrate their capacity for rule by dramatic displays of oratory, not dispassionate statements in print. A rare contemporary description of a speech by Anti-Federalist William Grayson captures the centrality of one's personal identity to the politics of the public sphere in gentry society.

> Col: Grayson's Trope of Rhetoric was more to the feelings of the Virgin-ians. He harangued the People at the Court House having in his Hand a snuff Box hardly so broad as a Moidore [a Portuguese coin]. The point of finger and Thumb are inserted with difficulty. Perhaps said he you may

48. Richard Henry Lee to William Shippen, Jr., Oct. 2, 1787 (*DHRC*, XIII, 289); Richard Henry Lee to Samuel Adams, Oct. 27, 1787 (XIII, 484); Harry Innes to John Brown, Dec. 7, 1787 (VIII, 223).

49. Valerius, *Virginia Independent Chronicle,* Jan. 23, 1788 (*DHRC,* VIII, 313–319).

50. On the notion of republicanism and depersonalization, see Warner, *Letters of the Republic.*

think it of Consequence that some other States have accepted of the new Constitution, what are they? When compared to Virginia they are no more than this snuff Box is to the Size of a Man.[51]

While the decision of leading politicians in Virginia to circulate their ideas in manuscript might not appear to share much with the more dramatic world of the courthouse steps, they were each crucial to success for a traditional gentry and embodied two rather different incarnations of the ideal of the public sphere as a realm in which society's virtuous few worked to produce rational agreement on matters of public concern. Members of the gentry were expected to use their power and prestige in a manner consistent with the public good. In a society in which honor was crucial, personal identity was central to the way members of the elite understood their public role. Thus, in correspondence with other men of standing, one might calmly debate issues of public concern. The anonymous world of print was not a medium in which gentlemanly exchange might flourish. In contrast to the contentious nature of the the anonymous world of print, the gentry public sphere was defined by its consensual character. If private correspondence represented one mode of the gentry ideal of the public sphere, then public speaking was its other modality. Here gentlemen demonstrated their capacity for sympathy, affirming in a highly visible way that they were capable of understanding and representing the popular will. Once consensus among the virtuous few was achieved through the exchange of letters, the consent of the people could be secured in dramatic ritual displays such as Grayson's courthouse oratory.[52]

The conception of public opinion defended by elite Anti-Federalists was not democratic. In their view, public opinion was the deliberative will of

51. Hugh Williamson to John Gray Blount, June 3, 1788 (*DHRC*, IX, 608–609).

52. On gentility and the culture of letter writing, see Robert A. Ferguson, *The American Enlightenment, 1750–1820* (Cambridge, Mass., 1997). On the role of honor in southern culture, see Bertram Wyatt-Brown, *Southern Honor: Ethics and Behavior in the Old South* (New York, 1982). As Jürgen Habermas notes, the bourgeois public sphere was preceded by a public sphere defined largely by spectacle and an emerging literary public sphere that took letter writing as its model (*The Structural Transformation of the Public Sphere: An Inquiry into a Category of Bourgeois Society,* trans. Thomas Burger and Frederick Lawrence [Cambridge, Mass., 1989], 7, 29, 49).

On Virginia politics as actual theater, see Rhys Isaac, *The Transformation of Virginia, 1740–1790* (Chapel Hill, N.C., 1982); A. G. Roeber, *Faithful Magistrates and Republican Lawyers: Creators of Virginia Legal Culture, 1680–1810* (Chapel Hill, N.C., 1981). On the notion of sympathy and oratory, see Jay Fliegelman, *Declaring Independence: Jefferson, Natural Language, and the Culture of Performance* (Stanford, Calif., 1993).

the people as revealed by the political process of selecting the most virtuous leaders—representatives from society's natural aristocracy who refined the public will. For precisely this reason, men like Richard Henry Lee and George Mason believed that matters of public concern ought to be discussed and debated in correspondence with other men of influence. For members of the elite, the public sphere was more likely to be understood as an extension of their own circle of contacts than as an anonymous world of print.

The ideal that the political process ought to refine the public will, not resemble it, was made explicit by the Massachusetts author Republican Federalist. For this author the state legislatures were vital forums in which the public will could be cultivated. Conceding that it was up to the people to adopt or reject the Constitution, he thought the decision to bypass the state legislatures was a serious mistake that deprived the people of the wisdom of those collective bodies. The legislatures "might at any time have considered the subject, expressed their sentiments on it, and recommended to the people." Such a policy would have had the salutary effect of allowing the legislatures to explain "to the people; and the publick opinion would have been thus *united*." In contrast to more popular Anti-Federalist authors, Republican Federalist actually preferred this mode of informing the public to the contentiousness of newspaper debates.[53]

For the Anti-Federalist elite, molding public opinion was vital to the preservation of liberty and virtue. Their commitment to the ideal of the small republic reflected their belief that public opinion could be most effectively molded within localities. When politics was removed from the locality, men of refinement would lose their advantages. Politics would invariably become impersonal, and demagoguery would triumph. Precisely for this reason, a number of leading Anti-Federalists showed so little faith in the impersonal politics of print. For those committed to an elitist conception of localism, the medium of print actually worked against their efforts to promote deference.

Modern accounts of Anti-Federalism have not paid sufficient attention to the distinctive character of elite Anti-Federalist thought, and monolithic treatments have blended elite and popular Anti-Federalist ideas indiscriminately. In other cases, elite Anti-Federalist thought has been treated as

53. Republican Federalist, no. 2, "To the Members of the Convention of Masachusetts," *Massachusetts Centinel*, Jan. 2, 1788 (*CA-F*, IV, 169). On the role of legislative bodies as deliberative assemblies capable of informing the public, see Habermas, *The Structural Transformation of the Public Sphere*, trans. Burger and Lawrence.

anomalous. Both of those approaches obscure the vital role of a small but highly influential group of elite Anti-Federalists in shaping the terms of public debate over the Constitution.

Most members of the Anti-Federalist elite framed constitutional issues in Whig republican terms. Although limited by constitutional charters, legislatures enjoyed considerable latitude when enacting laws for the common good. As long as such laws were the product of duly elected representative bodies, there was no contradiction between limits on the rights of citizens and the ideal of liberty. Religious tests are an excellent illustration of this dimension of Anti-Federalist thought. Government could exclude individuals who lacked sufficient virtue from holding office. Such a policy was, not incompatible with liberty, but an expression of a republican conception of liberty. This language of republican constitutionalism, however, was not monolithic. Indeed, elite constitutional thought reflected the uneven development of American constitutionalism. Some authors melded republican and liberal ideas into a coherent synthesis, but others combined them inconsistently. In a very few cases, Anti-Federalists employed a liberal conception of individual rights and a limited view of government.

The complex constellation of republican and liberal ideas challenges the notion that the opponents of the Constitution were simply country Whigs railing against a distant court faction. Anti-Federalists certainly borrowed rhetorical tropes from this language and a number of intellectual concepts as well. They took this familiar language and reshaped it to reflect their own cosmopolitan vision of how federalism and localism could be harnessed to protect American liberty. Federalism and localism were both crucial to elite Anti-Federalism, and recognizing their importance also challenges the idea that elite Anti-Federalists were simply men of little faith who mistrusted the people as much as they feared government. Responding to the Federalist charge that they were excessively jealous of their liberty and of government, John Tyler of Virginia affirmed that his fear of distant government was more than balanced by his faith in state government. "Gentlemen say we are jealous—I am not jealous of this House. I could trust my life with them." These Anti-Federalists showed a remarkable faith in the ability of state governments to act in the best interests of the people.[54]

The critique of aristocracy routinely invoked by Anti-Federalists had a special resonance with elites. It was not the ideal of natural aristocracy they feared, but rather the dangers of oligarchy. What elite Anti-Federalists feared

54. John Tyler, Speech in the Virginia State Convention, June 21, 1788, *Debates and Other Proceedings of the Convention of Virginia* (*DHRC*, X, 1527–1528).

most was corruption, the potential of any group of men, no matter how virtuous, to exalt their own interests or those of some faction and ignore the common good. Elite opponents of the Constitution were eager to preserve an aristocracy of virtue or merit—a natural aristocracy.

Elite Anti-Federalist thought was deeply conservative, echoing the traditional Whig view of balanced government. For Old Patriots the struggle between the many and the few that had defined politics since antiquity continued as the central reality of politics. Although America contained no titled aristocracy, government had to accommodate both natural aristocracy and democracy, and bicameralism was one structural means of balancing the interests of those two amorphous social classes. This conception of politics not only shaped the way elites viewed the legislature but also colored their view of the law. Judges reflected the virtues of natural aristocracy while juries embodied the advantages of a well-ordered democracy.

The political ideal of the small republic was crucial to Anti-Federalist political and constitutional theory. In such a society virtuous men would rise to positions of power and understand the interests of people. This goal could be achieved only when politics remained rooted in localities. The political sociology of elite Anti-Federalism was the mirror image of the idea of the filtration of talent championed by leading Federalists.

In addition to the traditional republican notion of disinterested virtue, politicians had to demonstrate a capacity for sympathy with those they represented. Those two qualities allowed individuals to secure the consent of the people without force. This conception of the public sphere was shaped by a particular gentry ideal informed by a strong dose of localism. The more distant and impersonal politics became, the less likely it was for elites to triumph, and the anonymity of print actually weakened the ability of elites to function as the spokesmen for local views. The Constitution threatened this distinctive vision of localism, because it would no longer be possible to reconcile natural aristocracy with democracy.

CHAPTER 3 :

POPULAR ANTI-FEDERALIST

POLITICAL AND CONSTITUTIONAL

THOUGHT

Contemporary observers on both sides of the ratification debate were struck by the intensity of popular opposition to the Constitution. Indeed, the essence of popular Anti-Federalism was its democratic character. While traveling in western Pennsylvania, Thomas Rodney, a leading Delaware Anti-Federalist, noted that "the inferior class are totally against" the Constitution, their opposition springing "from their current Sentiment against proud and Lordly ideas." Many Federalists would have agreed with Rodney's analysis. John Montgomery, a Federalist from Carlisle, Pennsylvania, similarly observed that Anti-Federalists feared that the Constitution would make the farmers "dependents, who will be reduced to vassalage." In Massachusetts, Federalist George Minot offered a similar diagnosis, remarking that the language of the Constitution "alarmed the yeomanry" of his state. One sarcastic Federalist parodied Anti-Federalist writing, suggesting that the typical Anti-Federalist essay could be reduced to a simple recipe of the following proportions: "WELL-BORN, nine times—*Aristocracy*, eighteen times" and "*Great Men*, six times." The author assured readers that "these *words*" could be "served, after being once used, a dozen times to the same table and palate." In contrast to elite opposition to the Constitution, popular Anti-Federalism did not seek to balance the advantages of natural aristocracy and democracy: popular Anti-Federalists asserted the superiority of democracy and vigorously defended egalitarian ideals.[1]

1. Thomas Rodney Journal, May 10, 1788 (*DHRC*, II [microfiche], 676); John Montgom-

Popular opposition to the Constitution brought together a diverse coalition that included members of the middling sort as well as plebeian farmers and artisans. The most influential spokesmen for middling ideas were the new political men who dominated state politics in places like New York and Pennsylvania. These men served in state ratification conventions and authored the bulk of Anti-Federalist essays. The typical Anti-Federalist essay reflected the views of individuals like New York's Abraham Yates, a cobbler turned politician, or Pennsylvania's William Findley, a weaver turned lawyer. These spokesmen for the middling sort were beneficiaries of the democratization of politics after the Revolution. In every state, new men emerged to become symbols and champions of a more democratic style of politics. The middling sort dominated the political scene most effectively in New York and Pennsylvania, where, respectively, George Clinton and his allies and George Bryan and the members of the Constitutionalist party became the leaders of powerful political organizations that implemented the agenda of the middling sort.[2]

---

ery to James Wilson, Mar. 2, 1788 (*DHRC*, II, 701–706); George Minot Journal, January–February 1788, Sedgwick Papers, MHS; "A Receipt for an Antifederal Essay," *Pennsylvania Gazette* (Philadelphia), Nov. 14, 1787 (*DHRC*, XIV, 103). The tensions among Federalists have not received much attention. For an interesting account of the class divisions within Federalism in New York, see Alfred F. Young, *The Democratic Republicans of New York: The Origins, 1763–1797* (Chapel Hill, N.C., 1967). Studies of Federalist crowd behavior have attracted some interest; see Sean Wilentz, "Artisan Republican Festivals and the Rise of Class Conflict in New York City, 1788–1837," in Michael H. Frisch and Daniel J. Walkowitz, eds., *Working-Class America: Essays in Labor, Community, and American Society* (Urbana, Ill., 1983), 37–77. A slightly different view is presented by Paul A. Gilje, "The Common People and the Constitution: Popular Culture in New York City in the Eighteenth Century," in Gilje and William Pencak, eds., *New York in the Age of the Constitution, 1775–1800* (Rutherford, N.J., 1992), 48–73.

2. Historical scholarship on the socioeconomic character of eighteenth-century America is sharply divided between scholars who believe that the new nation was a prosperous society united by middle-class values and others who contend that the nation was riven by sharp social divisions and ideological discord. For a forceful statement of the middle-class thesis, see Gordon S. Wood, "Ideology and the Origins of Liberal America," *WMQ*, 3d Ser., XLIV (1987), 628–640. For the opposing view, stressing the importance of class tensions, see Gary B. Nash, "Also There at the Creation: Going beyond Gordon S. Wood," *WMQ*, 3d Ser., XLIV (1987), 602–611. On the rise of new men in post-Revolutionary politics, see Jackson Turner Main, "Government by the People: The American Revolution and the Democratization of the Legislatures," *WMQ*, 3d Ser., XXIII (1966), 391–407. For biographical information on Yates, see Stefan Bielinski, *Abraham Yates, Jr., and the New Political Order in Revolutionary New York* (Albany, N.Y., 1975); on Findley, see Gordon S. Wood, "Interests and

Middling democrats influenced the drafting of constitutions and shaped the legislative agenda throughout much of the Confederation period. The constitutionalism of the middling sort sought to restrict the powers of the executive and judicial branches and strengthen the legislatures.[3]

A number of historians have equated popular Anti-Federalism with an agrarian localist tradition distinctly hostile to the marketplace and commerce. This characterization distorts the ideology of middling democrats. The middling sort defended an ideal of economic harmony, in which farmers, artisans, and small merchants would all enjoy a comfortable competence. Middling Anti-Federalism was decidedly procommercial, and in both Pennsylvania and New York the Anti-Federalist coalition included a number of individuals involved in commerce and manufacturing. In Pennsylvania, John Nicholson, controller of the state and responsible for coordinating much of the Anti-Federalist campaign there, was a manufacturer. In New York, Melancton Smith, a merchant, was crucial in coordinating his state's campaign and became its most important spokesman for Anti-Federalism in its ratification convention. The producer ideology of the middling sort favored economic growth but did oppose unfair concentrations of wealth.[4]

Disinterestedness in the Making of the Constitution," in Richard Beeman, Stephen Botein, and Edward C. Carter II, eds., *Beyond Confederation: Origins of the Constitution and American National Identity* (Chapel Hill, N.C., 1987), 69–112. On Clinton, see John P. Kaminski, *George Clinton: Yeoman Politician of the New Republic* (Madison, Wis., 1993). On George Bryan, see Joseph S. Foster, *In Pursuit of Equal Liberty: George Bryan and the Revolution in Pennsylvania* (University Park, Pa., 1994).

3. Studies of American constitutionalism in this period include Gordon S. Wood, *The Creation of the American Republic, 1776–1787* (Chapel Hill, N.C., 1969); Donald S. Lutz. *Popular Consent and Popular Control: Whig Political Theory in the Early State Constitutions* (Baton Rouge, La., 1980); Willi Paul Adams, *The First American Constitutions: Republican Ideology and the Making of the State Constitutions in the Revolutionary Era* (Chapel Hill, N.C., 1980); Marc W. Kruman, *Between Authority and Liberty: State Constitution Making in Revolutionary America* (Chapel Hill, N.C., 1997).

4. The most influential effort to portray Anti-Federalists as agrarian localists committed to prodebtor paper money policies is Jackson Turner Main, *The Anti-Federalists: Critics of the Constitution, 1781–1788* (Chapel Hill, N.C., 1961), and *Political Parties before the Constitution* (Chapel Hill, N.C., 1973). Main's work employed statistical methods to create an aggregate picture of the voting behavior of legislators who became Anti-Federalists. A similar view informs the work of Van Beck Hall, *Politics without Parties: Massachusetts, 1780–1791* (Pittsburgh, 1972). The focus on the aggregate behavior of legislators obscures the role of an influential group of procommerce Anti-Federalist leaders in shaping the public debate over the Constitution. Both the agrarian localist and procommerce dimensions of Anti-Federalism are important to understanding the opposition to the Constitution. The two

Although small, one of the most important groups among middling Anti-Federalists was the printers. Newspapers such as Philadelphia's *Independent Gazetteer* and the *New-York Journal* were the leading forums for middling democratic Anti-Federalist ideas and provided ample space for Pennsylvania's Constitutionalists and New York's Clintonians to spread their ideas. Clintonians and Constitutionalists were also extremely well organized within their own states and were well connected with politicians in other states. Thus they not only shared political intelligence but also provided an informal distribution network that was particularly important for the circulation of pamphlets.

Of all the voices that protested the Constitution, the most difficult to recover is that of plebeian Anti-Federalists—the cottagers, tenant farmers, and less affluent mechanics who provided much of the base of grass-roots Anti-Federalist support. The numerical strength of this group was concentrated in the backcountry, and those regions were generally the least likely to have their own newspapers. The few newspapers outside cities and large towns were often founded by Federalist sympathizers eager to spread their values to the hinterlands. One of the great ironies of the publishing history of ratification is that the papers most sympathetic to the Anti-Federalist cause were in urban areas, not in the backcountry. With their access to the press blocked in the backcountry, plebeian ideas were generally underrepresented in print. Relatively few plebeian essays were republished outside their region, although their perspective did spill into the papers in states such as New York, Pennsylvania, and Massachusetts. Despite the difficulty of gaining access to the press, a few newspaper essays and pamphlets representing this viewpoint entered the national debate and gained broader circulation. In some cases plebeian ideas were picked up by radical polemicists whose works were widely reprinted and who crafted their essays to appeal to plebe-

---

most influential examples of the procommerce middling Anti-Federalists were John Nicholson in Pennsylvania and Melancton Smith in New York. On Nicholson, see Robert D. Arbuckle, *Pennsylvania Speculator and Patriot: The Entrepreneurial John Nicholson, 1757–1800* (University Park, Pa., 1975); and Steven R. Boyd, *The Politics of Opposition: Anti-Federalists and the Acceptance of the Constitution* (Millwood, N.Y., 1979). On Melancton Smith's role in New York, see Robin Brooks, "Melancton Smith: New York Anti-Federalist, 1744–1798" (Ph.D. diss., University of Rochester, 1964), and "Alexander Hamilton, Melancton Smith, and the Ratification of the Constitution in New York," *WMQ*, 3d Ser., XXIV (1967), 339–358. For cautionary remarks about using the behavior of legislators as proxies for their constituents, see Lee Benson, *Turner and Beard: American Historical Writing Reconsidered* (Glencoe, Ill., 1960).

ian tastes. Crowd behavior and the private correspondence of individuals on both sides of the debate who commented on the lower sort's views provide additional evidence about plebeian ideas.

Middling Constitutionalism

Most middling authors were willing to cede vast authority to state governments to legislate on behalf of the best interests of their citizens. Only a few authors expressed reservations about such grants of authority. The leading Anti-Federalist writers in Pennsylvania framed their discussions of liberty in Whig republican terms. No author was more explicit about this than was Pennsylvania's Old Whig, whose rhetorical identity made clear his commitment to traditional republican ideas. This author and his essays were a collective effort of prominent members of Pennsylvania's Constitutionalist party, including George Bryan, John Smilie, and James Hutchinson. Bryan was a vocal supporter of the state constitution, and Smilie was a leading spokesman for backcountry interests. Hutchinson, a physician, taught medicine at the University of Pennsylvania. An Old Whig's choice of pen name and method of argument affirmed a bond with the ideals of the Revolution. Indeed, this author reminded Americans that, before accepting the Constitution, they would do well "to read over the publications of the years, 1774, 1775, 1776 and 1777."[5]

An Old Whig had good reason to venerate his state constitution, one of the most democratic documents produced during the Revolution. The version of democratic theory embodied there was distinctly communitarian and consensual. Pennsylvania had to contend with a vocal and powerful tory minority and a sizable group of religious pacifists. Eager to prevent the tyranny they ascribed to the British, Pennsylvanians were equally wary of the dangers of internal subversion and counterrevolution. Thus, Pennsylvania enacted the most sweeping loyalty oaths of any state.

To justify their variant of constitutionalism, Pennsylvanians drew heavily on civic republican ideals. When entering civil society it was necessary to alienate a certain portion of one's natural liberty.

---

5. An Old Whig [George Bryan, John Smilie, and James Hutchinson?], no. 3, *IG*, Oct. 20, 1787 (*CA-F*, III, 29). For a brief comparison of the different situations faced by New York and Pennsylvania in the Revolutionary era, see Edward Countryman, "Confederation: State Governments and Their Problems," in Jack P. Greene and J. R. Pole, eds., *The Blackwell Encyclopedia of the American Revolution* (London, 1991), 332–345.

If they yield up all their natural rights they are absolute slaves to their governors. If they yield up less than is necessary, the government is so feeble, that it cannot protect them.—To yield up so much, as is necessary for the purposes of government; and to retain all beyond what is necessary, is the great point.[6]

Most Anti-Federalists would have accepted the important distinction between unalienable and alienable rights. Certain rights were unalienable and could never be ceded by individuals. Religious conscience was the most obvious example of a right that could not be renounced. Other rights were alienable but could be compromised only when the good of society demanded such sacrifices. Individual liberty could never be sacrificed for the good of a particular interest or faction. To guard against that danger, citizens had to remain active, vigilant, and even suspicious of government. Unrestrained by public virtue and constitutional safeguards, governments would inevitably trample upon individual liberty. Alienable rights were political rights, rights that resulted from the creation of a polity. Since they were inextricably linked to a properly functioning republican polity, they could never be exercised in such a way as to undermine that polity. Limits on liberty were permissible as long as laws were enacted by representatives of the people. Old Whig advised his readers, "If, indeed, government were really strengthened by such a surrender, if the body of the people were made more secure, or more happy by the means, we ought to make the sacrifice." He reiterated this by declaring, "If the good of his country should require it . . . every individual in the community ought to strip himself of some convenience for the sake of the public good." Republican notions of citizenship, of sacrificing some measure of one's liberty to serve the public good, were deemed essential. "Wherever the subject is convinced that nothing more is required from him, than what is necessary for the good of the community, he yields a chearful obedience, which is more useful than the constrained service of slaves." The "chearful obedience" described by An Old Whig was not identical to a Spartan ideal of virtue. While An Old Whig conceded that Americans were more virtuous than most nations, he did not ascribe heroic qualities to the typical citizen. He certainly placed no great faith in society's leaders' being incorruptible. Nor did he assert that it was necessary for citizens to have the same interests in order to achieve the virtue necessary for the survival of republican government.[7]

6. An Old Whig, no. 4, *IG*, Oct. 27, 1787 (*CA-F*, III, 33).
7. Ibid. (III, 32–34), no. 8, *IG*, Feb. 6, 1788 (III, 49).

Under ordinary circumstances, An Old Whig believed that liberty and virtue would not be antithetical, the two concepts being, in fact, complementary. In practice, An Old Whig contended that the sacrifice of individual freedom for the common good was, not a restriction on liberty, but the necessary condition for the exercise of liberty properly understood. The goal of constitutional reform ought to be "the forming of a plan of confederation, which may enable us at once to support our continental union with vigor and efficacy, and to maintain the rights of the separate states and the invaluable liberty of the subject." He conceded, "These ideas of political felicity, to some people, may seem, like the visions of an Utopian fancy." Yet, he went on to assert, "There is at least, this consolation in aiming at excellence, that, if we do not obtain our object, we can make considerable progress towards it." An Old Whig's constitutionalism placed great faith in the ability of the state governments to protect liberty and act on behalf of the common good. As long as the sacrifice of liberty did not impinge on unalienable rights and decisions were made by the legislature acting on behalf of the common good, there was no contradiction between those two goals.[8]

An Old Whig was not unmindful of the threat to liberty posed by government. His response, however, revealed considerable faith in the constitutional mechanisms provided by his own state constitution. Indeed, preserving the integrity of the Pennsylvania state constitution was central to his vision. Thus, An Old Whig did not look to Spartan virtue, but he did praise the reverence Spartans had for maintaining the purity of their constitution. One of the best expressions of this ideal was his support for the Pennsylvania Council of Censors, a hybrid legislative-judicial body whose function was to judge the constitutionality of legislation.[9]

The Pennsylvania Council of Censors also reflected the deep suspicion within popular constitutional thought toward judicial review. By placing his faith in an elected body to review the constitutionality of laws, An Old Whig displayed a distinctive hostility to the authority of judges and lauded the role of juries. "Judges" he wrote, "unincumbered by juries, have been ever found

8. Ibid., no. 4 (III, 32–34), no. 5, *IG*, Nov. 1, 1787 (III, 35), no. 8 (III, 49).

9. Anti-Federalists in Pennsylvania were strong supporters of the state constitution. Federalists generally opposed the state constitution. An Old Whig's reverence for constitutional purity partly reflected his desire to protect the state constitution against those who sought to replace it. On constitutional struggles in Pennsylvania, see Douglas M. Arnold, *A Republican Revolution: Ideology and Politics in Pennsylvania, 1776–1790* (New York, 1989); Richard Alan Ryerson, "Republican Theory and Partisan Reality in Revolutionary Pennsylvania: Toward a New View of the Constitutionalist Party," in Ronald Hoffman and Peter J. Albert, eds., *Sovereign States in an Age of Uncertainty* (Charlottesville, Va., 1981), 95–133.

much better friends to government than to the people." An Old Whig shared the middling democratic view of the jury as an authentic voice of the will of the community.[10]

No Anti-Federalist text has attracted more modern interest than *Observations . . . in a Number of Letters from the Federal Farmer to the Republican.* During ratification a number of prominent Federalists and Anti-Federalists praised this work, describing it as the most intellectually compelling and politically persuasive argument against the Constitution. The pamphlet was distributed in New York, Pennsylvania, Massachusetts, and Connecticut. A second installment, *Additional Letters,* was sent by New York Anti-Federalist John Lamb to leading opponents of the Constitution in Virginia, North Carolina, and New Hampshire. Although *Letters* was not widely reprinted in newspapers, the distribution of the pamphlet made it available to leading Anti-Federalists in most states. The identity of Federal Farmer remains a mystery and was the subject of some speculation at the time the essays first appeared. Several Massachusetts papers claimed that the letters were written by Richard Henry Lee with the help of "several persons of good sense in New York." Although modern scholars have not solved this riddle, the essays were most likely written by a New Yorker who was part of the Clintonian faction and might well have been Melancton Smith. There are important similarities in both tone and content between the writings of the Federal Farmer and Smith's speeches in the New York state ratification convention.[11]

The *Letters* was addressed to the Republican, a pen name that Clinton often employed. Federal Farmer's politics resembled those of George Clinton, the leading Anti-Federalist politician in New York. Indeed, Federal

10. An Old Whig, no. 1, *IG,* Oct. 12, 1787 (*CA-F,* III, 19); no. 2, *IG,* Oct. 17, 1787 (III, 24); no. 8 (III, 49). On the Council of Censors, see Lutz, *Popular Consent and Popular Control.*

11. Federal Farmer [Melancton Smith?], *Observations Leading to a Fair Examination of the System of Government Proposed by the Late Convention . . . Letters from the Federal Farmer to the Republican* (New York, 1787) (nos. 1–5), *An Additional Number of Letters from the Federal Farmer to the Republican . . .* (New York, 1788) (nos. 6–18). For a discussion of the circulation and reception of *Letters from the Federal Farmer,* see *DHRC,* XIV, 14–18. The identity of Federal Farmer has been a subject of considerable controversy. In "The Authorship of the *Letters from the Federal Farmer,*" *WMQ,* 3d Ser., XXXI (1974), 299–308, Gordon S. Wood suggested that *The Letters* was probably written by a New Yorker. Robert H. Webking has suggested that Federal Farmer might have been Melancton Smith, in "Melancton Smith and the *Letters from the Federal Farmer,*" *WMQ,* 3d Ser., XLIV (1987), 510–528. Smith now seems the most likely author of this important set of essays, although we still lack a positive identification. In constitutional theory, the essays more closely resemble the thought of middling democrats in New York than anything produced by Richard Henry Lee or any other members of the Virginia gentry.

Farmer came as close to voicing the views of Clintonians as did any Anti-Federalist author.[12]

One of the distinguishing characteristics of Federal Farmer's argument was his effort to persuade his readers that he was not just a dispassionate commentator on political matters but was the true voice of the middling sort. The middling sort, in his view, stood between the wealthy aristocrats and the debt-ridden lower sort. The stereotype of Anti-Federalists as Shaysites or debtors, a view perpetuated by Federalists, drew Federal Farmer's ire. He explicitly condemned "levellers" and "little insurgents, men in debt, who want no law, and who want a share of the property of others." Federal Farmer aligned himself with the "men of middling property, men not in debt on the one hand, and men, on the other content with republican government, and not aiming at immense fortunes, offices, or power." On the subject of paper money and bankruptcy law, Federal Farmer presented a view consistent with the many middling merchants who formed part of the Anti-Federalist coalition. He opposed paper money emissions and believed that bankruptcy law was best left to the states, who were better able to determine the best manner for handling such matters. It was not only those at the bottom of society who posed a threat to political stability. At the other extreme of the social spectrum and equally dangerous to republicanism were the aristocratic few, "men unfriendly to republican equality." Federal Farmer looked on the better sort with the same suspicion that characterized his view of the lower sort. The survival of republican government depended on those who stood somewhere between these two extremes: the middling sort.[13]

Federal Farmer's discussion of liberty and rights was among the most lucid of any Anti-Federalist author and went well beyond the discussion provided by An Old Whig to explore the relationship between rights and constitutionalism. His conception of liberty was also far more self-conscious about the need to protect the interests of the middling sort. Liberty would thrive only in a society in which men of middling fortunes directed the course of state action and defined the nature of the legal system.

Federal Farmer shared An Old Whig's faith in state constitutions and state legislatures to guard liberty. In the "state constitutions, certain rights have

12. [Smith?], *Letters from the Federal Farmer*, no. 5 (*CA-F*, II, 253). For examples of the Federal Farmer's views on paper money and bankruptcy, see *CA-F*, II, 225, 227, 229, 243, 340. His views echo Clinton's on a number of issues. On Clinton's political thought, see Kaminski, *George Clinton*, 96–109. Clinton was among the most important Anti-Federalist leaders, and Federal Farmer one of the most respected critics of the Constitution.

13. [Smith?], *Letters from the Federal Farmer*, no. 1 (*CA-F*, II, 226), no. 5 (II, 253).

been reserved in the people; or rather, they have been recognized and established in such a manner, that state legislatures are bound to respect them." He divided rights into three categories: "natural and inalienable" rights, "constitutional or fundamental" rights, and "common or legal" rights. The first type was never ceded when men entered civil society, and the second category of rights could not "be altered or abolished by the ordinary laws; but [by] the people." Trial by jury and habeas corpus were both examples of fundamental rights that had been established by written constitutions or sanctified by long usage as part of an unwritten constitution. This final class of rights included those which "individuals claim under laws which the ordinary legislature may alter or abolish at pleasure." Federal Farmer conceded to the states vast power to regulate their internal police. The concept of a broad police power was central to Federal Farmer's constitutionalism and included a range of governmental responsibilities, including the collection of internal taxes, the administration of justice, and the organization of the militia.[14]

Whatever suspicion Federal Farmer might have felt regarding the new government, he displayed great confidence in the state legislatures to act in conformity with the common good. This confidence did not diminish the need for a formal declaration of rights. Bills of rights served as a check on government and a means of alerting the people to the dangers to their liberty. One of their primary functions was to mark "the powers of the rulers and the rights of the people," which then became "visible boundaries, constantly seen by all, and any transgression of them is immediately discovered." For Federal Farmer, bills of rights were part of the secular creed of the nation and had to be reverenced, much like the Bible. The analogy between civil and political religion was made explicit when he wrote, "If a nation means its systems, religious or political, shall have duration, it ought to recognize the leading principles of them in the front page of every family book." Constitutionalism, like Protestantism, did not require a special caste of priestly interpreters. Republican principles were easily understood by anyone possessing the qualities of honesty and common sense. It was vital that these ideals be instilled in every citizen. Constitutions not only functioned as a social compact; they were instruments of civic education.[15]

The danger posed by the federal judiciary was often cited in popular Anti-Federalist thought as a serious defect of the Constitution: "It is true, the laws are made by the legislature; but the judges and juries, in their interpreta-

14. Ibid., no. 1 (II, 229), no. 4 (II, 248), no. 5 (II, 256), no. 6 (II, 261).
15. Ibid., no. 6 (II, 258), no. 16 (II, 324).

tions, and in directing the execution of them, have a very extensive influence for preserving or destroying liberty." In contrast to the Federalists, Federal Farmer believed that, the more popular an institution was, the less it threatened liberty. Thus, he asserted that abuses of power by judges were less easily corrected than were the excesses of the legislature. Although the actions of the legislature were immediately sensible, the decisions of judges might initially affect only "a single individual, and noticed only by his neighbors, and a few spectators in the court." To compound the danger, Americans "have been always jealous of the legislature, and especially the executive; but not always of the judiciary." The nature of law and American society were such that the courts posed one of the most serious threats to liberty.[16]

In contrast to elite Anti-Federalists who saw the jury as a check on the power of judges, Federal Farmer went much further, asserting the superiority of the jury and equating power of the jury with that of the legislative branch. "I hold," he wrote, "the established right of the jury by the common law, and the fundamental law of this country, to give a general verdict in all cases when they chuse to do it, to decide both as to law and fact." This practice was not only long sanctioned, but it was justified by the jury's role as an expression of the people's will: "Juries are constantly and frequently drawn from the body of the people, and freemen of the country; and by holding their jury's right to return a general verdict in all cases sacred, we secure to the people at large, their just and rightful controul in the judicial department." Expansive jury powers not only were necessary to control the judicial branch, but they were essential for democracy. "The body of the people, principally, bear the burdens of the community; they of right ought to have a controul in its important concerns." Federal Farmer's activist vision of the jury was part of a broader commitment to a notion of constitutionalism in which mediating elites would have little function. "It is true, the freemen of a country are not always minutely skilled in laws," he noted, "but they have common sense in its purity, which seldom or never errs in making and applying laws to the condition of the people." Federal Farmer conceded that there would always be a need to interpret the law. In those cases, he placed his faith in the jury, not the judiciary, to make decisions. Jury service also provided an important form of civic education. "This and the democratic branch in the legislature" were "the means by which the people are let into the knowledge of public affairs—are enabled to stand as the guardians of each others rights." In this sense the jury served as another forum, a variant of the public sphere in which citizens engaged in reasoned debate on

16. Ibid., no. 15 (II, 315, 316).

public matters. The jury served a double function—expressing the popular will and educating citizens in constitutional principles.[17]

The conception of the jury defended by Federal Farmer was not the localist ideal defended by the gentry. "When I speak of the jury trial of the vicinage or the trial of the fact in the neighbourhood,—I do not lay so much stress upon the circumstance of our being tried by our neighbours." It was far less important that juries be composed of local citizens than that they be composed of "the common people." For Federal Farmer, the values and ideals of the middling sort were shaped, not by attachment to locality, but by social position.[18]

The emphasis on the importance of the middling sort to Federal Farmer's constitutional vision also shaped how he understood the role of the militia. Ultimately, he concurred with other Anti-Federalists that the final check on a tyrannical government was the right of armed resistance. Federal Farmer also shared the frequently voiced fear that the new government had stripped this power away from the states, where it rightfully resided. Liberty could be maintained only in a federal system in which the states continued to be the dominant political units. State control of the militia was an important structural safeguard, a counterweight to the power of the central government. Federal Farmer asserted that it was essential that "the states shall form and train the militia." The ideals of middling democracy informed the way Federal Farmer understood the militia. One of the most fascinating aspects of Federal Farmer's theory was his insistence that the militia was, not a select body drawn from the people of the states, but the whole body of the citizens, excluding those who were not capable of displaying the virtue necessary for republican citizenship: "A militia, when properly formed, are in fact the people themselves, and render regular troops in great measure unnecessary." A select militia set off from the regular body of the people posed as serious a threat to liberty as did a standing army: "It is essential that the whole body of the people always possess arms, and be taught, alike, especially when young, how to use them." While Federal Farmer valorized the sturdy yeomanry who were the foundation of the militia, he also made clear the danger of includ-

17. Ibid., no. 15 (II, 315, 319, 320). On the notion of jury rights, and the representative character of the jury, see Chapter 2, n. 33, above. A few points are worth making about Federal Farmer's views of jury rights. Federal Farmer not only framed one of the most forceful statements of jury power; he also made one of most powerful arguments that those rights would be eroded by the federal courts. For a modern discussion of the relevance of jury rights to contemporary jurisprudence that relies heavily on Federal Farmer, see Akhil Reed Amar, "The Bill of Rights as a Constitution," *Yale Law Journal*, C (1991), 1131–1210.

18. [Smith?], *Letters from the Federal Farmer*, no. 4 (*CA-F*, II, 249).

ing men "not having permanent interests and attachments in the community" within the ranks of the militia. This was one reason why it was vital for the states to retain control of this power. It would be easy for a powerful government to create a select militia of individuals with no interest in preserving republicanism. State control of the militia "places the sword in the hands of the solid interest of the community, and not in the hands of men destitute of property, of principle, or of attachment to the society and government." Federal Farmer endorsed a right to bear arms, but he linked that right to an individual's responsibility to be trained in arms, submit to state control, and demonstrate he was not a dependent who might become a pawn or a hireling.[19]

One of the characteristics distinguishing middling democracy was its effort to chart a path between the elitism of traditional Whig republicanism and mobocracy. Ensuring that the militia remained under the authority of the states also reflected this concern. While middling Anti-Federalists opposed the notion of a select militia, they equally opposed the idea that citizens might spontaneously constitute themselves as militia units and challenge despotic authority on their own initiative. The fear of the mob led Federal Farmer to affirm the right of the community to exclude from the militia individuals whom it deemed dangerous or potentially dangerous to

19. Ibid, no. 17 (*CA-F*, II, 341–342). For a discussion of the controversy over a select militia, see Joyce Lee Malcolm, *To Keep and Bear Arms: The Origins of an Anglo-American Right* (Cambridge, Mass., 1994). A substantial effort has been devoted to exploring the liberal and republican origins of the Second Amendment. For an argument grounded in liberal theory that it represented an individual right to gun ownership, see Robert E. Shalhope, "The Ideological Origins of the Second Amendment," *JAH*, LXIX (1982–1983), 599–614; for the counterargument that the amendment was a collective militia right grounded in civic republican assumptions, see Lawrence Delbert Cress, "An Armed Community: The Origins and Meaning of the Right to Bear Arms," *JAH*, LXXI (1984–1985), 22–42. These two interpretations are discussed in Shalhope and Cress, "The Right to Bear Arms: An Exchange," *JAH*, LXXI (1984–1985), 587–593. A sensible effort to chart a middle ground between these positions may be found in David T. Hardy, "The Second Amendment and the Historiography of the Bill of Rights," *Journal of Law and Politics*, IV (1987), 1–62. Constitutional theorists have taken up those issues in order to evaluate contemporary policy on gun ownership and gun control. For a defense of the Second Amendment as the final check on tyranny, see Sanford Levinson, "The Embarrassing Second Amendment," *Yale Law Journal*, XCIX (1989), 637–659. Legal scholars championing the "standard model," an interpretation of the Second Amendment that recognizes the right of individual gun ownership, can be found in "Second Amendment Symposium," *Tennessee Law Review*, LXII (1995), 443–821. This interpretation relies heavily on Anti-Federalist ideas for support. For an attack on this model, see Garry Wills, "To Keep and Bear Arms," *New York Review of Books*, Sept. 21, 1995, and the responses by Sanford Levinson and Glen Harlan Reynolds, Nov. 16, 1995.

republican order. It was for this reason that the militia included only men with a permanent attachment to society. The jury and the militia were cast in terms that reflected his faith in state authority. In part, his preference for state over local solutions mirrored the belief of the middling sort that their values were universal and not rooted in any particular locality.

Another demonstration of how Federal Farmer's variant of middling democracy presupposed a fairly homogeneous population is evident in his discussion of religious tests for officeholding. He expressed his shock that neither the Congress nor the states could impose additional restrictions on the qualifications for officeholding. Officeholding was opened up to "Christians, Pagans, Mahometans, or Jews." While Federal Farmer welcomed a broad representation of different economic groups, he showed far less concern about including racial or religious diversity in the legislature. His commitment to a liberal, interest-oriented theory of politics embraced economic, not social, diversity. His support for the rights of conscience and freedom of worship did not mean that all individuals were entitled to full political participation. In all areas where individual liberty might have a direct impact on the ability of political society to preserve its republican character, Federal Farmer sided with the right of the community to regulate the behavior of individuals.[20]

On economic matters, Federal Farmer was decidedly liberal. Thus, he was also able to write, "Liberty, in its genuine sense, is security to enjoy the effects of our honest industry and labours, in a free and mild government, and personal security from all illegal restraint." Free governments, in Federal Farmer's view, were not activists in economic matters. Federal Farmer believed that people ought to "follow their private pursuits, and enjoy the fruits of their labour with very small deductions for the public use." In contrast to his traditional Whig republican understanding of political liberty, he approached economic liberty in far more liberal terms.[21]

A different interpretation of the nature of political liberty was elaborated by two other New York Anti-Federalist authors whose writings demonstrate a more expansive view of individual rights and a more limited view of the sphere of government authority. One short essay, signed by A Son of Liberty, expressed the fear that the power to tax would provide pretexts "by which our bed chambers will be subjected to be searched by brutal tools of power, under pretence, that they contain contraband or smuggled merchandize,

---

20. [Smith?], *Letters from the Federal Farmer,* no. 12 (*CA-F,* II, 295).
21. Ibid., no. 6 (II, 261), no. 7 (II, 264), no. 12 (II, 295).

and the most delicate part of our families, liable to every species of rude or indecent treatment." The fear that the extensive powers of taxation and the absence of protection against unreasonable searches would lead to massive assaults on individual freedom prompted a similar reaction from Brutus. Elaborating upon the type of analysis provided by A Son of Liberty, Brutus predicted that the new power to tax would endow the government with almost unlimited authority: "This power, exercised without limitation, will introduce itself into every corner of the city, and country—It will wait upon the ladies at their toilett, and will not leave them in any of their domestic concerns." The threat posed by such boundless authority would "enter the house of every gentleman, watch over his cellar." This power would even "attend him to his bed-chamber, and watch him while he sleeps." This fear that government might invade the most intimate areas of private life suggests that some Anti-Federalists were willing to carve out a larger zone of individual liberty exempt from legislative prerogatives. Tentatively, these Anti-Federalists suggested that there might be a line beyond which government simply could not go and so took an important, if only modest, first step, toward recognizing a broader sphere of individual liberty, a penumbra surrounding those natural and constitutional rights essential to freedom.[22]

The emergence of a genuinely libertarian impulse among a few Anti-Federalist authors in New York makes sense, given that state's political experiences. The actions of the British military during the Seven Years' War and the Revolution left a bitter taste in the mouths of many New Yorkers. The fears of Brutus and A Son of Liberty about intrusive government were not abstractions gleaned from political tracts. Their perspective reflected the experiences of men like Abraham Yates, an influential state politician and political organizer who was an outspoken opponent of the Constitution. When British troops had been billeted in Albany during the Seven Years' War, Yates felt the oppressive hand of the military firsthand. Yates blamed the miscarriage of his wife on the harassment of his family by British troops. The author who adopted the name A Son of Liberty underscored the degree to which the experience of war continued to shape the way New Yorkers approached constitutional issues. Having lived under a tyrannical British government,

22. A Son of Liberty, *New-York Journal,* Nov. 8, 1787 (*DHRC,* XIII, 481–482); Brutus, no. 6, *New-York Journal,* Dec. 27, 1787 (XV, 111–114). On the tradition of natural rights theory, see Knud Haakonssen, "From Natural Law to the Rights of Man: A European Perspective on American Debates," in Michael J. Lacey and Knud Haakonssen, eds., *A Culture of Rights: The Bill of Rights in Philosophy, Politics, and Law—1791 and 1991* (Cambridge, 1991), 19–61.

this Anti-Federalist author formulated a more libertarian view of rights, carving out a sphere of action immune from government interference.[23]

The Political Sociology of Middling Anti-Federalism

The fundamental defect of the new Constitution was its aristocratic character. "Every man of reflection must see," Federal Farmer concluded, "that the change now proposed, is a transfer of power from the many to the few."[24] While America enjoyed more equality than any other nation, it was not exempt from the tensions between patricians and plebeians that had divided almost every society in history. For Federal Farmer, the structure of the new government was designed to restore to members of the natural aristocracy the power that the Revolution had given to the people:

> The people of this country, in one sense, may all be democratic; but if we make the proper distinction between the few men of wealth and abilities, and consider them, as we ought, as the natural aristocracy of the country, and the great body of the people, the middle and lower classes, as the democracy, this federal representative branch will have but very little democracy in it.[25]

No Anti-Federalist author devoted more energy than did Federal Farmer to exploring the problem of aristocracy, whose meaning was bitterly contested by both sides in the debate over ratification. "There are three kinds of aristocracy spoken of in this country," Federal Farmer wrote. "The first is a constitutional one, which does not exist in the United States." A second was "an aristocratic faction; a junto of unprincipled men, often distinguished for their wealth or abilities, who combine together and make their object their private interests and aggrandizement." The last and perhaps most slippery use of the term was "natural aristocracy." The line dividing the natural aristocracy from the people "is in some degree arbitrary; we may place men on one side of this line, which others may place on the other." He realized that "in all disputes between the few and the many, a considerable number are wavering and uncertain themselves" and might wind up on one or the other side.[26]

23. Bielinski, *Abraham Yates*, 6. Some scholars have suggested that Brutus might have been Abraham Yates, but the identities of Brutus and A Son of Liberty remain a mystery.

24. [Smith?], *Letters from the Federal Farmer*, no. 4 (*CA-F*, II, 251).

25. Ibid., no. 3 (II, 235).

26. Ibid., no. 7 (II, 267).

America had rid herself of the first type of aristocracy, hereditary or constitutional, during the Revolution. The second type, oligarchy or aristocratic cabals, continued to present a serious problem. All Anti-Federalists, including the Anti-Federalist elite, wished to oppose this form. The notion that any body of men, even the most virtuous group of politicians, might succumb to the temptations of power and substitute their private interests for those of the commonweal was a commonplace republican concern. The third type described by Federal Farmer, natural aristocracy, identified an amorphous social class, variously described in popular Anti-Federalist discourse as the better sort or the wellborn. Popular Anti-Federalist constitutionalism parted company with elite thinking by attacking this notion of aristocracy.

The difference between Federal Farmer's constitutionalism and elite Anti-Federalist constitutionalism was evident in his discussion of virtue. In contrast to the Anti-Federalist elite, middling Anti-Federalists democratized the idea of virtue. The wisdom and knowledge necessary for public service might be found in any industrious member of the middling sort: "The knowledge, generally, necessary for men who make laws, is a knowledge of the common concerns, and particular circumstances of the people." If virtue was evenly diffused throughout the whole population, then "every order of men in the community" ought to be represented. The legislature ought to include not only members of the gentry, the learned professions and merchants, but farmers and mechanics as well. Federal Farmer's commitment to democracy did not embrace a radical egalitarianism. He conceded that there would always be some distinctions and that the legislature ought to include the most talented citizens. There was, however, an important distinction between a representative body that included the most respected artisans and yeomen, and a body drawn primarily from the natural aristocracy. The key point for Federal Farmer was that each class contained men with the necessary wisdom and virtue to serve as representatives.[27]

Federal Farmer believed that men of "wealth or abilities" were actually more likely to be involved in cabal and conspiracy. The great and wellborn were less likely to show the moderation that characterized men of middling fortunes. High station also bred contempt for those below them. Federal Farmer's critique was not the most radical attack on aristocracy framed by Anti-Federalists. He merely sought to reduce the power of natural aristocrats, not eliminate their influence entirely.[28]

27. Ibid., no. 2 (II, 230), no. 9 (II, 275, 276), no. 11 (II, 292).
28. Ibid., no. 11 (II, 288). Federal Farmer grudgingly accepted that it might be appropri-

In addition to democratizing virtue, Federal Farmer rejected the ideal of disinterestedness. He embraced an interest-oriented theory of representation that accepted that no group in society could rise above its interests. On this issue, Federal Farmer shared with many middling Anti-Federalists a theory of politics that was essentially liberal, not republican. Society was, not an organic whole, but an aggregation of separate interests. Precisely for this reason, Federal Farmer advocated representation for all of society's diverse interests. While he trusted the sturdy yeomanry to be the most reliable class, he acknowledged that "the several orders of men in society, which we call aristocratical, democratic, merchantile, mechanic," had their own interests and, if unchecked by other competing interests, were likely to "elevate themselves and oppress others." To counteract this tendency, it was necessary that "each order must have a share in the business of legislation actually and efficiently." Although Federal Farmer admitted that many would view such a suggestion as utopian, he strenuously argued, "It is deceiving a people to tell them they are electors, and can chuse their legislators, if they cannot, in the nature of things, chuse men from among themselves, and genuinely like themselves." Representatives had to resemble those they represented to protect their interests faithfully.[29]

Another important dimension of Federal Farmer's critique of aristocracy was his analysis of the dynamics of electoral politics: the Constitution could not be analyzed apart from the sociological realities of America politics. Congress, he argued, would be dominated by aristocrats. In large electoral districts, men drawn from the ranks of the natural aristocracy would have unfair advantages over men drawn from the middling sort: "A man that is known among a few thousands of people, may be quite unknown among thirty or forty thousand." The inevitable result would be that "those few who have become eminent for their civil or military rank, or their popular legal abilities," would win election. Few individuals from the less opulent walks of life would be elected. Increasing the size of the legislature would solve this problem and allow more interests to be represented and would also facilitate the creation of smaller electoral districts in which men of middling fortunes would be more likely to succeed in election. The transformation of state politics after the Revolution provided ample evidence for this view, and leading Federalists would have agreed with Federal Farmer's diagnosis of the dominant political trend in post-Revolutionary society. Where Federal

---

ate for the senate to represent property interests, with the lower house to serve as the voice of the people and guardians of their liberty.

29. Ibid., no. 7 (II, 266–268).

Farmer parted company with Federalists was in his positive assessment of this trend.[30]

The conception of society implicit in Federal Farmer's social vision was not the harmonious ranked order that many elite Anti-Federalists still cherished. His frank acceptance of interest and economic diversity led him to reject the notions of deference and hierarchy associated with traditional Whig thought. Although the most important distinction in society was between the many and the few, Federal Farmer also recognized that there were many economic interests that had to be properly represented. His language was distinctly eighteenth-century in this regard, since he used the plural concept of classes or orders. While he recognized that all classes were antagonistic in some sense, his conception of class was still fairly inchoate.

To protect the democratic achievements of the Revolution required more than simply making Congress more democratic. The issue of federalism was closely related to the problem of democracy. The further power was from the states, the more likely the elite would dominate the government. "The federal government will be principally in the hands of the natural aristocracy, and the state governments in the hands of the democracy." In addition to increasing the number of representatives, Federal Farmer advocated returning more power to the states. Restoring balance within the federal system would also improve the character of representation, because "nineteen-twentieths of the representatives of the people" were in the various state legislatures and had "a near connection" and "immediate intercourse with the people." As a result, it was the state government that would "possess the confidence of the people, and be considered generally as their immediate guardians."[31]

Centinel and Philadelphiensis: Voices of Radical Democracy

One of the most important voices among the Anti-Federalists was a group of radical polemicists, authors whose writings were among the most widely reprinted during ratification. Popular Anti-Federalism occupied a spectrum that ran from middling authors on one end to plebeian populists on the other. Authors such as Centinel, An Officer of the Late Continental Army, and Philadelphiensis stood somewhere between those poles.

The most prolific and influential of those authors was Centinel. Eighteen installments of his writing appeared during ratification. Not only was Cen-

30. Ibid., no. 9 (II, 276).
31. Ibid., no. 2 (II, 232–233), no. 10 (II, 282).

tinel one of the first Anti-Federalist essayists to enter the fray, but the earliest installments of his writings were among the most widely reprinted in newspapers and were also included in a number of pamphlet anthologies. Federalists and Anti-Federalists each concurred that Centinel was among the most effective spokesmen for the opposition to the Constitution.

As far as the content of his writing was concerned, Centinel's arguments were hardly unique. On most issues he employed many of the same criticisms about consolidation, aristocracy, and the absence of a bill of rights invoked by other Anti-Federalist authors. What distinguished Centinel's writing was its radicalism and polemical flair. Indeed, more than any other author, Centinel crafted his appeals in such a way that parts of his essays appealed to the middling sort and plebeians. The appeal to diverse audiences accounted for the popularity and influence of his writings. Understanding his meaning necessarily involves exploring the diverse readerships he sought to influence and persuade.

Among widely reprinted Anti-Federalists essayists, none employed a more assertive and class-conscious rhetoric. The chief threat to liberty in his view was aristocracy. "In many of the states, particularly in this and the northern states, there are aristocratic junto's of the *well-born few,* who had been zealously endeavoring since the establishment of their constitutions, to humble that offensive *upstart, equal liberty.*" Centinel linked democracy and federalism. It was the state governments that represented the democratic achievements of the Revolution. He was especially impressed by the example of Pennsylvania. The freemen of Pennsylvania were fortunate to live under a state constitution that protected their liberty and afforded them adequate representation. Centinel attacked the Constitution for threatening the state governments and for creating an aristocratic government. In his view, Federalist ideas were inspired by John Adams, who hoped to model American government on the British constitution.[32]

One of the most interesting features of Centinel's political philosophy, reflecting his experience of Pennsylvania, was his call for a unicameral legislature. His explanation of its advantages used an argument important to popular constitutional thought, the belief that the structure of government had to be simple to promote greater popular participation. Centinel disagreed with the bicameralism endorsed by elite Anti-Federalists. For Centinel, the most important check on government was, not bicameralism, but the close ties between representatives and the people. When government was

32. Centinel [Samuel Bryan?], no. 3, "To the People of Pennsylvania," *IG,* Nov. 8, 1787 (*CA-F,* II, 156).

simple, the people would serve as the guardian of their own liberties. "If imitating the constitution of Pennsylvania, you vest all the legislative power in one body of men," and make sure that this body was "elected for a short period, and necessarily excluded by rotation from permanency, and guarded from precipitancy and surprise by delays imposed on its proceedings, you will create the most perfect responsibility." The goal of this more radical variant of constitutionalism was to make government simple and guarantee that representatives were tied to their constituents. The call for a cooling-off period, in effect building in a delay for legislation, was intended to give legislators the time to ascertain the people's views on public issues and more faithfully represent their wishes. By contrast, the Constitution created a legislature specifically designed to exclude the people from consultation. The Congress was contrived to frustrate the will of the people and would be "composed of the *better sort,* the *well born.*"[33]

Pennsylvanians, Centinel reminded his readers, enjoyed the "peculiar felicity of living under the most perfect system of local government in the world." Centinel feared that the "ambitious," particularly in his own state, "have been united in a constant conspiracy to destroy" the Pennsylvania constitution, which Centinel believed was the "great palladium of equal liberty." Although history provided countless examples of republics in which "the few generally prevail over the many," Pennsylvania was exceptional, since "in Pennsylvania the reverse has happened; here the *well born* have been baffled in all their efforts to prostrate the altar of liberty." Since the state constitutions represented the democratic reforms of the Revolution, it was vital to protect them and prevent the adoption of a document that would have diminished their power. Protecting the rights of the states was another means of guarding the rights of the people against the ambitious designs of an aristocratic elite. Although framing his ideas in more egalitarian terms, Centinel shared with many middling democrats a belief that the states were the best guardians of popular liberty.[34]

His conception of liberty reflected the republican vision of other Pennsylvania Anti-Federalists. In much the same way An Old Whig counseled the need to surrender liberty when the good of the commonweal demanded, Centinel supported the Pennsylvania Test Acts, which barred individuals who would not take a loyalty oath from enjoying the full benefits of citizenship. The acts disenfranchised and levied heavy penalties on a number of the state's religious and ethnic minorities as well as a number of former tories.

33. Ibid., no. 1, "To the Freemen of Pennsylvania," *IG,* Oct. 5, 1787 (II, 139, 142).
34. Ibid., no. 9, "To the People of Pennsylvania," *IG,* Jan. 8, 1788 (II, 179–180).

Federalists charged that the Anti-Federalists had "violated the rights of conscience, by imposing a wicked and tyrannical test law upon the Quakers, Menonists, and other sects of Christians." Centinel responded to that accusation with an attack on the Federalists, accusing them of seeking to "destroy the harmony of Pennsylvania, and forward the vassalage of her citizens to the *rich and aspiring*." Centinel affirmed the necessity and legality of the Test Acts. "I shall only observe that the circumstance of the times justified, nay made it indispensably necessary." The justification was obvious to "common sense and agreeable to the great law of self-preservation to draw a line of discrimination, and exclude from our councils and places of power and trust, those persons who were inimical to our cause." While such a policy was appropriate to "civil war," Centinel admitted that "sound policy dictates the repeal of such laws as soon as it can be done consistent with the public safety." By failing to support the Revolutionary cause, the individuals excluded by the Test Acts were placed outside the republican polity. Only individuals demonstrating their capacity for republican virtue were entitled to full citizenship. The right of the community to legislate for the public welfare took precedence over the liberties of the disenfranchised Quakers, Germans, and former tories.[35]

Although reasonably procommercial in his views, Centinel fell short of supporting the sort of liberal ideas espoused by elite spokesmen such as Agrippa: he shared Federal Farmer's belief in economic growth. While he accepted the necessity of commerce for economic prosperity, he was distinctly hostile to the values of the merchant class. He chided it for seeking "pre-eminence and superiority" when "already possessed of a competency." Something about commercial activity prevented citizens from seeing their true interests: "The merchant, immersed in schemes of wealth, seldom extends his views beyond the immediate object of gain; he blindly pursues his seeming interest, and sees not the latent mischief." Centinel's attack on mer-

---

35. Ibid., no. 22, *IG*, Nov. 14, 1788 (*DHFFE*, I, 341–342). In the view of constitutional historian James H. Hutson, the Anti-Federalist support for loyalty oaths, which effectively disenfranchised Quakers and many German religious sects, calls into question their commitment to liberty; see "The Birth of the Bill of Rights: The State of Current Scholarship," *Prologue*, XX (1988), 150. In this, Hutson follows the judgment of Leonard W. Levy: see *Original Intent and the Framers' Constitution* (New York, 1988). For critiques of Levy, see David M. Rabban, "The Ahistorical Historian: Leonard Levy on Freedom of Expression in Early American History," *Stanford Law Review*, XXXVII (1985), 795–856; Saul Cornell, "Moving beyond the Canon: Anti-Federalists, the Bill of Rights, and the Promise of Post-Modern Historiography," *Law and History Review*, XII (1994), 1–28. For a useful discussion of the debate over the Test Acts in Pennsylvania, see Arnold, *A Republican Revolution*, 103–119.

chants and commerce was not simply a rote recitation of country criticism of the intrigues of court. He was not against commerce, but was against the unrestrained excesses of the commercial spirit: "Commerce is the handmaid of liberty." The danger was that ambition and the lust for dominion created "a monopolizing spirit" that might "shackle commerce with every device of avarice" and destroy equal liberty and republicanism. It is interesting that Centinel chose to contrast the notion of a competency with the avaricious spirit that drove some merchants to seek great wealth. When individuals sought a competency, their industry promoted economic growth. The accumulation of great wealth, by contrast, sapped the spirit of initiative and threatened republicanism. Centinel's vision of commerce was tempered by republican values and more closely resembled the producer ethic of artisans than it did the liberal vision of a commercial republic celebrated by wealthy merchants. When individuals pursued a competency, the different interests in society were harmonized and produced general economic prosperity. As long as wealth was fairly evenly distributed, Centinel thought that it was essential for government not "to govern too much" in economic matters, as was possible in America because of the unique circumstances of her settlement and history. "Under the benign influence of liberty," America presented a situation "of which history furnishes no parallel: It is here that human nature may be viewed in all its glory." The relative equality of America nurtured liberty and prosperity. "Here the human mind, untrammeled by the restraints of arbitrary power, expands every faculty: as the field to fame and riches is open to all, it stimulates universal exertion." By concentrating power in the hands of the wealthy and weakening state control of the economy, the Constitution threatened this vision of equality.[36]

No form of liberty was more important than freedom of the press. Arguing that "liberty only flourishes where reason and knowledge are encouraged" hardly seemed novel. The notion of virtue that Centinel championed reflected his emphasis on the importance of the public sphere. He echoed earlier writers who noted that a "republican, or free government, can only exist where the body of the people are virtuous." He conceded that virtue was easier to attain when "property is pretty equally divided." Yet virtue, for Centinel, was not cast in neo-Harringtonian terms. It was not simply property that was central to the survival of republicanism. The concept of virtue

36. Centinel [Samuel Bryan?], no. 6, "To the People of Pennsylvania," *Pennsylvania Packet, and Daily Advertiser* (Philadelphia), Dec. 25, 1787 (*CA-F,* II, 172), no. 4, "To the People of Pennsylvania," *IG,* Nov. 30, 1787 (II, 162), no. 8, "To the People of Pennsylvania," *IG,* Jan. 2, 1788 (II, 176, 178).

had been transformed by Centinel to account for the centrality of public opinion to republicanism. In America, "the people are the sovereign and their sense or opinion is the criterion of every public measure." In America public opinion played an unprecedented role in supporting government and preserving liberty.[37]

Public opinion was even more crucial than it had been in any other republic. "In a confederated government of such extent as the United States," it was vital that "the freest communication of sentiment and information should be maintained." Centinel envisioned the public sphere of print as an important means of cementing the nation together. Print afforded a means of achieving social cohesion without a strong coercive authority.[38]

Ratification proved the danger of allowing the press to become a tool of party or faction: the suppression of Anti-Federalist writing facilitated ratification in a number of states. Centinel complained that "the liberties of this country are brought to an awful crisis," for it was precisely the Federalists' ability to dominate the press that allowed supporters of the Constitution to isolate and "overwhelm the enlightened opposition."[39]

Writing as Centinel, Bryan formulated the most sophisticated critique of the failure of the public sphere to function as a neutral medium for rational discourse. While most Anti-Federalist authors simply repeated a familiar litany of charges about the bias of printers, few diagnosed the underlying social forces that had effectively corrupted the public sphere. Indeed, most Anti-Federalists approached the problem as though an absence of virtuous printers was primarily to blame for the inability of Anti-Federalists to get their message into print. For Centinel, it was the economic clout of Federalists that enabled them to dominate the public sphere. "The free and independent papers were attempted to be demolished by withdrawing all the subscriptions."[40]

Not just the press but also the people needed to recognize the importance of public opinion in a republic. There was a danger that "the people are too apt to yield an implicit assent to the opinion" of natural aristocrats. Com-

37. Ibid., no. 1 (II, 139), no. 3 (II, 159).

38. Ibid., no. 1 (II, 137), no. 3 (II, 159), no. 18, "To the People of Pennsylvania," *IG*, Apr. 9, 1788 (II, 205).

39. Ibid., no. 18 (II, 205).

40. Ibid., no. 12, "To the People of Pennsylvania," *IG*, Jan. 23, 1788 (II, 189); Saul Cornell, "Reflections on 'The Late Remarkable Revolution in Government': Aedanus Burke and Samuel Bryan's Unpublished History of the Ratification of the Federal Constitution," *Pennsylvania Magazine of History and Biography*, CXII (1988), 129; compare the remarks of Philadelphiensis [Benjamin Workman?], no. 1, *IG*, Nov. 7, 1787 (*CA-F*, III, 105).

menting on the Massachusetts state convention, Centinel regretted that men of modest backgrounds had to battle "great learning, eloquence and sophistry in the shape of lawyers, doctors and divines, who were capable and seemed disposed to delude by deceptive glosses and specious reasoning." Recognizing that natural aristocrats possessed clear advantages in public debate did not mean that Centinel lacked faith in the people; it merely signaled his belief that republicanizing the people had been only partially completed during the Revolution. On this issue, Centinel shared a view common among many radicals, who believed a fair contest was impossible until the contest had been truly equalized. Until then, deference and the artificial advantages of wealth and education rendered the contest extremely unequal.[41]

The other Anti-Federalist author who devoted considerable attention to the politics of the public sphere was Philadelphiensis. In contrast to members of the Anti-Federalist elite, Philadelphiensis defended the anonymous world of print in forceful terms. Although he invoked the republican ideal of virtue, Philadelphiensis framed his defense of print in democratic terms. Newspapers created a public forum in which men of humble origins might come forward and challenge the authority of their social betters. Under the cloak of anonymity, one could appeal directly to the people and rouse them to action. Given the value that Philadelphiensis attached to print, it is easy to see why he reacted so strongly to the suggestion that newspapers no longer carry anonymous essays, and he attacked that policy as an example of the designs of the "well born" who sought to silence their opposition. "It is of no importance whether or not a writer gives his name"; the attention of the citizens ought to be on "the illustrations and arguments he affords us, and not with his name." Federalist printers would discourage "men of ability, of a modest, timid, or diffident cast of mind" from entering the public debate and "publishing their sentiments." In theory, the anonymity of the press allowed all citizens, regardless of their social status, to speak as equals. Anonymity was therefore essential to the preservation of an emerging public sphere of rational debate in which all citizens participated in political disputation. Pseudonyms were essential in post-Revolutionary society, Philadelphiensis argued, since many had not yet cast off habits learned under monarchy. Anonymity countered the persistence of deference: any citizen could adopt a rhetorical identity and make his case before the people. Theoretically, even women or slaves might gain a voice in public matters by

41. Centinel, no. 1 (*CA-F,* II, 137), no. 15, "To the People of Pennsylvania," *IG,* Feb. 22, 1788 (II, 197).

assuming a fictive identity. When understood in those terms, the public sphere of print became a powerful engine of democratic change.[42]

The centrality of print to his vision was reflected in his choice of a medical metaphor to describe its function. A free press was, he wrote, "the primary artery" responsible for supplying information, the "life blood" of the Republic, to the most remote parts of the body politic. A vibrant public sphere could bind the nation together, alert citizens of threats to their liberty, and improve the public mind by reasoned debate. The public sphere solved the central problem of Anti-Federalist political thought: how to ensure the survival of federalism without creating a powerful central government. It should be no surprise, then, that middling Anti-Federalists devoted so much attention to the threat to freedom of the press posed by the Constitution.

> In America the freedom of the press is peculiarly interesting: to a people scattered over such a vast continent, what means of information or redress have they, when a conspiracy has been formed against their sacred rights and privileges? None but the press. This is the herald that sounds the alarm, and rouses freemen to guard their liberty.[43]

It was not merely America's unique physical environment that made a free press essential. Although Anti-Federalists might differ about the character of the ideal small republic, they all accepted that the individual states came closest to approximating that ideal. Thus, it was imperative that America remain a federal republic in which power was rooted in the various localities and states. Centralization, the solution that most Federalists favored, posed a serious threat to individual liberty and to the nature of representation. How to keep power in the states and localities and still hold the Union together— that was the central problem facing Anti-Federalist political and constitutional thought. Although not every Anti-Federalist author or spokesman successfully grappled with the problem, the farthest-sighted theorists recognized that only a vigorous public sphere could accomplish those seemingly contradictory goals. Not only did the public sphere provide an alternative to the Federalist reliance on power, but an expanded and invigorated public sphere would strengthen the ideals of liberty and virtue crucial to Anti-Federalist republicanism.[44]

42. Philadelphiensis, no. 1 (*CA-F,* III, 103–105).

43. Ibid. (III, 105), no. 6, *IG,* Dec. 27, 1787 (III, 120), no. 8, *IG,* Jan. 24, 1788 (III, 124).

44. The public sphere included the world of print—newspapers, pamphlets, and broadsides—as well as other forums, such as debating societies, clubs, coffeehouses, and taverns. See the discussion in Jürgen Habermas, *The Structural Transformation of the Public Sphere:*

Plebeian Populism

Many of the ideas developed by Centinel were taken up by plebeian authors who carried the egalitarianism of Centinel several steps further. The literary form that best suited their assault on the Constitution was satire, and many of the sharpest attacks on the Constitution were parodies of Federalist writing. One of them was written by William Petrikin, a self-described "mechanic" and tenant farmer from Carlisle, Pennsylvania. His pamphlet, *The Government of Nature Delineated*, attacked the Constitution and Federalists in a trenchant satire—and also revealed important dimensions of plebeian constitutionalism.[45]

Aristocrotis, the pen name Petrikin chose, burlesqued the haughty style of Federalists. In the mask of an ultra-Federalist, Aristocrotis addressed his remarks to the "well-born," those of "illustrious descent," "the full-blooded gentry," and "money men" who have the "necessary qualifications of authority; such as the dictatorial air, the magisterial voice, the imperious tone, the haughty countenance." Petrikin went further than Federal Farmer, Old Whig, or even Centinel in attacking the concept of natural aristocracy and the notion (as Aristocrotis puts it) that "nature hath placed proper degrees and subordinations amongst mankind." Any notion of deference was cast aside in Petrikin's scathing assault on Federalist aristocratic pretensions. He derided Federalists for their elitism. Aristocrotis censured the "plebeians" and "ignoble obscure . . . persons" who dared to question the federal Constitution's principles. In his eyes, the charge of aristocracy was a class indictment.[46]

According to Aristocrotis, the mock champion of Federalist elitism, the Revolution had given the people "exorbitant power," and choosing to elect "their own rulers" only led to "the subversion of all order and good government." The greatest evil flowing from the excess of democracy was the necessity of pandering to the mob, the vulgar practice of "electioneering." By avoiding annual elections and giving Congress the power to determine the

---

An Inquiry into a Category of Bourgeois Society, trans. Thomas Burger and Frederick Lawrence (Cambridge, Mass., 1989).

45. On the social history of Carlisle and Petrikin's place within that world, see Saul Cornell, "Aristocracy Assailed: The Ideology of Backcountry Anti-Federalism," *JAH,* LXXVI (1989–1990), 1148–1172. Petrikin's own class consciousness is evident in his correspondence; see William Petrikin to John Nicholson, Feb. 24, 1788 (*DHRC,* II, 695), May 8, 1788 (*DHRC,* II [microfiche], 675).

46. Aristocrotis [William Petrikin], *The Government of Nature Delineated . . .* (Carlisle, Pa., 1788) (*CA-F,* III, 197–198, 204–205).

manner and place of holding elections, the Constitution would restore the ignorant rabble to the proper place of subordination. To assure this outcome, the government was provided with extensive powers to tax. Burdened by onerous taxes, the people would be forced to "attend to their own business" and would have little time for "dabbling in politics."[47]

To enforce the dictates of this new, despotic government, the Constitution established a standing army and wrested control of the militia away from the states. Federal control of the militia was necessary to disarm the "the peasants; viz. the farmers, mechanics, labourers." It was prudent to disarm them, since "it would be dangerous to trust such a rabble as this with arms in their hands." Petrikin's assault on the Federalists' notion of the militia reveals an important aspect of plebeian thinking; he did not follow the example of Federal Farmer and other middling Anti-Federalists and exclude from the militia individuals from the lower sort.[48]

The middling democratic vision of the jury evidenced in the writings of Federal Farmer was recast by Aristocrotis in aggressively populist terms. The power of juries was "a gross violation of common sense." The vast powers possessed by juries in Revolutionary America were foolish: "In the first place it is absurd, that twelve ignorant plebeians, should be constituted judges of a law, which passed through so many learned hands;—first a learned legislature." Then "learned writers have explained and commented on it.—Third, learned lawyers twisted, turned and new modeled it—and lastly, a learned judge opened up and explained it." It was preposterous that, "after all these learned discussions, an illiterate jury" composed of men of no property "must determine whether it applies to the fact or not." Aristocrotis pointed out that empowering juries to determine both the facts and the law in most situations would create a situation where an "insignificant cottager" might successfully challenge a "learned gentleman." Giving juries the power to determine both matters of fact and law would, Petrikin believed, serve as a counterweight to the power of society's existing elite. Under such a scheme, it would be possible for a simple cottager to challenge the authority of a rich merchant or large landowner. Similarly, populists showed a distinctive distrust of judicial review, seeing the courts as the preserve of a small, aristocratic elite. Anti-Federalists like Petrikin preferred to allow the legislature the power to override pronouncements of the court, and juries the power to determine both matters of fact and law. Neither jury service nor the militia

47. Ibid. (III, 198, 202).
48. Ibid. (III, 203).

was tied to property requirements. In both cases plebeian populists asserted a more radical democratic egalitarian constitutional vision.[49]

Petrikin shared with middling Anti-Federalists a narrow vision of religious tolerance. He accepted the common Anti-Federalist argument that religious tests helped promote virtue, but recast this argument in an interesting fashion: religion had often served as a check on rulers by providing a basis for popular resistance. Weakening religion was therefore useful to those who sought to diminish the power of the people. He went on to attack the Constitutional Convention for its deism. The populist view of religion held by Petrikin was not especially tolerant of religious diversity: governments were not only entitled to but actually had a responsibility to exclude from office those individuals who were incapable of displaying the necessary virtue.

Plebeian Anti-Federalists rejected the moderation of middling democracy in favor of a more radical localist variant of direct democracy. It was the will of the local community, not the numerical majority in either the state or the nation, that they sought to empower. In contrast to middling democrats, plebeians were not especially interested in protecting the power of the state governments: local institutions such as the jury, the militia, or the crowd embodied the true voice of the people. Plebeian Anti-Federalist constitutional thought demonstrates the potential conflict between federalism and localism. When localism and federalism came into conflict, plebeians were more apt to favor the former.[50]

The Carlisle Riot: The Constitutionalism of the Crowd

To understand the perspective of plebeians requires moving beyond the surviving literary texts to explore the social texts they created to express their frustration with the Constitution. Reading public rituals and crowd behavior as texts provides important insights into plebeian constitutional thought.

49. Ibid. (III, 204).
50. Popular traditions of social justice are discussed by E. P. Thompson, "The Moral Economy of the English Crowd in the Eighteenth Century," *Past and Present*, no. 50 (February 1971), 76–136; "Eighteenth-Century English Society: Class Struggle without Class?" *Social History*, III (1978), 133–165; "Patrician Society, Plebeian Culture," *Journal of Social History*, VII (1973–1974), 382–405. For a stimulating discussion of the transplantation of English traditions of popular justice to America in the same period, see Alfred F. Young, "English Plebeian Culture and Eighteenth-Century American Radicalism," in Margaret Jacob and James Jacob, eds., *The Origins of Anglo-American Radicalism* (London, 1984), 185–212.

The dramatic differences separating plebeian constitutionalism from that of elite and middling Anti-Federalists are evident in the events arising out of the riot in Carlisle, Pennsylvania, in late 1787. That riot yields up a vivid glimpse of the radicalism latent in so much popular Anti-Federalism, illustrating how plebeian Anti-Federalists in Carlisle understood constitutional questions. Anti-Federalists in Carlisle actually acted out the suggestions of the most radical essayists in the popular press.[51]

A violent encounter between Federalists and Anti-Federalists in the streets of Carlisle occurred the day after Christmas 1787. It became one of the most widely reported events during ratification. The Federalist account of the event by An Old Man was printed thirty-eight times, more than most Federalist or Anti-Federalist essays.[52]

Violence erupted after Federalists sought to celebrate their victory in the Pennsylvania state ratification convention. Local Anti-Federalists, smarting from their recent defeat, were determined to send a firm message to their opponents. Federalists might have carried the state of Pennsylvania, but opposition to the Constitution in many parts of the state, particularly Carlisle, was still intense. The initial confrontation with Federalists in the streets of Carlisle resulted in an exchange of blows and the destruction of a cannon the Federalists had procured for the occasion. One author in the local press added, "It was laughable to see Lawyers, Doctors, Colonels, Captins etc. etc. leave the scene of their rejoicing in such haste."[53]

The situation remained tense even afterward. The next day the opponents of the Constitution staged a demonstration to signify their continuing hostility to the aristocratic designs of Federalists. Anti-Federalist rioters burned effigies of James Wilson and Thomas McKean, two of the state's leading Federalists. Before "execution," the effigies of these respected members of the Pennsylvania Federalist elite were whipped and paraded around as common criminals. Subjecting respected political figures to symbolic humiliations usually reserved for individuals of the lowest social standing enacted a colorful ritual of status reversal and thereby reinforced the populist democratic ideals of plebeians. By their actions, the rioters explicitly rejected Federalist pleas for deference to society's natural aristocracy. The crowd, refusing to defer to its betters, proudly asserted that it "would pay no respect to their rank, nor make any allowance for their delicate constitutions." The punish-

---

51. For a discussion of the Carlisle riot and the political ideology of plebeian Anti-Federalists, see Cornell, "Aristocracy Assailed," *JAH*, LXXVI (1989–1990), 1148–1172.

52. An Old Man, *Carlisle Gazette* (Pennsylvania), Jan. 2, 1788 (*DHRC*, XV, 225–228).

53. One of the People, *IG*, Feb. 7, 1788.

ment meted out by the crowd was appropriate for those who sought to "undermine the liberties of their country." Like legal punishment, this ritual reaffirmed the values of the community and provided a warning against others who might contemplate similar betrayals of the people's trust.[54]

Plebeian Anti-Federalists favored the use of crowd action. Through popular rituals of plebeian culture, particularly traditions such as "rough music," the symbolic humiliation of individuals who had offended the "people," crowds affirmed community values and punished individuals who transgressed those beliefs. In some instances, crowds used those rituals to voice new political grievances as well as to defend social customs. Since the victims of those actions were often individuals of higher social status, the message conveyed was an egalitarian and class-conscious hostility to established elites. Plebeian action was an explicit rejection of deference and an affirmation of the ability of common folk to judge their social betters. The rioters were animated by a radical egalitarianism far beyond anything even middling democrats were willing to accept. Plebeians rejected the need for any mediating class of political leaders, even one drawn from the middling sort. The only way to preserve that vision was to keep politics rooted in the locality, where the voice of the people could be heard without any intermediaries.[55]

The debate in the local press and the actions of local Anti-Federalists provided an unusual occasion for plebeian Anti-Federalists to articulate their approach to a range of constitutional issues. In Carlisle, the radical egalitarianism and localism of plebeians was not a subject of speculation in print, but was put into action.

Plebeian Anti-Federalists insisted that Federalists should have sought community approval before staging their celebration. A spokesman for the Anti-Federalists queried his opponents, "if a town meeting was called to consult the people, whether they approved of the measure or not." When Anti-Federalists confronted Federalists in the streets of Carlisle, the spokesman reminded supporters of the Constitution that their "conduct was con-

54. Ibid.
55. For an important discussion of the crowd in America, see Pauline Maier, *From Resistance to Revolution: Colonial Radicals and the Development of American Opposition to Britain, 1765–1776* (New York, 1972); Edward Countryman, "The Problem of the Early American Crowd," *Journal of American Studies,* VII (1973), 77–90; Paul A. Gilje, *The Road to Mobocracy: Popular Disorder in New York City, 1763–1834* (Chapel Hill, N.C., 1987). Although historians have explored the moral economy of the crowd in great detail, they have devoted little attention to the constitutionalism implicit in the actions of crowds. For a thought-provoking exploration of this dimension of popular constitutional ideas, see Hendrik Hartog, "Pigs and Positivism," *Wisconsin Law Review,* 1985, 899–935.

trary to the minds of three-fourths of the inhabitants, and must therefore produce bad consequences if they persisted." When Federalists disregarded their warnings, the opponents of the Constitution enforced the will of the community with extralegal crowd action. Interestingly, Anti-Federalists viewed themselves as "friends of liberty," consciously linking their actions to the traditions of crowd activity associated with the Revolution.[56]

Plebeian populists saw no problem with limiting the Federalists' right of assembly or speech. Their reaction to local Federalists did not mark them as hypocrites; rather, their denial of liberty to their Federalist opponents was perfectly consistent with their own claim to be "friends of liberty." They believed that the community enjoyed extensive power to regulate behavior to promote the public good. The actions of Federalists were bound to inflame passions and produce violence, and hence it was legitimate to limit their celebration. In effect, Anti-Federalists exercised a heckler's veto. Their conception of liberty was hardly liberal, but perfectly consistent with republican notions of constitutionalism. Plebeian Anti-Federalists employed a more extreme version of the same logic that justified loyalty oaths: in both instances the rights of the community trumped those of the individual. Interestingly, Carlisle Anti-Federalists did not apply the same standard to publications. Although they resented the pro-Federalist bias of the *Carlisle Gazette*, they did not seek to silence it. Federalist crowds in New York did not exercise a similar restraint when they ransacked the printing shop of Thomas Greenleaf, publisher of the Anti-Federalist *New York-Journal*. Carlisle Anti-Federalists treated unpopular speech, at least in the streets, differently from speech in the press. Public demonstrations had to be compatible with community norms, but debate in the press was subject to different rules.[57]

During the altercation in the streets of Carlisle, the opponents of the Constitution confiscated a cannon, burning its carriage and spiking the barrel. Their justification is also revealing about plebeian constitutionalism. The gathering declared that "the cannon was the property of the United

56. One of the People [William Petrikin?], *Carlisle Gazette*, Jan. 9, 1788 (*DHRC*, II, 675); The Scourge [Petrikin], *Carlisle Gazette*, Jan. 23, 1788 (*DHRC*, II, 685).

57. On the attitude of local Anti-Federalists toward the press, see William Petrikin to John Nicholson, Feb. 24, 1788 (*DHRC*, II, 695), May 8, 1788 (II [microfiche], 675). The crowd attack on Thomas Greenleaf is discussed in Linda Grant De Pauw, *The Eleventh Pillar: New York State and the Federal Constitution* (Ithaca, N.Y., 1966), 270. Plebeian Anti-Federalism represented a form of consensual communitarianism. For another example of this strain in early American history, see Michael Zuckerman, *Peaceable Kingdoms: New England Towns in the Eighteenth Century* (New York, 1970). For a modern analogue, see Catharine A. MacKinnon, *Feminism Unmodified: Discourses on Life and Law* (Cambridge, Mass., 1987).

States, that what belonged to the United States belonged to the People; that they were the People, and consequently had a right" to confiscate it. Property rights, while important, were clearly not sacrosanct. The confiscation testified to an expansive view of the community's right to limit property rights, as made explicit by one author, who enjoined Anti-Federalists: "Act with a spirit becoming freemen; convince the world and your adversaries to, who wish to become your tyrants—That you are not insensible of the invaluable blessings of liberty—That you esteem life and property, but secondary objects; when your liberty comes to be attacked."[58]

The aftermath of the riot also reveals important aspects of plebeian constitutionalism. Several of the rioters were arrested and charged with assaulting Federalists and behaving in a riotous manner. The incarceration of the rioters set in motion a series of events that demonstrated in compelling terms the latent radicalism in plebeian constitutionalism. The arrest warrant was issued by Chief Justice Thomas McKean, and the rioters demanded that they have an immediate local hearing and confront their accusers in court. The presiding judge was uncertain about his jurisdiction in a case in which a warrant had been issued by another judicial body. Pending the outcome of his consultations with the judges of the supreme court, the local magistrate offered the defendants the opportunity to make bail, which they refused. The confinement of the rioters prompted Anti-Federalists in and around Carlisle to action. As one contemporary account noted, "Immediately the country took the alarm on hearing that a number of persons was confined in prison for opposing a measure that was intended to give sanction to the proposed Federal Constitution." The different militia companies in the surrounding areas sent representatives to consult with one another on what action would be appropriate. The militia then appointed representatives to meet with leading Federalists to discuss how to settle the matter, and an agreement was reached. Accordingly, and to celebrate their victory, a large contingent of the militia marched into town and released the prisoners.[59]

58. Another of the People, *Carlisle Gazette*, Jan. 16, 1788 (*DHRC*, II, 681); The Scourge [Petrikin?], *Carlisle Gazette*, Jan. 25, 1788 (II, 688).

59. A copy of the petition may be found in *DHRC*, II, 708. Details of the prisoners' release can be obtained in the "The Release of the Prisoners," *Carlisle Gazette*, Mar. 5, 1788 (*DHRC*, II, 699–701). Contemporary estimates of the size of the crowd that marched to the jail to secure the release of prisoners vary from 250 to 1,500. For more detail, see *DHRC*, II (microfiche), 491, 544, 554, 556, 629, 652. For examples of Federalist hostility toward the marchers, see John Montgomery to James Wilson, Mar. 2, 1788 (*DHRC*, II, 701–706); John Shippen to Joseph Shippen, Mar. 3, 1788 (II, 706–707). The legitimacy of self-created societies would become an important issue during the Jeffersonian period.

The response of area Anti-Federalists demonstrates the radical potential in the plebeian view of the militia. Their reaction to the judge's ruling and their decision to plead their own case revealed a general hostility to the judiciary and to lawyers. Nor were the rioters especially impressed that the state courts would protect their interests. They demanded a hearing in their own community; and, when they were denied that, citizens acting through the militia bypassed the existing structure of both the state and local courts and turned to the militia to settle the matter. In this instance, plebeians viewed the local militia as the final check on tyranny.

The radical egalitarianism and localist democracy championed by plebeians shared little with the state-centered solutions envisioned by middling democrats. The actions of the militia were not guided by the state, but reflected the views of the local units. Appointing representatives from each militia unit was a form of Leveller democracy, a populist impulse swelling up from below. The attitude toward the courts evidenced a similar form of localist democracy, for it was local juries to which plebeians looked to administer justice. Federalism, a concept crucial to both middling and elite Anti-Federalist constitutionalism, was far less important to plebeians. Localism, not federalism, was the animating impulse behind plebeian constitutionalism.

For local Federalists the events in Carlisle merely confirmed their suspicion that the opponents of the Constitution were bent on establishing mobocracy. Plebeians saw those events in a different light. The negotiation and release of the prisoners was an example of direct democracy in action. For plebeians in Carlisle, the final outcome of the clash with Federalists not only vindicated their radical conception of constitutionalism; it strengthened their resolve to oppose the Constitution.[60]

Plebeian Radicalism and the Public Sphere

Even if the actions of Anti-Federalists in Carlisle were not typical, their ideas were certainly not unique. The radical democratic ethos espoused by

60. On localist democracy and its relationship to Anti-Federalist thought, see Joshua Miller, *The Rise and Fall of Democracy in Early America, 1630–1789: The Legacy for Contemporary Politics* (University Park, Pa., 1991); Christopher M. Duncan, *The Anti-Federalists and Early American Political Thought* (DeKalb, Ill., 1995). Miller and Duncan link Anti-Federalist notions of community to Puritan covenant theology. Although a case might be made for such legacy in New England, this type of link does not seem plausible for other regions of the nation.

plebeians found its way into newspapers in most states. If anything, those views were probably underrepresented in the press, because most Anti-Federalist editors were either members of the elite or identified with the ideas of middling democrats.

Plebeians in Carlisle certainly took their victory as a sign that their struggle to challenge the Constitution was far from over. William Petrikin, a leader of the riot, observed that, in its aftermath, "almost every day" thereafter "some new society" committed to opposing the Constitution was "being formed" to oppose "this detastable Fedrall conspiracy." He boasted that he had formed "a volunteer" militia "company all Anti-Federalist" and that the company had drafted "a private article oblidgeing ourselves to oppose the establishment of the new Constitution at the risque of our live and Fortunes." William Bard, a representative from Franklin County, endorsed Petrikin's analysis: "I am very confident that on the West side of the Susquehanna in this state there is at least nine out of every ten that would at the risk of their lives and property be as willing to oppose the new constitution as they were the British in their late designs." Another Anti-Federalist affirmed, "The affear at Carlisle may give you a Specimen of the temper that prevales hear." One contemporary observer, Benjamin Blyth, noted that many "will defend their Established Constitutional Liberty with the risk of their Lives." For those Anti-Federalists, the right to bear arms included the right of citizens to organize spontaneously as militia units to defend their liberties. According to this interpretation, the militia became the ultimate check on tyranny, an expression of a permanent right of revolution.[61]

The plebeian public sphere was shaped by an extreme form of democratic localism. While plebeian Anti-Federalists looked to the press for information, they counted on direct action by the people as the best means for discerning the will of the people. Local institutions such as the militia or the jury, or even the crowd, were ultimately more important to this vision of the

---

61. William Petrikin to John Nicholson, Carlisle, Feb. 24, 1788 (*DHRC*, II, 694–696); "Extract of a Letter from Franklin County [Pa.], Apr. 24, 1788," *Cumberland Gazette* (Portland, Maine), May 22, 1788; Benjamin Blyth, Sr., to John Nicholson, Feb. 11, 1788 (*DHRC*, II, 714–715). For another confirmation of backcountry hostility, see Richard Baird to John Nicholson, Feb. 1, 1788 (II, 712–713). In addition to the disturbances in Carlisle, Anti-Federalist crowd actions took place in Huntingdon County, Pa., South Carolina, North Carolina, and Rhode Island. For Huntingdon County, see *FJ*, Mar. 19, 1788 (II, 718). On South Carolina, see Aedanus Burke to John Lamb, June 23, 1788, Lamb Papers, NYHS. On the Dobbs County, N.C., election riot, see Robert Allen Rutland, *The Ordeal of the Constitution: The Antifederalists and the Ratification Struggle of 1787–1788* (Norman, Okla., 1966), 271–272. On Rhode Island, see *Providence Gazette: and Country Journal*, July 12, 1788.

public sphere than was the anonymity of the world of print. Rather than refine the public will, the plebeian public sphere sought literally to embody it through direct local action.

It is not surprising that the most receptive discussion of the Carlisle riot by an influential Anti-Federalist author was penned by Centinel, who reminded Federalists that "the great body of the people are awakened to a due sense of their danger, and are determined to assert their liberty, if necessary by the sword," against a "junto composed of the lordly and high minded gentry." Centinel recommended that "societies ought to be instituted in every county and a reciprocity of sentiments and information maintained between such societies." Plebeians interpreted Centinel's suggestion as encouragement to bypass the existing institutional structures of the courts and militia. What many viewed as mobocracy, Centinel lauded as an expression of the popular will. To those who raised the specter of anarchy, including both elite and middling Anti-Federalists, Centinel replied, "A state of anarchy from its very nature, can never be of long continuance." He concluded, "It would be infinitely better to incur it; for even then there would be at least the chance of good government rising out of licentiousness." Accepting anarchy as a temporary, and admittedly unpleasant, alternative to tyranny, set Centinel apart from both elite and middling Anti-Federalist thinkers. In contrast to most writers, who denounced mobs, Shaysites, and the Carlisle rioters, Centinel exhorted Federalists "to take warning from the fate of the Carlisle junto."[62]

Middling Anti-Federalists were less apt to sympathize with the direct crowd action taken by the Carlisle rioters, and the leading spokesmen in Pennsylvania were acutely aware of the dangers of plebeian radicalism. They themselves had been victims of the ire of Federalist crowds in Philadelphia and recognized that such action could just as easily undermine liberty as defend freedom. The most important and influential statement of middling Anti-Federalist ideas, "The Address and Reasons of Dissent of the Minority,"

62. Centinel, no. 7 (*CA-F,* II, 175), no. 9 (II, 181), no. 11 (II, 185), no. 13 (II, 192). Centinel also noted that Shays's Rebellion frightened many Anti-Federalists into accepting the Constitution, in no. 9 (II, 181), no. 15 (II, 196–197). The fact that Bryan could adopt two so radically different points of view further confirms the need to pay attention to the way authors crafted distinctive rhetorical identities aimed at specific audiences. The more moderate "Address and Reasons of Dissent of the Minority of the Convention of Philadelpia to Their Constituents" was written for the middling legislators who attended the Pennsylvania state convention. Centinel crafted his essays to appeal to both the middling sort and plebeian populists.

attacked crowd action. "The Dissent" denounced the action of the Federalist mob in Philadelphia that had attacked Anti-Federalist legislators. It reminded readers that "every measure was taken to intimidate the people opposing" the proposal to convene a state convention to consider the Constitution. Freedom of debate had been threatened, and "the public papers teemed with the most violent threats against those who should dare to think for themselves, and *tar and feathers* were liberally promised to all those who would not immediately join in supporting the proposed government." Of the twenty-three nays at the convention, twenty-one signed "The Dissent," including several well-known state politicians: William Findley, John Smilie, and Robert Whitehill. These popular spokesmen for the western yeomanry had been victims of Federalist mobs and were aware that mobocracy might easily be exploited by tyrants as well as patriots.[63]

The widespread coverage of the Carlisle riot in the press brought plebeian action into the public sphere of political debate. Whatever Anti-Federalists in Carlisle thought about their actions, the reports of the riot had become another text whose meaning they could no longer control. Federalists interpreted events in Carlisle as a confirmation of their own charge that Anti-Federalism inevitably led to Shaysism. The response of elite and middling Anti-Federalists to plebeian radicalism was more complicated and ultimately at least as important as the plebeian ideas that the rioters had brought into public view. Although it is difficult to gauge the popularity of plebeian populist ideas, the impact of the Carlisle riot on others within the Anti-Federalist coalition was profound.

The specter of mobocracy frightened many Anti-Federalists, including members of the established elite and spokesmen for the middling sort. Ironically, the Carlisle riot only intensified the desire of middling and elite Anti-Federalists to seek compromise and avert further violence.

To members of the Anti-Federalist elite, the right to bear arms and the militia were legal only within the structures provided by the states. Extralegal actions, such as those of Anti-Federalists in Carlisle, were little more than mobocracy. For Elbridge Gerry, the Carlisle riot was a bitter reminder

63. [Samuel Bryan], "The Address and Reasons of Dissent of the Minority of the Convention of Philadelphia to Their Constituents," *Pennsylvania Packet*, Dec. 18, 1787 (*CA-F*, III, 148). For another example of similar sentiments, see "Fair Play," *IG*, Oct. 4, 1787 (*DHRC*, II, 154). For a discussion of the impact of the Carlisle riot on Anti-Federalism in Maryland, see Eric Robert Papenfuse, "Unleashing the 'Wildness': The Mobilization of Grassroots Antifederalism in Maryland," *Journal of the Early Republic*, XVI (1996), 73–106.

of the leveling tendencies among the populace. Although an outspoken opponent of the Constitution, Gerry shared the Federalist belief that the nation's political problems stemmed from "the excess of democracy." When he learned that the "people threatened the Justice in Carlisle to pull down his House, and the houses of the federalists," he expressed grave concern that they "shall be in civil War," adding his hope, "May God avert the evil." Rather than solidifying opposition to the Constitution, the plebeian radicalism of the Carlisle rioters divided the Anti-Federalists.[64]

The middling sort rejected the plebeian conception of the public sphere, believing that the public sphere's function would best be executed through the medium of print, where it could be both local and democratic but not succumb to the dangers posed by mobocracy. A public sphere of political debate could cement the Union together without relying on a powerful government that would threaten liberty. As with nearly every aspect of thinking of the middling sort, its support for localism was tied to its views of federalism and tempered by anxiety about the threat posed by plebeian populism. While those of the middling sort viewed the public sphere in more democratic terms than did elites, they did not see it as a simple plebiscite. The public sphere was an arena of rational discourse, in which middling politicians would dominate. This vision of democracy was certainly not identical to mob rule.[65]

The beliefs of plebeian populists did not provide the basis for building a democratic coalition, but instead split the two most democratic wings of the Anti-Federalist coalition apart. Middling democrats rejected the radical notion that the militia and the right to bear arms could be exercised in the manner suggested by the Carlisle rioters. This tension within popular Anti-Federalism would have profound consequences for how opposition to the Constitution evolved after ratification. Ultimately, the plebeian vision of the public sphere was not compatible with the ideal embraced by middling democrats, and the tension between those two conceptions of politics drove a deep wedge within the Anti-Federalist coalition, dividing plebeian and middling democrats from one another. The principal beneficiaries of this

64. Gerry's statements about the dangers of an excess of democracy and the leveling spirit may be found in James Madison's *Notes of Debates in the Federal Convention of 1787*, ed. Adrienne Koch (Athens, Ohio, 1966), 39. His comments on events in Carlisle appear in Elbridge Gerry to S. R. Gerry, Jan. 28, 1788, Samuel R. Gerry Papers, MHS. The threat made against the judge presiding over the case of the rioters was reported in *IG*, Jan. 12, 1788 (*DHRC*, II [microfiche], 328. Gerry's republicanism is discussed at length by George Athan Billias, *Elbridge Gerry: Founding Father and Republican Statesman* (New York, 1976).

65. Philadelphiensis, no. 1 (*CA-F*, III, 104).

schism were elite Anti-Federalists who were able to forge a more effective coalition with spokesmen for the middling sort.

Middling and plebeian Anti-Federalists each championed a democratic critique of the Constitution. A principal target of their attack was natural aristocracy: authors such as Federal Farmer, Centinel, and Aristocrotis challenged an amorphous social class of natural aristocrats who sought to use the new government to further their own interests. Although the middling sort and plebeians shared a commitment to a more democratic and egalitarian constitutional theory, they interpreted the ideas of democracy, federalism, and liberty differently.

Spokesmen for the middling sort, such as Federal Farmer, were among the most sophisticated and original thinkers within the ranks of Anti-Federalists. The version of democracy championed by such writers was not that of populist democracy. Nor was middling democracy tied to an agrarian vision. Authors such as Federal Farmer consciously framed their appeals to persuade the middling sort, which might include artisans and small merchants as well as the broad ranks of the yeomanry. The ideal of liberty defended by middling democrats sought to restrict government interference with the economy and basic rights while defending the legislature's right to enact laws consistent with the public good. Within the ranks of the middling democrats there was some variability on this issue. In general, New Yorkers such as Federal Farmer were more libertarian than were Pennsylvanians such as An Old Whig.

On the nature of representation there was considerable agreement among middling democrats about the dangers of the aristocratic character of the new government. Only a government in which the middling sort was broadly represented would safeguard liberty or produce the requisite virtue necessary for the survival of republicanism.

Federalism was crucial to the middling idea of democracy, and the states approximated the ideal of the small republic that middling Anti-Federalists championed. In a federal system in which the states retained the bulk of their authority, liberty would be guarded by bodies that the middling sort would dominate, such as the legislature and the jury. The farthest-sighted thinkers among middling democrats also recognized that an energetic public sphere nurtured by an active press could help liberty to flourish in such a federal republic. The anonymity of print allowed men of middling rank to step forward and defend their ideas and effectively limited the undue advantages possessed by natural aristocrats. Finally, the idea of the public sphere allowed middling democrats to reject the notion that the nation needed a strong, coercive central authority. Middling democrats championed the idea of a federal republic in which the public sphere would unify the nation.

Plebeians advocated the most radical form of direct democracy within the opposition to the Constitution. In contrast to spokesmen for the middling sort, plebeians made no effort to exclude the lower sort from involvement in the militia, jury service, or suffrage. While supporting state government, plebeians embraced a more radical democratic localist ideology. The locality, not the state, was the appropriate unit of political organization. There were also important differences in how the two approaches to democracy handled the problem of rights. The particular conception of liberty embodied in plebeian constitutionalism was a consensual communitarianism that showed far less concern for individual rights than did the constitutionalism of many of the middling sort. When the rights of the individual and the will of the local community conflicted, plebeians were far more willing to sacrifice individual liberty. Their willingness to engage in crowd action was the most dramatic example of their radical localist vision. The crowd was not, however, the only means of collecting the will of the people. The local jury and the militia also provided forms of direct democratic action that plebeians endorsed. Their idea of public opinion also was shaped by this localist conception of politics. Although they supported a free press, they did not view the public sphere as a medium for the refinement of opinion, but saw in it a forum in which the will of the people could be directly ascertained: the plebeian public sphere was little more than a plebiscite. For plebeians there was no particular advantage to print. Public opinion might just as easily be obtained by assembling the people in the streets.

The differences between these two variants of popular constitutionalism influenced the evolution of Anti-Federalism and the subsequent history of popular dissent in American politics. The tensions between plebeian democracy and middling democracy would continue to be a source of division long after the Constitution was ratified.

CHAPTER 4 :

COURTS, CONVENTIONS,

AND CONSTITUTIONALISM

The Politics of the Public Sphere

Anti-Federalist writing included an alarming catalog of horrors that would befall the nation if the Constitution were adopted. Although the list of evils conjured up by opponents of the Constitution was quite extensive, the most frequently repeated charges were not framed in hysterical terms but were presented as sober predictions. That specter of a powerful, distant government capable of using its extensive powers of taxation, control of the judiciary, and standing army to enforce its arbitrary decrees did not require readers to engage in a paranoid flight of fancy. Most Americans had only to recall the period of British rule to visualize the dangers Anti-Federalists decried.

Although many of the fears of Anti-Federalists echoed familiar complaints drawn from the tradition of country protest, that catalog of horrors was not simply a tired recitation of political clichés. The most ominous threat detected by Anti-Federalists was all the more insidious because it was essentially covert. Nothing better demonstrated the cunning of their opponents than the effort to undermine freedom of the press. The enormity of this threat was the reason that Anti-Federalists devoted so much energy to exposing the mechanisms by which the destruction of the press could be accomplished under the new government. The Constitution threatened to eviscerate the public sphere and make it impossible for the people to resist the imposition of tyranny.

Anti-Federalists complained bitterly that the Federalist-dominated press refused to provide equal space to opponents of the Constitution. The charge was repeated in both public and private statements. Thus, Aedanus Burke, an influential South Carolina Anti-Federalist, queried Pennsylvania's Samuel Bryan "if any and what arts" were "used by the federalists to mislead or deceive the people to adopt it" or to "suppress the publications or objections of the other party." Burke also inquired about "impediments in the Printing offices" and "the conduct and character of the Printers in general in this business." "Were Printers under any and what fear or restraint to publish against the New-System? Or did the Printers act independently or otherwise?"[1]

Although modern accounts have tended to dismiss Anti-Federalist complaints as either paranoia or propaganda, the surviving evidence about publication tends to support the indictment. Anti-Federalists did have trouble getting their message into print. The perception that few papers would publish Anti-Federalist material was fairly accurate. One-quarter of all papers published no Anti-Federalist material. The median number of essays published by those editors who did open their pages to Anti-Federalist authors was only four. In the view of Centinel the actions of printers were part of a Federalist conspiracy to prevent Anti-Federalists from rallying the people against the Constitution. Centinel claimed that every means of intimidation was used to frustrate the efforts of printers to publish material against the Constitution, including physical harassment and the threat of economic boycott.[2]

Further evidence of a conspiracy was provided by the actions of the postmaster general. His adoption of a new method for distributing the mails infuriated Anti-Federalists and intensified their belief in a Federalist conspiracy. The controversy over the mails seemed to provide concrete proof of Anti-Federalist allegations that Federalists sought to use government power to crush opposition to the Constitution. Both of those controversies help to account for some of the intensity and passion of Anti-Federalist rhetoric about the press. The actions of Federalists seemed to confirm the direst predictions made by any Anti-Federalist writer about the dangers of accepting the Constitution. If this was the situation during ratification, what chance would an opposition have under the new Constitution?

1. Saul Cornell, "Reflections on 'The Late Remarkable Revolution in Government': Aedanus Burke and Samuel Bryan's Unpublished History of the Ratification of the Federal Constitution," *Pennsylvania Magazine of History and Biography*, CXII (1988), 122–123, 129.

2. Centinel [Samuel Bryan?], no. 12, "To the People of Pennsylvania," *IG*, Jan. 23, 1788 (*CA-F*, II, 187–190). Data on republication were obtained from the *DHRC* volumes and files of the DHRC project. It is true that some papers published few, if any, political materials. Anti-Federalists would have taken little solace from this fact, since they believed that it was the duty of all printers to provide open access to essays on important public subjects.

Postmaster General Ebenezer Hazard believed that his decision to switch from stagecoach deliveries to postriders was merely a prudent economy to improve the efficiency of the mail and cut costs. To his Anti-Federalist enemies, however, the decision was a deliberate attempt to interfere with the traditional prerogatives of printers and obstruct the free flow of political information. Rather than improving the efficiency of the mails, Hazard's reforms actually resulted in widespread delays and increased the opportunities for corruption. In many instances papers were simply discarded by postriders or sold by individuals for personal profit.[3]

A Friend to the People believed that the actions of the postmaster general were motivated by the "advocates of despotic power" who had "found their efforts to shackle the press unsuccessful in many of the States." Frustrated in their efforts, the "next step was as much as possible to cut off all communication of sentiment, and to prevent any publications" from circulating to other states. Centinel thus believed that Hazard's actions limited the influence of newspapers "to the places of their publication, whilst falsehood and deception have had universal circulation, without the opportunity of refutation." The actions of the Post Office constituted a "violation of their duty and integrity" and had "prostituted their of——ces to forward the nefarious design of enslaving their countrymen, by thus cutting off all communication by the usual vehicle between the patriots." Another author in the *Freeman's Journal* believed this "stretch of arbitrary power" surpassed that of the British "before the Revolution." Such a policy was disastrous. "By this manoeuvre all communication is cut off between the States, so that the despots may assemble an *army* and subjugate the freemen of one state, before their friends in another hear of it."[4]

The controversy over the Post Office seemed to vindicate the conspiratorial rhetoric of the most polemical Anti-Federalist authors. This point did not go unnoticed by Federalists. George Washington feared that the controversy over the Post Office fueled Anti-Federalist complaints, making "very plausible pretexts for dealing out their scandals, and exciting jealousies, by inducing a belief that the suppression of intelligence at that critical juncture, was a wicked trick of policy, contrived by an Aristocratic Junto." The paranoia often attributed to Anti-Federalists by modern scholars seems less exaggerated when one considers the publishing history of ratification.

3. On the controversy over the Post Office, see *DHRC*, XVI, 540–541.

4. A Friend to the People, *FJ*, Apr. 16, 1788 (*DHRC*, XVI, 586); Centinel [Samuel Bryan?], no. 11, "To the People of Pennsylvania," *FJ*, Jan. 16, 1788 (*CA-F*, II, 187); Centinel, no. 15, "To the People of Pennsylvania," *IG*, Feb. 22, 1788 (II, 196).

Anti-Federalists might have been mistaken about the motives of many of their opponents; they were not, however, wrong about their impact on the campaign. The Anti-Federalists did have a much more difficult time finding outlets for their materials.[5]

The actions of the postmaster general and bias of the Federalist press intensified Anti-Federalist concerns about the dangers posed by the Constitution. If Anti-Federalists faced major obstacles to publication during ratification, the prospects after adoption seemed even more dire. Anti-Federalists believed that, once adopted, the new Constitution would pose a whole range of threats to freedom of the press. In response to the Federalist question—"What controul can proceed from the federal government to shackle or destroy that sacred palladium of national freedom?"—Anti-Federalists were prepared with a detailed set of responses. An Old Whig rattled off a number of measures that might be taken to limit freedom of the press, including licensing of printers and burdensome security bonds to compel good behavior. One of the most common fears expressed by Anti-Federalists was that taxation could be used as a weapon against a free press. Federal Farmer observed, "I am not clear, that congress is restrained from laying any duties whatever on printing, and from laying duties particularly heavy on certain pieces printed."[6]

The likelihood of a new Stamp Act enforced by a powerful standing army was only one of the threats envisioned by Anti-Federalists. A Democratic Federalist believed that, if "the enormous power of the new confederation" were extended directly to "*individuals* as well as to the *States* of America, a thousand means may be devised to destroy effectually the liberty of the press." Implicit in this argument was the belief that the states were more likely to guard the liberties of their citizens than was a distant government—a par-

5. George Washington to John Jay, July 18, 1788 (*DHRC*, XVI, 595). On the paranoia and exaggerated quality of Anti-Federalist rhetoric, see Cecelia M. Kenyon, "Men of Little Faith: The Anti-Federalists on the Nature of Representative Government," *WMQ*, 3d Ser., XII (1955), 3–43. This also informs the interpretation of Jack N. Rakove, *Original Meanings: Politics and Ideas in the Making of the Constitution* (New York, 1996). For a fascinating effort to locate conspiracy theory in the context of eighteenth-century theories of causation, see Gordon S. Wood, "Conspiracy and the Paranoid Style: Causality and Deceit in the Eighteenth Century." *WMQ*, 3d Ser., XXXIX (1982), 401–441.

6. Old Whig [George Bryan, John Smilie, and James Hutchinson?], no. 3, *IG*, Oct. 20, 1787 (*CA-F*, III, 27); Federal Farmer [Melancton Smith?], *Observations Leading to a Fair Examination of the System of Government Proposed by the Late Convention . . . Letters from the Federal Farmer to the Republican* (New York, 1787), no. 4 (II, 250). See also Robert Whitehill, Speech in the Pennsylvania State Ratification Convention (*DHRC*, II, 454); Deliberator, *FJ*, Feb. 20, 1788 (*CA-F*, III, 179).

ticularly compelling claim, given the absence of a written bill of rights. The power of the judiciary and the imprecision of the text of the Constitution only amplified that danger. "There is no knowing what corrupt and wicked judges may do," especially "when they are not restrained by express laws."[7]

The most likely and in most respects the most perfidious means of undermining the freedom of the press was the use of libel, especially seditious libel prosecutions. The power to prosecute libels was particularly dangerous because it allowed the government to single out specific individuals for punishment and effectively divide opposition. Since libel law might not immediately be invoked, it was far easier to lull the people into a false sense of security. Philadelphiensis warned citizens, "When Government thinks proper, under the pretence of writing a libel, etc. it may imprison, inflict the most cruel and unusual punishment, seize property, carry on prosecutions, etc. and the unfortunate citizen has no *magna charta*, no *bill of rights*, to protect him."[8]

Although both Federalists and Anti-Federalists agreed that the preservation of republicanism and liberty demanded a responsible free press, there was an important difference between their views of seditious libel. Federalists generally defended a conception of libel based in Blackstone, whereas Anti-Federalists looked to the model established in the case of John Peter Zenger.

The Federalist view of the doctrine of seditious libel was succinctly articulated by James Wilson, who asserted the classic Blackstonian view that "the idea of the liberty of the press is not carried so far as this in any country" as to abandon the notion of seditious libel. He went on to remind his Anti-Federalist opponents, "What is meant by the liberty of the press is, that there should be no antecedent restraint upon it; but that every author is responsible when he attacks the security or welfare of the government." Essentially, Blackstonian doctrine asserted the continuing validity of the idea of seditious libel and affirmed that freedom of the press only prevented prior restraint and licensing of the press.[9]

Most Anti-Federalists accepted the precedent of the Zenger trial, which legitimated truth as a defense against libel and accepted the role of the jury as

7. A Democratic Federalist, *Pennsylvania Herald, and General Advertiser* (Philadelphia), Oct. 17, 1787 (*CA-F*, III, 59).

8. Philadelphiensis [Benjamin Workman?], no. 9, *IG*, Feb. 7, 1788 (*CA-F*, III, 129).

9. James Wilson, Speech in the Pennsylvania State Convention (*DHRC*, II, 455). By the time he published his lectures on law, Wilson had clearly moved to embrace Zengerian ideals; on this point, see Norman L. Rosenberg, *Protecting the Best Men: An Interpretive History of the Law of Libel* (Chapel Hill, N.C., 1986), 65–69.

an arbiter of both the facts and the law in libel cases. Empowered to determine not only whether the utterance had been made but also whether the utterance was libelous, Zengerian principles provided an appropriate republican safeguard against tyranny. It was up to the community to decide whether an utterance was libelous, not the government. The Anti-Federalist debt to Zengerian principles is evident in Arthur Lee's Cincinnatus essays. In his discussion of the freedom of the press, Cincinnatus wrote: "It was the jury only, that saved Zenger . . . it can only be a jury that will save any future printer from the fangs of power." For Lee, trial by jury in cases of seditious libel served as an important check on arbitrary government. Like many Anti-Federalists, Lee was unwilling to abandon the concept of seditious libel entirely. To do so would remove an important structural check on the possible licentiousness of the press. Even "the sacred palladium of public liberty," freedom of the press, was subject to the limits set by the community. By allowing the jury to determine when a statement was libelous, the people retained the right to police themselves and set restrictions on the exercise of individual liberty when the good of the community demanded such limitations. Trials in state courts would provide the necessary protection for individuals and simultaneously allow the people to police themselves and the press. State libel, unlike federal libel, did not trouble most Anti-Federalists.[10]

Thus, fearful of the potential abuse of seditious libel prosecutions, most Anti-Federalists were not willing to reject the doctrine of seditious libel in toto, nor was there any need to dispense with the concept of libel as long as the right of trial by jury in state courts was preserved. Pennsylvanian John Smilie wondered, "What security would a printer have, tried in one of their courts?" The answer for Smilie was simple: none. The reason that the federal government could not be trusted was equally clear: "An aristocratical government cannot bear the liberty of the press." Only the state governments could form juries that truly represented the opinions of the people. Juries would both reflect the will of the people and deliberate in a rational manner on the nature of the alleged crime.[11]

Although there was little disagreement that federal juries could not be trusted, there was no consensus whether juries had to be drawn from specific localities or merely from the states in which the charges were brought.

10. Cincinnatus [Arthur Lee], no. 1, "To James Wilson, Esq.," *New-York Journal*, Nov. 1, 1787 (*CA-F*, VI, 9). For a useful overview of the Zenger case and the relationship between libertarian thought and civic republican ideals in America, see Rosenberg, *Protecting the Best Men*, 35–40.

11. John Smilie, Speech in the Pennsylvania State Convention (*DHRC*, II, 441, 453).

For some Anti-Federalists it was sufficient safeguard to demand that juries be drawn from the states, but others favored a more localist conception, arguing for the necessity of drawing jurors from the county in which the offense occurred.[12]

Apprehensions about the threat to liberty posed by seditious libel were uttered by many Anti-Federalist authors. The most intense criticism of this aspect of the Constitution, however, was expounded by Pennsylvania Anti-Federalists. Publishers and printers in that state had good reason to fear the danger such prosecutions posed: libel was an especially volatile issue in Pennsylvania. The leading Anti-Federalist printer, Eleazer Oswald, had once before faced a politically motivated libel charge, in 1782. Then, the printer had infuriated Supreme Court Justice Thomas McKean by publishing an account of a trial in which the judge had impugned the character of some Revolutionary war veterans. The judge hauled Oswald into court and charged him with libel. Oswald responded by publishing an account of his own experiences in McKean's court that excoriated the judge's efforts to use libel to silence political dissent. In effect, Oswald sought to try his case in the court of public opinion. Using the press to rally support for his cause, Oswald bypassed the authority of the court and appealed to the jurors who would decide his fate. Despite the best efforts of the attorney general to persuade a grand jury to bring forward a charge of libel, Oswald escaped prosecution.[13]

The Oswald case of 1782 colored the way Pennsylvania Anti-Federalists interpreted the Constitution's power over the press. McKean's prominent support for the Constitution only lent additional credence to Anti-Federalist fears that the Constitution had been crafted by men who intended to use the law of libel to stifle all political opposition.

Anti-Federalists did not have to wait long to see their worst fears about the Federalist view of libel invoked against them. Even as the news of the ratification of the ninth state reached Pennsylvania, Oswald became embroiled in another libel controversy. Once again, the law of libel appeared to be used as a political weapon, and its primary target was an influential Anti-Federalist publisher.

Until Oswald's prosecution for libel, the constitutional disagreements

12. For discussion of threats to jury trial by the Constitution, and as a form of judicial control, see above, Chapters 2 and 3.

13. A Friend to the Army, *IG*, Oct. 1, 1782, The Printer, Jan. 4, 11, 1783. The events of the 1782 Oswald libel case are discussed briefly in Robert L. Brunhouse, *The Counter-Revolution in Pennsylvania, 1776–1790* (Harrisburg, Pa., 1942), 126.

between Federalists and Anti-Federalists had been largely theoretical. The debate was conducted in the pages of newspapers and on the floor of the individual state ratification conventions. The Oswald case was the first instance in which Federalist and Anti-Federalist constitutional philosophies were put to a test in court. It is not surprising, therefore, that the controversy arising out of the Oswald libel prosecution spilled over into the press and eventually found its way into the halls of the Pennsylvania State Assembly. The public debate over the law of libel conducted in the court, the press, and the State Assembly provided an occasion for Anti-Federalists to distinguish their conception of law from that of their opponents. The case not only was a landmark in the history of the law of libel, but it also allowed the middling democrats who dominated Pennsylvania Anti-Federalism to assert their own distinctly democratic vision of constitutional theory.

The Oswald Libel Case of 1788

The second Oswald libel case, in 1788, developed out of a personal conflict between Eleazer Oswald, the publisher of the *Independent Gazetteer*, and Andrew Brown, the former editor of the *Federal Gazette*. Oswald had published a number of essays critical of Brown, and the aggrieved Federalist editor demanded that Oswald reveal the names of those authors who had attacked him or face possible libel charges. Oswald defended the principle of anonymous speech against the efforts of his Federalist adversaries to force him to reveal the identity of his authors; he refused to disclose his author's identities and further infuriated Brown with his ridicule, calling the printer a "*hand-maid* of some of my enemies among the federalists." Brown followed through on his threat to bring a charge of libel.[14]

Initially the libel case came before George Bryan, the prominent Anti-Federalist leader, who released Oswald on his own recognizance. Oswald was confident that the jury would once again prove his salvation. In 1782, Oswald had escaped libel prosecution by appealing to the grand jury, which refused to indict him for libeling his enemies. Were Brown's case against him to go to trial, it was very likely that Oswald would evade prison, as in 1782. Oswald now made a tactical blunder when he challenged his old nemesis Chief Justice Thomas McKean's impartiality in the press. McKean ruled that the attack on the neutrality of the court was an instance of contempt, and he or-

14. A Gentleman of the Law, *The Case of the Commonwealth against Oswald* . . . (Philadelphia, 1788), 3.

dered Oswald imprisoned without a jury trial. McKean invoked the doctrine of constructive contempt, which allowed judges to construe statements outside the courtroom as contempt if they interfered with court proceedings. Thus, McKean's use of a contempt citation effectively denied Oswald a jury trial. Oswald was fined ten pounds and sentenced to a month in prison.[15]

One of the leading Anti-Federalist printers in the nation, Oswald believed that the prosecution was politically motivated. His strategy was exactly the same one he had used successfully in 1782: he sought to make the trial proceedings as public as possible. The libel suit against him had been brought "the moment the *federal* intelligence came to hand" that the new Constitution had been ratified by nine states. Emboldened by their political victory, Federalists took this opportunity, Oswald charged, to settle an old score with him. Oswald was confident that the machinations of his opponents would come to nothing and asserted confidently that, "if former prejudices should be found to operate against me on the bench," he would be content to let his fate rest with "a jury of my country, properly elected and empannelled, a jury of freemen and independent citizens." He informed his audience, "I have escaped the jaws of persecution through this channel on certain memorable occasions." The decision to use his paper to rally public support for his cause made perfect sense, for Oswald believed that the role of newspapers was to shape and influence public opinion. In this sense the public sphere of print and the role of the jury were mutually dependent. For Oswald, not only was the jury intended to be a mirror of society; it was itself a quasi-representative body entitled to judge the constitutionality of law. While McKean believed that Oswald had compromised the independence of the judicial process, Oswald felt it was merely another manifestation of the political process. Accordingly, Oswald believed the job of the press was to educate citizens politically so they could exercise their function on the jury. McKean hoped to confine the jury's role and insulate it from the world of print, a forum that could not be controlled by judges trained in the law.[16]

Had Oswald not provided McKean with a pretext for issuing a contempt citation, the case might have been a simple replay of the earlier case. The use of contempt to prosecute Oswald changed things dramatically, and the case became a subject of public debate and considerable controversy. Reactions to the case, however, went beyond discussion of the technical issues in the case: a wide-ranging discussion of the nature of libel, the role of juries, the use of constructive contempt, and the meaning of freedom of the press

15. Ibid., 9.
16. Ibid., 3.

ensued. In attacking McKean, Anti-Federalists presented a more expansive, libertarian view of the freedom of the press. Anti-Federalists also reasserted an expansive view of the rights of juries and their own distinctive approach to constitutional interpretation.

While a number of writers defended Oswald in traditional Zengerian terms, a few Anti-Federalist writers moved beyond this defense and put forth a new, more liberal theory of freedom of the press. Oswald had himself begun to question whether the use of libel was "Incompatible with law and liberty." One author, A Pennsylvanian, developed Oswald's argument even further. He began by observing, "An idea has been circulated that too great a latitude is allowed to the press, and that its *licentiousness* ought to be restrained." In practice, this "idea" constrained the freedom of the press, since it was "extremely difficult to draw a line of distinction between what is termed the *liberty* and licentiousness of the press." While most Anti-Federalists accepted the need to draw such a line, this author proclaimed: "There is no middle line—Restrain the *licentiousness*, and you in effect demolish the *liberty* of the press."[17]

The second aspect of the Oswald case that provoked considerable public commentary was the use of constructive contempt judgments against a defendant. This issue touched on a number of Anti-Federalist concerns: the roles of judges and juries and the proper method of interpreting constitutional texts. McKean sought to diminish the role of juries, and he defended the use of constructive contempt as indispensable to his judicial authority. Oswald's public statements, although not made in court before McKean, had effectively undermined that judicial process and authority. Throughout the proceedings McKean defended the authority of his office. "Judges discharge their functions under the solemn obligations of an oath: and, if their virtue entitles them to their station, they can neither be corrupted by favour to swerve from, nor influenced by fear to desert, their duty." Punishing Oswald was thus necessary to preserve the authority of the court. Oswald's public appeal was an instance of contempt because it had the effect of "prejudicing the public" regarding "the merits of a case" and hence interfered with the

17. Ibid., 4; *Respublica versus Oswald,* in Alexander J. Dallas, *Reports of Cases Ruled and Adjudged in the Several Courts of the United States, and of Pennsylvania* . . . , I (Philadelphia, 1788), 319; *IG,* July 1, 1788; A Pennsylvanian, *IG,* Sept. 27, 1788. The response to the Oswald case casts doubt on Leonard W. Levy's claim that "in the entire body of Anti-Federalist publications no one had come to grips with any real problems connected with freedom of the press" (*Emergence of a Free Press* [New York, 1985], 244). For a critique of Levy, see David M. Rabban, "The Ahistorical Historian: Leonard Levy on Freedom of Expression in Early American History," *Stanford Law Review,* XXXVII (1985), 795–856.

"administration of justice." McKean asserted the right of the judiciary to determine the law on this matter and denied that Oswald was entitled to a jury trial. "Whether the publication amounts to a contempt, or not, is a point of law, which, after all, is the province of the judges, and not of the jury, to determine." McKean sought to reduce the prerogatives of juries and expand the powers of judges.[18]

Federalists placed far less trust in popular tribunals and preferred to expand the scope of judicial authority. Their worst scenario of all was to drag legal issues into the court of popular opinion. McKean and his allies had correctly interpreted the Anti-Federalist strategy. Oswald's supporters sought to use the press to shape the views of jurors who would then interpret both the facts of the case and the law. Such tactics made perfect sense, given the Anti-Federalists' theory of libel and their more democratic approach to constitutional matters, which was closely tied to a notion of an expansive public sphere. For middling democrats such as Oswald, a vibrant public sphere was essential to educate citizens and alert them to threats to their liberty. Far from undermining the authority of law, Oswald's actions helped the jury serve its proper constitutional function.

The use of constructive contempt was perceived by Anti-Federalists to be an effort by the judiciary to increase its authority. McKean's actions seemed to vindicate their claim that Federalists intended to use the interpretive authority of judges to expand the powers of government. Amicus reminded Pennsylvanians, "There is but one way of being guilty of what is called a contempt of the court, by some act of violence or indecent expression, in the presence and hearing of the court, whilst sitting, or by refusing to obey the process of the court." Federalists appeared to be trying to circumvent the requirements for a jury trial by invoking this unfamiliar legal concept. McKean's actions justified the Anti-Federalist's belief that a powerful judiciary would pervert the plain meaning of constitutional texts. X. Z. attacked the use of "implied power" and was particularly incensed that "the party, pretending to be offended, is to decide on the offence." Framing the issue in democratic terms, X. Z. noted, "Gentlemen of the robe have too generally lofty ideas on this subject." McKean's actions were typical of the judges who were incapable of sympathizing with the common man. "Amongst the *great*," X. Z. wrote, "the inferior class of mankind are viewed as a lower order of beings." Furthermore, "gentlemen of the bar are very ingenious in producing cases and opinions in Court, to support particular points." Against the legalism and latitudinarian constructions favored by Federalist

18. *Respublica versus Oswald,* in Dallas, *Reports,* 326.

judges, X. Z. exhorted Pennsylvanians to recall that "no opinion must ever be permitted to overrule the fundamental liberties of our country, or to destroy the express words of our constitution." Anti-Federalists were proponents of a constitutional plain style and committed to a form of constitutional literalism, and they accordingly opposed the sort of broad interpretive latitude that McKean defended. X. Z. complained that, by "this sort of logic, the whole constitution may be converted to a very ductile code." Fortunately, a properly worded constitution, such as framed by Pennsylvanians, did not easily lend itself to interpretive abuse. Affirming the strong textualist stance taken by most Anti-Federalists, X. Z. asserted that the Pennsylvania constitution's "words are too stubborn to bend to every blast of invention."[19]

McKean's behavior led some commentators to champion a more democratic vision of the law. An author who adopted the name One of the Common People warned readers, "It is the fashionable opinion of the times, that the common people cannot understand, and ought not to inquire into the proceedings of those in power." In particular, Federalist judges and lawyers wished to lessen the power of juries and thereby exclude the people from an active role in legal proceedings. McKean's use of a constructive contempt citation and his refusal to allow Oswald a jury suggested that he did not trust the people to fulfill their obligations as jurors. "*Judges* were sworn to act rightly and honestly, and *therefore* could not be biased: But his honor was graciously pleased to express his great doubts, whether *jurymen* paid so sacred regard to *their* oaths." Contrary to the excessive legalism of Federalists, Anti-Federalist supporters of Oswald maintained that the law was a matter of common sense and that men of sound mind and virtuous character could interpret it without formal legal training or education. In a republic, there was no need of a special priestly class to interpret the law.[20]

Many of the issues debated in the press were replayed in the Pennsylvania Assembly, which took up the Oswald case. Federalists asserted the Blackstonian doctrine that "true liberty" was "equally endangered by tyranny on the one hand, and by licentiousness on the other." Indeed, Federalist opponents of Oswald went further: "To censure the licentiousness, is to maintain the *liberty* of the press." The argument against Oswald was peppered with historical evidence about the law of libel in England and America. Supporters of McKean challenged the claims made in the press that Blackstone was a "courtly" writer who stood against true Whig republican principles of the American Revolution. In their view the Pennsylvania constitution embraced

19. Amicus, *IG*, Sept 23, 1788; X. Z., *IG*, July 28, 1788.
20. One of the Common People, *IG*, Aug. 7, 1788.

a neo-Blackstonian understanding of freedom of the press. McKean accepted that the law protected only "a candid commentary" but did not shield "every endeavour to bias and intimidate," arguing that it was the job of the courts to "enquire into the motives of such publications, and to distinguish between those which are meant for use and reformation, and with an eye solely to the public good, and those which are intended merely to delude and defame." The Federalists accepted the neo-Blackstonian reading of the Pennsylvania constitution's declaration protecting freedom of the press as a limit on prior restraint, not a rejection of the idea of seditious libel. One of McKean's supporters in the Assembly recognized that Oswald had intended to subvert the judicial process by appealing his case directly to the people. Such a move was "certainly calculated to draw the administration of justice from proper tribunals; and in their place substitute newspaper altercations." Federalists sought to limit popular involvement in judicial proceedings. The jury's role would be to decide on the facts of the case and not pass judgment on technical matters of law that were best left to judges. Above all, Federalists did not wish to see the law politicized. The prospect that legal matters would become the subject of debate in the press and that jurors would be influenced by those debates horrified them. This was precisely the sort of democratic excess that the federal Constitution was intended to check.[21]

McKean's actions shocked and outraged Oswald's Anti-Federalist allies in the Assembly. William Findley, a leading Anti-Federalist spokesman, challenged McKean's supporters, lambasted McKean, and reiterated themes that Anti-Federalists had repeated throughout ratification. Against McKean's neo-Blackstonian emphasis on the common law, which elevated the role of the judiciary, Findley championed "the rights and immunities which formed the great object of the revolution." Findley dismissed the common law as a relic of British monarchism. The Revolution represented a distinct break with this tradition, which belonged to "the dark and distant period of juridical history."[22]

Findley did more than simply restate the familiar Zengerian principles that defined the Anti-Federalist view of libel. He also pressed many of the themes that had been presented in response to the Oswald case in the press. His critique of the common law went beyond exposing its contamination by outdated antirepublican ideas. Invoking the common law was a familiar tactic of those judges who were eager to manipulate the plain sense of the Constitution through speculative constructions of legal principle. In opposi-

21. *Respublica versus Oswald,* in Dallas, *Reports,* 325, 326.
22. Rosenberg, *Protecting the Best Men,* 62–65.

tion to the legalistic cast of Federalist arguments, Findley affirmed a constitutional plain style, championing the belief that legal principles were "capable of an easy and equivocal definition." "Every man," Findley alleged, "who possessed a competent share of common sense, and understood the rules of grammar" could determine the meaning of the Constitution. He denounced "the sophistry of the schools and the jargon of the law" and warned that many legal techniques were designed to "pervert or corrupt the explicit language" of the text. Pennsylvania's constitution had been drafted by middling democrats like Findley. The language of that document, unlike the ambiguity of the federal Constitution, was set down in a plain style and included a bill of rights explicitly limiting the scope of government powers. For Findley, "there was nothing ambiguous or uncertain" about the rights guaranteed by the state constitution. It would be "fatal to the cause of liberty," he declared, "if it was once established, that the technical learning of a lawyer is necessary to comprehend the principles" sown in "this great compact between the people and their rulers." The text of the Constitution and the principles of natural rights evident to anyone who possessed common sense were the foundations of law, not the accumulated wisdom of the common law. The Federalists' use of the common law was part of a larger effort to reduce popular involvement in judicial proceedings.[23]

Reducing the powers of jury and strengthening those of the judiciary were part of the Federalist goal of creating a more aristocratic style of government. Findley even went so far as to affirm that "the law of the land was not, in fact, contradistinguished from the judgement of his peers, but merely a diversity in the mode of expressing the same thing." The jury, like the legislature, was an authentic voice of the people. Findley shared the view of other Anti-Federalists that the jury could function like a sitting constitutional convention, an authoritative interpreter of the meaning of constitutional documents.[24]

The Oswald libel case seemed to vindicate Anti-Federalists' worst fears about their opponents. The chasm between the Federalists' Blackstonian views and the Anti-Federalists' Zengerian principles could hardly be wider. A few of Oswald's Anti-Federalist supporters even broke with Zengerian ideals and challenged the very idea of political libel. This new, more liberal conception of freedom of the press not only represented an important step in the transformation of an alternative to Federalist constitutionalism; it was an important step in the growth of a new theory of the public sphere.

23. Ibid.
24. *Respublica versus Oswald*, in Dallas, *Reports*, 319; *IG*, July 1, 1788.

During ratification Eleazer Oswald had framed his ideals in republican terms. He defended printers whose "true dignity consists in looking after and supporting the general good, in which every citizen in a greater or lesser degree is equally interested." Although his paper became one of the most important vehicles for Anti-Federalist ideas, Oswald prided himself on publishing both Federalist and Anti-Federalist materials. After ratification, that republican conception of the press would give way to a more partisan one. So in the aftermath of the libel suit, Oswald's paper too became a far more partisan platform. Rather than each printer striving to embody the ideal of disinterestedness, individual printers would champion particular ideas, and the public will would emerge out of this conflict.[25]

Anti-Federalists had not devoted much attention to analyzing the function of the press, but during ratification most Anti-Federalists bitterly complained about its partiality. In nearly every instance, they attacked the antirepublican bias of Federalist printers. Writing shortly after ratification, Samuel Bryan (the author of the Centinel essays) suggested a different way of understanding the dynamics of the public sphere.

> The Printers were certainly most of them more willing to publish for, then against the new Constitution. They depended more upon the People in the Towns than in the Country. The Towns people withdrew their Subscriptions from those who printed Papers against, and violent Threats were thrown out against the Antis and Attempts were made to injure them in their Business.[26]

Federalists controlled access to newspapers because of their economic clout. Appeals to republican virtue were of little consequence; only by recognizing the role of economic interests could Anti-Federalists effectively combat Federalists. With the benefit of hindsight, Bryan had clearly come to recognize that the press and the public sphere would not regulate themselves and that republican injunctions were insufficient to challenge the power of the marketplace. The lesson of ratification was clear: in the future, control of the diffusion of knowledge would become essential for politicians. The old republican conception of the press would have to yield to a new, more modern and liberal conception of the press as an agent of particular interests seeking to manage public opinion in a marketplace of ideas. The notion of a public sphere, a site of rational dialogue on matters of common concern, would

25. Eleazer Oswald's Statement, *IG*, Mar. 12, 1788 (*DHRC*, XVI, 557–559).

26. Cornell, "Reflections on 'The Late Remarkable Revolution in Government,'" *PMHB*, CXII (1988) 122–123, 129.

come more closely to resemble a marketplace of ideas in which partisan interests vied for the sympathies of the public. The transformation from public sphere to marketplace of ideas would not be accomplished for some time, but the politics of ratification were indispensable in leading some influential figures to begin to rethink the nature of the public sphere.

The Aborted Second Convention Movement

Just as the Oswald libel case was concluding in September 1788, Pennsylvania Anti-Federalists faced a new, more pressing problem: what to do about the adoption of the Constitution. During ratification, a number of Anti-Federalists actively agitated for a second convention to revise the Constitution. Other Anti-Federalists concentrated their attention on the prospect of amendments and looked to the First Congress as the appropriate battleground. Ratification had entered a new phase after February 1789, when the Massachusetts state convention decided to ratify with an implicit understanding that a set of recommended amendments would be taken up by the First Congress. Although that decision did not quash the movement for a second convention, it shifted energy and attention away from it. Not until the New York convention met in July did a second convention garner renewed interest. Initially, New York Anti-Federalists had proposed recommendatory, explanatory, and conditional amendments. When that proposal seemed unlikely to pass, Melancton Smith suggested that ratification be conditional and that a second constitutional convention consider amendments. The proposal also called for the temporary suspension of congressional power over the militia, elections, and taxation until the question of amendments was settled. Federalists responded with a call for ratification "in full confidence" that amendments would be taken up by the Congress. Smith next called for a conditional ratification, including a right to secede if two-thirds of the states did not petition Congress to call a second convention to take up amendments. The right of secession was defeated, as was the conditional adoption. Ultimately, New York followed the Massachusetts model of recommending amendments. The New York convention, however, did publish a circular letter calling for a second constitutional convention to consider the subject of amendments, which would then be taken up by Congress. Efforts to organize a national second convention movement were coordinated by New York Anti-Federalist John Lamb, who corresponded with Anti-Federalist leaders from South Carolina, North Carolina, Virginia, Maryland, Pennsylvania, and New Hampshire.[27]

The first and only state to convene such a convention was Pennsylvania, where delegates from all over the state convened at Harrisburg in September 1788 to take up the subject of amendments. The outcome of the Harrisburg convention was crucial to the future of Anti-Federalism. If Harrisburg should succeed, it would be a model for a broad national movement for a second convention and create the nucleus of an anticonstitutional movement.

The dynamics of the Harrisburg convention also illustrate the continuing importance of the tension between elite and popular opposition to the Constitution and the vital role that middling democrats played in mediating between those two poles of Anti-Federalism.

Plebeian populists looked forward to Harrisburg as an opportunity to further their own radical agenda. Carlisle Anti-Federalists, encouraged by the news of a convention in nearby Harrisburg, offered up a toast calling for amendments that might "render the proposed Constitution of the United States truly democratical." Leading Anti-Federalists throughout Pennsylvania and several newcomers to Pennsylvania politics attended. One of the newcomers was a feisty representative from Carlisle, the leader of the Carlisle riot, William Petrikin. Like other plebeian populists, Petrikin was eager to persuade the delegates to adopt a radical program to unite Anti-Federalists throughout the country and scrap the system of government so recently adopted.[28]

At Harrisburg, Petrikin felt betrayed by the moderate forces, who "did more injury to our cause than all the strategems of our advarsaries." His disappointment was hard to contain: "Our friends throughout the state expected something decisive from us and we spent our whole time Canvassing for places in Congress." While moderates directed their energies to working through the system, Petrikin confessed that he had "expected the intention of our meeting was to unite the opposition in the different parts of

27. For the text of the New York circular letter, see *DHFFE,* I, 44–45. For a general discussion of the dynamics of this process, see Steven R. Boyd, *The Politics of Opposition: Antifederalists and the Acceptance of the Constitution* (Millwood, N.Y., 1979), 131–133.

28. *Carlisle Gazette* (Pennsylvania), July 9, 1788. A number of documents relating to the Harrisburg Convention have been reproduced in *DHFFE,* I, 257–281. Other accounts of Harrisburg include Paul Leicester Ford, *The Origins, Purpose, and Result of the Harrisburg Convention of 1788: A Study in Popular Government* (Brooklyn, N.Y., 1890); Linda Grant DePauw, "The Anticlimax of Antifederalism: The Abortive Second Convention Movement, 1788–89," *Prologue,* II (1970), 98–114; Boyd, *The Politics of Opposition,* 142–144.

the state that they might act in concert—to form committees and associations and open a Chanel of communication through-out the united states if posible." In contrast to the other delegates, who "courted preferment," Petrikin proudly recommended that Anti-Federalists continue to organize into committees of correspondence and militia units. His radical localist agenda was not compatible with the state-centered view of politics championed by more experienced politicians. Echoing the spirit of Anti-Federalists in Carlisle who took their political grievances into the streets, Petrikin declared, "If a party of Feds and anties happens to meet upon any convival or public occasion the feds is sure to get a compleat dressing befor they dissmiss."[29]

The moderate forces at Harrisburg were led by Charles Pettit, an established politician and close ally of the middling democrats who dominated Pennsylvania politics. Pettit sought to distance himself from events like the Carlisle riot and avert any actions that might possibly promote anarchy. Middling politicians like Pettit were alarmed by the depth of hostility in the backcountry and feared anarchy. Writing to one of the leading spokesmen for Pennsylvania's middling democrats, Robert Whitehill, to express his grave reservations about continued resistance to the new Constitution, Pettit stressed his own belief that to "reject the New Plan and attempt again to resort to the old" would be disastrous and would "throw us into a State of Nature, filled with internal Discord." Pettit underscored the fact that "a Politician will readily imagine the Danger of such a Situation." He captured the view of many leading Anti-Federalists when he later confided to George Washington, "Even after the vote of adoption by the State Convention, a large proportion of the people, especially in the western counties, shewed a disposition to resist the operation of it, in a manner which I thought indicated danger to the peace of the State." For Pettit, the willingness of plebeian populists to take their grievances into the streets was an example of mobocracy, not republicanism, and had to be prevented at all costs. The memory of the Carlisle riot, a scant six months earlier, loomed large in the minds of Petitt and Whitehill. Middling democrats appreciated that latent radicalism unleashed by the riot could undermine their more moderate democratic agenda.[30]

The Harrisburg convention recommended a set of amendments to be submitted to the state legislature, which would then be transmitted to Con-

29. William Petrikin to John Nicholson, Mar. 23, 1789 (*DHFFE*, I, 406–407).

30. Charles Pettit to Robert Whitehill, June 5, 1788 (*DHRC*, XVIII, 154–155); Pettit to George Washington, Mar. 19, 1791 (II [microfiche], 706).

gress. Mild in tone and conciliatory, the content of those amendments would have satisfied all but the most radical voices within the Anti-Federalist coalition. Although disappointing to William Petrikin, they were true to the spirit of more mainstream critics of the Constitution: the amendments would tip the balance of power within the federal system in favor of the states. Their goals were to limit the new government to powers expressly delegated and explicitly prohibit the expansion of federal power "under color or pretense of construction or fiction." All the rights protected under the state constitutions were explicitly affirmed. The power to regulate the election of senators and representatives was returned to the states. Poll taxes were prohibited, and direct taxation was restricted to cases in which states failed to meet congressional requisitions. A prohibition of standing armies in times of peace and state control over the militia were also recommended. Control over the federal district was restricted to those regulations pertaining to "police and good order." Inferior federal courts were restricted to admiralty jurisdiction, and appeals restricted to matters of law. Full congressional approval of treaties was mandated, extending the existing provision for Senate approval. Thus, the pattern of amendments suggested by the Harrisburg convention conformed to the general model that emerged from the individual state ratification conventions: protection for individual liberty, restrictions on the elastic clauses within the Constitution, and a shift in the balance of power between the states and the federal government.[31]

For plebeian populists, the decision of the Harrisburg convention was a betrayal. They continued to organize themselves into committees of correspondence and local militia units—they had not accepted the effective transfer of sovereignty to a government they believed would not be truly representative. They continued to affirm a belief in the legitimacy of the people to resist unjust exercises of arbitrary authority. Their radical localist vision of democracy did not easily integrate into the Anti-Federalist agenda to work as a loyal opposition to amend the Constitution.

Pettit and middling democrats hoped that the struggle for amendments might actually revitalize an alternative politics, to combat the politics that inspired Federalists to create a stronger central government. The struggle between Federalists and Anti-Federalists was merely another expression of a more basic tension: those who believed that the stability of government depended upon force versus those who thought that government could rest on the confidence and affections of the people. Pettit was not naive. He

31. On the Harrisburg convention, see the documents in *DHFFE*, I, 257–281.

conceded that the Confederation was faulty and that its framers had relied too heavily on a degree of "Virtue, Public Spirit and other Attributes of Patriotism" that the people had been unable to supply. Pettit accepted that "those Ties are so far dissolved as to have lost their Force." Still, the Federalist solution was a cure worse than the disease.[32]

Rather than depend on stronger coercive authority, Pettit placed his faith in a revitalized public sphere, one that would unite individual communities. The amendment process was a means of reestablishing the social ties necessary to bring the nation together on a more solid and permanent basis. Pettit hoped to create a network of local organizations to work together for a common end. The goals of such an organization, however, were radically different from what William Petrikin envisioned. Pettit looked to the states and the federal system as the best means to assure that localism would not disrupt the Union. Pettit hoped that the individual counties would convene meetings to discuss the amendments and then send delegations to convene at the state level to make appropriate recommendations. Pettit showed a remarkable faith in the ability of reasoned debate to produce a consensus. In place of the republican reliance on virtue, the flaw that had crippled the Confederation government, Pettit and other middling democrats hoped to substitute an invigorated public sphere. The meetings within local communities working through the state structure, Pettit hoped, would energize the political process and unite the nation. The public sphere in this vision was grounded in locality, even as it created ties among different localities. In contrast to the plebiscite envisioned by plebeian populists, Pettit favored a deliberative democracy. With such a system, there would be no need for a strong central government: the public sphere, not virtue, would be the new foundation for American republicanism.

Although fearful of anarchy, Pettit remained sanguine and committed to democracy. Federalists in Pennsylvania were less optimistic, and their experience with backcountry unrest led them to an even more negative view of democracy. Before the Harrisburg convention, there was considerable concern among Federalists that continued Anti-Federalist agitation might lead to anarchy. One contemporary observer conjectured, "Blood and slaughter seem unavoidable unless speedily counteracted by sufficient authority." Given such fears, it is easy to appreciate why Pennsylvania Federalist John Armstrong might concede in private, "The philosophy that teaches the equality of mankind and the dignity of human nature is founded in vanity."

32. Pettit to Whitehill, June 5, 1788 (*DHRC*, XVIII, 154).

In Armstrong's view, the recent events had demonstrated that "there is infinitely more truth in the opposite doctrine, that the many were made for the few, and that we are better governed by rods than by reason." Armstrong was not unaware that many of his views were too dangerous to broach in public. "These ideas" were kept private, and he advised Horatio Gates that he would express such sentiments only to "a tried and bosom friend."[33]

Federalist attitudes toward plebeian radicalism diverged from those of more moderate Anti-Federalists in one important respect. While each side might have breathed easier once the threat of civil war and anarchy had been averted, Federalists perceived recent events in ironic terms, particularly plebeian radicalism. In the view of Federalist John Montgomery, the violence at Carlisle had prompted a number of Anti-Federalists of "respectable characters, whose minds were for some time greatly adverse to that Constitution," to seek a moderate position: violence had made these men as "anxious to preserve peace and good order, as any others." Public disorder strengthened, not weakened, the desire to create political stability. "Upon the whole, seeming evil has often since the Revolution been productive of real good in our public affairs." The local success of plebeian radicals in Carlisle thus weakened their position in the broader political arena.[34]

Ironically, the very success of the plebeian radicalism of the Carlisle rioters ultimately proved their own undoing. The fear of anarchy led the middling democrats who dominated the proceedings at Harrisburg to turn their energies to creating an effective loyal opposition, contributing to the demise of the drive for a second convention: opposition would not take the form of an anti-Constitution movement. Rather than encourage extralegal action by backcountry populists, leading Anti-Federalists opted to compromise and take up their role as a loyal opposition party.

The publication of the Harrisburg convention's resolves eased political tensions considerably. Federalist Richard Peters wrote to George Washington to express his happiness: "Our Anti-Federalists have changed their battery. They are now very Federal. They want amendments and they must get into the seats of government to bring them about." Anti-Federalists resolved to work through the electoral system to achieve the amendments they desired. Middling democrats were optimistic after Harrisburg, and the moderate tone adopted by the delegates to Harrisburg did not blunt their desire to

33. —— to Francis Hopkinson, Aug. 17, 1788 (*DHFFE*, I, 252); John Armstrong, Jr., to Horatio Gates, New York, May 30 1788 (I, 238).

34. John Montgomery to James Wilson, Mar. 2, 1788 (*DHRC*, II, 704).

assert their own political and constitutional visions. Rejecting the radicalism of plebeian populism actually enabled middling Anti-Federalists to carry forward with their own distinctive agenda.[35]

It is possible to find among the vast writings of Anti-Federalists numerous hysterical and outlandish claims about the dire consequences that would follow ratification of the Constitution. When those exaggerated claims are accorded equal weight with the more typical Anti-Federalist arguments, it is easy to construct an image of the opponents of the Constitution as exemplars of the paranoid style of politics or as men of little faith. Both of those views, however, obscure the fact that most Anti-Federalists raised a far more sober and specific set of concerns. When Anti-Federalists worried about the absence of a bill of rights, they focused on such threats as the absence of a guarantee for trial by jury and the failure to protect freedom of the press. Nothing seemed more likely to imperil liberty than the prospect that the new government might use the law of libel as a political weapon to suppress dissent. Anti-Federalists did not have to wait long to see it used exactly so by their enemies. The prosecution of Eleazer Oswald was concrete evidence that Federalists would use the law of libel as a political tool.

Before the Oswald libel case, the argument between Federalists and Anti-Federalists had been largely speculative. The prosecution of Oswald brought Federalists and Anti-Federalists face to face in court, pitting Federalist adherence to Blackstonian ideals against Anti-Federalist Zengerian precedents. Anti-Federalists formulated a more trenchant critique of Federalist jurisprudence, and they moved beyond Zengerian ideals to frame a more liberal theory of freedom of the press and assert a more democratic vision of constitutional law.

As the furor over the Oswald case was abating, Pennsylvania Anti-Federalists turned once more to national politics. The Harrisburg convention was a turning point in the evolution of Anti-Federalism. Before Harrisburg, many within the Anti-Federalist coalition were dedicated to calling a second convention to frame substantive amendments to the Constitution. Some even recommended scrapping the Constitution and beginning anew. At the very least, before Harrisburg, an anti-Constitution party was plausible.

But those radical alternatives were decisively rejected. The middling democrats who dominated that meeting recognized that such a party would only encourage plebeian populists to push their more radical goals, and they feared the destabilizing impact. Middling Anti-Federalists also recognized

35. Richard Peters to George Washington, Sept. 17, 1788 (*DHFFE*, I, 275).

that continued agitation for a second convention would only distract them from the important political battles ahead and inflame popular passions, ultimately weakening their ability to mount an effective opposition. The prospect of extralegal action by plebeian populists worried middling democrats, and their chosen path would minimize that danger. Instead of an anti-Constitution party, a loyal opposition emerged from Harrisburg.

As in their response to the Oswald case, middling democrats in the Harrisburg convention demonstrated their willingness to pursue their own agenda. Anti-Federalists continued to defend a more democratic vision of politics and law and employed a variety of tactics to fulfill it. They sought to rally popular support by championing their cause in the press, defending their views in the courts, and pursuing an aggressive democratic program in the legislature. What they refused to countenance was extralegal crowd action. Their politics embraced several related goals: amending the federal Constitution, defending the prerogatives of the jury, and asserting the superiority of the legislature over the judiciary. All were compatible with their stance as a loyal opposition. Crucial thereto was their emphasis on the centrality of the public sphere to American constitutionalism. Protecting the public sphere against Federalists and creating institutions to knit localities and states together became a major focus of their loyal opposition. The public sphere would provide a means of unifying the nation without a strong central government. Faith in the public sphere had come to replace an earlier faith in republican virtue.

The transformation of Anti-Federalism into a loyal opposition was gradual. Ratification of the Constitution did not eliminate the underlying tensions between Federalists and Anti-Federalists. Plebeian populists were discouraged by the moderation of middling democrats. The strategy adopted by middling democrats did not, however, mark the demise of plebeian populism; their radical egalitarian and localist agenda did not disappear. Popular unrest, temporarily muted, would remain dormant until the Whiskey Rebellion sparked another, wider popular upheaval.

PART TWO :
ANTI-FEDERALISM
TRANSFORMED

CHAPTER 5

THE EMERGENCE OF

A LOYAL OPPOSITION

The Debate over the Meaning of Representation

Anti-Federalist ideas did not simply disappear after the Constitution was ratified. The first controversy under the new government, the proper mode of electing representatives to the new Congress, was framed in terms that drew heavily from Anti-Federalist ideas and rhetoric. This dispute demonstrated once again the heterogeneity of Anti-Federalist thought. The tensions between popular and elite thought evident during ratification reappeared as different authors argued over the appropriate means for selecting representatives. As during ratification, the two most pervasive voices dominating public debate were the elite and the middling Anti-Federalists, who invoked different visions of politics. Middling Anti-Federalists championed a distinctly democratic notion of representation, and elites defended traditional gentry notions of virtue. Although there was little agreement among Anti-Federalists over exactly what defined a good representative, there was a broad consensus that individuals had to be rooted in the localities they represented. For middling democrats the goal of such a localist vision was to ensure that representation included the people. When government was close to the people, it would be possible for men of more modest means to enter politics. The opposite was the case for elite Anti-Federalists: by keeping politics local, they believed it would be possible to select members of the natural aristocracy. Those selected would have the confidence of the people and be able to sympathize with those they represented. Federalists, by contrast, supported a more pyramidal structure, one that deliberately sought to increase the distance between elected officials and those they represented. The goal for Federalists was to use the political system to winnow away those unqualified to represent society, and produce a class of politicians more likely to be men of expansive views. Purged of local influences, these national-minded politicians would be better able to discern the common good. Given the differences separating Anti-Federalist from Federalist views of representation, considerable disagreement over how to structure the first congressional elections was inevitable. Federalists generally argued for at-large election while Anti-Federalists championed election by district. The debate over the best way to elect candidates was particularly vociferous in Pennsylvania, Maryland, and Massachusetts.

An anonymous Federalist writer in the *Pennsylvania Mercury* strongly opposed electoral districts and favored at-large elections: "In this mode the characters most noted for wisdom and virtue will be brought forth, local prejudices will be destroyed." Another Federalist author, Numa, reminded Pennsylvanians that it would be a mistake to be "misled by the local prejudices or interests." In the Federalist plan, "none but men of real character and abilities will be returned, for such men are generally best known throughout every part of a state." Such a view had been central to Federalist thinking throughout the struggle over ratification.[1]

The heated debate within the press even spilled over into the Pennsylvania state legislature. Federalist William Lewis attacked the idea that representatives ought to be elected from "those particular districts into which a county for the convenience of its inhabitants are divided." In response, Anti-Federalist William Findley reminded members of the Assembly that at-large elections "went to extend the influence of the general government, without taking proper care to conciliate the minds of the people." The only means of providing for an effective and actual representation of the people's interests was to allow them to vote for a "man who has their confidence, who either resides among them, or is well known to them by the common interest and concern which he has with them." Furthermore, Findley asked his Federalist adversaries, "how can our Representatives know what is proper" if drawn from the state at large? Representatives had to be "possessed of local and common, as well as a general knowledge, and how is this to be obtained so fairly as by dividing the people into districts?" The legislature, in Findley's view, had not only to represent local interests but to include men who

1. *Pennsylvania Mercury and Universal Advertiser* (Philadelphia), Sept. 16, 1788 (*DHFFE*, I, 274); Numa, *Pennsylvania Gazette* (Philadelphia), July 16, 1788 (I, 246).

resembled those they served. George Clymer, a prominent Federalist, challenged Findley and argued that "the necessity of having the state of Pennsylvania well represented in the next Congress" necessitated the election of men who could command the respect of representatives from other states. The interests of Pennsylvania would be better served if her delegation were composed of men of reputation. Under such a system, it was "more likely a good and respectable representation was to be obtained." Clymer did not espouse a localist conception of politics, but defended a more nationalist and decidedly elitist vision. It was the respect of other members of the national legislature, not one's constituents, that Clymer thought was crucial to the interests of Pennsylvania and its citizens.[2]

James Madison's comments on the conflict in Pennsylvania demonstrate his own opposition to the localist orientation of Anti-Federalists. Madison approved of the at-large system and believed that, if Pennsylvania followed that model, it would "confine the choice to characters of general notoriety, and so far be favorable to merit." Such a system would, he cautioned, probably antagonize Anti-Federalists and be "liable to some popular objections urged against the tendency of the new system." Madison saw more clearly than any other contemporary that Federalist and Anti-Federalist visions were fundamentally at odds over the issue of representation.[3]

The Pennsylvania debate over representation conveyed a distinctly class-conscious message. Federalists objected to the Anti-Federalist proposal for electing representatives and sought to portray their opponents as populist demagogues who not only pandered to the people but were themselves crude and ill suited to positions of authority. One Federalist took great pains to equate Anti-Federalist localism with a lack of breeding and refinement. This sardonic Federalist, pretending to be a member of the Harrisburg convention, mocked William Findley's low social breeding and his heavy Scotch-Irish accent. In his eyes, that crude accent was one of Findley's main qualifications for office. "It was right that Findly should be put in nomination, because he can . . . say, 'Myster Spacker,' and avoid being 'parsenal,' and will do great credit to the western country."[4]

The debate over the mode of election in Pennsylvania pitted two different

2. Thomas Lloyd, *Debates of the General Assembly of Pennsylvania*, IV (Philadelphia, 1788) (*DHFFE*, I, 283, 287, 288).

3. James Madison to Thomas Jefferson, Oct. 8, 1788 (*DHFFE*, I, 302–303). For additional evidence that at-large elections were viewed as consistent with the spirit of the new Constitution, see Francis Corbin to James Madison, Nov. 12, 1788 (*DHFFE*, II, 371).

4. "Observations by a Member of the Convention at Harrisburg," *Pittsburgh Gazette*, Sept. 20, 1788 (*DHFFE*, I, 280).

views of representation against each other. Anti-Federalists were localists who favored districtwide elections because they would ensure that representatives were rooted in local communities and resembled their constituents. This mode of election would produce a more democratic legislature, in which men of middling fortunes would be more likely to succeed.

The debate over representation in the Pennsylvania press spilled over into neighboring Maryland. As was so often the case, arguments that entered the public sphere were easily appropriated by others. One Maryland author writing in the *Maryland Journal* invoked the argument of a Pennsylvania Federalist to support his claim that "elections by districts" were "contrary to the spirit and intention of the Federal Constitution." In the view of Maryland Federalists the spirit of Anti-Federalism was alive and as strong as ever. "A Marylander" attacked the Anti-Federalists, challenging their loyalty to the Constitution and arguing that their persistent calls for a second convention to discuss amendments were evidence of their implacable hostility to the new government. Such a policy demonstrated the dangers of Anti-Federalism. "When a man advocates a new general convention, to which the members from different states would come, bound down by instructions of a local nature, and thereby prevent any agreement, which can only take place from a spirit of mutual conciliation and concession; such a man may safely be termed antifederal." For him, the spirit of Anti-Federalism was its narrow-mindedness—a natural outgrowth of its localism. An additional argument in favor of at-large elections was ensuring that representatives were of the "first rank." This author feared that the Anti-Federalist proposal would not produce the independent-minded man, but instead would favor the man who has "nothing to recommend him but his supposed humility." Such a man "will not be too proud to court what are generally called the *poor folks*." Maryland Federalists attacked their opponents on two related grounds: excessive localism and democracy.[5]

The tension between Federalist and Anti-Federalist theories of representation was also central to the public debate over the mode of elections in Massachusetts. The Federalist vision of representation was aptly summarized by Honorius, who advocated "selecting the *best* and most *competent* characters." At-large election "will naturally expand the views of every ELEC-

5. *Maryland Journal, and the Baltimore Advertiser,* Nov. 14, 1788 (*DHFFE*, II, 125; A Marylander, *Maryland Gazette* (Annapolis), Dec. 30, 1788 (II, 165); Aristrides [Alexander Contee Hanson?], *Maryland Gazette,* Jan. 1, 1789 (II, 177); "The Moral Politician," no. 1, *Maryland Journal,* Feb. 13, 1789 (II, 220).

TOR." The minds of the electorate would be improved "by giving his suffrage not merely for his own townsman, but for the man of abilities, honor, integrity, wherever he may reside, and whatever may be his rank or profession in life." The goal would be to eliminate "that bane of our country in times past, *local prejudice.*" Honorius went further: "Every real Federalist must be decidedly in favor of those measures that bear the strongest impression of federal features—for whatever plan has a tendency to *socialize* the citizens, to *obliterate jealousies* and *unreasonable local attachments*" would help the Constitution succeed. One Federalist, Nathaniel W. Appleton, even went so far as to oppose explicitly "the division of the state into districts," a move he argued was inconsistent with the intent of the Constitution. "Confining the choice of a candidate to his own district, is, in my opinion, contrary to the true spirit of the Constitution, which aims at being as *national* as possible."[6]

One of the most interesting and original statements of the Federalist vision of representation was developed by Jonathan Jackson, who not only ran as a candidate for Congress but also authored a fascinating political tract, *Thoughts upon the Political Situation of the United States of America.* In that work, he attacked the excesses of democracy and sought to defend natural aristocracy. In his view the Constitution had not gone far enough: it was vital that the system of representation select individuals from the ranks of the natural aristocracy. Jackson's theory recommended that representatives should be "refined, again and again, from the rude digested first choice of the people." In a letter to a friend, he reiterated his fear that "an excess of republicanism," or what "might more properly be styled *unchecked democracy,* has threatened the ruin of our country, and had almost effected it," even arguing that "the word liberty" had been "much abused and little understood" in recent debates. Similarly, "aristocracy is a term" that had "never been well defined" and was "little understood by most of us." Jackson sought a method of election that took the logic of Federalists James Madison and James Wilson to its conclusion. His solution to the problem of excessive localism was particularly ingenious, since it used localist impulses to defeat localism

6. Honorius, *Herald of Freedom, and the Federal Advertiser* (Boston), Nov. 3, 1788 (*DHFFE,* I, 469–470); Nathaniel W. Appleton to Noah Webster, Nov. 30, 1789 (II, 506). Although Federalists lost the battle to secure election at large, they won a considerable victory in the construction of districts that favored the profederal commercial interests of the state. Electoral districts were created that favored the coastal regions over the Anti-Federalist regions of Maine and western Massachusetts; for a discussion of this process, see *DHFFE,* I, 476–477.

and promote a nationalist ethos. Voters were to be divided into squads of ten and elect a single spokesman, who would then gather with the representatives of other squads. This refinement would continue until a small number of highly qualified persons were selected as representatives of the state. The base of this pyramid would be broad; it embraced local representation while neutralizing its pernicious tendencies. It differed from Anti-Federalist localism: the goal was, not to incorporate local ideas, but rather to exclude them by filtering them out. His ideal was identical to one that Wilson and Madison had defended during ratification: the creation of representatives of pronounced knowledge, wisdom, and talents. Jackson's improvement upon the federal system would tame the excesses of democracy by guaranteeing that elected officials would be from society's natural aristocracy. In this way, the balance between the interests of the many and the few would be maintained and the general good of society more likely be promoted.[7]

The Anti-Federalist point of view was defended by Real Farmer: "A diversity of interests subsists among the citizens in every state." After discussing those interests, particularly the difference between the mercantile and landed interests, the author reiterated that the assembly ought to be a perfect likeness of the people. "In order that an equal and *real* representation may, in any measure, be secured, it seems to be necessary that the travel to elections should be rendered as short as may be, and that the circles or districts, in which Representatives shall be chosen, should be as small as the nature of the case, and the Constitution, will admit of. By this means, the citizens will more generally know, and be known by, their representatives." He closed his essay with a reminder "that the various classes of citizens may be *really* represented in government" so that "every department thereof may be filled with men of virtue, moderation, and discernment." The Anti-Federalist response to Federalists in Massachusetts repeated the arguments that middling democrats had used elsewhere. It was necessary for government to possess the confidence of the people. This could be accomplished only if representatives were drawn from localities and resembled the people at large. The ideal of virtue at the heart of this vision was far more egalitarian than the Federalist vision of politics. Virtue was not exclusively associated with gentlemen. The localist character of Anti-Federalist theories of representa-

---

7. A Native of Boston [Jonathan Jackson], *Thoughts upon the Political Situation of the United States of America* . . . (Worcester, Mass., 1788), 69, 106–111; Jonathan Jackson to William Eustis, December 1788 (*DHFFE,* I, 591, 594). Jackson came in second in the election in a field of eight candidates and was eventually elected to state office from Essex; see *DHFFE,* I, 615. For more information on Jackson's political career, see *DHFFE,* I, 752.

tion contrasted with the Federalist vision of a government composed of men, not rooted in their locality, but of pronounced national vision.[8]

Rats versus Antirats

With the debate over the method of selecting representatives concluded, attention was now concentrated on what sort of men should be elected. This issue was enmeshed with the question of amendments and kept the issues raised during ratification alive. Anti-Federalist authors were eager to keep public attention focused on the necessity for amendments, whereas Federalists sought to discredit Anti-Federalists by portraying them as anti-Constitution. In Massachusetts, Honestus, an Anti-Federalist, challenged the effort to hang on supporters of amendments "the opprobrious epithet of *Antifederalists*." "I am sensible it is rather unfashionable among some circles, to adhere to our old republican principles," he wrote. "A republican and an Antifederalist with them are synonymous. The term Anti-Federalist has of late been used by such persons to weaken the influence of some of our old tried republicans." This rhetorical move, casting aside the pejorative label of Anti-Federalist and recasting the debate to make republicanism the central issue, was a favorite tactic of a number of influential Anti-Federalist authors. When phrased in this way, the important issue was, not one's stance on the Constitution, but rather who was the more faithful adherent of the principles of Revolutionary republicanism.[9]

The rhetorical structure of public debate carried over many themes from ratification into the elections for the First Congress. A number of Federalist writers in the *Massachusetts Centinel* linked Anti-Federalism with Shaysism, a twist that had been used effectively by many writers during ratification. One author calling himself "Good Old '75" asserted, "The Antifederalists of *Massachusetts* to a man are insurgents." An Elector to the Federal Mechanics of This Town warned against choosing men who were associated with the evils of "*insurgents, mobs, Antifederalists, paper money,* or *tender laws.*" Linking Anti-Federalism with mobocracy thus prompted two rather different responses from authors who drew on middling and elite Anti-Federalist rhetorical themes.[10]

8. Real Farmer, *Hampshire Chronicle* (Springfield, Mass.), Oct. 22, 1788 (*DHFFE*, I, 468–469).

9. Honestus [Benjamin Austin?], *Independent Chronicle: And the Universal Advertiser* (Boston), Oct. 30, 1788 (*DHFFE*, I, 473–476).

10. *Massachusetts Centinel* (Boston), Dec. 17, 1788 (*DHFFE*, I, 562–563).

The debate in Massachusetts also became highly personal, focusing attention on the two men most closely identified with Anti-Federalist views, Samuel Adams and Elbridge Gerry. Defenses of Adams and Gerry followed two different ideological strategies. One approach used the republican rhetoric of virtue to demonstrate that Adams and Gerry were men of principle who would not be influenced by either popularity or interest. Another, quite different rhetorical strategy portrayed the enemies of those men as aristocrats hostile to popular liberty. The two different approaches made sense, given the complex nature of Massachusetts Anti-Federalism, which included both a popular democratic wing and a more conservative elite strain. Once again, plebeian views were largely muffled. The dominant popular voices in the public sphere were the established elite and middling Anti-Federalists.

"So are they all 'honorable,' " a writer styling himself Truth asserted, "who basely mean to pierce the heart of liberty with a dagger when they appear merely to aim the stroke at the character of Adams." While acknowledging Adams's reservations about the Constitution, Truth attacked "the blind idolatry with which many have affected to contemplate this fancied model of perfection." Instead, Truth counseled moderation: "Let us be wise and temperate; but in justice to him, let the citizens of Boston respect and revere the man, whose resolution has been invincible, and whose wisdom has been only equalled by his virtue." This defense of Adams drew on many of the republican themes that the Old Patriots had used during ratification, stressing the ideals of virtue and the refusal to succumb to popular enthusiasms.[11]

A different, more popular rhetorical strategy was used by A Republican, who attacked "these aristocratical tyrants" who were "ever insulting and abusing the old patriots and true friends of our country, because they are not as despotically inclined as themselves." The assaults on the character of Anti-Federalist leaders were intended to discredit individuals friendly to the people: "A republican is called a Shayite and a destroyer of all government." By undermining confidence in these popular leaders, those eager to prevent amendments could secure their ultimate objective, the creation of an aristocratic or monarchic government. "Thus notwithstanding it is the wish of the people that the alterations recommended should take place, these arbitrary aristocratics are perpetually scribbling in the little papers to induce the people to neglect the true patriots of our country, that themselves may be chosen into the federal legislature."[12]

Elbridge Gerry's highly visible role as an Anti-Federalist became a central

11. "Truth," *Boston Gazette, and the Country Journal,* Sept. 1, 1788 (*DHFFE,* I, 452–453).
12. A Republican, *Boston Gazette,* Sept. 1, 1788 (*DHFFE,* I, 453–454).

issue in his election. Federalists sought to damage Gerry's reputation by hammering away at his opposition to the Constitution. X denounced Gerry: "Those who mean to destroy the new Constitution ought to vote for Mr. Gerry. All who are in debt and wish for paper money, all who are for tender acts, all Shayites and such, ought to vote for Mr. Gerry."[13]

Gerry's own defense of his Anti-Federalism asserted his disinterestedness and explicitly affirmed that his opposition to the Constitution did not proceed from any leveling or radical democratic ideas. "A government too democratical have I ever deprecated," he explained. His desire for amendments was motivated by a desire to "secure the *governed* from the rapacity and domination of lawless and insolent ambition." Another author, claiming to be "An Independent Man," praised Gerry as a disinterested gentleman. In private, a number of Gerry's friends urged him to ignore the attacks on his character and remain true to his republican principles. Samuel Osgood reminded Gerry, "A true Republican never ought to be so offended with the people as to forsake them or withdraw from their service." Calumny was inevitable in popular governments. "Such governments are at times, and always will be, tumultuous. The only way to render them good for anything is for the cool and rational part of society to adhere together."[14]

Some writers extolled Gerry as a model republican statesmen who pursued the public interest without regard to popularity. The author who took the classical identity Marcellus interpreted the attacks on Gerry as a corruption of the public sphere itself. Slander and calumny were universal, making it impossible for virtuous men to serve the public and pursue the good of the commonweal. Marcellus identified Gerry as one such man: "a gentleman of clear head, and upright heart, a patriot of 75, a man who wishes for an energetic government" balanced by "proper checks and balances."[15]

Despite Gerry's own explicit disavowals of democracy, a number of writers employed a more democratic rhetoric to defend him. The very presence of such diametrically opposed arguments provided further evidence that, once they entered the public sphere, authors were no longer in control of their arguments. In Gerry's case, it seemed, he could not even control how his own persona was constructed in public debate. Adolphus attacked the "proud aristocratical gentry, who think the yeomanry of the country unfit, totally unfit, to have any part in the government; and the many idle and

13. "X to the Electors of Middlesex," *Herald of Freedom*, Jan. 16, 1789 (*DHFFE*, I, 646).

14. "Elbridge Gerry to the Electors of Middlesex," *Independent Chronicle*, Jan. 22, 1789 (*DHFFE*, I, 647); Samuel Osgood to Elbridge Gerry, Feb. 19, 1789 (I, 657).

15. Marcellus, *Herald of Freedom*, Jan. 23, 1789.

worthless minions, who expect an unearned living from the industry of the people." Another defense of Gerry, by Countryman, writing in a plainer style, also acknowledged Gerry's elite status, while affirming that his attitudes were not typical of the better sort. "He has been so long in public life, that he knows how to do, and how to talk, and how to figure, and how to write, as well as any of the great ones that was with him in Congress." The difference between Gerry and these others, Countryman noted, was that Gerry's loyalty was to the public, not to his class interest. Unlike those "great ones," Gerry would "not say what all the rest of the great folks say, if he think they are not right."[16]

Public efforts to defend Gerry followed a bifurcated rhetorical strategy that reflected the importance of two competing discourses, one decidedly elitist, the other more democratic. Gerry's candidacy brought forth a variety of responses; he became a public symbol whose meaning was bitterly contested. Federalists and former opponents of the Constitution sought to control the way that symbol was interpreted, as each vied to define the legacy of Anti-Federalism. Federalist efforts to discredit Anti-Federalism sought to link it with Shaysism and charged Gerry with being a demagogue engaged in rank political opportunism. Some defenses of Gerry continued to cast the essential divide in American politics as a struggle between the many and the few. Other supporters, including Gerry himself, avoided the class-conscious rhetoric favored by many former Anti-Federalists and chose instead to invoke the ideal of a disinterested republican statesman, a spokesman for the old republican values of the Revolution. Those two different rhetorical traditions, each tied to a different political ideology, were emblematic of the tensions that continued to divide Anti-Federalists. The transition into a loyal opposition did little, if anything, to narrow this rift within opposition thought. The one Anti-Federalist voice that seemed silent in this public debate was that of plebeians. The only invocation of plebeian ideals was negative, part of the Federalist campaign to discredit Anti-Federalism.

The debates over the appropriate mode of elections and the contest for seats in Congress demonstrated the continuing relevance of Anti-Federalist ideas. They also established in compelling terms the necessity of jettisoning the label "Anti-Federalist," which would only continue to be a political liability. This fact was obvious to the former opponents of the Constitution. Indeed, once in Congress, Gerry sought to put his own coloring on the relevance of the old categories of Federalist and Anti-Federalist. He chose a

16. Adolphus, *Independent Chronicle,* Jan. 1, 1789 (*DHFFE,* I, 636–638); Countryman, *Boston Gazette,* Jan. 26, 1789 (I, 649).

witty yet accurate terminology for capturing the differences separating the two sides in ratification.

> The federalists were for ratifying the Constitution as it stood, and the others not until amendments were made. Their names then ought not to have been distinguished by federalists and anti-federalists, but rats and anti-rats.[17]

The battle between rats and antirats would continue during the First Congress but would evolve in ways that fulfilled many of the Anti-Federalists' most dire predictions about the dangers posed by the power of the new federal government even as it shocked some who had been ardent supporters of the Constitution.

Anti-Federalism and the Politics of the First Congress

Elections to the First Congress were profoundly influenced by the politics of ratification. In many instances, a candidate's original stance on the Constitution was at least as important as any other issue put before the public. Despite the efforts of Federalists to discredit those who had been Anti-Federalists, the new Senate contained two vocal Anti-Federalists, and the new House contained a distinct Anti-Federalist minority of fourteen representatives. Although not the only voting bloc to emerge in the House, the voting pattern of these individuals consistently reflected their Anti-Federalist commitments. On a number of issues ranging from the right of the president to declare days of thanksgiving to his power to remove heads of executive departments without congressional approval and administer the Post Office, former Anti-Federalists broadcast their objections in terms reminiscent of the recent debate over ratification.[18]

17. *Annals of Congress*, August 1789, I, 731.

18. For a review of the literature on voting patterns and alignments during the First Congress that makes a forceful argument that an identifiable group of Anti-Federalist legislators voted in accordance with a distinctive Anti-Federalist ideology, see John H. Aldrich and Ruth W. Grant, "The Anti-Federalists, the First Congress, and the First Parties," *Journal of Politics*, LV (1993), 295–326. Earlier quantitative studies of politics in the First Congress downplayed the role of Anti-Federalism. See Mary Ryan, "Party Formation in the United States Congress, 1789 to 1796: A Quantitative Analysis," *WMQ*, 3d Ser., XXVIII (1971), 523–542; Rudolph M. Bell, *Party and Faction in American Politics: The House of Representatives, 1789–1801* (Westport, Conn., 1973); John F. Hoadley, *Origins of American Political Parties in Congress, 1789–1803* (Lexington, Ky., 1986). While the patterns of voting in the First

One struggle within the Congress that prompted participants to return to the issues debated during ratification was the move to provide an honorific title of address for the new president, George Washington. Thomas Tudor Tucker posed a series of queries to his fellow congressmen: "Will it not alarm our fellow-citizens?" "Will they not say, they have been deceived by the convention that framed the Constitution?" "Shall we not justify the fears of those who were opposed to the Constitution, because they considered it as insidious and hostile to the liberties of the people?" The debate over the appropriate mode of address for the new president, an issue of considerable symbolic importance, was only one of many debates where the participants invoked issues at the core of the old struggle between Federalists and Anti-Federalists.[19]

The debate most self-consciously linked to the ratification contest concerned amendments to the Constitution. The job of framing amendments that would satisfy the Anti-Federalist objections fell to James Madison, who was eager to prevent Anti-Federalists from obtaining structural changes in the federal system that would weaken the new government.

The terms of the debate over the Bill of Rights in the First Congress were largely derivative of the arguments between Federalists and Anti-Federalists. Describing the politics there, one contemporary observed, "The Antis viz. Gerry Tucker etc. appear determined to obstruct and embarrass the Business as much as possible." Pennsylvania's Frederick A. Muhlenberg even believed that the Anti-Federalist sympathies of some members had become more pronounced as a result of the political conflicts of the First Congress. "Mr. Gerry and Tucker had each of them a long string of Amendts. which were not comprised in the Report of the Special Committee, and which they stiled amendments proposed by the several States. There was a curious medley of them, and such as even our Minority in Pennsylvania would rather have pronounced dangerous."[20]

Congress do not support the idea that interest groups were functioning as part of a fully formed party system, they do suggest a core of Anti-Federalist voters on a range of constitutional questions. On the persistence of an antiparty political culture, see Ronald P. Formisano, "Deferential-Participant Politics: The Early Republic's Political Culture, 1789–1840," *American Political Science Review*, LXVIII (1974), 473–487.

19. *Annals of Congress*, I, 319, 759.

20. John Brown to William Irvine, Aug. 17, 1789, in Helen E. Veit, Kenneth R. Bowling, and Charlene Bangs Bickford, eds., *Creating the Bill of Rights: The Documentary Record from the First Federal Congress* (Baltimore, 1991), 279 (hereafter cited as *CBR*); Frederick A. Muhlenberg to Benjamin Rush, Aug. 18, 1789 (*CBR*, 280). The best account of the politics of the struggle over the Bill of Rights is Kenneth R. Bowling, "'A Tub to the Whale': The

A distinctive Anti-Federalist agenda emerged. The goal of Anti-Federalists was to limit the powers of the new government and bolster the states so that they would continue to be in a position to protect the liberty of their citizens. William Grayson confided to Patrick Henry that amendments being considered in Congress "shall affect personal liberty alone, leaving the great points of the Jud[iciar]y and direct taxation etc. to stand as they are." This claim reiterated the central concern of Anti-Federalists: that the organization of federal authority was essential to the preservation of liberty. Grayson's observation that the proposed amendments "are good for nothing, and I believe as many others do, that they will do more harm than benefit" reflected his concern that issues of taxation and the structure of the new federal judiciary could render all other amendments protecting personal liberty nugatory. Grayson explicitly faulted Congress for failing to address Anti-Federalist concerns about those potential threats to liberty. Taxation and impartial administration of justice had been central in the Revolutionary struggle with Britain and were crucial to the Anti-Federalist critique of the Constitution. To Grayson, the threat that the new government would overstep its bounds and use the power of taxation arbitrarily and oppressively negated any paper check on governmental authority. This threat was compounded by the nature of federal judicial power. Where the only legal recourse to challenge federal authority would be through the federal courts, without structural change mere parchment barriers could not protect liberty. Anti-Federalists' view of liberty and rights was still closely akin to the one patriot leaders espoused in 1776. Grayson's concerns about the judiciary and taxation can be understood only within the context of this tradition. Written guarantees of individual liberty were meaningless if the new government contained large, unrestricted grants of authority, especially in the area of taxation.[21]

Founding Fathers and the Adoption of the Federal Bill of Rights," *Journal of the Early Republic*, VIII, (1988), 223–251. For a general discussion of the constitutional issues at stake in the debate over the Bill of Rights, see Michael J. Lacey and Knud Haakonssen, eds., *A Culture of Rights: The Bill of Rights in Philosophy, Politics, and Law—1791 and 1991* (Cambridge, 1991).

21. William Grayson to Patrick Henry, June 12, Sept. 29, 1789, *CBR*, 248–249, 300. Leonard W. Levy cites Grayson's attitude toward the Bill of Rights as an example of Anti-Federalist indifference to individual liberty; see *Original Intent and the Framers' Constitution* (New York, 1988), 169–172. On the importance of Levy's work to scholarship on the Bill of Rights, see James H. Hutson, "The Birth of the Bill of Rights: The State of Current Scholarship," *Prologue*, XX (1988), 143–161. For two critiques of Levy's thesis, see David M. Rabban, "The Ahistorical Historian: Leonard Levy on Freedom of Expression in Early

No issue was more bitterly contested than the Anti-Federalist effort to limit the powers of the new government to those expressly delegated by the Constitution. Madison's response was an amendment: "The powers not delegated by this Constitution, nor prohibited by it to the states, are reserved to the states respectively." Anti-Federalist Thomas Tudor Tucker moved to insert the word "expressly" between "not" and "delegated." Madison responded, "This question was agitated in the Convention of Virginia; it was brought forward by those who were opposed to the Constitution, and was finally given up by them." Without the insertion of the word "expressly," many Anti-Federalists believed that amendments were of little consequence: the new government would eventually absorb all power within its orbit. Tucker's argument with Madison foreshadowed later arguments over the proper strategy for interpreting what would become the Tenth Amendment. More than any other issue, the notion of restricting the powers of the government to those expressly delegated by the Constitution would define the core around which a distinctively Anti-Federalist interpretation of federalism would evolve into a dissenting constitutional discourse.[22]

Thomas Tudor Tucker championed another Anti-Federalist cause when he sought to curtail Congress's power to levy taxes, insisting that such a power be exercised only if a state neglected to comply with congressional requisitions. Tucker echoed a common theme heard during ratification, that it was impossible to construct a system of taxation that would operate fairly on all inhabitants. The power of direct taxation would invest the federal government with too great a power: "Whenever Congress shall exercise this power, it will raise commotions in the states." Such a policy would empower the new government to weaken the states and could become a means of punishing them as well. Like many Anti-Federalists, Tucker sought to have the states determine how taxes would be assessed. Only if a state failed to provide its requisition would direct taxation become an option for Congress.[23]

American History," *Stanford Law Review,* XXXVII (1985), 795–856; Saul Cornell, "Moving beyond the Canon of Traditional Constitutional History: Anti-Federalists, the Bill of Rights, and the Promise of Post-Modern Historiography," *Law and History Review,* XII (1994), 1–28. The perspective of legal scholar John Phillip Reid is crucial to understanding the way that Anti-Federalists conceptualized liberty; see his *Constitutional History of the American Revolution: The Authority of Rights* (Madison, Wis., 1986), and *The Concept of Liberty in the Age of the American Revolution* (Chicago, 1988).

22. *Gazette of the United States* (New York), Aug. 22, 1789 (*CBR,* 193); *Congressional Register,* Aug. 18, 1789 (*CBR,* 197); Madison's Resolution, June 8, 1789 (*CBR,* 14).

23. *Gazette of the United States,* Aug. 26, 1789 (*CBR,* 207).

Another important Anti-Federalist concern was the threat posed by federal oversight of elections. Aedanus Burke sought an amendment that would ensure that "Congress shall not alter, modify or interfere in the times, places or manner of holding elections of senators or representatives, except when any state shall refuse, or neglect, or be unable by invasion or rebellion to make such election." This was not the only concern about representation under the Constitution. Anti-Federalists also were concerned that, once elected, even the most virtuous representatives might be corrupted. Simply correcting the dangers posed by federal oversight of elections was only a partial solution. Equally important was the the effort to bind legislators through the use of instructions. Tucker moved that the right of assembly be linked to a right to instruct representatives. Gerry supported the move and argued that not only should such a right be protected but that it should be augmented by a right to bind representatives to particular positions. Aedanus Burke supported the measure, arguing that, without it and other substantial changes in the Constitution, it was unlikely that amendments would give "satisfaction to our constituents."[24]

State control of the militia was another Anti-Federalist concern that resurfaced. Elbridge Gerry reminded members of Congress of the indispensable role that a militia played in a republican government. "What, sir, is the use of a militia? It is to prevent the establishment of a standing army, the bane of liberty." The importance of this issue was difficult to overstate. "Whenever government[s] mean to invade the rights and liberties of the people, they always attempt to destroy the militia, in order to raise an army upon their ruins." Gerry sought to define the role of the militia such that it would continue to be a creature of the states. The proposal to exempt individuals with religious scruples from having to serve in the militia struck Gerry as a dangerous concession of power to the new government. "This clause would give an opportunity to the people in power to destroy the constitution itself. They can declare who are those religiously scrupulous, and prevent them from bearing arms." Having disarmed the militia, it would be easy to create a powerful standing army. A sacred tenet of republican faith was that standing armies were dangerous to liberty, and Gerry feared that the language of the proposed amendment opened that door.[25]

Throughout the debate over amendments, Anti-Federalist congressmen sought to secure structural changes that would augment the power of the

24. *House Journal,* 161 (*CBR,* 35); *Congressional Register,* Aug. 15, 1789 (*CBR,* 165–166, 175).
25. *Congressional Register,* Aug. 17, 1789 (*CBR,* 182).

states and to block any wording that might provide the new government with a pretext for expanding its authority. In every instance Madison and his allies effectively blunted the Anti-Federalist agenda.

Anti-Federalists were not satisfied with Madison's amendments. Elbridge Gerry reminded his fellow congressmen, "Those who were called anti-federalists at that time, complained that they had injustice done them by the title, because they were in favor of a Federal Government, and the others were in favor [o]f a national one." A number of prominent Anti-Federalists, including Gerry, believed that the amendments adopted by the First Congress failed to achieve the structural changes necessary to protect the rights of individuals and the power of the states. Still, few, if any, prominent Anti-Federalist politicians were willing to challenge the legitimacy of the Constitution, a move that would have undermined the new government.[26]

It is easy to understand the dissatisfaction of many Anti-Federalists with the final form of the Bill of Rights presented by Congress. In the view of Aedanus Burke, those amendments "likely to be adopted by this house, are very far from giving satisfaction to our constituents." The amendments adopted were not "those solid and substantial amendments which the people expect; they are little better than whip-syllabub, and frothy and full of wind, formed only to please the palate, or they are like a tub thrown out to a whale, to secure the freight of the ship and its peaceable voyage."[27]

Richard Henry Lee, like other Anti-Federalists, assessed the amendments approved by Congress even less optimistically. "The idea of subsequent Amendments was delusion altogether, and so intended by the greater part of those who arrogated to themselves the name of Federalists." He echoed the arguments of his fellow Virginians: "The great points of free election, Jury trial in criminal cases much loosened, the unlimited right of Taxation, and Standing Armies in peace, remain as they were. Some valuable Rights are indeed *declared*, but the powers that remain are very sufficient to render them nugatory at pleasure." Lee's judgment reflected the Anti-Federalist belief that, without serious structural change, a declaration of rights would remain a flimsy barrier against encroachments on popular liberty.[28]

Some Anti-Federalists were more sanguine, and George Mason was more optimistic than many: "I received much Satisfaction from the Amendments to the federal Constitution, which have lately passed the House of Represen-

26. *Annals of Congress*, I, 731.
27. *Gazette of the United States*, Aug. 19, 1789 (*CBR*, 175).
28. Richard Henry Lee to Patrick Henry, Sept. 14, 1789 (*CBR*, 295).

tatives." Yet, even Mason believed that such amendments were still woefully inadequate on a number of points:

> With two or three further Amendments such as confining the federal Judiciary to Admiralty and Maritime Jurisdiction, and to Subjects merely federal—fixing the Mode of Elections either in the Constitution itself (which I think would be preferable) or securing the Regulation of them to the respective States—Requiring more than a bare Majority to make Navigation and Commercial laws, and appointing a constitutional amenable Council to the President, and lodging with them most of the Executive Powers now rested in the Senate—I cou'd chearfully put my Hand and Heart to the new Government.[29]

Mason reiterated the Anti-Federalists' concerns about the structural defects of the new government, particularly their fears that the judiciary represented a palpable threat and that the new Constitution failed to provide adequate representation.

It was not only Anti-Federalists who viewed the final amendments as little more than a political expediency. Federalist George Clymer wrote to Tench Coxe, describing "Madison's amendments" as a mere placebo: "Like a sensible physician," Madison "has given his malades imaginaires bread pills powder of paste and neutral mixtures to keep them in play." Thus, even some influential Federalists supported the view that Madison's amendments were designed to assuage Anti-Federalist fears without answering Anti-Federalist objections.[30]

Anti-Federalists were united in seeking substantial amendments to the Constitution. Understanding the logic of their demand for a Bill of Rights is essential in order to appreciate their reaction to the draft proposed by James Madison. The final form adopted by Congress failed to remedy many of the most serious defects identified by Anti-Federalist critics. That Anti-Federalists were dissatisfied with the version of amendments did not mean that their earlier support for a Bill of Rights was hollow or a cynical maneuver. Their disappointment made perfect sense, given their beliefs that liberty could be protected only in a properly structured federal system.

With the controversy over amendments concluded, the stage was set for a new political debate. With the amended Constitution now firmly in place, the most pressing issue facing former Federalists and Anti-Federalists was

29. George Mason to Samuel Griffin, Sept. 8, 1789 (*CBR*, 292).
30. George Clymer to Tench Coxe, June 28, 1789 (*CBR*, 255).

how to interpret the new frame of government. The old divisions between Anti-Federalists and Federalists did not disappear, but were radically transformed by the conclusion of the debate over amendments. The last remaining issue directly inherited from ratification was now settled. Increasingly, the struggle turned on how the Constitution would be interpreted by citizens, Congress, and the courts.

One of the most interesting sources for charting the gradual transition from a distinctively Anti-Federalist style of opposition to a new Democratic-Republican constitutional opposition is the detailed diary kept by Senator William Maclay of Pennsylvania. A supporter of the Constitution in 1787–1788 and a Democratic-Republican during the 1790s, Maclay's observations about politics provide important clues to the evolution of political discourse in this period. Early in his diary, Maclay described Virginia's Richard Henry Lee as "a notorious Antifederalist" and Massachusetts's Elbridge Gerry as "highly Antifederal." Yet, as new issues came before Congress, Maclay's description of the terms of political debate changed. He noted the emergence of a new group, which he described as the "Court party." This group was committed to strengthening the executive branch and generally expanding the powers of the federal government. Maclay even found himself in agreement with the "notorious Antifederalist" from Virginia, Lee. Maclay was flattered that Lee had adopted his own argument against this new, emerging court party. Maclay's shifting response to Lee suggests an erosion of the older lines of political controversy. The emergence of new divisions and alliances did not completely obliterate old animosities. While Maclay showed considerable sympathy for Lee, he took exception to William Grayson's suggestion that the court party was merely carrying forward the designs of the original supporters of the Constitution. Having himself supported the Constitution, Maclay rejected this argument. He thought Grayson's reference to Patrick Henry's charge that "consolidation is the object of the New Government" was "remarkable." Certainly, not all former Anti-Federalists were of a single mind in interpreting new developments in Congress. Clearly, Lee's more conciliatory approach seemed more likely to win over those former Federalists who opposed the emerging "court interest." That Maclay sided with the former Anti-Federalists in opposing the court faction did not mean that he had adopted Anti-Federalist principles. Maclay clearly believed that new political divisions had emerged in Congress. For many Anti-Federalists, the actions of the court faction vindicated their earlier stance during ratification; the most politically astute realized that it was vital to forge a working alliance with those members of the old Federalist coalition who were alarmed by the rise of a court-style political faction. Doubtless, for some, such a move grew out of political expediency, but for others it arose out of a recognition that some who supported the Constitution might not have intended to create a court-style government.[31]

Maclay was especially puzzled by the newfound affection for British government expressed by members of the court party. He was particularly confused by the "conduct of [William] Patterson," who had "been characterized to me as a Staunch Revolution man and Genuine Whig." Despite this reputation, Patterson "has in every republican Question deserted and in some instances betrayed Us." A clear pattern had emerged in the First Congress, and Maclay sincerely believed that "the desi[gns] of a certain party" were to use "the General Power to carry the Constitution into effect by a constructive interpretation." This strategy "wou[l]d extend to every Case That Congress may deem necessar[y] or expedient." In Maclay's view, the Supreme Court's interpretation of the Constitution proved to be an "open point," an "unguarded pass" that if unchecked would render "the General Government compleatly incontrolable." Maclay was astonished that politicians boasted that they had "cheated the People" and established "a form of Government over them which none of them expected." Ultimately, Maclay believed, the arrogance of this new faction would be its undoing: "I think they have made but a bungling hand of it." In their arrogance, the supporters of the court faction had confessed their true intentions. It would now be possible to alert the people and rally those who sought to preserve the spirit of the Constitution against those who would use it as an engine of aristocratic influence. The idea that the court interest had departed from traditional Whig republican ideals and now intended to transform the Constitution through "constructive interpretation" was a stance that former Anti-Federalists could readily accept. The rise of a court "faction" made possible a rapprochement between former Anti-Federalists and many who had originally supported the Constitution.[32]

The development of the court party had profound consequences for both former Anti-Federalists and Federalists. At the same time that the court was energizing former Anti-Federalists, it was providing the basis for those original supporters of the Constitution who feared greater centralization to reassess their views of their former Anti-Federalist opponents. Once again, a common enemy effectively united what might otherwise have remained a loose and, in many respects, incompatible coalition of interests. The stage

31. Kenneth R. Bowling and Helen E. Veit, eds., *The Diary of William Maclay and Other Notes on Senate Debates*, vol. IX of *DHFFC*, 10, 50, 113–115.

32. Ibid., 114–115, 382–383.

was set for the creation of a dissenting political and constitutional movement that would draw on a rich ideological legacy that included a generous dose of Anti-Federalism.

The death of Anti-Federalism as an active political movement provided the means for resurrecting the spirit of Anti-Federalism. While the decision to assume the role of a loyal constitutional opposition was crucial to this transformation, the rehabilitation also benefited from the efforts of Thomas Jefferson and James Madison. Jefferson had conditionally supported the Constitution and was among the most outspoken proponents of incorporating a bill of rights. Madison had been one of the most outspoken supporters of the Constitution and critics of Anti-Federalism. Confronting the threat of the new court faction of Federalists, both men reassessed their views of Anti-Federalism.[33]

By 1792, Jefferson reevaluated his initial assessment of Anti-Federalist arguments. Writing to Washington, he confided, "The Antifederal champions are now strengthened in argument by the fulfilment of their predictions." By contrast, "the republican federalists who espoused the same government for its intrinsic merits, are disarmed of their weapons." Jefferson had come to believe that Anti-Federalist "prophecy" had now "become true history."[34]

A similar effort at reevaluating the legitimacy of Anti-Federalism was undertaken by James Madison in his 1792 essay "A Candid State of Parties." Madison laid out for the public his own analysis of the evolution of American political life since the Revolution. His explanation of the transition from the political situation of the 1780s to that of the 1790s was one of

33. Useful works on the character of Jeffersonian political thought include Lance Banning, *The Jeffersonian Persuasion: Evolution of a Party Ideology* (Ithaca, N.Y., 1978); Banning, "Jeffersonian Ideology Revisited: Liberal and Classical Ideas in the New American Republic," *WMQ*, 3d Ser., XLIII (1986), 3–19; Joyce Appleby, *Capitalism and a New Social Order: The Republican Vision of the 1790s* (New York, 1984); Appleby, "Republicanism in Old and New Contexts," *WMQ*, 3d Ser., XLIII (1980), 20–34; John Ashworth, "The Jeffersonians: Classical Republicans or Liberal Capitalists?" *Journal of American Studies*, XVIII (1984), 425–435. On the ideological division between Federalists and Jeffersonians, see Richard Buel, Jr., *Securing the Revolution: Ideology in American Politics, 1789–1815* (Ithaca, N.Y., 1972); John Zvesper, *Political Philosophy and Rhetoric: A Study of the Origins of American Party Politics* (New York, 1977); James Roger Sharp, *American Politics in the Early Republic: The New Nation in Crisis* (New Haven, Conn., 1993); Stanley Elkins and Eric McKitrick, *The Age of Federalism* (New York, 1993); Simon P. Newman, *Parades and the Politics of the Street: Festive Culture in the Early American Republic* (Philadelphia, 1997).

34. Thomas Jefferson to George Washington, May 23, 1792, in Merrill D. Peterson, ed., *Thomas Jefferson: Writings* (New York, 1984), 988.

the most important contemporary discussions of how Anti-Federalism had been transformed into a loyal opposition.[35]

Madison contrasted the local character of partisan politics during the Confederation period with the national scope of politics during the struggle over ratification. The debate over the Constitution, he maintained, had transformed the nature of American politics: "The Federal Constitution, proposed in the latter year, gave birth to a second and most interesting division of the people. Every one remembers it, because every one was involved in it." As for the Federalists of 1788, Madison wrote, "Among those who embraced the Constitution, the great body were unquestionably friends to republican liberty; tho' there were, no doubt, some who were openly or secretly attached to monarchy and aristocracy." While defending the supporters of the Constitution, Madison conceded an essential point that had been central to the Anti-Federalist critique: the desire of some Federalists to use the Constitution as the instrument of an aristocratic counterrevolution. At the same time that Madison revised his estimation of the Federalists, he conceded a new respect for the Anti-Federalists. Madison's assessment of the Anti-Federalists was unusually generous, given his frustration with them during ratification. "Among those who opposed the constitution, the great body were certainly well affected to the union and to good government, tho' there might be a few who had a leaning unfavourable to both." The adoption of the Constitution, Madison asserted, had effectively rendered these older labels obsolete.[36]

---

35. Two rather different interpretations of the trajectory of James Madison's constitutional thinking have emerged in scholarly discussion of Madison. Jack N. Rakove, "The Madisonian Moment," *University of Chicago Law Review*, LV (1988), 473–505, stresses Madison's pragmatic responses to changing circumstances but highlights his nationalism. A different view of Madison, stressing his intellectual consistency and qualified support for nationalism, may be found in Lance Banning, *The Sacred Fire of Liberty: James Madison and the Founding of the Federal Republic* (Ithaca, N.Y., 1995). Banning questions the view that Madison became more Anti-Federalist in his thinking about federalism. Among those scholars who see Madison moving toward a more Anti-Federalist viewpoint are Marvin Meyers, *The Mind of the Founder: Sources of the Political Thought of James Madison*, rev. ed. (Hanover, N.H., 1981), xviii, xli; Elkins and McKitrick, *The Age of Federalism*, 270. For two other efforts to deal with the transformation of Madison's thought in the 1790s, see Douglas W. Jaenicke, "Madison v. Madison: The Party Essays v. 'The Federalist Papers,' " in Richard Maidment and John Zvesper, eds., *Reflections on the Constitution: The American Constitution after Two Hundred Years* (Manchester, 1989), 116–147; Zvesper, "The Madisonian Systems," *Western Political Quarterly*, XXXVII (1984), 236–256.

36. James Madison, "A Candid State of Parties," *National Gazette* (Philadelphia), Sept. 22, 1792 (William T. Hutchinson et al., eds., *Papers of James Madison* (Chicago, Charlottesville, Va., [1962–], XIV, 370–372).

Madison preferred to characterize the two sides as the "antirepublican party" and the "Republican party." The "antirepublican party," Madison observed, included those who "from natural temper, or from the habits of life are, more partial to the opulent than to the other classes of society." The leaders had "debauched themselves into a persuasion that mankind are incapable of governing themselves" and "that government can be carried on only by the pageantry of rank, the influence of money and emoluments, and the terror of military force."[37]

The willingness of former Anti-Federalists to support the amended Constitution allowed Madison and Jefferson to recognize the legitimacy of Anti-Federalist fears. The creation of a Democratic-Republican opposition was an amalgam of ideas drawn from various parts of Anti-Federalism and those more closely associated with Jefferson and Madison.[38]

While Jefferson and Madison worked to forge a new coalition that included former opponents of the Constitution, Federalists seized the opportunity that this new alliance created to attack the opposition. Federalists freely used the charge of Anti-Federalism to undermine their opposition. The term "Anti-Federalist" continued to be a political slur. In the controversial elections of 1792, the charge of Anti-Federalism once again circulated to discredit opposition to the Federalist agenda. The choice of the popular Anti-Federalist politician George Clinton to oppose John Adams for the vice-presidency served only to intensify the debate over the continuing status of Anti-Federalism in American politics. The list of evils paraded before the people by Clinton's enemies was lengthy. The New Yorker's Anti-Federalism was linked to a variety of other unsavory characters opposed to true republican principles, including "demagogues, democrats, mobocrats, non-contents, dis-contents, mal-contents, enemies to the government, hostile to the constitution, friends of anarchy, haters of good order, promoters of confusion, exciters of mobs, sowers of sedition." In response, Clinton supporters strenuously insisted that no virtuous citizen in America would claim to be an Anti-Federalist if that meant opposing the amended Constitution.[39]

Former Anti-Federalists worked hard to stress that the original opponents of the Constitution were now its greatest supporters. William Findley cap-

37. Ibid.
38. Ibid.
39. For a useful discussion of this campaign, see Sharp, *American Politics in the Early Republic*, 56–57. On the use of the epithet "Anti-Federalist," see Donald Stewart, *The Opposition Press of the Federalist Period* (Albany, N.Y., 1969), 43, 321, 452. On the effort to discredit Clinton by charging him with Anti-Federalist sympathies, see John P. Kaminski, *George Clinton: Yeoman Politician of the New Republic* (Madison, Wis., 1993), 229–239.

tured the attitudes of many former opponents when he rejected the present validity of the label "Anti-Federalist," sharing the view of most Anti-Federalists, who were never comfortable with the label in the first place. Anti-Federalists had always maintained that they were the true supporters of federalist ideas. Eager to rid themselves of the opprobrium attached to the epithet "Anti-Federalist," they still adhered to many of the same constitutional principles. Findley argued that the term "Anti-Federalism" had become an anachronism: it deserved an honorable place in history, but it no longer was useful in the political struggles of the post-Constitution period. "The artful cry of the danger of antifederalism is gradually ceasing to have its effect," he was happy to report. "The more the people examine, the more they are convinced, that no body of antifederalists exists in the United States, and that no design for overturning the government has been entertained since the commencement of its operation." No former Anti-Federalist wished to oppose the amended Constitution; the goal was to maintain a loyal opposition that would actually preserve the Constitution against its current enemies. The key was to limit the government to those powers that the people acting through their state conventions had intended to cede to the federal government.[40]

Even as Findley acknowledged the merits of the amended Constitution, he reiterated his fear about the continuing danger of the Federalist agenda. If anything, that program appeared more sinister than in the predictions made in 1787.

> Those who opposed adopting the government without amendments, in their zealous criticism on the Constitution, said the time might come, when an insidious faction would get into the legislature, and expound these expressions in such a manner as to bottom a subversion of the governments on them; but those who advocated the Constitution in the State Convention, pronounced this apprehension to be absurd.

Findley not only felt that Anti-Federalist warnings had been prescient; he was somewhat astonished that this view was shared by many so others. Neither party expected "that what the one thought might possibly happen at some future period, and the other believed to be impossible, should be realized so soon."[41]

Most Anti-Federalists followed Findley's explanation of the nature of

40. A Citizen [William Findley], *A Review of the Revenue System Adopted by the First Congress under the Federal Constitution* . . . (Philadelphia, 1794), 116.

41. Ibid., 74.

Anti-Federalist opposition to the Constitution: "Those who were designated antifederalists when the Constitution was in a probationary state, were not opposed to a Federal government, but . . . they objected to the proposed instrument as not being defined with that precision, nor guarded with those restraints that were necessary." He was quick to add that the majority of Americans shared this view, and the demands for amendments by the states demonstrated that this was "the general opinion in the majority of the states." Anti-Federalists sought "greater precision in the definition of the powers, and more explicit guards were recommended." Once those objections were "removed, those who had been called antifederalists are not only well satisfied, but zealously attached to the government." Although Findley was satisfied with the amended Constitution, he retained some concerns. The failure of the amendments to eliminate all Anti-Federalist concerns, to restrain those sections of the Constitution that sanctioned broad grants of authority to the federal government, worried Findley. With amendments adopted, "the monarchical party," Findley remarked, was forced to place its hopes in "the ambiguity of the Constitution." The adoption of the Constitution necessarily inaugurated a debate over the politics of constitutional interpretation, because amendments had not prevented the danger from constructive interpretations.[42]

Despite the intensity of Anti-Federalist opposition to the Constitution, no Anti-Constitution party emerged after ratification. With the demise of the second-convention movement, Anti-Federalists turned their attention to seeking office under the new government. Federalist efforts to discredit Anti-Federalists only further diminished the likelihood of a distinctive Anti-Federalist party's emerging. Instead, Anti-Federalists set about becoming a loyal opposition. A number of other factors facilitated this transformation. The rapid adoption of the Bill of Rights, even if it failed to satisfy many Anti-Federalists, deprived them of an important rallying point. Reverence for the principles of constitutionalism and a belief that, when properly amended, the new frame of government would effectively protect liberty further weakened the chances of an Anti-Federal party's forming. The respect accorded George Washington, the new president, also worked against continued opposition. When coupled with renewed economic prosperity, all of those factors helped promote the formal demise of Anti-Federalism. Yet, though Anti-Federalism did not generate an Anti-Constitution party, the term "Anti-Federalist," the various texts produced by the Anti-Federalists during

42. Ibid., 116, 117.

ratification, and the alternative constitutional discourses that shaped Anti-Federalism did not simply disappear. The emergence of a court faction among Federalists caused many former supporters of the Constitution to re-think the original Anti-Federalist critique. The efforts of former Federalists, most notably James Madison, and former Anti-Federalists, such as William Findley, were crucial to the creation of a Democratic-Republican opposition. That loyal opposition drew important ideas and rhetorical themes from Anti-Federalism and adapted them to the exigencies of political conflict in the 1790s.[43]

43. For a useful overview of all these points, particularly the last factor, see Lance Banning, "Republican Ideology and the Triumph of the Constitution, 1789 to 1793," *WMQ,* 3d Ser., XXXI (1974), 167–188.

CHAPTER 6 :

ANTI-FEDERALIST

VOICES WITHIN

DEMOCRATIC-

REPUBLICANISM

Areas that had been strongly Anti-Federalist in 1788 would in the 1790s cast their votes for Democratic-Republicanism in key states such as Virginia, New York, and Pennsylvania. Many of the most influential figures in this movement had been vocal Anti-Federalists, and those spokesmen were influential at both the state and national level. Men such as John Taylor, William Findley, and Albert Gallatin were especially effective at getting their message into print and influencing public debate. Publishers Eleazer Oswald and Thomas Greenleaf continued to provide a platform for those ideas. The *Independent Gazetteer* in Philadelphia and the *New-York Journal,* the two papers most sympathetic to the Anti-Federalist cause, became leading voices of opposition to the Federalist agenda, and other papers joined them. Oswald also published some of the most important pamphlets critical of Federalist policy, including works by John Taylor and George Logan. As a result of these efforts, many Anti-Federalist ideas and themes would inform political and constitutional debate through the decade.[1]

1. The two best state studies demonstrating the continuities between Anti-Federalism and Jeffersonianism at the state level are Alfred F. Young, *The Democratic Republicans of New York: The Origins, 1763–1797* (Chapel Hill, N.C., 1967); Richard R. Beeman, *The Old Dominion and the New Nation, 1781–1801* (Lexington, Ky., 1972). For a more general regional assessment of the Upper South, see Norman K. Risjord, *Chesapeake Politics, 1781–1800* (New York, 1978). A number of the most influential and interesting figures within the Democratic-Republican movement had either been Anti-Federalists or acknowledged a debt to Anti-Federalist ideas. On the importance of these individuals, see Robert E. Shalhope, "Republi-

Although there were important commonalities, it would be a mistake to conflate Democratic-Republicanism and Anti-Federalism. Democratic-Republicanism also included many who had supported the Constitution in 1788, most notably James Madison and Thomas Jefferson. During ratification Madison had been a vocal opponent of Anti-Federalism. Jefferson stood on the sidelines in France during ratification, steering a course somewhere between the two opposing camps. Both men came to reassess Anti-Federalism. Democratic-Republicanism also attracted other groups that had supported the Constitution, including urban artisans. What had seemed wild exaggeration in 1788 was becoming a terrifying reality. The Federalist agenda and political program to strengthen the new federal government seemed to fulfill the ominous predictions made by Anti-Federalists during ratification. This new alliance in opposition to the Federalists during the 1790s was even more heterogeneous than Anti-Federalism had been.

Uniting the diverse coalition that rose in opposition to the Federalist agenda was a daunting task. If anything, the difficulties confronting Democratic-Republicans were more intimidating than those faced by Anti-Federalists, but the Democratic-Republicans would prove far more effective organizers. In part, their success was due to their recognition that control of the public sphere was crucial. In contrast to Anti-Federalists, Democratic-Republicans made a concerted effort to create a network of newspapers and political societies to help spread their message and increase public awareness about political matters. In addition, they founded a semiofficial publication, the *National Gazette,* to help refine and spread their message. Of equal importance was the creation of dozens of political societies, committed to educating the public and disseminating information. The Democratic-Republicans turned their attention to the public sphere to generate an effective opposition to Federalists intent on undermining liberty. Democratic-

canism, Liberalism, and Democracy: The Political Culture of the New Nation," in Milton M. Klein, Richard D. Brown, and John B. Hench, eds., *The Republican Synthesis Revisited: Essays in Honor of George Athan Billias* (Worcester, Mass., 1992), 37–90. On the ideological continuities between Anti-Federalism and Jeffersonianism, see John Zvesper, *Political Philosophy and Rhetoric: A Study of the Origins of American Party Politics* (New York, 1977). On republicanism, see Lance Banning, *The Jeffersonian Persuasion: Evolution of a Party Ideology* (Ithaca, N.Y., 1978), and "The Persistence of Anti-Federalism after 1789," in Richard Beeman, Stephen Botein, and Edward C. Carter II, eds., *Beyond Confederation: Origins of the Constitution and American National Identity* (Chapel Hill, N.C., 1987), 295–314; James Roger Sharp, *American Politics in the Early Republic: The New Nation in Crisis* (New Haven, Conn., 1993). On agrarian democracy, see Richard E. Ellis, *The Jeffersonian Crisis: Courts and Politics in the Young Republic* (New York, 1971).

Republicans took the inchoate notion of the public sphere of Anti-Federalists and fashioned it into a vital part of their political and constitutional philosophy. A vigorous public sphere provided a counterbalance to the Federalist vision of a strong central government.[2]

Hamiltonianism and the Democratic-Republican Opposition

Democratic-Republicans opposed Alexander Hamilton's aggressive economic agenda, which was designed to place the new government on a solid economic basis and forge strong ties between the new government and financial interests. One of the cornerstones of this plan was assumption of the Revolutionary war debt of the states, a plan intended to strengthen the financial power of the federal government. Another aspect called for redeeming the full value of depreciated federal securities, which would have generated enormous profit for speculators. To facilitate this economic program Hamilton and his allies also favored the creation of a national bank, which would foster confidence in the economic stability of the new government. The government would deposit its funds in the bank and supervise its operations; the directors would be drawn from private stockholders. The bank would also print and back a national currency.

The controversy over the funding issue was extremely bitter. Few, if any, mainstream politicians were willing to repudiate the war debt by failing to pay security holders. There was, however, serious disagreement over how to deal with rank speculation in securities. Many of the original holders of the securities had sold them for a fraction of their original value as government paper depreciated over the postwar period. Speculation in the heavily discounted paper instruments created a powerful constituency for redeeming the securities at face value. Hamilton and his allies made forceful arguments that the economic stability of the new nation depended on establishing sound credit, a policy that lent support to the decision to fund the debt at face value. Hamilton championed the bank as a means of stabilizing the new economy, in order simultaneously to bolster the confidence of the wealthy and draw the support of domestic and foreign creditors to the new government.[3]

2. On the organization of the Democratic-Republican opposition, see Noble E. Cunningham, Jr., *The Jeffersonian Republicans: The Formation of Party Organization, 1789–1801* (Chapel Hill, N.C., 1957), 23, 142. Cunningham downplays the vital role of former Anti-Federalists such as William Findley, John Taylor, and George Clinton.

3. The best narrative of the events of this period is Stanley Elkins and Eric McKitrick, *The*

Opposition to Hamilton provided a core around which former Anti-Federalists and many who had originally supported the Constitution could rally. Hamilton's distinctive approach to political economy threatened the values crucial to Democratic-Republicans. One of the most important dangers was the attempt to destroy the liberty essential for the survival of the public sphere. By weakening the public sphere and replacing it with a powerful central government, Hamilton would undermine the basis for opposition itself.

Former Anti-Federalists were leaders in shaping the public response to Hamilton. One of the most astonishing things about the large corpus of Anti-Federalist writing from the period 1787–1788 is the absence of systematic discussions of political economy. Relatively few authors had explored economic issues more than cursorily. Apart from a critique of excessive taxation, most Anti-Federalists provided little guidance on what sort of political economy would be compatible with their constitutional vision. Indeed, there was no common economic vision uniting Anti-Federalists. Southern Anti-Federalists such as Richard Henry Lee adhered to an agrarian vision strongly indebted to country ideology and suspicious of commerce. Elite Anti-Federalists in New England, most notably Elbridge Gerry, were procommercial, seeking to reconcile commerce with Whig republican ideals of virtue. Middling democrats, such as Federal Farmer, defended a pro-commerical ideology reflecting the ideals of merchants and independent yeomen. William Findley championed a variant of this progrowth commercialism but tempered it with a producer ideology opposing excessive concentrations of wealth. Finally, plebeians affirmed the traditions of a moral economy against the intrusion of market values. Once again, the theory of the small republic allowed individuals who might otherwise share little to support a federal system in which the preponderance of power would remain with the states. Such a system could accommodate the diverse approaches to political economy taken by Anti-Federalists.[4]

Age of Federalism (New York, 1993). On the tone of politics in this period, see John R. Howe, Jr., "Republican Thought and the Political Violence of the 1790's," *American Quarterly*, XIX (1967), 147–165; Marshall Smelser, "The Federalist Period as an Age of Passion," *AQ*, X (1958), 391–419.

4. On the political thought of Hamilton, see Gerald Stourzh, *Alexander Hamilton and the Idea of Republican Government* (Stanford, Calif., 1970). One issue that prompted much comment by Anti-Federalists was taxation; on this point see Thomas P. Slaughter, "The Tax Man Cometh: Ideological Opposition to Internal Taxes, 1760–1790," *WMQ*, 3d Ser., XLI (1984), 566–591. Efforts to reconstruct a more systematic and coherent account of Anti-Federalist political economy include Cathy D. Matson and Peter S. Onuf, *A Union of Inter-*

The most important published attacks on Hamilton's economic program were written by Democratic-Republicans who had been prominent Anti-Federalists: John Taylor of Caroline, Albert Gallatin, and William Findley. This debate also appears to have reached down into the popular plebeian world of tavern life. One of the most fascinating critiques of the Hamiltonian scheme was written by William Manning, a tavernkeeper from Billerica, Massachusetts, who provides a rare glimpse into how a self-described member of the "laboring sort" understood the issues of the 1790s. Manning stood somewhere between plebeian populism and middling democracy, appropriately for a man whose own social status was midway between the respectable middling sort and the lower sort. The analyses of Federalist political economy by these four individuals demonstrate the continuing importance of the class and regional differences inherited from Anti-Federalism. While united in their opposition to Hamilton, each of these men drew upon different variants of Anti-Federalist discourse to voice his disagreement. John Taylor advocated an agrarian political economy. Albert Gallatin was a spokesman for the commercial interests of the Middle Atlantic and New England. William Findley championed those middling democrats whose vision was less commercial than Gallatin's. William Manning upheld the traditions of the moral economy more closely associated with plebeian culture.[5]

---

ests: Political and Economic Thought in Revolutionary America (Lawrence, Kans., 1990); and John E. Crowley, The Privileges of Independence: Neomercantilism and the American Revolution (Baltimore, 1993), both of which stress the commercial character of Anti-Federalist thought. For studies that stress the agrarian character of Anti-Federalism, see Jackson Turner Main, The Antifederalists: Critics of the Constitution, 1781–1788 (Chapel Hill, N.C., 1961); Main, Political Parties before the Constitution (Chapel Hill, N.C., 1973); Van Beck Hall, Politics without Parties: Massachusetts, 1780–1791 (Pittsburgh, 1972); Roger H. Brown, Redeeming the Republic: Federalists, Taxation, and the Origins of the Constitution (Baltimore, 1993).

5. On Findley's political thought, see Gordon S. Wood, "Interests and Disinterestedness in the Making of the Constitution," in Beeman, Botein, and Carter, eds., Beyond Confederation, 69–109; Shalhope, "Republicanism, Liberalism, and Democracy," in Klein, Brown, and Hench, eds., The Republican Synthesis Revisited, 37–90. On Manning, see Michael Merrill and Sean Wilentz, eds., The Key of Liberty: The Life and Democratic Writings of William Manning, "A Laborer," 1747–1814 (Cambridge, Mass., 1993). Merrill and Wilentz express puzzlement over the fact that Manning seemed happy with the amended Constitution even though his townsmen voted against the Constitution in 1788. This stance seems perfectly consistent with the vast majority of other Anti-Federalists. Indeed, Anti-Federalists such as William Findley made exactly the same distinction as Manning did, differentiating between the Constitution as originally proposed and the final, amended version.

In a series of newspaper essays and pamphlets from 1793 through 1795, John Taylor hammered away at the corrupt policies inaugurated by Federalists. Beginning with a series of essays signed "Franklin" in the *National Gazette,* Taylor's attack on Hamilton fused the antiaristocratic elements of Anti-Federalism with a critique of finance drawn from traditional English country polemics. In Taylor's view, the Hamiltonian program was "literally copied from the monarchical system of Britain." Such a system "may produce a revolution as complete, as if it had been effected by force." Taylor attacked the creation of an English system of finance, which would inevitably corrupt the American political system. The supporters of the bank were "a powerful faction" whose designs were "dangerous to the rights and interests of the community" and who were intent on "the establishment of an institution, in express violation" of the Constitution, that would become "an engine of corruption" and ultimately result in the collapse of "the foundation of public virtue."[6]

Taylor's hostility to the bank, grounded in an agrarian vision deeply suspicious of commerce and finance, lambasted the "paper fabrick" that supported a "paper interest" inimical to the commonweal. This artificial interest, or paper faction, brought together individuals committed to the "private and exclusive benefit of themselves and not for the public good." The paper interest included "not only stockholders themselves, but public officers who wish for higher salaries, paper men and speculators who will gain by an increase of the public debt." All of these groups lusted "after aristocracy and monarchy." Taylor detected in the new Hamiltonian program a systematic conspiracy to destroy the Constitution's republican principles and replace them with a "court-style" English government. He outlined the main goals of this plot with logical precision:[7]

The funding system was intended to effect, what the bank was contrived to accelerate. 1. Accumulation of great wealth in a few hands. 2. A political moneyed engine. 3. A suppression of the republican state assemblies, by

6. *National Gazette* (Philadelphia), Feb. 20, 1793; [John Taylor], *An Examination of the Late Proceedings in Congress, respecting the Official Conduct of the Secretary of the Treasury* (Richmond, Va., 1793), 27. On Taylor's political thought, see Robert E. Shalhope, *John Taylor of Caroline: Pastoral Republican* (Columbia, S.C., 1980); and, more generally, Banning, *Jeffersonian Persuasion,* 195.

7. [John Taylor], *Definition on Parties; or, The Political Effects of the Paper System Considered* (Philadelphia, 1794); [Taylor], *An Enquiry into the Principles and Tendency of Certain Public Measures* (Philadelphia, 1794), 85–87.

depriving them of political importance, resulting from the imposition and dispensation of taxes.[8]

Taylor's critique drew on the tradition of country polemics. There was, however, an important Anti-Federalist strain in his constitutionalism, clear in the third point of his indictment. Taylor's political vision was rooted in an Anti-Federalist conception of federalism. The court faction's use of taxation was designed to reduce the state assemblies to mere ciphers in a consolidated system of government. State legislatures, the only truly representative bodies in the new federal system, would be rendered impotent by the machinations and manipulations of the paper interest. Taylor believed that state legislatures provided a means of collecting the will of the people and improving it through reasoned debate. In this regard, the state legislatures expressed the deliberative will of the people. Hamilton's system threatened this vital means of collecting and organizing public opinion. In short, Taylor argued that Hamilton's program would undermine the public sphere itself.

One of the most important aspects of Taylor's constitutional theory was his exposition of states' rights. Indeed, in his attack on the federal carriage tax, Taylor moved well beyond Luther Martin's variant of states' rights Anti-Federalism. Anti-Federalists feared that Congress could not enact taxes without unfairly burdening some states. Taylor revived this argument and asserted that the Constitution mandated that taxes apply uniformly to all of society's interests. Mindful that southern property, particularly slaves, might be the object of specific taxes, the Constitution had enshrined the idea that "all should feel the taxes to be imposed, with the utmost attainable degree of equality." Any departure from this principle would make one region "monarch of the rest" and risk creating "an aristocracy of states." The antiaristocratic rhetoric of Anti-Federalism was recast into a distinctive states' rights idiom. In opposition to Hamilton's scheme, which threatened to undermine the equality of the states, Taylor championed a new, more systematic theory of states' rights.[9]

Many of Taylor's country republican themes had figured prominently in Anti-Federalist rhetoric. His critique of Hamiltonian economics, however, went further than any of the polemics of 1787–1788. Such rhetoric in the 1790s became even more closely identified with Taylor's effort to recast the debate over the meaning of federalism in terms of a more systematic theory

8. [Taylor], *An Enquiry*, 47.

9. John Taylor, *An Argument respecting the Constitutionality of the Carriage Tax* . . . (Richmond, Va., [1795]), 16. See also Harry Innes to John Brown, Dec. 7, 1787 (*DHRC*, VIII, 221); and William Grayson, Speech in the Virginia Convention (X, 1374–1375, 1496).

of states' rights. The particular variant of this emerging theory reflected the views of one important segment of the Democratic-Republican opposition—southern agrarians.

Democratic-Republicanism, while important in the South, also drew on considerable support in the Middle Atlantic, where many Anti-Federalists had strong mercantile connections. The most influential spokesman was Albert Gallatin. In contrast to the polemical fervor of Taylor's published writings, Gallatin adopted a calm, detached tone in his own attack on the Hamiltonian system. His pamphlet, *A Sketch of the Finances of the United States,* contained a detailed analysis of Hamilton's financial program that not only challenged the underlying principles of Federalist economics but disputed the actual accounting procedures employed by the secretary of the Treasury.[10]

The hostility toward banks that characterized agrarian political economy was entirely absent from Gallatin. Gallatin had been an important supporter of Pennsylvania's efforts to charter its own bank, and he believed that banks could promote the public interest by facilitating economic growth. Banks were "of great commercial utility, by bringing into circulation moneys which otherwise would remain inactive." As agents of economic expansion, guided by sound and prudent policies to provide capital for all of society's citizens, banks were positive instruments of a republican political economy. Gallatin was aware that "the assistance to be received from the bank may, however, be abused both by government and by individuals." The Bank of the United States, unfortunately, had become a "political engine," and, instead of "adding to the capital of the nation," it had actually drained capital away from productive investment.[11]

Unlike Hamilton, Gallatin opposed a large funded public debt. He noted that a public debt did not "increase the existing amount of cultivated lands, of houses, of consumable commodities; it makes not the smallest addition either to the wealth or to the annual labor of a nation." Gallatin's political economy was shaped by his Genevan Protestant upbringing. His political economy shared attributes with the writings of commercial-minded Anti-Federalists: each opposed conspicuous consumption and policies that concentrated wealth in a small class of speculators. He differentiated between productive investment and financial manipulation, attacking speculators who lived "to consume, to spend more," and denounced the luxury of those

10. Albert Gallatin, *Sketch of the Finances of the United States* (1796), in Henry Adams, ed., *The Writings of Albert Gallatin,* III (Philadelphia, 1879), 69–205.

11. Ibid., 135, 145.

who made their money through such means. Gallatin's condemnation of the "elegant houses" built by speculators was based on several related assumptions. Extravagance not only encouraged corruption; it drained money away from more productive investments. Such conspicuous consumption "afford[ed] no additional revenue to the nation" and depleted capital available for other uses.[12]

Cognizant that the debt needed to be eliminated, Gallatin sought a scheme of taxation that would not burden any one region unfairly. With Taylor, Gallatin recognized that issues of federalism could not easily be disentangled from questions of political economy. America's federal system was the only means of dealing with the economic and cultural diversity of American life. He reasoned that, since tariffs were more onerous for the South, a flat per-acre land tax could be enacted that would fall more heavily on northern land, thereby equalizing the burden. The final component of his plan called for the sale of western lands, whose revenues would be applied to reduce the debt.[13]

Gallatin argued that productive investments facilitated by banks actually enriched the wealth of the nation and were useful to citizens from all social classes. The Federalist variant of banking defended by Hamilton actually amounted to a transfer of wealth to that small class of speculators who then engaged in conspicuous consumption and political machinations. Gallatin earnestly believed in a proper role for banking in a republic. It was a vision of political economy that stood in opposition to Hamiltonian economics but differed from the agrarianism of men such as John Taylor. Once again, the nature of federalism allowed individuals with quite different ideas to join together to oppose a more centralized vision of political and economic development. Gallatin's political economy fused liberal and republican ideals. It shared with liberalism a progrowth, procommercial orientation while committed to the sanctity of contractual obligation. These liberal principles, however, were tempered by a Whig republican understanding that government could direct economic development to encourage socially desirable ends. In this vision the states, not the federal government, would take the lead in economic development, a stance that was a clear inheritance from Anti-Federalism. Allowing the states to take the lead meant that Taylor's and

12. Ibid., 145–147.

13. For a good, concise overview of Gallatin's political economy, see John R. Nelson, Jr., *Liberty and Property: Political Economy and Policymaking in the New Nation, 1789–1812*, Johns Hopkins University Studies in Historical and Political Science, 105th Ser., no. 2 (Baltimore, 1987); and Edwin Gwynne Burrows, "Albert Gallatin and the Political Economy of Republicanism, 1761–1800" (Ph.D. diss., Columbia University, 1974).

Gallatin's different visions could exist alongside each other. Solutions appropriate for Virginia would not work for Pennsylvania. The genius of the federal system was to allow each of the states to organize economic activity so as to reflect their differences within America.

The federalism and localism that animated Democratic-Republican thought depended on the public sphere to knit the nation together in a manner consistent with its liberty. Gallatin opposed Hamilton's policies for creating artificial unity. In response to Hamilton's notion that a funded public debt would bind creditors to the nation, Gallatin argued that this bond was contrived and hence undesirable. It concentrated wealth in the hands of a few citizens rather than harmonized different economic interests and increased the wealth of the entire community. "So far as that interest is artificial, so far as it is distinct from the general interest, it may perhaps act against that general interest and become as pernicious as it is supposed to have been useful." The Union was now more divided by "the jealousies, the apprehensions, the discontents" created by Hamilton's program. For Gallatin, Hamilton's economic program actually undermined the ideal of union by making it more difficult to identify and cultivate the common interests of the nation. In part, Hamilton's economic agenda had corrupted the public sphere itself, preventing the type of rational exchange of information that would have allowed Americans to work in consort to unite the nation. By imposing a solution instead of allowing the states to work out their own solutions, Hamilton substituted power for the ideal of rational debate that defined the public sphere for so many middling democrats.[14]

Yet another critique of Hamiltonian economics was formulated by William Findley, who followed a different strain of middling democratic thought. The secretary of the Treasury had justified his policy as necessary to protect the honor and reputation of the nation. Findley doubted that a nation could be honorable if it violated the principles of justice and equity. In his view, honor demanded paying the original holders of Continental securities the amount they had earned for their sacrifices on behalf of the nation. He queried his readers about the fortunes of "those who had been rendered or kept poor by their meritorious and hazardous service to the public in times of national distress." The model of contractualism implicit in Hamilton's economic philosophy was incompatible with republican values. The original holders of government securities faced "unavoidable circumstances"; they were forced "to sell their claims to the wealthy for a trifle." Findley dwelt on the principles of "justice and equity," in contrast to the

14. Gallatin, *Sketch of the Finances,* in Adams, ed., *Writings,* III, 149.

"disgraceful speculation and venal bargaining" and "scramble for public securities" that characterized Hamilton's program. The emphasis on justice and equity reflected the continued importance of republican ideals about the relationship of politics to the economy. Ultimately, the economy had to serve the interest of the commonweal.[15]

Findley's belief that government should promote equity did not mean that he was not committed to an expansive economy. Indeed, part of the problem with Hamilton's program was that it would weaken the nation's finances. Hamilton's funding scheme increased the amount of debt and the need for burdensome taxes, which placed a more onerous burden on the states and their citizens. Hamilton argued that the debt would attract foreign investors and raise the value of American securities. Findley conceded that this might have a short-term benefit, but, like all artificial growth spurred by speculation, this temporary boom would be followed by an inevitable economic downturn.[16]

Findley's political economy shared with Gallatin's a progrowth ideal of economic development. Findley was certainly not an enemy to banking, as long as it intended to promote the interests of the middling sort. In contrast to Gallatin's parsimony, however, Findley favored the limited use of paper money as one such instrument of growth. Hamilton's use of the national debt had not enlarged the amount of money in circulation, nor had it encouraged individuals to invest in land, manufacturing, or the purchase of homesteads. Almost any other policy, Findley concluded, including money lent at moderate interest, would have accomplished those desirable social ends more effectively than the system of finance envisioned by Hamilton. In all of his economic suggestions, Findley sought to promote policies favorable to the middling ranks of society. Hamiltonian economics made little sense and had actually hurt the economy. The secretary of the Treasury's policies had not expanded America's markets. Findley believed that it was the middling classes who increased the productive wealth of society by their labor. Hamilton's economic policy made the wealthy richer. Ultimately, by

15. A Citizen [William Findley], *A Review of the Revenue System Adopted by the First Congress under the Federal Constitution* . . . (Philadelphia, 1794), 12, 28. On the importance of equity to eighteenth-century conceptions of law, see Peter Charles Hoffer, *The Law's Conscience: Equitable Constitutionalism in America* (Chapel Hill, N.C., 1990).

16. A Citizen [Findley], *Review of the Revenue System*, 37, 39, 77, 81, 114. Many of Findley's ideas were developed in the earlier controversy in Pennsylvania over the Bank of North America. See Matthew Carey, ed., *Debates and Proceedings of the General Assembly of Pennsylvania, on the Memorials Praying a Repeal or Suspension of the Law Annulling the Charter of the Bank* (Philadelphia, 1786). For a discussion of Centinel, see Chapter 4, above.

encouraging the wealthy to increase their consumption of imported luxuries, it had actually weakened the balance of trade. One additional problem with the debt was the incentive it had created to burden the people with new taxes. Since new taxes were needed to fund the debt, the program amounted to a transfer of wealth from the many to the few. Findley's political economy expressed the vision of middling democrats who sought to expand opportunities for a broad range of citizens. Progrowth policies had to benefit the middling sort, who were not only the numerical majority but the group most responsible for the stability of government. Political economy, in Findley's view, ought to be guided by those goals. When the marketplace threatened those values, government could step in to promote justice or equity.[17]

Findley was optimistic about the eventual outcome of the struggle against the Federalist program. His discussion drew freely from Anti-Federalist rhetoric.

> Monarchy and aristocracy cannot yet come to perfection in the American soil. Our citizens are possessed of too much information, and have too high a sense of their individual rights and independence, to suffer themselves to be governed by a junto, who have found the means of monopolizing the public wealth.[18]

The vitality of the public sphere would alert citizens to the dangers to their liberty. Despite his general optimism, Findley was concerned that Federalists continued to dominate the press and employ it to further their plans. The ability to manipulate the press was especially troubling, because it undermined the ability of the opposition to alert the public to the threats posed by Hamilton and his supporters. "The courtly gazette and others of the same character, supported by the *speculating order* in the towns where they have the greatest influence, are still industriously employed in promoting the monarchical plan, by more successful artifices." To exercise the "constitutional watchfulness" and "jealousy" necessary to prevent further Federalist usurpations, it was vital to protect the freedom of the press.[19]

Findley's diagnosis of the dangers of Federalist political economy echoed many of Gallatin's concerns. Federalist policy failed to create additional wealth, but concentrated it in the hands of a small, aristocratic class of speculators. The secretary of the Treasury's policies also imposed national solutions, in place of local ones, thereby weakening the proper basis of union

---

17. A Citizen [Findley], *Review of the Revenue System*, 12, 13.
18. Ibid., 83.
19. Ibid., 103.

and substituting an artificial set of interests that would only increase jealousy and conflict. "Our government being of a particular structure, and depending on the confidence of the people, should be carefully administered to preserve that confidence." Hamilton's program "diminished the confidence of the majority of the people, and weakened their interest in supporting the government." Findley reiterated the basic tenet of Anti-Federalist constitutionalism: government depended on the confidence of the people. Hamilton's nationalist goals undermined it and substituted a system of coercion that included higher taxes to be enforced by a powerful central government, precisely the concerns of Anti-Federalists in 1787–1788. What men like Findley had come to realize since ratification was that opposition to Hamilton depended on control of the press and the vitality of public debate.[20]

A more populist critique of Hamiltonianism was formulated by William Manning, the tavernkeeper from Billerica, Massachusetts. Manning's response to Hamilton's economic program confirms Findley's belief that the press was crucial to their cause. An avid newspaper reader, he was inspired to author his own attack on Federalist economic policy after "Reading the Many Altercations proposals and Disputes in the publick papers about funding and the Manner of paying the Continental and State Debts." Manning's world, the tavern, constituted an important part of an alternative plebeian public sphere. Here the ideas of middling democracy of men such as Findley intermingled with a more popular democratic plebeian culture. Although men like Manning clearly were avid readers of the press, they did not passively consume newspapers. Manning was an active reader who tried, unsuccessfully, on several occasions to publish his writings. Although his ideas stopped short of the most ardent plebeian populists', they were still far more radical than those of middling democrats such as Findley.[21]

20. Ibid., 125.

21. Ruth Bogin, ed., " 'Measures So Glareingly Unjust': A Response to Hamilton's Funding Plan by William Manning," *WMQ*, 3d Ser., XLVI (1989), 320, 322. For two studies of Manning that stress his radicalism, see Merrill and Wilentz, eds., *The Key of Liberty*; and, for a different view, Christopher L. Tomlins, *Law, Labor, and Ideology in the Early American Republic* (New York, 1993). For a view casting Manning as more of a democratic capitalist and protoliberal, see Gordon S. Wood, "The Enemy Is Us: Democratic Capitalism in the Early Republic," *Journal of the Early Republic*, XVI (1996), 293–308. For a study of another popular political vision with many similarities to Manning's, see Mark Haddon Jones, "Herman Husband: Millenarian, Carolina Regulator, and Whiskey Rebel" (Ph.D. diss., Northern Illinois University, 1983). On the rituals of popular political culture during this period, see Simon P. Newman, *Parades and the Politics of the Street: Festive Culture in the Early American Republic* (Philadelphia, 1997). Manning's choice of terminology is revealing;

Manning could not but "Vue with Abhorance all the arguments that have as yet bin offered in favour of paying the Hole Sume to the present holders." Such a policy violated the ideals of equity and justice and also threatened to undermine the entire political system created by the Revolution. Like Findley, Manning believed that Hamilton's argument that honor and justice demanded that current owners of securities be paid fully was spurious. To begin with, the government had already broken its promise to the original holders by allowing the securities to depreciate. The idea that the original holders had freely parted with their securities when they sold them at a discount to speculators led Manning to compare such a transaction to "persons beset with Robers" who "prudently Delivered up their purses Rather than their Lives." To the argument that funding the debt was needed to ensure that foreign creditors retain faith in the American economy, Manning protested, "Let other Nations Do as they will." Manning shared Findley's belief that honor required justice and equity, without which it would be impossible to "Maintain publick or private Credit." William Manning's beliefs were even more profoundly shaped by the values of a moral economy than were Findley's.[22]

Manning believed that Hamilton's policies had doubly injured the people. Not only had they provided a windfall for speculators, but new taxes enacted to pay off the speculators bore down hardest on the people. "It would Eventually prove the Destruction of our Dear bought Libertyes and of all the State Governments." Manning reiterated the quintessential Anti-Federalist concern that taxation could be used to destroy liberty and state authority. He accepted the orthodox Anti-Federalist argument that the state governments were more responsive to the people and hence were less likely to trample on popular liberty.[23]

Hamilton's policies were, in Manning's view, a logical extension of the original intent of the framers of the Constitution. Manning believed that the federal Constitution had established a government "at Such a Distance from the Influence of the Common people" that the wealthy "think their Interests and Influence will always be the gratest Sway." Precisely because the state governments were more responsive to the popular will, the wealthy desired to weaken state power.[24]

---

he employed the terms "laborers," "common people," "the many," and "the middling sort" as synonyms.

22. Bogin, ed., " 'Measures So Glareingly Unjust,' " *WMQ*, 3d Ser., XLVI (1989), 322.

23. Ibid., 320.

24. Ibid., 329–330. For a very similar critique by another popular voice in the 1790s, see

Manning's hostility to the bank echoed the critique of William Findley. Rather than expand the medium of circulation and lend money in amounts useful to small landowners and tradesmen, banks in Hamilton's scheme merely favored the interests of the wealthy. As Manning noted, "The Marchents are furnished with a Mediam that answers their End—while the Cuntry people have none." While individuals like Gallatin and Findley strove to maintain a sense of equality between debtors and creditors, Manning unabashedly favored the debtor classes. "If the Measure of Government Must favour one Side or the other the Debttors aught to have it." Manning's critique of Hamilton reflected a producer ideology of those at the bottom of the economic order.[25]

Manning put forth a radical labor theory of value. He discriminated between those producers who created wealth and others who lived off the wealth of the producing classes. Manning's division of society into productive and unproductive classes had important political consequences: "Those that Labour for a Living and those who git one without or as they are generally tarmed the few and the Many." Hamilton's economic plan would strengthen the power of the few at the expense of the many.[26]

Manning did not wish to see America default on her debts. To fund the debt, he proposed a scale of depreciation to fund the securities that would discriminate between original holders of securities and "Sharpers taikeing advantage of their Ignorance." Hostile to formal legal proceedings in debt cases (a stance typical of the middling and lower sort), Manning advocated that controversies over restitution be brought to local courts composed of juries empowered to decide debt cases. He also advocated the use of paper money to relieve the shortage of specie and make payment easier.[27]

Ultimately, Manning believed that the effort to subvert the ideals of liberty would be unsuccessful. He shared with other former Anti-Federalists who joined the Democratic-Republican opposition a faith in the public sphere as a bulwark against tyranny: Americans were too aware of their rights and the principles of constitutionalism to succumb to the Federalists' plans for undermining republicanism. "It is Not ondly implyed But fully Expressed in allmost all the Constitutions on the Continant—that Men are

the trial of David Brown in 1799, in Irving Mark and Eugene L. Schwaab, eds., *The Faith of Our Fathers: An Anthology Expressing the Aspirations of the American Common Man, 1790–1860* (New York, 1952), 44–47.

25. Bogin, ed., " 'Measures So Glareingly Unjust,' " *WMQ*, 3d Ser., XLVI (1989), 330–331.
26. Ibid., 329.
27. Ibid., 322, 329–330.

born free and Equel . . . and that government was Instituted to for the Common Good." The "general knowledg of these rights," particularly "amongue the Labourers," meant, "We Shall soone Unite." In Manning's view the most important countervailing force to Hamilton was, not the individual states, but the public sphere, which ensured that people were aware of their rights. For Manning, written constitutions, the widespread participation of citizens in juries, and the press all nurtured a public awareness about liberty. The vitality of the public sphere encouraged the people to remain alert and fostered a pervasive rights-consciousness. In America, constitutionalism had become tied to the existence of a public sphere of political inquiry.[28]

Strict Construction and the Original Understanding

Hamilton's proposal to charter a national bank became the first major conflict over how the new Constitution would be interpreted. The government, Hamilton claimed, enjoyed a wide latitude in interpreting it. As long as the goal pursued by the federal government was within its orbit, it was up to Congress to determine the means to accomplish its goals. Unless a power was expressly forbidden by the Constitution, and was "not immoral, or not contrary to the essential ends of political society," it was legal. In short, the federal government was limited in its ends but had tremendous discretion to employ whatever means appropriate to accomplish them.[29]

One of the most important voices to rise up in opposition to Hamiltonian constitutionalism was John Taylor, who proved himself a tireless opponent of the secretary of the Treasury. In a spate of pamphlets and newspaper essays Taylor developed a different approach to Hamiltonian broad construction. In expounding that theory, Taylor elaborated his own variant of states' rights federalism. Taylor also reiterated the textual literalism that led many Anti-Federalists to embrace a form of strict construction. He advised his readers, "Search our political scripture, consider it text by text." Such an inquiry would only confirm that the funding plan would have shocked "every convention which sifted and considered" the Constitution. Taylor's constitutional theory was grounded in a historical search for the original understanding of the Constitution embodied in individual state ratification conventions. While such a theory might shed light on the intent of particular

28. Ibid., 329–330

29. Alexander Hamilton, "Opinion on the Constitutionality of an Act to Establish a Bank" (1791), in Harold C. Syrett et al., eds., *The Papers of Alexander Hamilton*, 27 vols. (New York, 1961–1987), VIII, 63–134 (quotation on 98).

constitutional provisions, no one during ratification had anticipated the situation that Democratic-Republicans now faced. In 1788 Anti-Federalists devoted their energies to opposing the Constitution, not formulating contingency plans to meet a set of threats they hoped to avoid by defeating the Constitution. The assurances of Federalists in 1788 were of little help, since the supporters of the Constitution denied that the new government would pose a threat to liberty. Faced with Hamilton's unconstitutional policies, Taylor was forced to push the logic of Anti-Federalism beyond anything contemplated in 1788. Two avenues were available to challenge such constitutional usurpations. The first was to elect representatives to the federal government who would act consistent with the original understanding of the constitution. The other was the state legislatures. Although Taylor was vague about how that right would be exercised, he insisted, "The state legislatures have at least as good a right to judge of every infraction of the constitution, as Congress itself." Taylor's defense of the state legislatures as the appropriate guardians of federalism would become an important principle for later theorists seeking to define a dissenting constitutionalism.[30]

A different approach to Hamilton's broad construction was taken by James Madison, whose own theory of strict construction became another cornerstone of Democratic-Republican jurisprudence. In explaining the nature of constitutional interpretation, Madison noted that the overarching principle was that the grant of power to the new federal government was intended to be limited: "It is not a general grant, out of which particular powers are excepted; it is a grant of particular powers only, leaving the general mass in other hands." This interpretation was justified by the original understanding of the Constitution at the time of ratification. "So it had been understood by its friends and foes, and so it was to be interpreted." Madison appealed to an underlying consensus that had made adoption possible. In essence, Madison laid the foundation for interpreting the Constitution as the product of dialogue between Federalists and Anti-Federalists.[31]

30. [Taylor], *An Enquiry,* 48, 55. One difference between Taylor and Martin worth noting is Martin's particular concern about the interests of the small states. Virginians, by contrast, tended to fear that the interests of the more populous large states would be adversely affected under the federal system.

31. *Annals of Congress,* I, February 1791, 1896. On Madison's commitment to a form of strict construction before the drafting of the Constitution, see Lance Banning, "James Madison and the Nationalists, 1780–1783," *WMQ,* 3d Ser., XL (1983), 227–255, and "The Hamiltonian Madison: A Reconsideration," *VMHB,* XCII (1984), 3–28. Madison's theory of strict construction was not the same as the textual literalism that animated much Anti-Federalism. Madison was far less optimistic about the ability to draw a precise line that

To buttress his theory of constitutional interpretation, Madison introduced a historical component into his argument. He turned to the published records of the state ratification conventions: Pennsylvania, Virginia, and North Carolina. Madison's approach necessarily led to a reconsideration of the original Anti-Federalist critique. He asserted that, "in controverted cases, the meaning of the parties to the instrument" was the appropriate guide. A corollary of this principle was that "contemporary and concurrent expositions are a reasonable evidence of the meaning of the parties." Madison's theory of original intent opened the door for a reassessment of both the Anti-Federalist critique of the Constitution and the Federalist reply. Although the term "Anti-Federalist" remained controversial, the constitutional position taken by the Anti-Federalists during ratification enjoyed a privileged status as part of the original understanding of the Constitution. Determining the original understanding meant investigating the debates of 1787–1788, recognizing the give-and-take between the original participants in that struggle.[32]

When the issue of the constitutionality of the bank came before Congress, there were no clear rules how to construe the Constitution. Even for those who believed in consulting the ideas of the participants in the original debate, it was not clear what texts ought to be consulted. Pamphlet editions of a number of Federalist and Anti-Federalist essays were still extant in individual libraries, and a number of the state ratification convention debates had recently been printed, but the only text readily available was *The Federalist*.

A number of participants in the debate over the bank quoted from *The Federalist*. Yet, not everyone viewed Publius as the best guide to the original meaning of the Constitution. Elbridge Gerry dismissed *The Federalist* as a "political heresy." That work, Gerry observed, "was calculated to lull the conscience of those who differed in opinion with him at that time; and having accomplished his object, he is probably desirous that it may die with the opposition itself." Gerry also reminded members of Congress that the intent of the Philadelphia Convention would be impossible to reconstruct, because "the memories of different gentlemen would probably vary." Even the state ratification conventions were unreliable. The proceedings of those

---

could demarcate the separation of state from national authority. Madison was also far less suspicious of judicial review than were most Anti-Federalists. Democratic-Republican constitutionalism drew on Anti-Federalist and Madisonian interpretive strategies. For a more comprehensive discussion of the constitutional issues arising in the debate over the bank, see Benjamin B. Klubes, "The First Federal Congress and the First National Bank: A Case Study in Constitutional Interpretation," *Journal of the Early Republic*, X (1990), 19–42.

32. *Annals of Congress*, I, February 1791, 1896, 1901

conventions, "as published by the short hand writers, were generally partial and mutilated." That partiality was troubling. In the case of Pennsylvania, there was not "a word against the ratification of the Constitution; although we all know that arguments were warmly urged on both sides." Gerry's comments pointed out the serious problem attending any effort to use the memories of the participants or the published writings produced during ratification to ascertain the public mind after adoption. The problem, however, was that Democratic-Republican constitutional theory had asserted that ascertaining the public mind at the time of ratification was crucial to the meaning. This issue would prove nettlesome for those seeking to ground constitutional dissent on a solid historical foundation.[33]

The development of a theory of strict construction necessarily involved reconciling the vaguely formulated theory of constitutional interpretation associated with Anti-Federalist fears about the dangers of constructive interpretation, with a more formal approach to constitutional theory framed by Madison. Although Madison became the leading theorist of strict construction, the variant of this approach to constitutionalism forced him closer to Anti-Federalist ideas. During ratification Anti-Federalists had insisted that the government had to be restricted to those powers expressly delegated by the Constitution. Federalists, including Madison, had argued that such a move would cripple the government, placing it in the same situation as under the Articles of Confederation. After the debate over the bank, Madison came to accept the Anti-Federalist dictum that the government had to be restricted to express powers. Adopting this stance did not in Madison's view require a shift; he believed that his position was perfectly consistent with his approach since the Confederation period. He had always embraced the idea that constitutional documents ought be construed strictly. Yet circumstances now forced Madison to embrace a variant of strict construction that closely resembled that of Anti-Federalists. In the midst of the debate over ratification, Madison had dismissed the Anti-Federalist approach to strict construction, which he feared might become a rigid textual literalism. For Madison, Anti-Federalist strict construction had seemed both diffuse and unworkable. In 1788 he had derided Anti-Federalist fears that language of the Constitution invited unscrupulous politicians and judges to expand the powers of government under the cloak of constructive interpretation. The controversy over the bank changed everything. From Madison's point of view, his drift toward an Anti-Federalist approach to strict construction did not depart from his earlier position, but was a necessary adaptation to a crisis

33. Ibid., 1950, 1952–1953.

precipitated by Hamilton's actions. In effect, Hamilton undermined the assumption upon which Madison's earlier constitutional theory had rested.

In private Madison conceded that Hamilton's philosophy had changed the issues at stake. The broad construction embraced by Hamilton effectively transformed American constitutionalism. As a result it was "no longer a Govert. possessing special power taken from the General Mass, but one possessing the genl. mass with special powers reserved." There was no small irony in Madison's position. The defeat of the Anti-Federalist goal of restricting the government to powers expressly delegated had been largely orchestrated by Madison. Now faced with the threat posed by Hamilton, Madison recast his theory of strict construction in terms that were essentially Anti-Federalist. In effect, Democratic-Republicans would assert that the original understanding of the Constitution was that it was limited to powers expressly delegated. To make this case, they would turn to the original debate over the Constitution, giving particular weight to the deliberations of the various state constitutional conventions. In so doing, Democratic-Republicans helped construct the notion of a founding dialogue, an original understanding out of which Anti-Federalist fears and Federalist assurances fixed the meaning of the Constitution.[34]

Anti-Federalism was certainly not the sole source of Democratic-Republican ideas. Still, Anti-Federalism provided this movement with important spokesmen who reshaped many ideas from the original debate over the Constitution and adapted them to the struggle against Hamilton and his Federalist allies. The coalition that opposed Hamilton included a range of different positions on a variety of issues, and opposition could proceed from a diversity of political and economic assumptions. All of the class and regional tensions that plagued Anti-Federalism were reproduced within Democratic-

34. Ibid., 1896; James Madison to Henry Lee, Jan. 21, 1792, in William T. Hutchinson et al., eds., *The Papers of James Madison* (Chicago, Charlottesville, Va., 1962–), XIV, 193, Madison to Edmund Pendelton, Jan. 21, 1792, XIV, 195. Scholars have been divided over the relationship between Madison's earlier constitutional thought and his position in the 1790s. For scholars who stress Madison's Anti-Federalist turn, see Marvin Meyers, ed., *The Mind of the Founder: Sources of the Political Thought of James Madison*, rev. ed. (Hanover, N.H., 1981); Elkins and McKitrick, *The Age of Federalism*, 266, 270. More pragmatic accounts of Madison's shift are provided by Jack N. Rakove, "The Madisonian Moment," *University of Chicago Law Review*, LV (1988), 473–505; and John Zvesper, "The Madisonian Systems," *Western Political Quarterly*, XXXVII (1984), 236–256. The most forceful supporter of the idea that Madison's position was entirely consistent during this period is Lance Banning, *The Sacred Fire of Liberty: James Madison and the Founding of the Federal Republic* (Ithaca, N.Y., 1995).

Republicanism. Hamilton's aggressive economic agenda did force opposition thinkers to refine their views of the connection between politics and economics. The concept of federalism defended by those voices of opposition provided a broad umbrella under which different groups could gather to challenge Hamilton's agenda. Democratic-Republicans were also united behind a vibrant public sphere of political debate as an alternative to the strong government championed by Hamilton.

John Taylor's political economy cast Hamiltonian policy in terms that drew upon an older tradition of country polemics against the court. Hamilton's bank, he argued, had created a new "speculating order" whose interests were inimical to the people and whose power posed a threat to the state governments. The emphasis on federalism is crucial to understanding Taylor's particular effort to recast traditional agrarian political economy. Although he borrowed from an older tradition of country protest, his approach to political economy was, not static, but progrowth. Federalism was the key to reconciling these seemingly contradictory impulses. When economic decisions were left to the states, government could act to foster economic growth consistent with republican values.

Albert Gallatin defended a commercial vision compatible with middling democracy, opposing Hamilton's scheme because he believed it would not foster growth. Instead of encouraging productive economic investment, Federalist political economy furthered the efforts to centralize control of the economy and create economic institutions that would serve the interests of the wealthy. Although he shared many concerns with Gallatin, William Findley's approach to political economy was more strongly influenced by a producer ethic that acknowledged that contracts could be overridden in extraordinary circumstances. His was a hybrid of traditional republican ideas and newer liberal conceptions of the market. Findley, like Gallatin, could work with a more traditional agrarian like Taylor because of their mutual commitment to a particular ideal of federalism. When economic matters were left to the states, the economy would prosper, because it was easier to devise strategies to encourage investment and enact taxes that would not unduly burden the people. In American society, economic solutions, like political ones, had to be local to work.

Although Findley might have been one of the most democratic voices among established political figures, the spectrum of democratic political sentiment extended well beyond his version of middling democracy. At the extreme of the political spectrum were plebeian populists, for whom the notions of a moral economy continued to shape economic ideals, where government or the community could actively intervene to promote equity.

Somewhere between Findley and plebeian populists stood William Manning, who went further than most middling democrats in conceptualizing politics as a struggle between the many and the few. While Manning shared with middling democrats and gentry opponents of Hamilton a commitment to strong state governments, his political and constitutional philosophy was not primarily built upon a state-centered vision of federalism. He was far closer to plebeian populists, who looked to localities, not states, for a more active, participatory ideal of democracy.

Issues of political economy inevitably led back to the problem of federalism. All of the critiques of Hamiltonian economics interpreted the effort to centralize economic policy as a threat to their vision of federalism. The creation of a national bank not only seemed misguided from the point of view of fashioning a policy that could accommodate the diversity of American economic life, but it also threatened to create an institution that would sap the vitality of local and state politics. All of those figures believed that in the long term the bank would corrupt American politics, contributing to a further centralization. In place of centralization, Democratic-Republicans looked to the public sphere as an alternative: it could unite Americans without centralizing authority and rally the people against the Federalist agenda. The broad dissemination of information and the knowledge of their rights would, in the end, lead the people to reject the Federalist conspiracy against their liberties.

In debating the merits of Hamilton's program, the question of how to interpret the Constitution came to the fore. Anti-Federalists had placed their faith in a constitutional plain style and in the idea of written constitutions as explicit limits on governmental power. To implement this idea Anti-Federalists tried to amend the Constitution to restrict its authority to those powers expressly delegated by the states and the people. That effort to limit the new government was opposed by Madison during the debate over the Bill of Rights. There was no small irony that the man who had done so much to prevent the word "expressly" from being inserted into the Tenth Amendment would come to adopt the strategy favored by Anti-Federalists as the only means capable of preventing Federalists from subverting the Constitution. The emergence of a doctrine of strict construction, following the Anti-Federalist notion that the federal powers were restricted to those expressly delegated, came to be integral to an emerging opposition constitutional philosophy.

Anti-Federalist ideas were central to this evolving opposition discourse in another way. Against the constructive interpretation favored by Federalists, Democratic-Republicans asserted that the Constitution had to be interpreted according to the original understanding during ratification. Ascertaining that meaning required balancing the original give-and-take between Anti-Federalists and Federalists. The assurances of Federalists were read as a direct response to the fears of Anti-Federalists. The original meaning of the Constitution therefore issued from the dialogue between Anti-Federalists and Federalists.

The threat posed by the Federalists did little to lessen the differences between elites and popular spokesmen for an emerging opposition tradition. In particular, the tensions within popular thought between middling democrats and plebeians raised by ratification, though dormant, were not resolved by the decision to act as a loyal opposition. The radical potential of plebeian populism continued to smolder under the surface of the opposition.

CHAPTER 7 :

THE LIMITS OF

DISSENTING

CONSTITUTIONALISM

The Democratic-Republican Societies

If Hamilton's policies seemed to vindicate their predictions about the danger posed by the Constitution, Anti-Federalists gained little solace from their foresight. Exploiting the ambiguities within the Constitution to facilitate his economic agenda, Hamilton and his allies within the emerging court party were threatening the survival of republican government. The subversion of the Constitution through constructive interpretation alarmed Democratic-Republicans. Unchecked, Hamilton and the Federalists would destroy the federal system and create the sort of consolidated national government that Anti-Federalists had prophesied. Facing the challenges of Federalist excesses, Democratic-Republicans were forced to define a constitutional strategy to check them. The public sphere would be a linchpin in that strategy. If public opinion could be marshaled and focused, Democratic-Republicans could rein in their opponents. The press would continue to play a central role in this struggle. To reinforce those efforts, Democratic-Republicans organized themselves into political societies to spread information and rally public support for their cause. They would tap the strong localist impulses in American politics and channel them to oppose the nationalist policies of Federalists. The rise of the Democratic-Republican Societies was therefore a crucial phase in the evolution of a loyal opposition. What Democratic-Republicans could not have predicted was how controversial the societies would become. Federalist denunciations of the societies were to be expected, but Democratic-Republicans were unprepared for the way that the societies would provide a forum for plebeians to advance a far more radical political agenda. Rather than solidify opposition to the Federalists, the rise of the Democratic-Republican Societies brought Democratic-Republicanism into direct conflict with plebeian populists.

In 1793 and 1794, forty-six Democratic-Republican Societies were formed across America with the avowed intent of alerting the public mind to important political matters. The societies drew on a broad base for support, and prominent former Anti-Federalists assumed leading roles in many of them. The societies set out to reinvigorate the public sphere and provide an alternative model of how society might be united without resorting to the authoritarianism favored by Federalists.

The role of the Democratic-Republican Societies in opposition politics was succinctly stated by a circular published by the Philadelphia society: "A constant circulation of useful information, and a liberal communication of republican sentiments, were thought to be the best antidotes to any political poison, with which the vital principles of civil liberty might be attacked." The New York Democratic-Republican Society made it clear that public opinion *"is the foundation of all our liberties,* and constitutes the only solid ground-work of all our Rights." The notion of a public sphere, a realm of "careful and attentive deliberation," in which citizens were to "impartially weight the arguments on both sides of all questions, and decide as the scale of reason is found to preponderate," was a key element of the societies. Democratic-Republicanism recognized that the public sphere had been transformed into a partisan political arena, where Federalists sought to overawe their opponents. The creation of Democratic-Republican Societies was necessary because "the presses teem with publications in justification of every measure of the government, however impolitic or arbitrary." The society went further, charging that Federalists "distribute their aristocratic writings in every corner of the union."[1]

The emergence of the Democratic-Republican Societies struck Federalists as a sign that the opposition was wedded to the Jacobin doctrines of the French Revolution. Although a number of the societies praised the French Revolution, they owed less to French ideas than to an emerging political awareness about the importance of the public sphere to American constitutionalism. In this sense, the societies represented a new development in

1. Philip S. Foner, ed., *The Democratic-Republican Societies, 1790–1800: A Documentary Sourcebook of Constitutions, Declarations, Addresses, Resolutions, and Toasts* (Wesport, Conn., 1976), 66, 179.

American political thought, distinguishing themselves from earlier efforts at political organization such as the Revolutionary Committees of Correspondence. The primary goal of the societies was to shape public debate and rouse citizens to action by alerting them to public threats.

Leading Federalists, including Washington, denounced the clubs as "self-created societies," which corrupted, not revitalized, the political system. For Federalists the opposition was an example of the continuing danger of faction and mobocracy, merely carrying forward the Anti-Federalist agenda. No Federalist was more scornful of the Democratic-Republican Societies than Fisher Ames. In his view, they were little more than thinly veiled efforts to spread Anti-Federalist ideas. When Congress debated endorsing Washington's denunciations of the Democratic-Republican Societies, Ames echoed the president's condemnation. The societies had undermined government by "perverting the truth and spreading jealousy and intrigue through the land." At the root of this corrosive influence, a leveling democratic impulse had inspired Anti-Federalists and Jacobins and now inspired Democratic-Republicanism. Ames linked all three of these movements together and hoped that the excesses of the societies would finally make it possible to "purify Congress from the sour leaven of antifederalism."[2]

Democratic-Republicans denied that they were following an Anti-Federalist agenda and defended the role of the societies in spreading political knowledge and rousing citizens to assert their rights and remain politically active. The Philadelphia Democratic-Republican Society included former Anti-Federalists and individuals with no prior connection to Anti-Federalism. They objected to "the old cry of anarchy and anti-federalism." In response to the suggestion that the societies were schools of sedition, the Philadelphia society expressed its regrets that "aristocracy has ever been disposed to proclaim every real or imaginary delinquency on the part of the people, a reason for depriving them of their rights." The New York Democratic-Republican Society, which also contained a number of former Anti-Federalists, replied to the charge of Anti-Federalism in more detail. The society acknowledged that there were "many, very many, members of these societies, who were warm advocates for the adoption of the Constitution." "But suppose there were none but those who . . . *were stiled anti-*

2. Ibid., 31; Fisher Ames, "Debate over the Propriety of Replies to the President's Speeches" (1794), in W. B. Allen ed., *Works of Fisher Ames*, 2 vols. (Indianapolis, Ind., 1983), II, 1061. On the connections between Anti-Federalism and Jacobinism, see Bifrons Janus [Ames], untitled essay, Against Jacobins (1794?), II, 974–984; Ames to Christopher Gore, Dec. 17, 1794, II, 1087.

federalists." The society asked a simple question: What was Anti-Federalism? The opponents of the Constitution desired amendments that had eventually been adopted. There was now widespread agreement that those amendments had been both necessary and salutary. Anti-Federalists were in this account the most loyal supporters of the Constitution with amendments. Indeed, by calling attention to the earlier Federalist opposition to amendments, it was possible to suggest that it was, not Anti-Federalists, but their adversaries who were the enemies of liberty. The most important division was, not between Federalists and Anti-Federalists, but between the supporters and opponents of amendments. Anti-Federalists had been "branded with the disgraceful epithets of—Enemies to the Constitution and government of their country." "For what reason? Because they had the daring impertinence, the unpardonable audacity, the unprecedented effrontery, freely to declare their sentiments on a subject of equal importance to both parties, and left to the unbiased discussion of each person of every class and denomination." Democratic-Republicans used the Federalist smear campaign to demonstrate how their opponents sought to narrow political discussion and stifle free political debate. While distancing themselves from any suggestion that they continued to harbor anticonstitutional sentiments, they sought to defend the original stance taken by Anti-Federalists.[3]

The Democratic-Republican Society of Vermont responded to the charge of Anti-Federalism by confessing that there was not a single individual who had opposed the Constitution within its ranks. Nevertheless, it praised those who had been Anti-Federalists, declaring that, "though we are not antifederalists," those who had originally opposed the Constitution were "friends and supporters of government, upon true republican principles." Having defended the honor of former Anti-Federalists from Federalist slurs, Vermonters believed it would be best for all concerned if "the term was obliterated from the memory of every American." For Democratic-Republicans the principles of Anti-Federalism had to be defended, even as the term "Anti-Federalist" had to be cast aside. For them, the term had no currency: having ceased to have any value, it was best that it be retired from circulation.[4]

One of the most interesting debates over the Democratic-Republican Societies occurred in the House in response to Washington's denunciation of "self-created societies." Sympathizers defended the societies as a necessary adaptation to the problem of sustaining a republican society over a large and

3. Foner, ed., *The Democratic-Republican Societies,* 94–95, 173–174.
4. Ibid., 313.

heterogeneous territory. In particular, the societies provided a means for sparsely populated areas and those without institutions like New England's town meetings to bring together citizens to debate matters of public concern. In response to the efforts of Congress to censure the societies, Democratic-Republicans challenged the right of legislative bodies to censure popular organizations. William Giles of Virginia went further, reminding the House that the move to censure the societies was an unwarranted extension of the powers of Congress. "We are neither authorized by the Constitution, nor paid by the citizens of the United States, for assuming the office of censorship. . . . If such a clause had been inserted in the Constitution, it never would have gone through. The people never would have suffered it." A very similar argument was made by Madison to Congress: "When the people have formed a Constitution, they retain those rights which they have not expressly delegated." Madison's phrasing is revealing: the censure of the societies was an extension of government power by positive construction. The powers of Congress, Madison insisted, were restricted to those expressly delegated. This had been the position that Anti-Federalists had supported and Madison rejected during the debate over amendments. Faced with the threat of Federalists' efforts to expand the scope of government power, Madison was forced to adopt the Anti-Federalist understanding of strict construction: the powers of the federal government were limited to those expressly delegated by the Constitution.[5]

It was not only unlawful for Congress to censure the societies but unnecessary. The societies, Madison argued, will "stand or fall by the public opinion." Madison not only placed greater faith in the ability of the public sphere to police itself, but he firmly believed that, "in a Republic, light will prevail over darkness, truth over error." For Madison, public opinion was the key to the survival of republicanism in America, and, increasingly, he placed greater emphasis on it. Protecting the public sphere came to be an important part of the political and constitutional philosophy that animated Democratic-Republican opposition.[6]

5. *Annals of Congress*, I, 759, September 1794, 914, November 1794, 918, 934.

6. For a brief but thoughtful discussion of the centrality of public opinion to opposition thought in the 1790s, see Richard Buel, Jr., *Securing the Revolution: Ideology in American Politics, 1789–1815* (Ithaca, N.Y., 1972). On Madison's views of public opinion, see Chapter 10, below. On the role of voluntary societies in the 1790s and their connection to the politics of the public sphere, see John L. Brooke, "Ancient Lodges and Self-Created Societies: Voluntary Association and the Public Sphere in the Early Republic," in Ronald Hoffman and Peter J. Albert, eds., *Launching the "Extended Republic": The Federalist Era* (Charlottesville, Va., 1996), 273–359.

The Whiskey Rebellion

In 1791 Congress had followed the recommendation of Secretary of the Treasury Alexander Hamilton and passed an excise tax on whiskey. The tax fell heavily on western farmers whose well-being depended on distilling grain into spirits and was especially odious to westerners, because the government excisemen collected the tax from the producers of the grain, not the retailers who sold the whiskey. The specter of excisemen harassing farmers had been frequently invoked by Anti-Federalists during ratification. The provisions for prosecuting tax evasion also seemed to vindicate fears voiced by Anti-Federalists: tax evaders were to be prosecuted in the nearest federal court, bypassing local judges and juries.

Farmers, particularly in western Pennsylvania, were extremely resentful of the tax. Hostility to Hamilton's program smoldered, and political passions ran high in the three years after its passage, but protests against the excise had remained essentially peaceful. Denunciations of Federalist policy appeared in the press, and petitions called for the repeal of the law. The rituals of plebeian protest included the burning of excisemen in effigy. In several parts of western Pennsylvania, local Democratic-Republican Societies added their voices to the rising chorus of opposition to Hamilton's program.[7]

The tenuous peace in western Pennsylvania that had existed since 1791 was shattered in July 1794 when armed tax resisters marched on the home of tax collector John Neville. This violent encounter set in motion a chain of events: seven thousand western Pennsylvania tax protesters would march on Pittsburgh, and President Washington would call out the milita from four states to suppress the western insurrection.

The decision of the Washington administration to use troops to put down the rebellion only heightened political tensions and vindicated the worst fears of Democratic-Republicans about the nefarious designs of Hamilton and his allies. Federalists blamed the uprising on the opposition and were especially critical of the role of the Democratic-Republican Societies. In defending themselves against Federalist attacks, opposition thinkers clarified their political and constitutional positions.

The Whiskey Rebellion was pivotal in the transformation of opposi-

---

7. The best narrative account of the rebellion is Thomas P. Slaughter, *The Whiskey Rebellion: Frontier Epilogue to the American Revolution* (New York, 1986). And see also Dorothy Elaine Fennell, "From Rebelliousness to Insurrection: A Social History of the Whiskey Rebellion, 1765–1802" (Ph.D. diss., University of Pittsburgh, 1981); Robert Eugene Harper, "The Class Structure of Western Pennsylvania in the Late Eighteenth Century" (Ph.D. diss., University of Pittsburgh, 1969).

tion political and constitutional thought. The most violent and sustained popular protest since Independence, the rebellion attracted the attention of Americans from all walks of life. Reactions to it varied enormously. For Federalists, the rebellion demonstrated the dangers of opposition thought, of excessive democracy, and provided a sobering reminder of the necessity of a strong central government to counteract the powerful centrifugal forces that threatened to pull the nation apart. Washington and Hamilton blamed the Democratic-Republican Societies for agitating the public mind and fomenting antigovernment attitudes. Democratic-Republicans were divided over the meaning of the rebellion. Although most sympathized with the grievances of the rebels, few supported extralegal crowd action. Thus, for Democratic-Republicans, the rebellion was equally ominous, reaffirming the threat of plebeian populism. In place of the radical localism of plebeian populists, Democratic-Republicans championed the public sphere as a means of creating an enlightened opposition compatible with the ideals of federalism and republicanism.

The unrest was most intense in areas that had strongly supported Anti-Federalism during the struggle over ratification. Much of that unrest was in western Pennsylvania, and William Findley and Albert Gallatin, two of the most important spokesmen for that wing of Democratic-Republican opposition, assumed prominent roles in this controversy. In defending themselves against Federalist accusations, both men defended their particular variants of middling democracy and their visions of federalism. Both men also took great pains to distance themselves from the popular plebeian radicalism that supported extralegal action. Once again, as in the Carlisle riot, violence drove a wedge between the two most democratic factions within the opposition tradition.

The public controversy that swirled about after the suppression of the rebellion focused an inordinate amount of attention on how popular political meetings and political societies influenced events leading up to the rebellion. In effect, Federalists denounced the efforts by their opponents to use the public sphere for partisan purposes. Democratic-Republicans, by contrast, attacked Federalists for once again trying to substitute force for persuasion and thereby undermining the structure of the public sphere and the principles of liberty and federalism.

Gallatin and Findley both defended their involvement in public meetings, at which, they claimed, their actions were not only legal but necessary. In the case of the Whiskey Rebellion, Gallatin drew a sharp line between "publication of sentiments and acting." He went further: "We must distinguish between an opinion merely that this or that measure is wrong," a proper and legitimate exercise of freedom of speech, "and an opinion to which is annexed a declaration that those who give that opinion mean to act in a certain manner or advise others to act." A number of the protesters in western Pennsylvania expressly linked their actions to the Revolutionary struggle against Britain, in some cases even resurrecting the custom of raising liberty poles as a form of symbolic protest. Gallatin's view of the raising of liberty poles during the protests over the excise reflected this distinction between thought and action. Those actions might be taken as "tokens of sedition," but might also in some cases have been "a harmless frolic." As far as public meetings were concerned, Gallatin asserted that it was vital for men of moderate temperament to attend such meetings precisely because they could act as a check on those "violent characters" who took a leading role at them. "Moderate men and friends to order were cautious" and unlikely to attend, Gallatin noted. Gallatin's analysis of politics out-of-doors reflected the centrality that a particular conception of the public sphere had come to play in the thinking of Democratic-Republicans. Gallatin blamed the insurrection on "ignorant men" and defended the participation of sober men of moderate temperament. In Gallatin's opinion the involvement of such men, of middling fortune and democratic views, was absolutely necessary if the public sphere was to function as a stabilizing influence. Political meetings were, according to him, not the cause of unrest, but one of the most important means for controlling violence. Without the participation of men like Gallatin, public meetings could not exercise their indispensable role as vehicles for collecting and improving the public mind.[8]

Gallatin was eager to prevent the Federalists from using the disturbances in the West as a pretext for pursuing their goal of expanding the power of the national government. He reminded the Pennsylvania Assembly, "Despotic governments eagerly seize every opportunity which the faults and the temporary folly of any part of the nation may afford them, in order to add new energy to their powers and to justify the arbitrary exercise of a jurisdiction extended to new objects." Once again federalism was seen as essential to preserving a particular vision of republicanism and democracy, an aspect evident in Gallatin's opposition to the use of federal courts to prosecute the

---

8. Alexander Addison to General Lee, in Steven R. Boyd, ed., *The Whiskey Rebellion: Past and Present Perspectives* (Westport, Conn., 1985), 54. Gallatin argued against the move to invalidate elections in counties that had experienced civil unrest and also sought to ensure that jury trials occurred within western localities. Albert Gallatin, "The Speech of Albert Gallatin . . ." (1795), in Henry Adams, ed., *The Writings of Albert Gallatin* (Philadelphia, 1879), III, 5–6, 14, 23, 46.

participants in the disturbances in western Pennsylvania. The effort to by-pass the state judiciaries and the local jury system struck Gallatin as foreboding a larger effort to shift power to a distant government. "They are to be tried, not in their own county," Gallatin objected, "and their fate depends on the verdict, not of a jury of their own vicinage, acquainted with their private character and the whole tenor of their lives, but on men selected from amongst strangers." This criticism echoed complaints made during ratification by many Anti-Federalists. Once again, Federalists sought to undermine the federal and local character of politics and substitute a single federal standard. This policy threatened to rend asunder "those bonds of amity and benevolence that can alone insure the existence of the Americans as an united nation." The Federalist policy of a strong government would serve only to polarize and divide the nation further.[9]

William Findley echoed many of the themes that Gallatin dwelt on, but his analysis of the insurrection reflected his more democratic and egalitarian politics. In much the same way that Gallatin tried to acknowledge the legitimate grievances of western folk without sanctioning extralegal action, so Findley sought to strike a balance, supporting the grievances of the rebels while distancing himself from their actions. Findley was acutely aware of the dangers of mobocracy. During ratification, he joined with other middling democrats who represented the western part of the state and denounced the Federalist mob in Philadelphia that had intimidated Anti-Federalist delegates to the assembly. He readily appreciated that the fury of a mob could just as easily be exploited by the enemies of the people as serve the friends of the people. His own account of the insurrection described those responsible for tarring and feathering excise men as an "armed banditti."[10]

In contrast to Federalists who blamed the Democratic-Republican Societies for causing the rebellion, Findley adopted a stance similar to Gallatin's, insisting that the meetings had helped contain the potential violence by spreading responsible political ideas. For Findley, the public sphere provided a desirable alternative to federal troops, better for maintaining order and respect for the law. Findley defended his participation in popular meetings as not only constitutional but politically prudent as well. "It may be plead, that popular meetings are often conducted with indiscretion, and have a tendency to promote licentiousness. . . . But it does not therefore

9. "The Speech of Gallatin," in Adams, ed., *Writings of Gallatin*, III, 47, 48, 50.

10. William Findley, *History of the Insurrection in the Four Western Counties of Pennsylvania . . .* (Philadelphia, 1796), 59.

follow, that such meetings should be prohibited by law or denounced by government." He shared Gallatin's belief that his participation might exercise a moderating influence, strenuously asserting that his involvement served to calm popular passions and that popular meetings were salutary. "On the whole a much greater proportion of useful information had been disseminated among the people, respecting their political duties and interests than formerly, that the number of those who had qualified themselves for giving information, and who were industrious in instructing their neighbours, were greatly encreased." Had the meetings "been more generally attended by men of discretion, they might have been advantageous." The public sphere, including societies and newspapers, was not the cause of rebellion. Had people in western Pennsylvania had greater access to such information, they had been less likely to join the rebellion.[11]

Findley's democratic and egalitarian beliefs led him to bridle at Federalist denunciations of popular meetings and self-created democratic societies. The goal of these attacks was to undermine the constitutional right of the people to associate and demonstrate. Such attacks had the effect of "reducing the people to mere machines, and subverting the very existence of liberty." Findley spoke out for the need for the people to remain vigilant, even jealous of their rulers. Under a representative government, the people retained the right to withdraw consent from their representatives at any time. "It is equally absurd to assert," Findley declared, "that because our laws are enacted by our own representatives, therefore we ought to submit to them without remonstrance." Such a policy assumed "that a government of representatives can never mistake the true interests of their constituents, nor be corrupted or fall into partial combinations." Although Findley did not believe that a representative was merely an agent of his constituents, he placed considerable faith in the people and believed that a representative was obliged to make the feelings of the people his primary guide in political matters.[12]

Findley's role for middling politicians in the public sphere and his views of democracy were closely connected. While he believed, like other members of the Democratic-Republican elite, that the public sphere provided a means

11. Ibid., 48, 176. This view was shared by William Manning, who believed that it was the isolation and absence of information that contributed to the outbreak of Rebellion. See Samuel Eliot Morison, ed., "William Manning's 'The Key of Libberty,'" *WMQ*, 3d Ser., XIII (1956), 241; and the preface to Michael Merrill and Sean Wilentz, eds., *The Key of Liberty: The Life and Democratic Writings of William Manning, "A Laborer," 1747–1814* (Cambridge, Mass., 1993), 123.

12. Findley, *History of the Insurrection*, 48, 49.

of refining and shaping the will of the public, his conception of how that would occur was far less one-sided. For democrats such as Findley, the public sphere was more egalitarian. The men most capable in that venue were, in his view, not natural aristocrats, but men of middling fortunes. Moreover, the goal of refining the public will existed in delicate balance with the need to represent that will.[13]

This democratic vision of government separated Findley from the more established political elite. Hugh Henry Brackenridge (Findley's rival in Pennsylvania politics) made clear the differences between those like James Madison who continued to believe in natural aristocracy and those like Findley who championed a more egalitarian middling democracy. Brackenridge denounced the political views of former Anti-Federalists like William Findley and John Smilie. The notion that Findley was a genuinely popular leader who sought to represent accurately the feelings of his constituents struck Brackenridge as exactly the pandering to the mob that disinterested republican statesmen had to avoid. "It was not anything celestial in the form or talents of these men that made them popular, it was their standing with a party and consulting the prejudices of the people. The moment they opposed the feelings of the multitude, they were dammed." Like many more elite politicians, Brackenridge believed that representatives had to represent the will of the people in its refined state, not its raw, undigested actual state.[14]

At least part of the blame for the Whiskey Rebellion rested with Federalists who had misled the public about the scope of federal authority under the new Constitution. Findley explained: "Many of the uninformed people, being told by the warm advocates of the federal government, that after it was ratified we would have no more excises, considered the excise law therefore as unconstitutional. . . . It is not easy to convince people that a law, in their opinion unjust and oppressive in its operation, is at the same time constitutional." Thus the political crisis caused by the rebellion was a combination of Federalist duplicity and popular ignorance. Once again, Findley sought to position himself as a spokesman for an enlightened and moderate middle position, one typical of the vast majority of citizens who constituted the substantial yeomanry. Focusing on Federalist duplicity and popular ignorance as the primary causes of the rebellion, Findley made clear his faith that both of those threats to liberty might be eliminated by a more vigorous and

---

13. Ibid.

14. Hugh Henry Brackenridge, *Incidents of the Insurrection in the Western Parts of Pennsylvania in the Year 1794*, rpt. in Boyd, ed., *The Whiskey Rebellion: Pespectives*, 64.

open public sphere of political debate, where the machinations of Federalists and the misunderstandings of the people could be exposed and corrected.[15]

Thus, Findley also blamed the rebellion on a popular misconception about constitutional government. "The great error among the people was an opinion, that an immoral law might be opposed and yet the government respected." In essence, Findley repudiated the essential principle of plebeian populist constitutionalism, wherein the will of the people could be reconstituted spontaneously in local organizations such as the militia, the jury, or even the crowd. By contrast, responsible politicians and men of moderate temperament recognized the danger of such a policy. "All men of discretion" realized that, "if they permitted government to be violently opposed, even in the execution of an obnoxious law, the same spirit would naturally lead to the destruction of all security and order; they saw by experience that in a state of anarchy the name of liberty would be prophaned to sanction the most despotic tyranny." The radicalism of plebeian populists contrasted with the more moderate stance of established political leaders, who realized that the challenge to the authority of the excise officers undermined their own authority as well and was destructive of all public order.[16]

Although Federalists linked the rebellion with lingering Anti-Federalist feeling, Findley reiterated the point that former opponents of the Constitution had made repeatedly after ratification: opposition to the Constitution had been motivated by a commitment to federalism, not opposition to it. "From mistaken party spleen," Findley wrote, "myself and others who acted the part I did, have been called Antifederalists, as a name of reproach, yet I do, and always did, treat the appellation with contempt. If I erred, it was from an excess of zeal for federalism, and a jealousy least the federal republican principles of the government were not sufficiently guarded, and in this we agree with the majority of the citizens of the United States."[17]

Findley's democratic ideals might have been among the most egalitarian within the Democratic-Republican leadership, yet his democratic beliefs stopped well short of those of the grass-roots supporters of the Whiskey Rebellion. The plebeian populists who took up arms against the new government were committed to a radical localist vision of democracy. The Whiskey Rebellion put middling democrats and plebeian populists on a collision course.

15. Findley, *History of the Insurrection*, 43.
16. Ibid., 177, 184, 300.
17. Ibid., 258.

Implicitly, Findley's *History of the Whiskey Insurrection* was more than a defense of his own involvement in events leading up to the suppression of the rebellion; it was also an attempt to demonstrate the profound differences that separated middling democrats from plebeian populists. The individual whom Findley singled out as the embodiment of those misguided principles was the radical Anti-Federalist from Carlisle, William Petrikin. The contrast between Findley's and Petrikin's views of the rebellion illustrates the irreconcilable tension between middling democracy and plebeian radicalism.[18]

In his own estimation, Findley had been unfairly branded an enemy of government and a supporter of rebellion because of a casual exchange of letters with Petrikin. Findley not only went out of his way to distance himself from any personal connection to Petrikin; he took great pains to show how his ideas shared little with the Carlisle radical. Findley believed that armed resistance was not only futile but unconstitutional. In fact, Findley feared the inflammatory rhetoric of Petrikin and other supporters of the rebellion. He informed the readers of his *History,* "What I knew from his character I was afraid he might take a warm part" in popular agitation. Findley counseled Petrikin against extralegal actions, believing that course "would tend to defeat our endeavors to restore order." It was in the best interests of all parties to prevent "the citizens of Cumberland country from doing any thing in imitation of the rioters." In his letter to Petrikin, Findley acknowledged, "On proper occasions I have endeavoured to inform the public mind so as to promote a repeal of the excise law." His opposition to the excise tax, however, did not include support for "riots or any thing that might tend to promote any unconstitutional exertions"; only legal action was appropriate to protest the excise law. In contrast to plebeian populists, Findley denied that the situation in western Pennsylvania resembled that of the colonists who opposed British tyranny a generation earlier: Americans enjoyed representation under the new government and were therefore bound to obey the law. Findley took great pains to distinguish between the orderly use of extralegal action

18. In addition to the evidence provided by Findley's history, a good deal of information about popular resistance to the Whiskey insurrection in Carlisle, including the role of William Petrikin, can be found in the indictments brought against the rebels. Attorney General William Rawle's legal papers contain a wealth of information about the political ideals of plebeian populists in this region: Rawle Family Papers, HSP. See also the federal indictment brought against Petrikin: *United States v. William Peterkin*, Criminal Case Files of the United States, Circuit Court for the Eastern District of Pennsylvania, 1791–1840, microfilm M986, reel 1, RG 21, National Archives.

during the Revolution and the "disorder and extravagance" and "the general dislike to the law" characteristic of recent actions in western Pennsylvania.[19]

For plebeian populists, however, the situation under the federal Constitution appeared quite similar to that faced by the colonists. For radical localists, a distant government could never represent their interests. Extralegal action during the rebellion was therefore perfectly consistent with plebeian constitutionalism. Erecting liberty poles, tarring and feathering excise men, and threatening pseudonymous notes were all actions drawn from the rich stock of plebeian rituals. Petrikin had employed many of those same techniques during the struggle against the Constitution. From his point of view, the excise was merely the most recent example of how the wellborn had created an oppressive government to do their bidding.

Petrikin's house in Carlisle became a meeting place for opponents of the Federalist policy who supported the Whiskey rebels. As a contemporary observer noted, on one occasion forty men left Petrikin's house and erected a liberty pole to which a board was fixed with the inscription "Liberty and Equality." Petrikin praised the actions of "the Glorious Sons of Liberty to the West." Rather than condemn the actions of the rebels, Petrikin advised that such behavior ought "not to be faulted," but "applauded and supported."[20]

The response of plebeian populists in Carlisle to the Whiskey Rebellion followed a strategy similar to that used to protest ratification of the Constitution. To demonstrate their solidarity with the rebels, Carlisle citizens once again turned to the rich stock of plebeian political ritual. Plebeian populists in Carlisle even singled out the same individual for symbolic execution that they had targeted several years before: Chief Justice Thomas McKean. An effigy of him was prepared for ritual execution and cremation and consigned to the flames, the crowd proclaiming, "Huzza, here is old McKean in blue Blazes." One individual even announced that "he would be dammed if some Lives should not be lost if Attempts were made to prevent putting up the said Pole." The crowd invited those who "who will sell Whiskey at nine pence a quart without paying Excise" to join the revelry and celebrate popular liberty.[21]

For Petrikin, erecting liberty poles was, not the end of protest, but merely the beginning. He sought to dissuade the local militia from joining federal forces marching against the rebels. Petrikin's vision of the militia as an agent

19. Findley, *History of the Insurrection*, 283–284, 285, 287.

20. Deposition of Francis Gibson, Oct. 11, 1794, Rawle Family Papers, I, 49; deposition of Samuel Irvine, Esq., I, 117.

21. Rawle Family Papers, I, 49, 117–119. See also the federal indictment brought against Petrikin, in *United States v. William Peterkin*.

of a radical democracy grew out of the same localist agenda that had inspired him to oppose the Constitution. He hoped that the militia might function as it did during the Carlisle riot, as an agent of local popular democratic agitation and organization. This time, however, Petrikin was disappointed. The militia did not oppose Washington's troops.[22]

At a meeting in Carlisle in which Petrikin and the prominent former Anti-Federalist leader Robert Whitehill participated, Petrikin urged local residents to side with the rebels against the government. As one participant noted, Petrikin "sd a great deal agst the excise law and against the Constitution." Against him, Whitehill "endeavored to show the impropriety of opposing" the law, arguing that "it would be better to submit," since continued opposition could "bring on a revolution." Petrikin, in turn, argued that "the show of Liberty to the West ought not to be falted," but "applauded and supported." To Whitehill's suggestion that continued resistance would start a revolution, Petrikin observed that "all Revns began by force and that it was as well it should begin." The actions of the government had convinced him: "It was time there should be a Revolution—that Congress ought either to Repeal the Law or allow these people to set up a government for themselves— and be separated from us." In his testimony, Whitehill recalled that Petrikin urged that "People in the West had better Separate themselves from the Government of the U. St. than undergo such hardships as they were subjected to, and they had better form of Govermt for themselves—that they should have a govermt who had no President no King."[23]

Petrikin's radicalism embraced not only the rituals of plebeian culture but an extreme form of democratic localism, and he continued to affirm the legitimacy of plebeian rituals of protest and extralegal action. The right of revolution had not been cast aside with the establishment of the Constitution. In contrast to Findley and Whitehill, Petrikin believed that westerners stood in the same relationship to the new government as the American colonists had with Britain. For these plebeian radicals, the federal government under the Federalist party was just as illegitimate as the government of George III. Indeed, in the view of one contemporary, the Whiskey rebels "flattered themselves that they were only carrying out Whig principles and following Whig examples in resisting the excise law." Petrikin's politics typified an important radical fringe within the ranks of Democratic-Republi-

---

22. Deposition of Francis W. Gibson, Oct. 11, 1794, Rawle Family Papers, I, 49; Testimony of Mr. Pollack, Mr. Laird, and Samuel Irwine, Esq., I, 117; Testimony of Robert Whitehill, I, 119.

23. Ibid.

canism. Not only did plebeian radicals propound the most extreme form of democratic views, but their radicalism served as a cautionary warning for more mainstream politicians. During ratification and at the Harrisburg convention Whitehill had seen the danger inherent in plebeian radicalism. The Whiskey Rebellion confirmed his worst fears and strengthened his resolve to promote a more moderate middling democratic agenda.[24]

The political vision of prominent state politicians like Findley, Gallatin, and Whitehill did not countenance the violence of the Whiskey rebels. While willing to concede that the excise tax was a mistake, they were not willing to support extralegal action to secure the repeal of the excise laws: the only recourse for redressing western grievances was constitutional means. Unlike under British colonial rule, the existence of representative institutions meant that extralegal action was no longer acceptable. Moreover, middling democrats viewed the actions of plebeian populists as a strategic blunder that only provided a pretext for Federalists to increase their assault on state authority and popular government.

Even William Manning's radical vision stopped short of endorsing the extralegal crowd action favored by plebeian populists. As with nearly everything Manning wrote, his views stood somewhere between the ideals of middling democracy championed by established politicians and the plebeian populism of individuals like Petrikin. In his view, the consequences of Shays's Rebellion and the Whiskey Rebellion were identical. He sympathized with the grievances that brought citizens into the streets in both instances but did not countenance mob activity. Manning realized that extralegal action only strengthened the hands of those hostile to popular liberty and democracy. Ultimately, Shays's Rebellion served to legitimate those eager to promote monarchy and aristocracy. The blame for both rebellions lay with the government. In both cases he believed that violence might have been averted if government had performed its representative function properly. "Insurrection would neaver have hapned if it had not bin for some unreasonable iritations imposed on the peopel." A government more responsive to the people, one that "had known the mindes of the peopel on it," would have settled the matter "for a trifel if fatherly and kinde measures had bin used."[25]

24. Rev. James Carnahan, quoted in Thomas P. Slaughter, "The Friends of Liberty, the Friends of Order, and the Whiskey Rebellion: A Historiographical Essay," in Boyd, ed., *The Whiskey Rebellion: Perspectives*, 13.

25. Morison, ed., "Manning's 'The Key of Libberty,'" *WMQ*, 3d Ser., XIII (1956), 241.

Apart from violence, there were many points upon which Manning and the rebels would have agreed. These commonalities are evident in the petitions and resolves drafted during the Whiskey insurrection. One particularly illuminating set of resolves was drafted by the inhabitants of Westpensbro and Newton, in Pennsylvania, sharing many of the themes that had informed the petitions of participants in Shays's Rebellion; they demonstrate the important continuities in popular radical discourse.[26]

In contrast to a policy of land sales that encouraged large-scale speculation, a "mode of selling Back Lands in Great Quantity to Companys," the Westpensbro and Newton petition called for a more equitable policy, which would follow that "Esensial Principal in Every Republican Government, Viz the Equal Division of Landed property which Ought to be Encouraged by Law." The resolves restated the Anti-Federalist commitment to a limited government, one in which policy served the interests of a broad section of the producing classes. The current policy was not "consistent with the Encouragement Dew to Industry" and was "Impolitic Because, it tends to Alienate the affection of the Common People to the federal Government by seeing themselves Deprived of Becoming Purchasers upon the same terms with the favourites of Government." To promote greater equity, the government should have discriminated between lands purchased solely for speculation and those actively farmed and improved. The resolves also protested the Hamiltonian funding scheme and favored the opposition's policy of discriminating between the original holders of securities and speculators. Public policy ought to foster a bond of affection between the people and government by encouraging the ownership of land. The resolves further asserted, "As virtue is the only Spring that supports a Republican government, and not power, the Laws should Recommend themselves to the affections of People by their propriety, Consequently it would make them easy in their Execution." The petition repeatedly stressed that free government had to rest on the affections of the people.[27]

Citizens were advised "not to Chuse at the Ensuing Election for members of Congress any Speculator in the funds, any stock holder in the Bank of the United States, nor any Land Jober, as these are a Class of men Who seems to Have a Separate Interest from the Mass of the People." Reiterating the arguments that had echoed in popular constitutional discourse since the debate

26. See Shays's Rebellion Petitions, Shays's Rebellion Folder, American Antiquarian Society, Worcester, Mass.; Westpensbro and Newton, Cumberland County, Pennsylvania, Resolves, Rawle Family Papers, I, 132.

27. Westpensbro and Newton Resolves, Rawle Family Papers, I, 33, 49, 117–119.

over the Bank of North America, the resolves asserted that only the election of individuals drawn from society's producing classes could ensure that representation would function properly. In contrast to Federalist political theory, the resolves affirmed a distinctly popular democratic view of republican government. When representatives resembled the people, literally shared their interests and burdens, they would enact laws that reflected popular needs. In a democratic republic, the people would not need to be coerced, because their interests and those of the government would be in harmony. In contrast to the Federalists' more elitist view of representation, the resolves boldly declared, "All Civil authority originates with and is received from the people in a Republican government, that Every law Made by the Representatives not agreeable to the Voice of those from whom they Derive their Authority is Tyranical and unjust." Thus, the resolves provide one of the clearest statements of popular political ideas framed during the Whiskey insurrection.[28]

A different dynamic defined the character of the Whiskey Rebellion in the South. The response of southern gentry to the Whiskey Rebellion is also instructive, since it demonstrates how a distinctively Anti-Federalist vision of federalism continued to shape individual responses to important political events. Judge Harry Innes of Kentucky was certainly no democrat. Yet, he used his role as a judge to moderate the severity of federal prosecutions against those who defied the excise law. Innes saw his role as a mediator between government and the people differently than did Pennsylvanians. Distillers in Kentucky, unlike distillers in western Pennsylvania, benefited from the fact that local elite showed little sympathy with the program of the federal government. The involvement of a number of prominent citizens in distilling also provided a shield for distillers of more modest means and influence. Innes clearly recognized that local juries would not indict citizens under an unpopular law. Rather than steer juries toward conviction, or deliver homilies on the need for juries to uphold unpopular laws, Innes reminded jurors that "trials by Jury have from time immemorial been considered as the basis of Liberty." Innes was quite explicit about the role that juries served in this system: "They are the great bulwark which intervenes between the Magistrate and the Citizen." Innes's efforts, together with local juries, effectively prevented the whiskey excise law from being enforced. In the fifty cases brought before the federal court in Kentucky, not a single defendant paid the full fines, penalties, or forfeitures prescribed by law. In

28. Ibid.

several cases in which juries found for the defendants, Judge Innes directed the accusers, often government informants, to pay the costs of litigation. Innes's commitment to local autonomy led him to use the legal system to support the resistance to unjust federal authority in an orderly manner.[29]

The defense of jury rights took on a vastly different meaning in western Kentucky than it had in western Pennsylvania. Once again, the genius of federalism brought together individuals who might otherwise have shared little. What Innes and Gallatin shared was a belief that political solutions were best left to states and localities. The political visions that led Innes and Gallatin to espouse this vision of federalism could hardly be more different. Anti-Federalism accommodated this sort of diversity and brought together a complex and diverse coalition that included the southern gentry and middling democrats.[30]

Federalism versus Localist Democracy

The Whiskey Rebellion acted like a prism, fracturing the Democratic-Republicanism coalition and revealing the many different hues that blended to constitute the opposition to the Federalists. For the Democratic-Republican elite and the middling democrats, the ideals of federalism and localism,

29. Harry Innes, grand jury address (draft), Innes Papers, Legal Files, box 8, MSS Division, LC; see also Mary K. Bonsteel Tachau, "A New Look at the Whiskey Rebellion," in Boyd, ed., *The Whiskey Rebellion: Perspectives,* 105, 106, 110.

30. Lance Banning, *The Jeffersonian Persuasion: Evolution of a Party Ideology* (Ithaca, N.Y., 1978), casts the Jeffersonians as civic republicans. Banning takes the agrarian republicanism of John Taylor as emblematic of Jeffersonian ideology. John Taylor's 1794 pamphlet *An Enquiry into the Principles and Tendency of Certain Public Measures* (Philadelphia, 1794) is the "nearest approach to an authorized statement of the republicans' reasons for opposing the Federalist System" (Banning, *Jeffersonian Persuasion,* 195). Joyce Appleby, *Capitalism and a New Social Order: The Republican Vision of the 1790s* (New York, 1984), characterizes the Jeffersonians as forward-looking liberals. For accounts that stress the importance of sectional and regional political cultures, see Buel, *Securing the Revolution;* John M. Murrin, "The Great Inversion, or Court versus Country: A Comparison of the Revolution Settlements in England (1668–1721) and America (1776–1816)," in J. G. A. Pocock, ed., *Three British Revolutions: 1641, 1688, 1776* (Princeton, N.J., 1980), 368–453; John Ashworth, "The Jeffersonians: Classical Republicans or Liberal Capitalists?" *Journal of American Studies,* XVIII (1984), 425–435. Richard E. Ellis, *The Jeffersonian Crisis: Courts and Politics in the Young Republic* (New York, 1971), notes a tension between moderate and radical Jeffersonians. Ellis's neo-Progressive framework casts politics as a struggle between radical agrarian democrats and moderate commercial conservatives. Such an account homogenizes agrarians and ignores the procommercial views of of the middling sort.

while distinct, were complementary. When federalism and localism came into conflict, Democratic-Republicans, like Anti-Federalists before them, generally favored the preservation of state autonomy within the federal system. While the different political and economic visions of the southern gentry and middling democrats could both be accommodated in a federal system, the Whiskey Rebellion provided dramatic evidence that, for the most radical wing of the opposition—plebeian populists—localism and federalism were not easily harmonized. The same conflicts that divided middling democrats from plebeian populists during ratification were reenacted on a much larger, more dramatic scale during the Whiskey Rebellion.

Democratic-Republicanism had proven extremely flexible, capable of uniting conservative southerners such as Harry Innes of Kentucky and John Taylor of Virginia with middling democrats such as William Findley. Democratic-Republicanism had even been able to accommodate the more egalitarian views of democrats such as William Manning. What the opposition could not handle was the radical localism of William Petrikin and the Whiskey rebels.

Judge Harry Innes of Kentucky provides an excellent example of a cosmopolitan conservative whose commitment to the ideals of federalism, localism, and strict construction of constitutional texts did not signal support for a democratic agenda. For members of the gentry, the necessity of promoting virtue continued to be an important part of their constitutionalism. This theme appeared repeatedly in Innes's grand jury charges. He took great pains to warn jurors, "So corrupt are the manners of our Citizens that their conduct may be termed licentiousness." Innes was convinced that "vice and immorality daily increase among us." One measure of the licentiousness of the people was the leveling egalitarian impulses he detected among some of the people. Innes expressed these fears in a letter to Jefferson drafted during the debates over the Kentucky constitution. Innes did not see recent events in Kentucky as a tribute to democracy.[31]

The people of Kentucky are all turned Politicians, from the highest in Office to the Peasant. The Peasantry are perfectly mad—extraordinary prejudices and without foundation have arisen against the present Officers of Government, the Lawyers and the Men of Fortune. They say *plain honest Farmers* are the only men who ought to be elected to form

31. Innes, Grand Jury Address, n.d., Innes Papers. For an informative discussion of his legal thought, see Mary K. Bonsteel Tachau, *Federal Courts in the Early Republic: Kentucky, 1789–1816* (Princeton, N.J., 1978), 39.

our Constitution. What will be the end of these prejudices it is difficult to say. They have given a very serious alarm to every thinking man.[32]

John Taylor of Caroline typifies another variant of this elitist tradition. His complaints about representation under the Constitution echoed a common Anti-Federalist complaint. Taylor concluded that it was "scarcely possible to communicate that regular and thorough information, of all transactions, from the seat of government to the extremities, so indispensably necessary to enable the constituent to judge with propriety of the conduct of his representative." Taylor's view of the representative function differed from middling or plebeian democrats' understanding of it. As far as the "great mass of society" was concerned, Taylor believed that it was "uninformed" and had to be molded by "those whom they have been long accustomed to look up to as leaders." Accordingly, Taylor turned to the state legislatures as representatives of the voice of the people. The legislature was in reality not merely an expression of the popular will but an improvement over a simple democratic assembly, since it represented "the people themselves in a state of refinement." Taylor's notion of representation was shaped by the same distorted mirror that other members of the gentry held up to the population: the image that this looking glass reflected was the gentry's values and ideals. Taylor shared Madison's idea that representation should refine popular views. Both men also came to see the issue of federalism in similar terms. What set Taylor apart from Madison was his localism: a belief, common among so many former Anti-Federalists, that the government needed to be closer to the people. In the context of a gentry society, Taylor believed it was possible to produce a refined elite at the local level. Implicitly, Taylor believed that the people would defer to their social betters, the natural aristocrats from a local gentry elite. This view of representation depended on a particular conception of federalism that accepted the diversity of America and the need for representatives to reflect that diversity adequately. It was, not democratic, but undeniably localist, a variant firmly grounded in a state-centered vision of federalism.[33]

William Findley's middling democracy also looked to the states as the primary political unit, and he shared the same commitment to federalism and strict construction of the Constitution. His view of the responsibilities of the legislators was more democratic than Taylor's and Innes's. "It is the duty of the legislature," Findley wrote, "not only to accommodate the laws to

32. Harry Innes to Jefferson, Aug. 27, 1791, in Julian P. Boyd et al., eds., *The Papers of Thomas Jefferson* (Princeton, N.J., 1950–), XXII, 86.

33. Taylor, *An Examination*, 5; Taylor, *An Enquiry*, 55.

the peoples' interests, but even, as far as possible, to their preconceptions; for as a republican government rests on the people's confidence, whatever weakens that confidence saps the foundations of the government." The politician's primary job was not simply to refine the popular will but to make the government faithfully represent that will. Government not only served the interests of the people, but it had to reflect their values. Findley's version of democracy accepted that a group of middling leaders would mediate between the people and the legislature. The qualities and attributes necessary for that role were not possessed by a natural aristocracy, but could be found in the many virtuous and solid citizens of middling ranks. This vision was also decidedly localist, since representatives could serve their function only if they were closely tethered to their constituents. Findley was active in the political life of Pennsylvania for more than four decades, serving at the state and the national level, and his confidence that the states were best suited to protect the interests of the people never wavered. Although more democratic, Findley shared with Innes and Taylor the view that the diversity of the nation could be accommodated only within a federal system.[34]

William Manning also placed his faith in the federal system and strict construction of the Constitution. When compared to a middling democrat such as Findley, Manning appears more egalitarian and localist. Politics was a perennial struggle between the laboring classes and those classes that were mere parasites on the productive classes. The wealthy sought to establish a government in which those with "property and high station" would "have wait or influence." "These Sentiments," he noted, had been "urged in such a masterly manner just before the adoption of the federal Constitution, and have bin so closely followed by the administration eversence." The Constitution was only the most recent example of this perennial struggle. The struggle between the "Rich and poor" had defined the course of history and continued to shape the most important political battles of his own day as well. He sought to reverse the tendency of the new Constitution to remove power from local governments and shift authority to a distant and unresponsive government.[35]

William Petrikin's support for the rebels represented another response, and his radicalism went much further than William Manning's. Petrikin supported extralegal crowd action and the use of the militia to bring about a

---

34. Findley, *History of the Insurrection*, 49.

35. Ruth Bogin, ed., " 'Measures So Glareingly Unjust': A Response to Hamilton's Funding Plan by William Manning," *WMQ*, 3d Ser., XLVI (1989), 330; Morison, ed., "Manning's 'The Key of Libberty,' " *WMQ*, 3d Ser., XIII (1956), 213.

radical localist democracy, in which the will of the people would be represented locally—in the militia, committees of correspondence, juries, and other local institutions. Petrikin, again in contrast to Manning, supported violence to help bring about this political vision. For individuals like Petrikin, the people retained the right to defend their liberty with arms. If government ceased to represent their interests, radical localists accepted a permanent right of revolution that included a right of secession. Community meetings, extralegal crowd actions, and, ultimately, armed resistance reflected a radical vision of participatory democracy rooted in the will of the community. While plebeian populists might have trusted their state governments more than the federal government, they were not committed to a federalism that accorded the states the central role in representing the will of the people.

The Whiskey Rebellion also demonstrated that the aspirations of plebeian populists were not compatible with those of middling democrats or the gentry elite. Violence in western Pennsylvania had the same negative impact on Democratic-Republicanism that the Carlisle riot had on Anti-Federalist democrats. Once again, the threat posed by plebeian populism divided radical and moderate democrats.

Federalists were content to put their faith in a more powerful government to compel popular allegiance. By contrast, Democratic-Republican constitutional and political philosophy rested in the belief that government had to secure the affections of the people. To secure consent without force, a means to ascertain and mobilize the popular will was necessary. Democratic-Republicans did not conceive of the public sphere as a replacement of governmental institutions such as the individual state legislatures, but viewed the press and the Democratic-Republican Societies as a way to empower the people to fulfill their role as guardians of their liberty. Democratic-Republicans recognized that their vision of federalism—a nation in which the center remained fairly weak and the individual states strong—required a vigorous public sphere. Middling democrats and members of the gentry elite hoped that Democratic-Republican Societies might tap the strength of localist impulses and harness their energy in a manner consistent with the constitutional structures of the federal system. Thus, while the societies were rooted in individual localities, they were intended to be part of an expanding public sphere of political discourse that would unite different communities.

That notion ran afoul of a more radical democratic localist ideology espoused by the Whiskey rebels and their supporters. For these plebeian populists, the will of the people required no refinement, but could be spontaneously reconstituted in such local institutions as the jury, the militia, or even the crowd. The plebeian understanding of the public sphere was ultimately not compatible with the Democratic-Republicans' vision of it. Indeed, while the Whiskey Rebellion did not mark an end to plebeian radicalism, it did sever the connection between plebeian radicalism and Anti-Federalism. After the rebellion, the Anti-Federalist heritage would increasingly become identified with a dissenting constitutional discourse used by elite and middling democrats to defend a vision of localism compatible with state authority. The original criticism voiced by Anti-Federalists during ratification, particularly the concerns expressed in the state ratification conventions, would come to occupy a central place in dissenting constitutional theory. The inclusion of this particular strain of Anti-Federalist thought in a distinctive canon of dissenting constitutional theory preserved Anti-Federalist ideas even as it narrowed the range of texts that would define it.

PART THREE :
THE ANTI-FEDERALIST
LEGACY

CHAPTER 8 :

THE FOUNDING

DIALOGUE AND

THE POLITICS OF

CONSTITUTIONAL

INTERPRETATION

Although the Whiskey Rebellion provided a dramatic, but temporary, distraction from the more protracted struggle between Federalists and their opponents, the most important battleground continued to be constitutional. Political issues in the 1790s were conceptualized in constitutional terms, and the opposition remained committed to defending the limitedness of the Constitution's grant of authority to the federal government. Proving that Federalists had perverted the meaning of the Constitution as understood at the time of ratification thus became an important part of the Democratic-Republican program.

The Irony of the Search for an Original Intent

During debate over the constitutionality of the Bank of the United States in 1791, Democratic-Republicans and Federalists each invoked the idea of original intent, albeit not devoting much energy to canvassing the writings of 1787–1788 for textual support. Defining exactly which, if any, texts would be used to identify the original understanding of the Constitution was a complicated and controversial issue. Equally contentious was defining the appropriate interpretive strategies to explicate those texts. In the struggle to define American constitutionalism, questions about the original intent of the parties to the Constitution would be central to jurisprudence at both the federal and state level. Congressional debates over the proper sphere of the new government's authority also forced a consideration of what the original understanding of the Constitution had been in 1788. While the struggle over the bank had prompted a few individuals to enter into the debate over the original meaning of the Constitution, this question assumed an even more prominent role in the debate over the Jay Treaty of 1795, the next great constitutional struggle of the 1790s.

Democratic-Republican opponents of the Washington administration in the House attacked the Jay Treaty, claiming that its generous terms of settlement with Great Britain struck an exceedingly poor bargain for America. Jay's negotiations, the opposition argued, demonstrated the pro-British bias of the Federalists. The House demanded evidence about Jay's instructions. Washington rebuffed the request, asserting that the president and Senate had the sole powers in making treaties. The House affirmed its right to exercise a check on the Senate and executive through its power to legislate on issues necessary to implement the treaty. The original understanding of the treaty-making clauses of the Constitution became an object of intense scrutiny and controversy.

In debating the meaning of the treaty-making power, the texts of ratification were recycled in ways that few of their authors might have predicted. The proliferation of different readings of Anti-Federalist texts, by Federalists and Democratic-Republicans alike, gave new life to Anti-Federalist arguments. At the same time, Publius was called on to testify for both Democratic-Republicans and Federalists. It seemed that, once an author's words entered the public sphere, they were set adrift on a vast sea of interpretive possibility. Authorship conferred no special authority to interpret a text, once published.

The range of sources invoked to establish the original understanding of the Constitution was staggering. One participant quipped that, since virtually every type of source had been introduced, "among the rest of his authorities, he was constantly expecting to hear him quote another, very common in the present times, the toasts" delivered by individuals both for and against the Constitution. This wry observation captures the sense in which virtually all of the available texts produced during ratification had the potential to be reinterpreted and reread in the struggle to ascertain the meaning of the Constitution. A multitude of ironies emerged from this debate. Federalists approvingly quoted the works of former Anti-Federalists while former Anti-Federalists made liberal use of the writings of Federalists. Federalists even charged Democratic-Republicans with employing a loose construction to justify their claim that the House enjoyed some jurisdiction in treaty making.[1]

Democratic-Republican congressman Jonathan Havens captured one of those ironies when he stated, "It was a very remarkable circumstance, that those who had been stigmatized by gentlemen as disorganizers of the Government, or as rebels against the constituted authorities, should be very strenuously contending for such a construction of the Constitution of the United States as would render all its parts harmonious." The irony was further compounded by the fact that "those who assumed to themselves the peculiar style of being defenders of the Constitution, and supporters of Government, should be contending for a construction of the Constitution as must render it inconsistent." The Democratic-Republican position, Havens argued, sought to interpret the role of the House in such a way that its powers were consistent with its larger constitutional function. The Federalists, on the other hand, sought to limit the powers of the lower house, the more democratic branch, in ways inconsistent with its larger constitutional role.[2]

Federalist William Smith appropriated Madison's injunction framed during the debate over the bank: arriving at the true meaning of the Constitution required uncovering "the general sense of the whole nation at the time the Constitution was formed." Smith advised his fellow congressmen to return to "the contemporaneous exposition of that instrument." Smith focused his attention on the fears of the Anti-Federalist critics of the Constitution, declaring that "he would then confidently appeal to the opinions of those who" at the time of adoption were "alarmed at the Treaty power." Smith used Anti-Federalist texts as a weapon against Democratic-Republicans: "The discussions which took place at the time of its adoption by the conventions of the several states, proved beyond a doubt, that the full extent of the power was then well understood, and thought by those who approved of the Constitution to be sufficiently guarded." Since the Anti-Federalists had raised this objection and the Constitution had still been ratified, Smith concluded that the objection had been effectively dismissed by the people. For additional support, Smith turned to the "amendments which had been proposed by the discontented." The Virginia convention's recommendation that the Constitution be amended so that commercial treaties required two-thirds of all senators, not merely two-thirds of those present, demonstrated that there was a broad consensus that the Senate was to have an exclusive

1. *Annals of Congress,* 4th Congress, 1st sess. (1796), 537, 759.
2. Ibid., 484, 486.

right to approve treaties, that the House was never intended to exercise a check on the Senate on this point. Further evidence could be adduced from the "Address and Reasons of Dissent of the Minority" and the proceedings of the Harrisburg convention. That body had proposed an amendment to require the consent of the House in approving treaties. Once again, Smith reasoned that, if these reforms had been proposed and not adopted, then the evidence was conclusive that the original intent of the people had been not to grant such powers to the House.[3]

A similar rhetorical strategy was adopted by the Massachusetts Federalist Theodore Sedgwick, who reminded the Congress that those who had been "unfriendly to the Constitution" and had intended to prevent its adoption "had stated to their constituents that the power of making Treaties, as confided to the President and Senate, was as extensive as was now contended for." While the opposition to the Constitution sought "to alarm the people with the dangerous extent, and what would be the pernicious exercise of this power," supporters made no effort to deny the scope of the power ascribed to the president and Senate. "They did no such thing; they admitted the power, proved the necessity of it, and contended that it would be safe in practice." The Federalist strategy of reading Anti-Federalist texts as proof that Democratic-Republican concerns had been given a fair hearing at ratification and were rejected put the former Anti-Federalists serving in Congress on the defensive. The authors of these particular texts, as it were, no longer were the masters of them. Once those texts became part of the public record, they could be read in ways that their authors would have found shocking. Authorship of a particular text conferred no intellectual ownership, and efforts to identify the original intent served only to underscore the impossibility of fixing the meaning of those texts. Rereadings and misreadings proliferated in direct proportion to the political significance of the text being discussed.[4]

3. Ibid. The major concern expressed by Anti-Federalists regarding the treaty power was that it might be used to extend federal power over the states by binding them to treaties negotiated without their input. Virginia Anti-Federalists showed the most concern with the dangers of the Senate's treaty power and the absence of House involvement. Virginians were especially worried about commercial treaties and the cessation of land claims. For some of the most important statements on these issues, see George Mason, "Objections to the Constitution of Government Formed by the Convention," *Massachusetts Centinel* (Boston), Nov. 21, 1787 (*CA-F*, II, 9–14); "The Society of Western Gentlemen Revise the Constitution," *Virginia Independent Chronicle* (Richmond), Apr. 30, May 7, 1778 (*DHRC*, IX, 771); and the following speeches and resolves introduced in the Virginia convention: *DHRC*, X, 1241, 1247, 1256, 1393, 1536, 1549.

4. *Annals of Congress*, 4th Congress, 1st sess. (1796), V, 523.

The presence of a number of former Anti-Federalists, including the authors of some of the texts being cited by Federalists, complicated the situation facing Democratic-Republicans. What opposition spokesmen tried to do was distance themselves from the claims they had made in 1788 and insist that, if such claims were to be invoked, they had to be properly contextualized. Two general points need to be kept in mind when seeking to situate Anti-Federalist objections within the context of the original debate over the Constitution. First, Anti-Federalist reservations about the treaty-making powers were an expression of a larger concern about the danger posed by the new government. Second, those fears had been addressed by Federalists, whose assurances were taken as proof that the alleged dangers were imaginary. Once again, Democratic-Republicans insisted that Anti-Federalist writings had to be read in conjunction with the responses of those Federalists who genuinely sought to quiet the apprehensions of their opponents. To cite Anti-Federalist writings by themselves obscured the fact that those writings had been part of a public debate. If one had to quote from only one side, then it was more appropriate to quote from the assurances provided by Federalists, not the fears expressed by Anti-Federalists. It was the founding dialogue between Anti-Federalists and Federalists that shaped the debate within the individual ratification conventions.

This interpretive strategy was adopted by William Findley, who sought to clarify the original understanding of Pennsylvania Anti-Federalists while establishing some distance from the documents produced on those particular occasions. Disagreeing that Anti-Federalist writings could be used to argue against some role for the House in foreign relations and treaty making, Findley expressed surprise that "the minority of the ratifying convention of Pennsylvania has been adduced to prove, that this was not believed to be the meaning of the Constitution at that time." He reminded the House that he had himself been one of the dissenting members of the Pennsylvania ratification convention, a statement consciously designed to reclaim ownership of a text he had helped produce. Findley acknowledged that the scope of the Senate's powers in making treaties had generated some concern, but he expressed his puzzlement with how the views of the minority were now being used: it was strange that "the sentiments of a minority, acting under peculiar circumstance of irritation," would "be quoted as a good authority for the true sense of the Constitution on this occasion." Such a construction was particularly strained, since the leading defender of the Constitution in Pennsylvania had confirmed the view now championed by Democratic-Republicans. Findley not only challenged the particular reading of the Anti-Federalist position but quoted the glosses on the treaty-making clause made by Federalists in 1788. He also disputed the logic of using Anti-Federalist writings in isolation and sought to expose the flaw in this argument. One could not read Anti-Federalist criticisms out of context, without considering the Federalist responses: Anti-Federalist objections had to be read alongside Federalist replies. One of the "advocates of the Constitution," who was "a celebrated politician" and "had an eminent hand in framing the Constitution, maintained that an effective, though indirect check on the exercise of the Treaty-making power, would naturally grow out of the exercise of the Legislative authority." Findley's rereading of the intent of the Pennsylvania minority invoked the sort of contextualist argument that had shaped Democratic-Republican constitutional interpretation since the conflict over the bank. Federalist and Anti-Federalist texts could not be understood apart from each another, but had to be read as part of a larger public debate.[5]

Albert Gallatin followed a strategy analogous to Findley's, querying the House about the report of the Harrisburg convention. Were they not, he wondered, "fully justifiable in their fears that part of the Constitution might be misconstrued?" The general principles asserted in Anti-Federalist writings such as the proceedings of the Harrisburg convention merely echoed those of the various state ratification conventions, whose deliberations were the ones that enjoyed legal standing in the quest for determining the original understanding of the Constitution. "The people and the State Conventions who ratified, who adopted the instrument, are alone parties to it, and their intentions alone might, with any degree of propriety, be resorted to." Anti-Federalist writings, wrenched from their original context, were an odd form of proof as to the original understanding of the Constitution. Indeed, Gallatin reiterated the point made by Findley: it was curious that, if only one side were to be quoted, it would be the opposers of the Constitution, not its original supporters. When severed from their original role in a particular public debate, Anti-Federalist texts lost their meaning. Once decontextualized, Gallatin argued, they were easily misinterpreted and manipulated to suit the agenda of Federalists.[6]

Democratic-Republican William Brent of Virginia adopted an interpretive strategy similar to Gallatin's. Brent was especially outraged by how the debates of state ratification conventions had been used by Federalists. Since those proceedings had been used "as an offensive weapon, he would endeavor to employ them as a defensive weapon." To prove that the Democratic-Republican construction was not novel, he referred to the original debates

5. Ibid., 592.
6. Ibid., 734–736.

cited by Federalists. Brent quoted from "a distinguished writer of the day, who was in opposition to the adoption of the Constitution." That writer had "construed the part of the Constitution now under consideration" in the same manner as the Republicans in Congress understood the powers of the House. After reading a long excerpt from *Letters from the Federal Farmer,* Brent noted that he "might have recourse to the pamphlet called *The Federalist,* as another authority to prove his construction." Frustrated by the misuse to which Anti-Federalist ideas had been put, he wondered: "If the public sentiments of that day is to be recurred to for an exposition of the Constitution, he wished to know whether the sentiments of the majority or minority were to be recurred to?" Brent answered his own rhetorical question. It was the intent of the majority that "must be considered as expressing the wishes of the people." The interpretive strategy favored by Gallatin and Brent followed a similar logic. The arguments of Anti-Federalists had to be understood within their original context, as part of a general indictment of certain defects in the Constitution. Those defects had been answered by Federalists. If any texts were quoted in isolation, they ought to be the texts that Federalists used to reassure the people, not the texts Anti-Federalists had written to sound an alarm.[7]

James Madison, who might well have trumped all other participants in this debate by invoking his authorship of *The Federalist,* refrained from playing this card in favor of a different tactic. In contrast to Gallatin, Madison argued that it would be "proper to attend to other amendments proposed by the ratifying Conventions which may throw light on their opinions and intentions on the subject in question." Madison considered the amendments proposed by Virginia, North Carolina, New York, Maryland, and New Hampshire. From these various proceedings, Madison identified a general principle of jealousy and asserted that there had been no intent absolutely to deprive the House of all control and extend "an absolute and unlimited power over all those great objects" to the Senate and executive.[8]

The difficult task of interpreting various provisions of the Constitution had prompted both Democratic-Republicans and Federalists to search beyond the Constitution and examine extratextual sources for insights into the

7. Ibid., 579–582.
8. Ibid., 778–779. In the view of Jack N. Rakove, the Federalists had the better originalist argument. Madison's originalism was "marred by unresolved problems." Moreover, "whatever clarity he gained by distinguishing framers from ratifiers was clouded by the difficulty of using the ambiguous debates and failed amendments of 1787–88 to offset an express constitutional provision" (*Original Meanings: Politics and Ideas in the Making of the Constitution* [New York, 1996], 364).

original understanding of the Constitution. A number of Federalists quoted Anti-Federalist essays and the deliberations of the state ratification conventions to prove that Democratic-Republicans were trying to revive arguments made at the time of ratification and rejected by the people. Democratic-Republicans responded by challenging the way Anti-Federalist texts were being read out of context, returning to a strategy crucial to their emerging constitutional philosophy since the debate over the bank: the original meaning of the Constitution was a product of give-and-take between Anti-Federalists and Federalists. Although no one seriously quoted the toasts given upon ratification, as one sarcastic participant in the debate over the Jay Treaty had recommended, a variety of quite different types of Anti-Federalist texts were invoked in these debates. The two most important published Anti-Federalist texts to resurface were "The Address and Reasons of Dissent of the Minority" and *Letters from the Federal Farmer*. The resolves of the Harrisburg convention were also cited as evidence of Anti-Federalist belief at the time of ratification. Some Democratic-Republicans even cited *The Federalist*, choosing to read Publius through the lens of his Anti-Federalist antagonists. In effect, Democratic-Republicans generated an Anti-Federalist interpretation of *The Federalist*, focusing on Publius's response to his opponents' complaints. Others focused on the argument between Anti-Federalists and Federalists within the individual state ratification conventions.[9]

Although a few influential speeches from the various conventions had found their way into print during ratification, the actual deliberations had not been widely available then. Their subsequent publication, however, had a profound impact on the dynamics of the public debate over the meaning of the Constitution. Although the published proceedings were attacked as both partisan and inaccurate, they were still accorded a privileged status because they were the only record of the deliberations of the people of the states, the parties that endowed the Constitution with legal force. The concerns expressed by Anti-Federalists in the surviving records of the state ratification conventions gradually surpassed the published writings of Anti-Federalist authors as the most important expressions of Anti-Federalist ideas. The emergence of the ratification debates as the chief texts for reconstructing the original understanding of the Constitution was crucial in the evolution of a coherent opposition constitutional theory. The most articulate spokesman for this emerging theory was James Madison. The emphasis on the intent of

9. H. Jefferson Powell "The Original Understanding of Original Intent," *Harvard Law Review*, XCVIII (1985), 885–948.

the ratifiers, particularly on the negotiations between Federalists and Anti-Federalists within individual conventions, became a cornerstone of Madison's own constitutional theory.

This was not a rarefied dispute confined to the halls of Congress. The issues also spilled over into popular political discourse. How these issues permeated popular political culture can be glimpsed in the writings of William Manning, the tavernkeeper from Billerica, Massachusetts. Manning admitted that his own knowledge of politics was gleaned from the popular press, and his writings provide a window into the way one important segment of the popular reading public perceived constitutional issues. Regarding the Constitutional Convention, he echoed a common Anti-Federalist complaint: the framers deliberately employed ambiguous language to facilitate their aristocratic designs. He confidently asserted, "The Convention who made it intended to destroy our free governments by, or they neaver would have spent 4 Months in making such an inexpliset thing." The Constitution was "made like A Fiddle, with but few Strings," so that those in power might "play any tune upon it they pleased." The ambiguity of the Constitution was a deliberate product of Federalist aristocratic machinations—confirmed by the practices of Federalists since ratification. Under the guise of constructive interpretations, Federalists were seeking to extend the powers of the federal government and trample on the people's liberties.[10]

The conflict over the Jay Treaty galvanized public attention. Opposition to it was intense, and effigies of Jay were burned in the streets in many cities. It is interesting that Manning's comments on the treaty placed the constitutional questions arising from the controversy at the center of the tempest. Manning echoed the stance of Democratic-Republican politicians. He shared the Democratic-Republican view that the House ought to have access to Jay's instructions. To support that position he invoked the very same approach to constitutional interpretation that defined the congressional debate, that the intent of the state ratification conventions ought to guide constitutional interpretation. It was "the sence and meening of the peopel when they excepted it" that was the final arbiter of the Constitution, not the intent of those who framed the document. Applauding the efforts of the House to check the Senate, he defended such actions as an appropriate exercise of the popular will, which would check the designs of the aristocratic faction in government. Concern about issues of constitutional inter-

10. Samuel Eliot Morison, "William Manning's 'The Key of Libberty,'" *WMQ*, 3d Ser., XIII (1956), 234–235.

pretation were clearly not something restricted to the courts or Congress. Manning's awareness of these issues testifies to the effectiveness of the press at bringing them to the attention of the public.[11]

During the debate over the Jay Treaty a diversity of texts was canvassed for evidence of the original undertanding of the Constitution. The easy availability of *The Federalist* and an emerging consensus on its value as an exposition of the Constitution led Democratic-Republicans and Federalists alike to search its pages for support for their own views. Reconstructing the original Anti-Federalist understanding of the Constitution was somewhat more difficult. Unlike *The Federalist,* Anti-Federalist texts had not been reprinted and did not go through multiple editions. The proceedings of the various state ratification conventions assumed position as the authoritative voice of Anti-Federalist dissent and assumed a quasi-legal standing as the record of the bodies that had endowed the Constitution with the force of law. Far from perfect, those texts became the primary sources by which the original Anti-Federalist critique of the Constitution entered constitutional debate. The primacy of the proceedings of the state conventions would remain unchallenged until the publication of Anti-Federalist Robert Yates's *Notes of the Federal Convention* a quarter-century later.[12]

The Sedition Act and the Transformation of Opposition Constitutionalism

No Federalist legislation passed since the adoption of the Constitution more inflamed political passions than the Alien and Sedition Acts, and the Sedition Act precipitated the most serious constitutional crisis in the period after ratification. The Alien and Sedition Acts forced opposition theorists to grapple with the meaning of dissent in novel ways. The meaning of "loyal opposition" was radically transformed and the course of American constitutionalism irrevocably altered by the response to those acts.

11. Ibid.
12. Modern constitutional theory has approached the problem of the slipperiness of constitutional texts from several perspectives. For hermeneutical approaches, see the essays in Sanford Levinson and Steven Mallioux, eds., *Interpreting Law and Literature: A Hermeneutic Reader* (Evanston, Ill., 1988). For neopragmatism, see Stanley Fish, *Doing What Comes Naturally: Change, Rhetoric, and the Practice of Theory in Literary and Legal Studies* (Durham, N.C., 1989). For deconstruction, see the essays in *Deconstruction and the Possibility of Justice, Cardozo Law Review,* XI (1990), 919–1726.

The Federalists' fears about foreign and domestic subversion had led them to pass pieces of legislation in 1798 making it more difficult to become a citizen and making seditious libel a federal crime. Federalists defended the Alien and Sedition Acts as necessary to prevent foreign agents, radical refugees, and their domestic allies from undermining American republicanism. The Sedition Act was interpreted by Democratic-Republicans as incontrovertible proof that their prognostications about the nefarious designs of Federalists had been correct. In challenging the constitutionality of the Sedition Act, Democratic-Republicans inaugurated a new phase of dissenting constitutional theory.

The most ardent Federalists believed that the act would help purify American politics and rid the nation of the last remnants of Anti-Federalist opposition. Fisher Ames actually welcomed the controversy over the Alien and Sedition Acts, because it would help clarify the lines of political division within American politics. He was eager to rid his own party of "trimmers" and believed that the severity of the Alien and Sedition laws would eliminate those not truly committed to the party's ideals. Ames derided the "theory of the Feds" who "help the government at a pinch, and then shout victory for two seconds,—after which, they coax and try to gain the *antis,* by yielding the very principles in dispute." In Ames's judgment, "The moderates are the meanest of cowards, the falsest of hypocrites." There was one virtue of the opposition: "The other side has none of them, though it abounds in every other kind of baseness. Their Guy Fauxes are no triflers. They have energy enough to vindicate the French, and, if opportunity favored, to imitate them." Ames continued to view politics in the 1790s through the same lens as he viewed the politics of ratification: "The implacable foes of the Constitution—foes before it was made, while it was making, and since,—became full of tender fears lest it should be violated by the alien and sedition laws." He dismissed the opposition's newfound fidelity to the Constitution as a disguise appropriated to hide the radical Anti-Federalist–Democratic-Republican agenda.[13]

One of the leading congressional spokesmen for the opposition, Albert Gallatin challenged the constitutionality of the Sedition Act by invoking the original understanding of the Bill of Rights: "The bill now under discussion justified the suspicions of those who, at the time of the adoption of the Constitution, had apprehended that the sense of that generally expressed clause might be distorted for that purpose." The First Congress recognized the legit-

13. Fisher Ames to Christopher Gore, Dec. 18, 1798, in W. B. Allen, ed., *Works of Fisher Ames,* 2 vols. (Indianapolis, Ind., 1983), II, 1302–1303.

imacy of the Anti-Federalist concerns over this issue and had adopted the First Amendment to correct this flaw: "It was in order to remove these fears, that the amendment, which declares that Congress shall pass no law abridging the freedom of speech or the liberty of the press, was proposed and adopted." Gallatin reiterated the Anti-Federalist fear that only strict adherence to the text of the Constitution could protect popular liberty: "It must be remembered that the only security of citizens against unconstitutional measures consists in a strict adherence to the Constitution." Ultimately, Gallatin observed, "their liberties were only protected by a *parchment*—by *words*—and that they may be destroyed whenever it shall be admitted that the strict and common sense of words may be construed away." Gallatin embraced the constitutional plain style that informed so much Anti-Federalist writing during ratification. The Federalists sought to subvert the Constitution through a process of construction. The only means of preventing this was to interpret the Constitution in strict terms. In doubtful circumstances the language of the text was to be construed so as to limit power, not increase it. Constitutional texts were drafted as limits on government, the line beyond which government could not go. They were not intended to provide pretexts for extending the power of government.[14]

While the conflict over the Alien and Sedition Acts did not prompt many Democratic-Republicans to abandon their faith in the Constitution and return to the doctrines of 1787–1788, it did lead many to assert that the worst nightmares predicted during ratification had finally been realized. In response to the Federalist measures, James Callender reminded readers that "that AWFUL SQUINTING foreseen by Patrick Henry" in the Virginia ratification convention, a tendency toward monarchism, had now been realized by Federalist policy. Callender denounced the Constitution in vigorous terms. He peppered his diatribe with a number of references to classic works of dissenting constitutional spokesmen, including William Findley and John Taylor. The threat of the Sedition Act surpassed any previous danger. It seemed to embody the Anti-Federalists' worst nightmare about the potential of the Constitution to be exploited by unscrupulous politicians eager to squelch liberty.[15]

14. *Annals of Congress*, 5th Congress, 2d and 3d sess. (1798), VIII, 2159, 3d sess. (1799), IX, 3002.

15. John C. Miller, *Crisis in Freedom: The Alien and Sedition Acts* (Boston, 1951); [James Callender], *The Prospect before Us*, I (Richmond, Va., 1800), title page (quote from Henry), 10–20, 83; *Aurora: General Advertiser* (Philadelphia), Mar. 15, 1800; *Examiner* (Richmond, Va.), Dec. 10, 1798; *Argus: Greenleaf's New Daily Advertiser* (New York), July 20, 1798.

Seventeen indictments were made under the Sedition Act, and among those were several figures with strong Anti-Federalist connections, including Congressman Matthew Lyon of Vermont and Ann Greenleaf, the widow of publisher Thomas Greenleaf. In addition, a number of other individuals singled out for punishment were recent immigrants who identified themselves with Anti-Federalist principles, including Thomas Cooper and James Callender. Although neither man had taken part in the struggle over the Constitution, both viewed the events of the 1790s as continuing the battle between Federalists and Anti-Federalists. Indeed, in many respects these men were more ardent champions of Anti-Federalist ideas than were many of the former opponents of the Constitution.[16]

Cooper's understanding of American politics was set out in *Some Information respecting America,* published abroad in 1794 after a short sojourn in America. It provided a general overview of American society and was generally laudatory about the achievements of American politics. Cooper noted that, apart from a few royalists, "the rest of the Americans are republicans." There were, however, two types of republicans, "one leaning to an extensive rather than a limitation of the powers of the legislative and executive government." That group favored British-style politics and sought to "introduce and extend the funding, the manufacturing, and commercial systems." They were "denominated the Federalists, partly because they were the chief introducers and supporters of the present federal government and the Constitution of 1787." Another style of republicans was called "Anti-Federalists: not because they are adverse to a federal government," but "in contradistinction rather to the denomination of the other class." The chief distinguishing characteristic of the Anti-Federalists was that they "were hostile to extensive powers given to government." Cooper associated Anti-Federalism with a desire to bring government closer to the people and a suspicion of the monopolizing spirit associated with high-toned government.[17]

In 1794, Cooper had settled in western Pennsylvania, where he found a

16. The role of this influential core of Jeffersonian opinion makers is discussed in Michael Durey, "Thomas Paine's Apostles: Radical Emigrés and the Triumph of Jeffersonian Republicanism," *WMQ*, 3d Ser., XLIV (1987) 661–688. Two of the most influential immigrants, James Callender and Thomas Cooper, each expressed considerable sympathy with the Anti-Federalist cause even though neither had participated directly in the struggle over ratification. For a more detailed discussion of Callender, see Michael Durey, *"With the Hammer of Truth": James Thomson Callender and America's Early National Heroes* (Charlottesville, Va., 1990). On Cooper, see Dumas Malone, *The Public Life of Thomas Cooper, 1783–1839* (New Haven, Conn., 1926), chaps. 3–4.

17. Thomas Cooper, *Some Information respecting America* . . . (Dublin, 1794), 67–68.

receptive audience for his ideas. Shortly after assuming the editorship of the *Northumberland Gazette* in 1799, he published a volume entitled *Political Essays*. In response to Federalist attacks on his *Essays,* Cooper lashed out at the Adams administration, and he was charged with seditious libel.[18]

During his trial for sedition, Cooper reiterated this understanding of the conflict between an essentially Anti-Federalist and a Federalist vision of politics. "This country is divided, and almost equally divided, into two grand parties; usually termed, whether properly or improperly, *Federalists* and *Anti-Federalists.*" Cooper then restated his earlier belief: "The one wishes to increase, the other to diminish, the powers of the executive; the one thinks that the people (the democracy of the country) has too much [power]." The contrast between the two extended to virtually every important political issue of the day: "The one thinks the liberties of our country endangered by the licentiousness, the other, by the restrictions of the press." While many former Anti-Federalists had earlier abandoned this label, Cooper showed no hesitancy about invoking the original opposition to the Constitution.[19]

James Callender, a Scottish immigrant and another prominent émigré editor who had not participated in the debate over the Constitution, also cast the political struggles of the 1790s in terms of the original debate between Federalists and Anti-Federalists. He went further than many Democratic-Republicans, reviving a more a radical variant of Anti-Federalist thought, in championing a simple, direct form of democracy uncomplicated by the system of checks and balances found in the federal Constitution.

Callender was sufficiently concerned about his vulnerability under the Alien Act to become a naturalized citizen in 1798. Believing that his vituperative attacks on high-ranking Federalists made him a likely target for prosecution under the Sedition Act, Callender left Philadelphia and resolved to refrain from publishing anything that might provoke an accusation of seditious libel. By 1799, he was safely established in the Republican stronghold of Virginia. He once again entered the political fray and joined the leading Republican paper in the state, the *Richmond Examiner*. As alleged in his trial, *The Prospect before Us* attacked President Adams, charging, "The reign of Mr. Adams has been one continued tempest of malignant passions." Ultimately,

18. Thomas Cooper, *Political Essays . . .* (Northumberland, Pa., 1799). For a general discussion of this phase of his career, see Malone, *The Public Life of Thomas Cooper,* chaps. 3–4.

19. "Trial of Thomas Cooper, for a Seditious Libel, in the Circuit Court of the United States for the Pennsylvania District, Philadelphia, 1800," in Francis Wharton, ed., *State Trials of the United States during the Administrations of Washington and Adams* (Philadelphia, 1849), 659–679 (quotations on 664).

Callender prophesied, the salvation of America depended on a choice "between Adams, war and beggary, and Jefferson, peace and competency."[20]

Callender went even further than Cooper in asserting a distinctly Anti-Federalist vision of the evolution of American politics. He departed from the conciliatory rhetoric characterizing nearly all writings by former Anti-Federalists. He showed no reverence for the Constitution, ridiculing the claim that it was a "government of *your own choice*." Quite the contrary was true: "The federal constitution, was crammed down the gullet of America." The Constitution had been "preferred by a *part* of the people" only and had met with "long and violent resistance to its adoption." Callender evoked the rhetoric of Patrick Henry's critique of the Constitution:

> It was the judgement of Patrick Henry, and it is mine, that the federal constitution, as it now stands, is good for almost nothing; that it as full of imperfections, as a sieve is full of holes; that unless the compact shall meet with numerous and material amendments, it must forever prove a thorn festering in the midriff of American prosperity.[21]

Callender was the last person prosecuted under the Sedition Act, and the only person prosecuted in the South; his case became one of the most celebrated of any brought. His defense team numbered some of the most celebrated legal minds in the country, including William Wirt, Patrick Henry's son-in-law, George Hay, son-in-law of James Monroe, and Philip Norborne Nicholas, the attorney general of Virginia. Wirt employed a classic Zengerian defense. He reminded the jury of its sacred obligation to judge both matters of fact and law and hoped that it might nullify the Sedition Act—that is, refuse to convict Callender. That effort was stymied by the court. A slightly different strategy was pursued by Hay, who proposed to call John Taylor of Caroline as his first witness, who would prove the truth of Callender's assertion that Adams was "a professed aristocrat." The effort to place Adams's political philosophy on trial also failed when the judge refused to allow Taylor to testify. The latter tactic would have used the trial as a public forum to rally public opinion to Callender's cause.[22]

---

20. "Trial of James Thompson Callender, for a Seditious Libel, in the Circuit Court of the United States for the Virginia District, Richmond, 1800," ibid., 688–690.

21. [Callender], *The Prospect before Us*, II, 56. For a more general discussion, see Durey, *"With the Hammer of Truth."*

22. The case solidified Republican opposition to the Federalist judiciary and eventually resulted in the impeachment (but acquittal) of Judge Samuel Chase, the former Anti-Federalist, who became one of the most outspoken and controversial converts to the Federalist cause. Chase's transformation from Anti-Federalist into Burkean conservative and

The main targets of Sedition cases were printers who published works critical of the administration, in most cases fairly prominent opposition figures. Although the Sedition Act did not generate the violence that the Whiskey Rebellion did, it did prompt a broader popular reaction than any other conflict since that episode. Popular opposition to the Sedition Act had taken a variety of forms, including public meetings and even a number of symbolic protests that drew on the rich legacy of plebeian and Revolutionary protest. The most important of those symbols was liberty poles. The raising of a liberty pole in Dedham, Massachusetts, home of the arch-Federalist Fisher Ames, prompted one of the most fascinating cases tried under the Sedition Act. Federalist ire was directed at David Brown, a self-described "laboring man" who had spoken in Dedham before the erecting of the liberty pole. In contrast to Manning, whose tavern provided him with a fixed political pulpit, Brown was an itinerant preacher who traveled across the state spreading his political gospel. His hostility to the Federalists was couched in terms nearly identical to those used by Manning. Brown denounced Federalist aristocrats, reminding his listeners, "There always has been an eternal struggle between the laboring part of the community and those lazy rascals that invented every means that the Devil, has put into their heads, to destroy the laboring part of the community." The efforts of Federalists to destroy liberty were in Brown's view doomed, since "seven-eights of the people are opposed to the measures of tyrants." Ultimately, the people would triumph because no government could long survive "after the confidence of the people was lost." While Brown clearly favored peaceful remonstrance and petition as the best method to secure the repeal of the Alien and Sedition laws, he hinted that, if government continued to reject such appeals, popular animosity might not be contained forever.[23]

For Federalists, Brown represented the sort of leveling egalitarian ideas that led to mobocracy. His use of the symbolism of the liberty pole seemed tame compared to the tar and feathers used by the Whiskey rebels to express their protest. Still, Federalists viewed Brown's plebeian rituals with horror. Their response to him was swift and decisive. Brown received the most

Federalist is detailed in Stephen B. Presser and Becky Bair Hurley, "Saving God's Republic: The Jurisprudence of Samuel Chase," *University of Illinois Law Review,* 1984, 771; Presser, *The Original Misunderstanding: The English, the Americans, and the Dialectic of Federalist Jurisprudence* (Durham, N.C., 1991).

23. MS Indictment of David Brown, June 1799, Federal Circuit Court, Boston, National Archives, Northeast Region. The original is missing, but much of it has been reprinted in Irving Mark and Eugene L. Schwab, eds., *The Faith of Our Fathers: An Anthology Expressing the Aspirations of the American Common Man, 1790–1860* (New York, 1952), 46.

severe sentence of any individual brought up on charges under the Sedition Act, eighteen months in prison, extended because he could not pay the fine of $480. Federalists argued that his crimes were particularly heinous because they were primarily directed at the "uninformed part of the community."[24]

Democratic-Republicans used all of the constitutional mechanisms for redress available to persuade Congress to repeal the law. Hostility to the acts was widespread. Newspapers teemed with denunciations of the Federalist policy. Mass meetings were organized, drawing crowds numbering as high as five thousand.

One of the most effective campaigns against the acts occurred in Kentucky, where, in the course of the public debate over the acts, a variety of remedies were proposed. Considerable effort was made to rouse public opinion, including public meetings and the press. Petitions and remonstrances were drafted to influence Congress directly, repeal of the law being the primary goal of the opposition. At the same time that they sought to persuade Congress to change its mind, others were thinking about other means for combating so egregious a violation of the Constitution. The normal remedies available were fairly limited. Some believed that the law should be declared unconstitutional by the federal courts while others had faith that individual juries might still nullify the law. When it became clear that those normal constitutional mechanisms would not work, opposition thinkers began the most serious reexamination of constitutional ideas since ratification.[25]

The Principles of '98

When the normal political and legal mechanisms for challenging the Sedition law failed, Democratic-Republicans were forced to think in novel ways about how to protect individual liberty and restore the federal government to its proper sphere of authority. It was only natural that Democratic-Republicans would see federalism as the most effective means of defending individual liberty from the Sedition Act. The principles of federalism had been central to opposition thought since ratification. The structure of the federal system was always seen as the final guarantor of individual liberty.

24. Ibid. On the Brown case, see James Morton Smith, *Freedom's Fetters: The Alien and Sedition Laws and American Civil Liberties* (Ithaca, N.Y., 1956). On the response of Federalists, see Ames to Gore, Dec. 18, 1798, in Allen, ed., *Works of Ames,* II, 1303.

25. On the Alien and Sedition Acts, see Miller, *Crisis in Freedom;* Smith, *Freedom's Fetters.* On the response of Kentucky, see James Morton Smith, "The Grass Roots Origins of the Kentucky Resolutions," *WMQ,* 3d Ser., XXVII (1970), 221–245.

Although this belief was a cardinal tenet of dissenting constitutionalism, relatively little attention had been devoted to exploring and analyzing how this checking function would operate when the normal mechanisms to guard liberty failed.

During ratification, numerous Anti-Federalist authors attacked the Constitution for creating a consolidated national government and thereby undermining the federal system. Those authors deliberately cast the future of federalism under the Constitution in the worst possible light. Their most frightening scenarios were part of a carefully orchestrated rhetorical strategy to defeat ratification. Authors deliberately avoided sketching possible remedies that might be available under the Constitution, in order to generate the greatest opposition to ratification. In the few instances in which Anti-Federalists discussed the options available to the states, the general consensus seemed to be that the only remedy was amendment. Such rhetoric obviously suited their needs in 1787–1788, when many Anti-Federalists believed it was possible to defeat or substantially alter the Constitution. By 1798, however, the democratic opposition faced a completely different situation.[26]

In response to the Sedition Act, Democratic-Republicans were forced to chart a new path, which drew some inspiration from the Anti-Federalist and earlier Democratic-Republican interpretations of the Constitution even as they marked out a new trajectory for opposition constitutionalism.[27]

26. On the tradition of states' rights, see Alpheus Thomas Mason, *The States Rights Debate: Antifederalism and the Constitution* (Englewood Cliffs, N.J., 1964). For an interesting discussion of Mason's shifting view of the Anti-Federalists that explores the libertarian and states' rights aspects of their thought, see H. L. Pohlman, "A. T. Mason and American Political Thought: A Non-Princetonian's View," *Constitutional Commentary,* VIII (1991), 51–63. For examples of scholarship that chart a direct connection between Anti-Federalism and Calhoun's theory of nullification, see Murray Dry, "The Debate over Ratification of the Constitution," in Jack P. Greene and J. R. Pole, eds., *The Blackwell Encyclopedia of the American Revolution* (London, 1991), 471–486; Morton J. Frisch, "The Persistence of Anti-Federalism between the Ratification of the Constitution and the Nullification Crisis," in Josephine F. Pacheco, ed., *Antifederalism: The Legacy of George Mason* (Fairfax, Va., 1992), 79–90; David F. Ericson, *The Shaping of American Liberalism: The Debates over Ratification, Nullification, and Slavery* (Chicago, 1993). A more reasonable genealogy for Calhoun connects nullification with the ideas of 1798, not 1788; on this point, see Don E. Fehrenbacher, *Constitutions and Constitutionalism in the Slaveholding South* (Athens, Ga., 1989)

27. On this point, see Kenneth M. Stampp, "The Concept of a Perpetual Union," *JAH,* LXV (1978–1979), 18. For a discussion of the importance of the principles of '98, see Richard E. Ellis, *The Jeffersonian Crisis: Courts and Politics in the Young Republic* (New York, 1971), 266–275; H. Jefferson Powell, "The Principles of '98: An Essay in Historical Retrieval," *Virginia Law Review,* LXXX (1994), 689–743.

Exactly how would the will of the people be determined in those extraordinary circumstances in which the states were called upon to exercise their role as the final check on tyranny? Would the judiciary, the legislature, or the people be the agents exercising the final check? During the debate over the Sedition Act, all of those had been proposed as answers. One of the most important efforts to sort out this problem and frame a response invoking the checking function of federalism was John Taylor's, in a letter to Thomas Jefferson: "The right of the state government to expound the Constitution might possibly be mad the basis toward a movement toward its amendment." Building upon the idea that the intent of the state ratification conventions ought to guide constitutional interpretation, Taylor took an important step toward the creation of a compact theory of federalism in asserting, "The people in state conventions are incontrovertibly the contacting parties, and, possessing the infringing rights, may proceed by orderly steps to attain the object." In making this argument, Taylor moved from a fairly abstract theory of states' rights federalism to a concrete assertion of what would become the core doctrine of the compact theory of states' rights.[28]

The compact theory of the Union was an important development in the creation of a dissenting constitutional theory to oppose the nationalism of Federalist constitutionalism. Taylor's suggestion that the states might provide a check on the unconstitutional acts of the federal government was not novel. Ironically, that had been one of the the arguments Federalists had used to satisfy their opponents in 1788. Taylor took the notion and reformulated it: the people acting in their corporate capacity as citizens of the individual states were the true parties to the compact that created the Union and could serve as a check on the federal government.

The task of formulating a constitutional response to the Alien and Sedition Acts that would make Taylor's theory viable fell to Madison and Jefferson in the Virginia and Kentucky Resolutions. Jefferson arranged for his friend John Breckinridge to introduce a set of resolutions attacking the

28. John Taylor to Thomas Jefferson, June 25, 1798, in William Dodd, ed., "John Taylor Correspondence," *John P. Branch Historical Papers of Randolph-Macon College*, II (1908), 271–276. On the importance of this letter to Jefferson's thought, see David N. Mayer, *The Constitutional Thought of Thomas Jefferson* (Charlottesville, Va., 1994), 199–208. Mayer links Jefferson's views to John Taylor's and stresses the relationship between states' rights and the preservation of liberty. This view is also endorsed by James Roger Sharp, *American Politics in the Early Republic: The New Nation in Crisis* (New Haven, Conn., 1993), chap. 9. Garrett Ward Sheldon, *The Political Philosophy of Thomas Jefferson* (Baltimore, 1991), stresses the democratic roots of this aspect of Jefferson's thought. Leonard W. Levy, *Jefferson and Civil Liberties: The Darker Side* (Cambridge, Mass., 1963), questions the libertarian views of Jefferson.

constitutionality of the acts in the Kentucky legislature. Another set of resolutions drafted by Madison was introduced into the Virginia legislature by John Taylor a month later, in December 1798. Neither Jefferson nor Madison took public credit for the documents. It seemed more prudent for both men to remain in the background while the legislatures of the two states appealed to the other states to oppose the acts. The Virginia and Kentucky Resolutions then circulated among the various state legislatures. Madison and Jefferson had hoped that the resolutions would rally opposition to Federalist policy, but they attracted no official support outside their states of origin and drew hostile replies from many legislatures, particularly those in the most ardently Federalist region of the nation, New England.

Both documents drew on the anticonsolidationist rhetoric that had defined dissenting constitutional discourse since ratification. In both cases, Jefferson and Madison asserted that the protection of individual liberty depended upon preserving the balance of power between the states and the federal government. States' rights and individual rights continued to be linked in opposition constitutional discourse. The two documents also adopted the compact theory of federalism, in which the states were cast as the original parties of the compact that created the Union. The people acting through the states had consented to alienate a portion of their power to the federal government for a limited set of objectives detailed by the Constitution. The original parties to this compact, the states, were therefore entitled to judge infractions that violated the original contract.

The Kentucky Resolutions affirmed, "The several states composing the United States of America are not united on the principle of unlimited submission to their general government." Jefferson's interpretation of the compact implied that individual states could judge for themselves the constitutionality of legislation. A corollary of this position was the view, "As in all other cases of compact among parties having no common judge, *each party has an equal right to judge for itself, as well of infractions as of the mode and measure of redress.*" Jefferson's original draft of the Kentucky Resolutions had called for state nullification of unconstitutional acts of Congress, but this language was omitted from the final version adopted by the Kentucky legislature. Asserting the right to judge infringements, even without an assertion of the right to nullify laws, did appear to give individual states a right to determine for themselves the constitutionality of federal laws.[29]

29. "Kentucky Resolutions of 1798," in Jefferson Powell, ed., *Languages of Power: A Sourcebook of Early American Constitutional History* (Durham, N.C., 1991), 130–133 (emphasis added).

James Madison's more temperate response in the Virginia Resolutions did not assert an individual state right, but noted that in extraordinary cases, when the Constitution's safeguards had broken down, the states "have the right, and are in duty bound to interpose for arresting the progress of the evil." By invoking the right of the states together, not of individual states, and employing the vague concept of interposition, Madison avoided language that would suggest the right of an individual state legally to nullify an unconstitutional law. The Virginia Resolutions shared with Jefferson's Kentucky Resolutions an emphasis on the compact theory of union. Madison declared that "the powers of the federal government" resulted "from the compact to which the states are parties, as limited by the plain sense and intention of the instrument constituting that compact."[30]

The efforts of the Kentucky and Virginia legislatures to seek redress were rebuffed by the other states and prompted Jefferson and Madison to compose a second set of resolutions. The term "nullification" was reintroduced in the Kentucky Resolutions of 1799. Once again, it was the state legislature that sought to sound the alarm. Asserting that the individual states could not only judge issues of constitutionality, the resolution also affirmed that in extreme circumstances nullification was the rightful remedy. The forcefulness of the term "nullification" was counterbalanced by the assertion that Kentucky would "bow to the laws of the Union" while continuing "to oppose, in a constitutional manner," unconstitutional acts. Jefferson even flirted with the notion of secession as the ultimate response to the tyranny of the Alien and Sedition Acts. Once again, Madison counseled Jefferson out of this radical position and helped avert a serious constitutional crisis.[31]

The revised position of Virginia was elaborated in the lengthy report prepared by Madison to the Virginia legislature. The "Report of 1800" was the logical culmination of more than a decade of theorizing about how to guarantee that the Constitution would secure individual liberty. The keys for Madison continued to be a strict construction of the Constitution and a defense of the federal system. Madison's analysis was grounded in the same

30. "Virginia Resolutions of 1798," ibid., 133–135.

31. Thomas Jefferson, "Draft of the Kentucky Resolutions [1798]," in Merrill D. Peterson, ed., *Thomas Jefferson: Writings* (New York, 1984), 449–456; "Kentucky Resolutions of 1799," in Powell, ed., *Languages of Power*, 138; Taylor to Jefferson, June 25, 1798, "John Taylor Correspondence," *Branch Papers*, II (1908), 271–276. On the Virginia and Kentucky Resolutions, see Adrienne Koch and Harry Ammon, "The Virginia and Kentucky Resolutions: An Episode in Jefferson's and Madison's Defense of Civil Liberties," *WMQ*, 3d Ser., V (1948), 145–176; Smith, *Freedom's Fetters*; Smith, "The Grass Roots Origins of the Kentucky Resolutions," *WMQ*, 3d Ser., XXVII (1970), 221–245.

theory of original intent that he had employed in the controversies over the bank and the Jay Treaty. The "Report of 1800" referred to the "co-temporary discussions and comments, which the Constitution underwent." The charge of consolidation continued to be central to this variant of dissenting constitutionalism. Consolidation had an "obvious tendency, and inevitable result." Such a policy "would be, to transform the republican system of the United States into a monarchy."[32]

Madison's variant of dissenting constitutional theory differed from Jefferson's in crucial respects. Unlike Jefferson, Madison displayed greater sympathy for the continuing importance of judicial review, and he affirmed the right of the judiciary to decide questions of constitutionality. He did, however, recognize the necessity for individual state legislatures to seek constitutional redress through the amendment process and petitions to the Congress. The importance of the states as a check on the federal government had been one of the chief arguments of the supporters of the Constitution to mollify the fears of its opponents. In 1788, Federalists reminded their opponents that state vigilance "would descry the first symptoms of usurpation" and "would sound the alarm to the public." Madison himself had been one of the most forceful voices to make that argument in 1788, and more than ten years later he was restating his own commitment to federalism even more assertively. In defending the rights of states, Madison was careful to note that in constitutional matters there was an important distinction between the ordinary acts of the legislature and the acts of the conventions that had ratified the Constitution. As a result, Madison was far more circumspect than Jefferson about asserting the rights of the state legislatures to judge constitutional matters.[33]

In discussing the dangers of consolidation, Madison noted that the undesirability of such an outcome had "been sufficiently decided by the general sentiment of America." His concern with the general sentiments of the people was closely related to a more general interest in protecting the public sphere of political debate, which he believed was vital to the survival of republicanism. "That right of freely examining public characters and measures, and of free communication," was in Madison's view "the only effectual guardian of every other right." The centrality of the press had been noted at the time of ratification, and the absence of safeguards for it singled out as an especially dangerous flaw in the design of the Constitution. The inclusion of an explicit provision guarding freedom of the press had been intended to

32. James Madison, "Report of 1800," in William T. Hutchinson et al., eds., *The Papers of James Madison* (Chicago, Charlottesville, Va., 1962–), XVII, 308, 315–316.

33. Ibid., 350.

mollify this concern. The understanding of freedom of the press, moreover, had been, not that of the common law, but a more expansive ideal that reflected the more democratic character of American republicanism.[34]

Madison's invocation of public opinion as the ultimate guardian of popular liberty informed the way he conceptualized both the Virginia Resolutions and the "Report of 1800." In contrast to the determinations of the courts, the Virginia Resolutions were "expressions of opinion, unaccompanied with any other effect, than what they may produce on opinion, by exciting reflection." Once again, Madison returned to his emphasis on the role of the public sphere as the ultimate guardian of liberty and the federal system. Madison invoked the original Federalist arguments "addressed to those, who apprehended danger to liberty, from the establishment of the general government over so great a country." He recast this original Anti-Federalist fear in terms of the central role that the state legislatures would play as public forums that would distill the popular will and channel it in a suitable manner. Madison echoed the assurances of Publius more than a decade earlier. Madison noted that at the time of ratification Federalists had asserted that the states would continue to play a critical role, being there to "sound the alarm to the public." In contrast to Jefferson's solution, which held up nullification and possibly secession as the ultimate checks, Madison returned to a theme that had defined much of his thinking in the postconstitutional period: the role of public opinion as the animating spirit of all politics.[35]

Although the thought of John Taylor and Jefferson was evolving toward a compact theory of federalism that would lead to a fully formed theory of state's rights, including the right of nullification, Madison's approach to federalism remained closely connected to a theory of the public sphere. For Madison, the survival of constitutional government depended upon an "enlightened public," which would recognize that republican government could be preserved only by "maintaining the different governments and departments within their respective limits." The only means for securing this goal was to protect and nurture the independence and vitality of the public sphere.

After ratification a distinctive opposition constitutional theory emerged that owed an enormous debt to Anti-Federalist ideas. The critique of consolida-

34. Ibid., 316, 326.

35. Ibid., 348, 350. On Madison's constitutional thought, see Donald O. Dewey, "James Madison Helps Clio Interpret the Constitution," *American Journal of Legal History*, XV (1971), 38–55; Lance Banning, *The Sacred Fire of Liberty: James Madison and the Founding of the Federal Republic* (Ithaca, N.Y., 1995); Kevin R. Gutzman, "A Troublesome Legacy: James Madison and the 'Principles of '98,' " *Journal of the Early Republic*, XV (1995), 569–589.

tion and the concern that the ambiguities within the Constitution might be exploited through constructive interpretation became the cornerstones of opposition constitutional thought. In the period between the controversy over the bank and the quarrel over the Jay Treaty, the original understanding of the Constitution at the time of ratification became crucial to this approach to constitutional theory. Thereby, the original Anti-Federalist critique of the Constitution was elevated to new prominence as part of the original public debate that defined the terms under which the people had ratified the Constitution.

Creating an opposition constitutional tradition required assembling a set of canonical texts that would legitimate the opposition's claim that its interpretation of the Constitution represented the true feelings of the people at the time of ratification. Although the published writings of Anti-Federalists were still occasionally consulted, the state ratification debates assumed a much more prominent role in public discussion. At the same time, a distinctive Anti-Federalist reading of *The Federalist* emerged: Publius was reincarnated as the first strict constructionist. *The Federalist* was cited as the semiofficial response of Federalists to Anti-Federalist complaints. When linked with Anti-Federalist criticisms, *The Federalist* was easily converted into a text supporting the agenda of Democratic-Republicans. These texts were put to good use to justify a theory of strict construction and a renewed concern about the dangers of consolidation. Essential features of a new theory of federalism had emerged and would become the cornerstone of an opposition constitutional tradition.

During the struggle over ratification, Anti-Federalists warned that the new Constitution would rob the states of their ability to represent and protect the interests of their citizens. Alarmed by the expansive and vague grants of authority to the new government, Anti-Federalists devoted all their energies to defeating the Constitution. Even after Anti-Federalists abandoned their hopes of blocking ratification and turned their attentions to securing substantial amendments, their dominant rhetorical strategy focused on the continuing danger posed by the Constitution. There was a strong incentive to accent the gravity of the threat posed by the Constitution. During the debate over amendments in the First Congress, the same logic prevailed. Anti-Federalists fought unsuccessfully to obtain structural changes that would weaken the authority of the federal government and enhance the abilities of the states to protect their citizens' and their own interests. In particular, the Anti-Federalists lobbied hard to change the wording of what would eventually become the Tenth Amendment—to restrict the powers of the new government to those expressly delegated by the Constitution. As during ratification, Anti-Federalists stressed the magnitude of the danger that the Constitution posed and increased their chances of obtaining major structural changes. What Anti-Federalists had not done in 1788 was explore what to do if the assurances provided by Federalists, which they discounted, failed to protect liberty. The situation in 1798, therefore, was distinctly different from that in 1788.

The language of dissent that emerged during the 1790s was transformed by the crisis of the Alien and Sedition Acts. The most important reformulation of these principles came in 1798, in the Virginia and Kentucky Resolutions. A number of Anti-Federalist ideas, including the attack on consolidation and a concern about the ambiguities within the Constitution, remained crucial to this theory. Yet, the basic terms of constitutional debate shifted as a new compact theory of the Union became a dominant feature of an emerging theory of states' rights. This new way of conceptualizing the nature of the Union prompted an examination of the remedies available to the people of the states in instances when the federal government exceeded its constitutional authority. With those changes in place, the way was clear for a fully articulated theory of states' rights.

Madison's response to the crisis of the Alien and Sedition Acts differed from Jefferson's and John Taylor's. Implicit in his understanding of the idea of original intent was the notion that the public discourse over the Constitution ought to constrain the interpretation of later generations. The public sphere assumed an even greater prominence in Madison's thinking during the Alien and Sedition crisis. Madisonian constitutionalism had come to rely on a vigorous public sphere as the ultimate check on political and constitutional tyranny. The public sphere would serve to unite the various state legislatures against unconstitutional acts of the federal government. The Madisonian synthesis of various strains of dissenting constitutionalism was further elaborated in the "Report of 1800" and would occupy a central place in the canon of opposition thought. Madison had appropriated and reshaped Anti-Federalist ideas and blended them with his own. For much of the next two decades, dissent would build on the foundations laid by Madison. With the framework created by Madison, Anti-Federalist ideas could be safely contained and directed at Federalists. Thus, Madisonian constitutionalism sought a middle path between the strong centripetal and centrifugal forces that threatened to pull the nation apart.

CHAPTER 9 :

DEMOCRATIC-REPUBLICAN

CONSTITUTIONALISM AND THE

PUBLIC SPHERE

Since ratification a number of voices had joined the chorus of dissent opposing Federalist policy. The Democratic-Republican coalition brought together former Anti-Federalists with many who had originally opposed Anti-Federalism. In the aftermath of the crisis prompted by the Alien and Sedition Acts, even the most sober Democratic-Republican political leaders were forced to conclude that Federalist policy had fulfilled the ominous predictions made by Anti-Federalists more than a decade earlier: constructive interpretation had become an engine to achieve the goal of undermining federalism and creating a consolidated national government.

Public Opinion and Dissenting Political Thought

The Alien and Sedition Acts prompted the most serious examination of the tenets of oppositional constitutional theory since ratification. Critics of the Sedition law revived many of the arguments Anti-Federalists had made during ratification, basing their critique of it on several related propositions. Democratic-Republicans denied that the federal government possessed a common law jurisdiction in criminal matters. The First Amendment explicitly prohibited Congress from curtailing freedom of the press. The effort of the government to expand the scope of its authority was also a violation of the Tenth Amendment. The wholesale assault on the press was especially ominous to Democratic-Republicans, since they viewed a free press as vital to protecting liberty. If unchecked, Federalist policy threatened to eviscerate the public sphere. Its destruction would intensify the centripetal forces of consolidation. The mutual dependence of liberty, federalism, and an energetic public sphere continued to be a central theme in opposition thought.

In contrast to the traditional ideas of virtue, Democratic-Republicans embraced a more dynamic ideal of the public sphere as creating the alert citizenry, informed by rational debate, necessary for the survival of the Republic. In the eyes of the opposition, the public sphere would provide a means of uniting the nation without a powerful centralizing authority, would best promote its notion of a federal republic. In contrast to a strong central government, Democratic-Republicans championed a more decentralized vision of federalism, under which liberty could be maintained and the diversity of the nation preserved. Stressing the centrality of public opinion allowed Democratic-Republicans to state their opposition without opening themselves to accusations of a narrow partisan or factional agenda. Rather than promote factionalism, opposition figures could frame their criticisms in appeals directed to the public. Public opinion had become a cornerstone of opposition thought, and protecting the integrity of the public sphere became a dominant objective of opposition theorists.[1]

The first systematic effort to analyze the role of public opinion was framed by James Madison during the period 1791–1793. Madison's unsigned essays published in the *National Gazette* (the paper he helped found to spread the Democratic-Republican message) rank among his most comprehensive analyses of republican government in the postratification period. Madison revisited many of the themes he had explored in *The Federalist*, extending his analysis and exploring old issues in new ways, but the concept of public opinion had not figured prominently there. Now Madison made public opinion central to his political and constitutional philosophy. The survival of republican government, he argued, rested on the integrity of those institutions that sustained a viable public sphere of rational political debate. The central problem for Madison remained how to protect individual liberty and encourage government to act in a manner consistent with the common good.

In his essay "Charters," he affirmed the centrality of public opinion to his ideal of republican government: "All power has been traced up to opinion." In "Public Opinion" he asserted, "Whatever facilitates a general intercourse

1. Richard D. Brown, *Knowledge Is Power: The Diffusion of Information in Early America* (New York, 1989).

of sentiments, as good roads, domestic commerce, a free press, and particularly a *circulation of newspapers through the entire body of the people*, and
Representatives going from, and returning among every part of them," was
"favorable to liberty." Both creating a network of papers that could spread
knowledge about politics and strengthening the state legislatures tended to
reinforce the public sphere by making it easier to collect and propound the
public will in its most refined form.[2]

Like nearly every aspect of republican government, Madison recognized
that public opinion could either strengthen liberty and virtue or become the
tool of designing and corrupt factions. Madison hoped to mold public
opinion and use public discourse to reinforce the attachment of the people
"to their governments as delineated in the *great charters*." Madison hoped
that the people would treat these—the state constitutions, the federal Constitution, and the Bill of Rights—"with a holy zeal," protecting these "political
scriptures from every attempt to add to or diminish from them." Madison's
language in "Charters" moved closer to the sort of textual literalism that had
characterized Anti-Federalist strict construction. The public sphere, in this
account, was closely linked to his understanding of American constitutionalism. The integrity of the Constitution could be preserved only by an
energetic public sphere that would educate citizens, creating a culture of
constitutionalism in which citizens were well versed in their rights. Madison
had not abandoned his earlier belief that constitutions were mere parchment barriers. What was new was his realization that constitutions might
strengthen a public sphere of political debate whereby citizens educated
themselves in political matters and participated in public deliberations.[3]

While he believed that it was vital to ascertain the will of the public,
Madison did not believe government ought to be only a mirror of popular
attitudes. The goal of public debate was to focus and sharpen public opinion. Institutions such as newspapers were certainly essential to shaping
the public sphere, but they were certainly not the only institutions that
helped collect and improve public opinion. Madison also believed with
other Democratic-Republicans in the importance of the state legislatures as
public forums, as organs for collecting the sense of the public mind and for
deliberating on matters of public concern. The state legislatures could thus
serve as a check on the federal government by generating declarations that

2. [James Madison], "Charters," *National Gazette* (Philadelphia), Jan. 18, 1792, "Public
Opinion," Dec. 19, 1791 (William T. Hutchinson et al., eds., *The Papers of James Madison*
[Chicago, Charlottesville, Va., 1962–], XIV, 170, 192).

3. [Madison], "Charters," *National Gazette,* Jan. 18, 1792 (ibid., XIV, 192).

would convey popular views to the national legislature. This aspect of Madison's constitutional theory would come to play an even more prominent role in the aftermath of the controversy over the Sedition Act. His "Report of 1800" defended freedom of the press and championed the role of the state legislatures as a means to mobilize popular support.

In his essay "Consolidation," Madison made explicit his belief that the state legislatures were vital instruments to ascertain and improve the public mind. Consolidation, by weakening and eventually obliterating the states, would silence the voice of the people, leaving government to pursue its own agenda independent of any popular check. In essence, Madison placed the public sphere at the center of Democratic-Republican political and constitutional theory. It would ultimately provide the only counterbalance to the power of government. Without a vibrant public sphere, federalism could not function, and the nation would invariably succumb to the powerful centripetal forces of consolidation.[4]

Madison's characterization of the role of the state legislature captured an important element of his thinking about the relationship between public opinion and the public sphere: he was profoundly suspicious of excessive localism. The public sphere provided a means of "eradicating local prejudices and mistaken rivalships." Ultimately, the public sphere would help create "one paramount Empire of reason, benevolence and brotherly affection." Madison remained fundamentally opposed to the centrifugal forces in American life. Excessive localism in his view was just as pernicious as excessive nationalism.[5]

Madison was not the only figure within the Democratic-Republican movement to realize the importance of an emerging public sphere of political debate. At roughly the same time that Madison was publishing his thoughts in the National Gazette, William Manning was working out his own ideas about politics, constitutionalism, and the public sphere. In his first piece on the Hamiltonian system, Manning noted that his thinking had

4. [Madison], "Consolidation," National Gazette, Dec. 3, 1791 (ibid., XIV, 137–139). On the centrality of public opinion to Democratic-Republican thought, see Richard Buel, Jr., Securing the Revolution: Ideology in American Politics, 1789–1815 (Ithaca, N.Y., 1972), 91–136. A useful introduction to Madison's thinking about public opinion may be found in Colleen A. Sheehan, "The Politics of Public Opinion: James Madison's Notes on Government," WMQ, 3d Ser., XLIX (1992), 609–627. Although both of these discussions are helpful about the importance of public opinion, neither connects this development to the emergence of a public sphere.

5. [Madison], "Consolidation," National Gazette, Dec. 3, 1791 (Hutchinson et al., eds., Papers of Madison, XIV, 137–139).

been shaped by the debates within the press, which inspired him to publish his own views. Manning recognized that the ultimate check on Federalists was the nature of American constitutionalism itself, particularly the way in which constitutional discourse had become part of public culture. In this view, he echoed Madison, that written constitutions and a public culture that encouraged citizens to reflect upon them were crucial to safeguard liberty. Not until the end of the decade, however, did Manning formulate a systematic analysis of how the public sphere could become the means for challenging the domination of the few and empowering the many.

Manning's study, "The Key of Libberty," touched on many of the themes that Madison discussed in the *National Gazette* essays. Although Manning shared Madison's belief in the centrality of public opinion in republican government, he envisioned a different type of republic, one in which democratic and egalitarian ideals would thrive. Thus, while the subject matter of Manning's writing was the same as in Madison's essays, the point of view is distinctive, reflecting a more populist interpretation of Democratic-Republicanism.[6]

In Madison's view, "Natural divisions exist in all political societies, which should be made mutual checks on each other." Manning shared Madison's belief that there was an inevitable tension between the many and the few. Manning cast this tension in terms far more sympathetic to the plight of the many and far more suspicious of the few. In "The Key of Libberty" he "Shews how the Few and Many Differ in their interests" and "those that live without Labour are ever opposed to the prinsaples and operation of a free Government." Where Madison saw the few threatened by the many, Manning believed that the many were dominated by the few.[7]

Manning envisioned a "reformation" in politics that would reduce the distance separating government officials from those they were elected to serve. He did not seek to refine the will of the public in the manner that Madison suggested. The transformation envisioned by Manning would make representatives "feel as acting in the presents of their Constituants

6. James Madison, "Notes for the *National Gazette* Essays," in Hutchinson et al., eds., *Papers of Madison*, XIV, 161–162; Samuel Eliot Morison, ed., "William Manning's 'The Key of Libberty,'" *WMQ*, 3d Ser., XIII (1956), 213, 220. Morison's transcription maintains the original spelling. For a modern edition, see Michael Merrill and Sean Wilentz, eds., *The Key of Liberty: The Life and Democratic Writings of William Manning, "A Laborer," 1747–1814* (Cambridge, Mass., 1993).

7. Madison, "Notes for the *National Gazette* Essays," in Hutchinson et al., eds., *Papers of Madison*, XIV, 161–162; Morison, ed., "Manning's 'Key of Libberty,'" *WMQ*, 3d Ser., XIII (1956), 217, 220.

and act as servents and not masters." Literally, the key to liberty for Manning was the press, which, if properly structured, could foster a viable localist democracy on a national scale. Power would remain with individual communities while knowledge would circulate freely among different communities, tying the Republic together without a powerful central authority. A reformed press would not "use all the arts and retrick hell can invent" to mislead and "to make the peopel believe falsehood." Once transformed, the press would become a means by which the people would regain control of their government.[8]

Manning's claim that "the gratest and best meens of obtaining the knowledge nesecary for a free man to have, is by Liberty of the Press" would not have shocked Madison. Yet, his interpretation of how public opinion ought to be channeled differed from the more elitist vision of Madison. In Manning's view, public opinion was not something to be managed from the top down, but rather was something to be organized from the bottom up. Manning believed that print provided a means by which the common people could organize and counter the natural advantages of the wealthy. For Manning the power of the few was multiplied by their ability to unite their efforts. The press would provide a similar opportunity for the common people. Manning advocated an expanded public sphere, but one that would not serve as an instrument for established elites to impose their views on the people. It was not necessary for the will of the people to be refined. Rather, he sought to expand the number of outlets, both for the publication of information and for collecting the ideas of the people.[9]

Manning advocated a national network of local societies, a Democratic-Republican alternative to organizations like the Society of the Cincinnati. Earlier efforts, including the Democratic-Republican Societies, had foundered because they lacked a "proper chanel of conveying their sentiments to the peopel." Manning proposed, instead, to create a new society that would bring together the advantages of political societies and a free press. The organization Manning imagined would include all laborers and true republicans across America. Access to information, he recognized, was restricted by the partisan nature of the press and the cost of papers. Manning's magazine would be cheap enough for common folk to purchase and would allow laborers from all localities to unite their interests and communicate with one another. While national in scope, this organization would em-

8. Morison, ed., "Manning's 'Key of Libberty,'" WMQ, 3d Ser., XIII (1956), 222, 232, 250.
9. Ibid. On Madison's views of the press, see [Madison], "Public Opinion," National Gazette, Dec. 19, 1791 (Hutchinson et al., eds., Papers of Madison, XIV, 170).

power the laboring sort of various localities. The magazine would have a national board of editors but would primarily serve as an outlet for a network of local correspondents.[10]

The more populist vision defended by Manning reflected a belief common among middling and plebeian Anti-Federalists that simple governments and laws were preferable to complex ones. As Manning remarked in the "Key," "In makeing laws in a free Government their cannot be two much pains or caution used to have them plain to be understood and not two numerous." Indeed, one of the means that the few used to dominate the many was the manipulation of the law. Thus, "The few have a grate advantage . . . in forming and constructing Constitutions and laws, and are highly interested in haveing them numerous, intricate and as inexplicit as possable." Lawyers, judges, and politicians perverted the plain sense, "construing and explaining away the true sence and meening of the constitutions and laws, and so raise themselves above the Lejeslative power." There was no need for a class of mediating elites in Manning's popular vision of constitutionalism, nor were judges and legislators necessary to refine the will of the public. Nothing better exemplified Manning's view of popular constitutionalism than the jury.[11]

The basic charters and texts defining constitutional government were to be written in a language accessible to all citizens. By encouraging citizens to be familiar with the basic texts of their government, society would encourage a pervasive consciousness about the rights of individuals and the limits on government. These ideals would be strengthened by a strong system of local juries. The job of the press would be to inform citizens. With open access to the press, juries could better execute the popular will in all legal matters. Manning shared with Anti-Federalists a belief in the primacy of jury power. It was only natural that the enemies of popular liberty, the Federalists, would seek to curtail the authority of juries and elevate the power of the judicial elite. Manning opposed this effort, viewing the jury as another part of the public sphere.[12]

Madison and Manning each believed the public sphere was crucial to the survival of republicanism. Both men also believed that print, particularly newspapers, would play a key role in ensuring the vitality of public discourse. A vibrant public sphere was essential to sustain a culture of constitutional-

10. Morison, ed., "Manning's 'Key of Libberty,' " *WMQ,* 3d Ser., XIII (1956), 231.

11. Ibid., 216, 222, 227. On the effort to weaken juries, see the 1799 revised version of the *Key of Liberty,* ed. Merrill and Wilentz, 141.

12. Ibid.

ism. While there were many similarities between these two men's approaches to the public sphere, there were also important differences separating them, reflecting their respective social positions. Madison's vision of the public sphere reflected his essentially elitist vision of politics, Manning's, by contrast, a more democratic perspective. Another difference was their attitudes toward localism. While Madison recognized the need for government to take stock of local differences, he believed that the goal of republicanism was to create an empire of reason that transcended local interests. Rather than diminish the dangers of excessive localism, Manning wished to keep government as close to the people as possible. He believed that the public sphere should provide empowerment, not refinement.

Responses to the Alien and Sedition Crisis

In response to the Sedition Act, opposition theorists developed in a more theoretically sophisticated manner a number of different aspects of their constitutional theory. Before the act, expressions of opposition constitutional theory were usually ad hoc. The act, by contrast, inaugurated a wider-ranging consideration of the meaning of loyal opposition and constitutional resistance. The national scope of the law meant that prosecutions were not limited to a single locality, and it thus allowed a wider public scrutiny of the law and fostered a more expansive consideration of the constitutional issues at stake. The prominence of many of the defendants indicted under the law also meant that some of the finest legal minds in America turned their energies to assisting those singled out for prosecution. As a result of this heightened inquiry, the meaning of freedom of the press and its place in American constitutionalism were subjected to the most thorough analysis since the adoption of the Constitution. The leading critics of the act probed the historical meaning of Anti-Federalism, the meaning of liberty, the nature of federalism, and the centrality of the public sphere to American constitutionalism.[13]

13. On the role that the Sedition Act played in galvanizing resistance to the Federalists, see James Morton Smith, *Freedom's Fetters: The Alien and Sedition Laws and American Civil Liberties*, rev. ed. (Ithaca, N.Y., 1966). The relationship between the response to the Sedition Act and the development of a new libertarian theory of press freedom is discussed in Leonard W. Levy, *Emergence of a Free Press* (New York, 1985); and Norman L. Rosenberg, *Protecting the Best Men: An Interpretive History of the Law of Libel* (Chapel Hill, N.C., 1986). George Hay, *An Essay on the Liberty of the Press* . . . (Philadelphia, 1799); and St. George Tucker's appendix to Tucker, *Blackstone's Commentaries: With Notes of Reference, to the*

The most important effort at a theory of the public sphere to counter the Federalist political and constitutional vision was elaborated by Tunis Wortman. His work, *A Treatise, concerning Political Enquiry, and the Liberty of the Press,* not only became the cornerstone of a new theory of freedom of the press, but it expounded the most sophisticated analysis of the centrality of the public sphere to Democratic-Republicanism.[14]

Wortman, a lawyer with a penchant for philosophical speculation, was an influential political force within the New York Democratic-Republican movement. Although he had been too young to participate fully in the battle over the Constitution, he emerged as an energetic and ambitious spokesman for the opposition in New York during the 1790s. Despite his youth, Wortman became the secretary for the New York Democratic-Republican Society.[15]

Wortman had published newspaper essays and addresses during the 1790s. Dismayed and outraged by Federalist actions, Wortman wrote to Albert Gallatin in February 1798, informing him of his plans to publish a "series of papers in favor of the republican cause." Wortman requested information from Gallatin so that he might publish an account "of the government from the period of the establishment of the present system." In particular, Wortman was interested in "facts and anecdotes respecting the secret convention, and its members, as far as that mysterious subject can be developed." Among the points that Wortman was particularly concerned to lay before the public were the "intrigues and artifices made use of for the purposes of compelling the adoption of the Constitution." Wortman accepted the view that the actions of the Federalists of 1788 were entirely consistent with Hamilton's program. The creation of the public debt and the funding system were, to Wortman, all part of the same goal of creating a consolidated national government. Wortman's perspective on the events of the 1790s was distinctly Anti-Federalist, tracing the origins of the struggle between Federalists and Democratic-Republicans to ratification. Wortman's query also suggests that many of the Anti-Federalist texts, including such widely distributed pieces as Luther Martin's *Genuine Information* and the

---

Constitution, and Laws of the Federal Government of the United States; and of the Commonwealth of Virginia, 5 vols. (Philadelphia, 1803), II, note G, were two of the most important constitutional responses to the Sedition Act.

14. Tunis Wortman, *A Treatise, concerning Political Enquiry, and the Liberty of the Press* (New York, 1800).

15. Biographical information on Wortman is sparse. For a brief but illuminating discussion of Wortman's political importance, see Alfred F. Young, *The Democratic Republicans of New York: The Origins, 1763–1797* (Chapel Hill, N.C., 1967), 394, 567.

essays of Centinel, were no longer easily available. Either would have afforded ample material to fashion an account of the origins of the Constitution from an Anti-Federalist point of view. Wortman's request also suggests that the manuscript notes of Robert Yates, an influential New York Anti-Federalist delegate to the Philadelphia Convention, were not available to others within the upper echelons of Democratic-Republican circles. The information therein would have provided an exceedingly detailed source for the account Wortman proposed to write.[16]

A year later, with the controversy over the Alien and Sedition Acts in mind, Wortman wrote to Gallatin again, this time describing a more specific project, "A Treatise Concerning Political Enquiry and the liberty of the press." Wortman hoped that his thoughts would be of interest to the general public and particularly wished to sway members of Congress. He enclosed a prospectus and was delighted to receive Gallatin's enthusiastic endorsement. When it was published in 1800, Wortman's work became one of the most important and influential statements of Republican political and constitutional theory and the most important defense of freedom of the press produced in America.[17]

Wortman's *Treatise* was both a prescriptive statement, presenting his own variant of democratic political theory, and an account of the role of freedom of the press in the American constitutional order since the adoption of the Constitution. The democratic theory as Wortman expounded it drew on well-established notions associated with middling democratic discourse and placed them within the context of a fully articulated theory of the centrality of the public sphere to democracy. Wortman went well beyond Madison's observations that all free governments rested on opinion. Wortman took the inchoate notions about public opinion of opposition theorists over the course of the 1790s and developed them into a systematic theory of politics.

The core of his theory was the belief: "With relation to government public opinion is omnipotent. It is the general will or acquiescence that supports every species of political institution." The most important consequence of this interpretation was a commitment to protect the public sphere so that it could improve the public mind. "Unless the public mind becomes enlightened, what principle or what law is possessed of sufficient energy to prevent it from leading to the most violent acts of outrage and desperation?" Such an improvement could occur only when there was a free exchange of ideas,

16. Tunis Wortman to Albert Gallatin, Feb. 23, 1798, Gallatin Papers, NYHS.
17. Ibid., Dec. 24, 30, 1799.

which, for Wortman, was the paramount value in society, superior even to the rights of property. "Of all the rights which can be attributed to man, that of communicating his sentiments is the most sacred and inestimable."[18]

Although Wortman recognized that clubs and societies contributed greatly to the expansion of the public sphere, he recognized also the primacy of printed discourse in shaping public opinion. "Next to the invention of Language and of Letters, that of Printing may justly be considered as the most powerful benefactor of mankind." Print allowed modern governments to surpass those of antiquity. Wortman contrasted Athens with America and found the former defective, because it lacked the advantages of print. "The information . . . acquired at the public assemblies, was neither so correct nor so extensive as that which is capable of being conveyed through the medium of the Press." Compared to oratory, print was "less liable to become converted into a pernicious engine of Design." That is, oratory was more inclined to sway the passions, whereas print was better calculated to persuade by reason.[19]

The centrality of public opinion led Wortman to assert the priority of the public over the private. In his letter to Gallatin describing his project on freedom of the press, Wortman ridiculed those whose time was consumed with "smoke and Madeira" or who were "drowning it in a bottle of Claret." In place of such self-indulgent practices, Wortman observed, "it is greatly to be wished that individuals of real discernment and talents should devote some of their time to purposes of general improvement." Wortman's emphasis on virtue and participation in the public sphere was not inspired by a traditional civic republican conception of politics. His understanding of virtue drew freely from Scottish moral sense theory and Wortman's own notions about the public sphere. "True virtue cannot require that men should become totally detached from themselves." Participation in politics did not demand self-sacrifice, but merely required that individuals discover their true interests. There was no area of human endeavor "in which every individual is more extensively concerned, or which may with greater correctness be considered as a common property." In his view, "Society should constitute an University of Politics, open to the instruction of each of its members."[20]

Wortman also drew upon the principle that man was inherently a social

18. Wortman, *Treatise*, 24, 25, 145, 146. In this sense Wortman's political theory broke with important aspects of both Lockean political theory and civic republicanism.
19. Ibid., 241–242, 245.
20. Wortman to Gallatin, Dec. 30, 1799, Gallatin Papers; Wortman, *Treatise*, 104, 145, 199.

being. Seen in those terms, the pursuit of the public good did not require the sacrifice of individual interest or the promotion of some transcendent common good, but rather required discovering the way to harmonize the differences within society. Thus, when Wortman wrote that the "Public Good must constitute the exclusive object to the attainment of which our enquiries should ultimately be directed," he expected that outcome would grow naturally from man's social felicity.[21]

The notion of politics and virtue that he defended rejected other facets of traditional civic republicanism. His political philosophy was grounded in distinctly modern liberal individualist terms. "It is to be observed, that the general superintendance of government, is rather of a *negative* than a *positive* kind. Its injunctions are, to abstain from the perpetration of vice, and not to perform particular acts of virtue." Indeed, he went further than any other Democratic-Republican theorist of his age in his limited, negative vision of the state. "Every unnecessary law is in its nature tyrannical—it is a wanton infringement of the rights of personal liberty." Balanced against this liberal individualist conception of rights was an emphasis on protecting and promoting rational debate within an expanded public sphere.[22]

The liberal individualism at the heart of Wortman's political philosophy shaped the way he conceptualized the public sphere. Wortman posed key questions about the nature of public opinion. Was it the opinion of "Society in its collective and organized capacity? Or does it designate the union or aggregation of individual sentiment?" Equally vital was how to ascertain public opinion, where to locate it within society: "Where shall we listen to the voice that can express it?" For Wortman, public opinion had to be understood as "an aggregation of individual sentiment." This individualism was wedded to a democratic theory of politics. "By Public opinion we are to understand that general determination of private understandings which is most extensively predominant." This particular conception allowed Wortman to make public opinion an expression of the democratic will of the people.[23]

The faith in cultivating the innate moral sense of individuals through rational debate was based upon his own interpretation of Scottish moral sense theory. Regarding political truth, he wrote, "Every truth is luminous; every principle is clear, perspicuous, and determinable; its doctrines are established in the common sentiments and feelings of mankind." This posi-

21. Wortman, *Treatise,* 29, 153.
22. Ibid., 27, 76.
23. Ibid., 118, 119.

tion was a logical outgrowth of his view that "the language of justice is uniformly legible; its characters are written by omnipotent wisdom, upon the tablets of our hearts."[24]

Wortman accepted that, when allowed to engage in rational debate, the people would arrive at opinions consistent with truth and justice. The only effective check on tyranny is an enlightened citizenry able freely to sift truth from error. Wortman used Scottish moral sense theory to reformulate the ideals of middling democrats in a new, more cogent idiom. While he acknowledged differences among the population, the most important one was education, which he was committed to improving. Morality, however, was a function, not of educational attainment, but of sentiment and hence was universal. Virtue and wisdom were therefore uniformly distributed throughout the various ranks of society.[25]

Wortman's commitment to middling democracy was most evident in his discussion of the connection between public opinion and representation. He favored an extension of suffrage, challenging the idea of property requirements. He attacked the idea that property gave one a greater stake in society and questioned whether property really made citizens independent: even without property, citizens have a stake in their life and liberty. If citizens could be counted on to serve their country and risk their lives in its defense, they demonstrated a sufficient stake. In any event, the possession of property was not fixed in America, he contended, displaying the characteristic view of middling democrats that wealth in America was more fluid. Those with wealth are as likely to lose it as those without might acquire it. Finally, he noted that those with property enjoyed sufficient power without having any special political privileges. He did share with middling democrats a mild disdain for those below them in rank, confessing to Albert Gallatin that one could not put much faith in the "dependent and laboring class." Still, his public support for political democracy was unqualified, and he forcefully argued that "every limitation of the representative principle is not only unjust, but highly pernicious."[26]

Wortman's middling democracy carried forward the suspicion of agrarian laws and the effort to divide property equally that had distinguished earlier proponents of this variant of democratic theory. Viewing such actions as both impractical and harmful, he declared, "The interference of

24. Ibid., 66.
25. Ibid., 56.
26. Wortman to Gallatin, Dec. 30, 1799, Gallatin Papers; Wortman, *Treatise*, 197.

Government upon such occasions would amount to the most atrocious and deprecable tyranny." At the same time, he remained suspicious of the wealthy, who, he believed, constituted a form of aristocracy every bit as dangerous as titled nobility. "The Aristocracy of Wealth," he argued, "exerts a pernicious empire over Manner and Morals."[27]

Wortman was not unaware that popular licentiousness and machinations on the part of powerful individuals could corrupt the public sphere, but he questioned the necessity of criminal prosecution to eradicate this threat. The best guard against licentiousness was truth. More public discussion, not less, was the proper means for securing liberty and eliminating licentiousness. Criminal sanctions on publication were a cure for licentiousness worse than the disease. In practice, he noted, there was little danger that the press would undermine government authority. Those in power had ample resources to defend themselves without resorting to criminal prosecutions. Government never lacked the services of those eager to court its favor and lavish praise on its measures.[28]

Persecutions by government not only were liable to abuse, but they dampened the progress of inquiry, making individuals timid. "Public prosecutions for libels are, therefore, more dangerous to Society than the misrepresentation which they are intended to punish." Public opinion provided the only effective check against government tyranny and also militated against popular upheavals by providing a channel for political passions that might otherwise be repressed and eventually erupt with violence.[29]

There was nothing naive or utopian about Wortman's attitude toward the press. He recognized that freedom carried with it the potential for abuse. The licentiousness of the press consisted not only in a "wanton or designing misrepresentation" of government's actions but also in an "interested partiality towards the Government." The experience of the recent past demonstrated to Wortman that there would always be far greater effort devoted to protecting government than to exposing those sycophants who were its tools. The only safe means for correcting both of those threats was to "trust to the wisdom of Public Opinion."[30]

When Wortman turned his attention to the Alien and Sedition Acts, he shifted away from an abstract philosophical discussion of political theory to

27. Wortman, *Treatise*, 197, 198.
28. Ibid., 149–165.
29. Ibid., 150, 170.
30. Ibid., 245, 250.

a much more concrete and specific examination of the constitutionality of the Federalists' legislative assault on freedom of the press. Central to Wortman's account was a careful exegesis of the nature and limits of federal authority under the Constitution.

The Constitution, Wortman wrote (reiterating standard dissenting constitutional discourse), was both "a compact of union between the States" and "the instrument which creates, defines, and limits the powers of the Government." His constitutionalism was built on the foundation laid by earlier opposition theorists: the compact theory of the Union and the critique of consolidation. The federal nature of the compact "implies that each of the contracting States retains its existence and its sovereignty, subject to the limitations imposed by the compact of Confederation, and is evidently distinguishable from Consolidation."[31]

Although Wortman's political ideals inclined toward a limited view of governmental authority, his constitutional theory reflected the assumptions that had defined dissenting constitutional thought since ratification. The state governments, he noted, "act without control in their spheres, and move independently within their orbits." By contrast: "The Government of the United States is a limited system. It was instituted for specific and particular purposes." His interpretation of federalism echoed earlier distinctly Anti-Federalist readings of the Tenth Amendment. "The powers vested in the general Government are such as expressly and particularly granted by the Constitution."[32]

The interpretation of the First Amendment Wortman proffered reflected his conception of federalism. The federal government simply did not have authority over the press. Wortman's strict construction eschewed the use of extrinsic textual evidence to support his case. Instead, he focused exclusively on the text of the Constitution and its amendments. He sought a holistic interpretation of how the Constitution tried to limit government and protect liberty. Every interpretation of the Constitution had to be understood as part of this larger goal. In his view, the terms "necessary" and "proper" were not meant to enlarge the powers of government, but merely to make it possible to execute the limited powers ceded to the new government. "We should always remember that one of the most invaluable advantages of a Written Constitution is the certainty with which it designates the powers of a Government." He went further: "Its principal and its only use is to mark with precision the

31. Ibid., 209–210.
32. Ibid., 210–212.

boundaries of Authority." Wortman affirmed the textual literalism and faith in a constitutional plain style that had been central to Anti-Federalism and continued to define so much dissenting constitutional theory. "Let us guard the sacred text against interpolations and commentaries."[33]

Rejecting Blackstonian libel theory had been commonplace among opposition constitutional theorists since ratification. To equate freedom of the press with a mere prohibition on prior restraint was to abolish press freedom in practice. The Constitution had intended to protect freedom of the press, not diminish it. Wortman also disputed the idea that there was a federal common law of crimes under which the Blackstonian ideal of libel might be invoked. The notion that the federal government was of limited delegated authority meant that there could be no federal common law of crimes.

One of the most interesting and complicated aspects of Wortman's constitutional theory was his view of the legality of state libel prosecutions. There, Wortman's political theory and constitutional philosophy were in conflict. The former, prescriptive theory pointed to the abolition of such prosecutions, but the latter, a descriptive account of the constitutionality of such actions, granted their legality, even as he labored to show that they were undesirable. Regarding libels, he wrote, "It is, therefore, to be presumed to have been intended that the States respectively should solely exercise the power of controuling the conduct of their own citizens in such cases." As a matter of principle, not law, however, he firmly believed that the use of criminal libel charges in political cases was destructive of free inquiry. He was adamant that "criminal prosecutions for Libels can never be necessary to preserve the public tranquility"; to guard against such dangers, "let the punishment of every breach of the peace be severe and certain." Actions, not ideas, were the proper subject of government prosecutions.[34]

33. Ibid., 231, 238, 239.

34. Ibid., 229–230, 253. This aspect of Wortman's thought has prompted the most controversy among modern scholars. For Leonard W. Levy, Wortman was an unqualified modern libertarian: see *Legacy of Suppression: Freedom of Speech and Press in Early America* (Cambridge, Mass., 1960), modified and presented in revised form in *Emergence of a Free Press*, 305, 327–331. Levy's original thesis was challenged by Walter Berns, "Freedom of the Press and the Alien and Sedition Laws: A Reappraisal," in Philip B. Kurland, ed., *The Supreme Court Review: 1970* (Chicago, 1970), 109–159. For an effort to reconcile these contradictions by placing his approach to freedom of the press in the context of republicanism, see Rosenberg, *Protecting the Best Men*. Wortman's republicanism, however, had incorporated a number of important liberal ideas. One way of understanding the complex connections among liberal, republican, and states' rights ideas is to recognize that Wortman

Private libel prosecutions, however, posed a different problem for Wortman. He conceded that it was appropriate to investigate the character of public officials. Such scrutiny was necessary in any free government, but should not deprive public officials of their right to guard their reputation. Attacks on public officials, he maintained, ought to be handled by private prosecutions by the injured party, and the determination of the libel ought to be the province of the jury. The right of trial by jury would afford appropriate protections for individuals. Wortman carried forward the emphasis on a broad purview for juries, a distinguishing characteristic of dissenting constitutionalism. Juries, in his view, were entitled to judge both the facts and the law of the case. It was completely within the province of juries, not judges, to decide when a publication was libelous.

Although Wortman went further than many in carving out a broad sphere of liberty for the press, his views on the use of political libel charges by individuals suggested that he had not completely shed all traces of earlier republican ideas about libel. It was left to the jury to determine community standards and protect the rights of individuals. It is important to note that the most celebrated libel prosecution in the postratification period prior to the Sedition Act had been a private action, not a state prosecution. Politically motivated private libel suits could have a devastating impact on printers— it was a private libel suit, not a criminal prosecution, that silenced Anti-Federalist printer Eleazer Oswald in 1788. Wortman's approach would not have barred such an action. The appropriate safeguard in those circumstances, Wortman argued, was access to jury trial, in which one's fellow citizens, not a judge, would determine whether an utterance was in fact libelous. In this regard, Wortman carried forward a stance that was central to the Anti-Federalist conceptualization of freedom of the press. The fact that Wortman's theory did not preclude such prosecution meant that his views of the press had not entirely broken with earlier views. Although Wortman's theory had made important strides toward articulating a genuinely liberal, libertarian conception of the press, his ideas were still rooted in earlier republican conceptions of constitutionalism.[35]

---

was working within the distinctive tradition of opposition thought in which all of these elements were combined. The goal of his theory of freedom of the press was to protect the public sphere.

35. Wortman, *Treatise*, 151, 202–203. On the Oswald trial, see Chapter 5, above. On Tucker's views of the relationship between judges and juries and the emergence of a distinctive judicial culture in Virginia, see A. G. Roeber, *Faithful Magistrates and Republican Lawyers: Creators of Virginia Legal Culture, 1680–1810* (Chapel Hill, N.C., 1981). On the attitudes of New York's Democratic-Republicans toward juries, see "Resolutions Adopted

The Anti-Federalist Blackstone: St. George Tucker
and a Democratic-Republican Jurisprudence

Many individuals voiced opposition to Federalist constitutional theory over the course of the 1790s and, by their end, had created a canon of dissenting texts and common interpretive assumptions about how those texts were to be used to understand the Constitution. Strict construction and the critique of consolidation were central to this constitutional philosophy. Both Jefferson and Madison recast these essentially Anti-Federalist notions in response to the crisis posed by the Alien and Sedition Acts. Thus, the principles of '98, further refined and elaborated by Madison in his "Report of 1800," defined the core of an alternative dissenting constitutional tradition against the one espoused by Federalists.

While the Madison synthesis provided a synoptic statement of dissenting constitutional principles, it fell well short of being a systematic theoretical alternative to an expanding body of Federalist jurisprudence. Creating such a treatise fell to another Virginian, St. George Tucker, whose monumental *Blackstone's Commentaries* became the philosophical core of dissenting constitutional theory. Although published in 1803, after Jefferson's election to the presidency, Tucker's work was drafted in the midst of the constitutional ferment of the 1790s. *Blackstone's Commentaries* was the fruit of more than ten years' labor. In 1790 Tucker became professor of law and police at the College of William and Mary, and he drew extensively from the lectures on law he delivered there during those turbulent days. In effect, Tucker synthesized the principles of 1788 and of 1798.

Among Tucker's reasons behind such a work was his belief that judges and lawyers were too dependent on the English jurist Blackstone. Relying on Blackstone was problematic. Blackstone's analyses of the common law of England were steeped in antirepublican sentiments, and they thus provided a poor guide to a version of the common law adapted to the republican soil of the New World.

Tucker's study of Blackstone was impressive in its scope and a model of legal erudition. It was also an instant publishing success. The first edition of the work sold out the entire run of five thousand. His work became the definitive American edition of Blackstone until midcentury. Indeed, as a comprehensive legal treatise on American constitutionalism, Tucker enjoyed

---

on the Need for Reform in Laws, Courts, and Juries, July 10, 1794," in Philip S. Foner, *The Democratic-Republican Societies, 1790–1800: A Documentary Sourcebook of Constitutions, Declarations, Addresses, Resolutions, and Toasts* (Westport, Conn., 1976), 240–242.

a virtual monopoly until Federalist James Kent published his *Commentaries on American Law* in 1826.[36]

Tucker's work had another important function: it became the most influential statement of opposition constitutional theory to appear after the election of Jefferson. Tucker's synthesis of the diverse strands of Democratic-Republican constitutional philosophy provided other thinkers with a starting point for future inquiry into a vision of American constitutionalism that owed an enormous debt to Anti-Federalism.

In an appendix to the second part of volume I, "Of the Right of Conscience; and of the Freedom of Speech and of the Press," Tucker confronted the problems raised by the Sedition Act, offering an expansive defense of the "liberty of speech and of discussion in all speculative matters." Tucker's libertarianism placed him at the forefront of contemporary thinking on this issue. The only restrictions on this right were when its exercise produced "the injury of any other individual, in his person, property, or good name."[37]

One of the most important points Tucker made regarding freedom of the press in America was that it rested on entirely different grounds from the common law understanding enshrined in Blackstone. The centrality of this right to American law was demonstrated by the place accorded freedom of the press in the various state constitutions. So vital was freedom of the press that the absence of an explicit protection for it in the Constitution provoked "great complaints" at the time of ratification. Tucker drew extensively on the Virginia state ratification convention to demonstrate that the promise of an explicit provision ensuring freedom of the press was instrumental in securing the ratification of the Constitution. Indeed, Tucker noted, the convention had affirmed its belief that this right could not be "cancelled, abridged,

36. For a discussion of the larger jurisprudential context in which Tucker wrote, see G. Edward White, *The Marshall Court and Cultural Change, 1815–1835,* History of the Supreme Court of the United States, III–IV (New York, 1988); Elizabeth Bauer, *Commentaries on the Constitution, 1790–1860* (New York, 1952); Bernard Schwartz, *Main Currents in American Legal Thought* (Durham, N.C., 1993); Craig Evan Klafter, *Reason over Precedents: Origins of American Legal Thought* (Westport, Conn., 1993). On Tucker, see Charles T. Cullen, *St. George Tucker and Law in Virginia, 1772–1804* (New York, 1987); Robert Morton Scott, "St. George Tucker and the Development of American Culture in Early Federal Virginia, 1790–1824" (Ph.D. diss., George Washington University, 1991). On the emergence of a distinctive southern tradition of jurisprudence, see Kermit L. Hall and James W. Ely, Jr., eds., *An Uncertain Tradition: Constitutionalism and the History of the South* (Athens, Ga., 1989). On the tradition of states' rights, see Richard E. Ellis, *The Union at Risk: Jacksonian Democracy, States' Rights, and the Nullification Crisis* (New York, 1987).

37. Tucker, *Blackstone's Commentaries,* II (*sic*), appendix, note G, "Of the Right of Conscience; and of the Freedom of Speech and of the Press," 11.

restrained, or modified" by the new government created by the Constitution. Tucker's framing of liberty of the press drew on the dissenting view of federalism that had evolved since the adoption of the Constitution. He reminded his readers that the Virginians had made clear the terms under which they had accepted the Constitution in their ratification convention. The Sedition Act violated this understanding. The powers claimed by Congress violated the limited nature of the Constitution's grant of authority, undermining the nature of the federal system and creating a national government in its place. Further, the government's actions undermined the nature of representation itself and thereby set the stage for the creation of a consolidated national government that would produce an aristocracy or monarchy.[38]

Comparisons with the English common law doctrine of libel were misleading, since American constitutionalism differed from English law. In America, Tucker observed, "the people, not the government possess the absolute sovereignty." Moreover: "In the United States, the great and essential rights of the people, are secured against legislative, as well as against executive ambition. They are secured, not by laws paramount to prerogative; but by constitutions paramount to laws." This concise statement of republican constitutional principles captured the essence of Tucker's vision of law.[39]

Tucker grounded his analysis in an appeal to the sense of the people at the time of ratification. The overarching principle of constitutional interpretation was to harmonize the various parts of the text of the Constitution to ensure that the federal government remained limited in power. In contrast to the states, the federal government was "possessed of particular and defined powers only; not of general and indefinite powers." Tucker shared the view that united opposition constitutional theorists: that federalism was one of the most important instruments for protecting liberty.[40]

At the end of his discussion of freedom of the press, Tucker consciously noted, "In contending therefore for the absolute freedom of the press, and its total exemption from all restraint, control, or jurisdiction of the federal government, the writer of these sheets most explicitly disavows the most distant approbation of its licentiousness." Tucker did not believe that the freedom of the press shielded those guilty of a personal libel of public individuals, who did not lose their right to protect their character from slander. "For injuries done the reputation of any person, as *an individual*,

38. Ibid., 14.
39. Ibid., 20.
40. Ibid., 24.

the state-courts are always open." Tucker's view thereof reflected a number of assumptions about the nature of liberty. That the states were the appropriate place to try such suits demonstrated his belief that, within the federal system, it was the states, not the federal government, that were the guardians of individual liberty. Although his ideal of freedom of the press was among the most expansive to be found in his day, the use of individual libel suits by public officials was more than a modest concession. Tucker's view of libel, like Tunis Wortman's, would not have spared Eleazer Oswald, the Anti-Federalist printer sued in 1788 for libel. As long as libel actions were conducted in state courts, however, Tucker was confident that their potential for political abuse was minimal. The conception of liberty that Tucker defended was therefore inextricably tied to his understanding of federalism.[41]

Tucker's debt to Anti-Federalism was even more explicit in a lengthy appendix on the federal Constitution. One of the most fascinating aspects of Tucker's analysis of ratification is the extraordinarily positive portrait of the Anti-Federalists.

> Party zeal never ran higher without an actual breach of peace. Had the opposers of the proposed constitution been as violent as its advocates, it is not impossible that matters would have proceeded to some pernicious lengths.[42]

In Tucker's accounts, the Anti-Federalists, not the Federalists, emerged as the voice of moderation and accommodation. The legitimacy of their opposition to the Constitution was evidenced by their numerical strength at the time of ratification: "In several of the states, the question was decided in favour of the constitution by a very small majority." Tucker expressed qualified support for Madison's view that state ratification conventions were an adequate proxy for the people's will. While not an absolutely accurate rendering of the voice of the people, the state conventions were the best expression of those sentiments. "The deputies in most of the counties were chosen according to the prevailing sentiments of the people in favour of the constitution, the opinions of the candidates being generally previously known." The state conventions were therefore indispensable in establishing the original intent of the people in adopting the new government.[43]

Another reason Tucker favored the state conventions was that these bod-

41. Ibid., 29, 30.
42. Ibid., I, appendix, note D, "View of the Constitution of the United States," 160.
43. Ibid., 160, 162–163, 167–168.

ies were constitutional bodies and their deliberations were less speculative than the philosophical musings of those writers who participated in the public debate over the Constitution. When seeking the original understanding of the Constitution, he wrote, "it would be more proper to rely on the authority of The American Congress or of the several State Conventions, than the opinions of any speculative writers." This approach further diminished the significance of the public essays that had defined the Constitution during ratification. By contrast, the published proceedings of the state ratification conventions assumed an even greater importance in his theory.[44]

Interestingly, Tucker made only one reference to a published Anti-Federalist text in his appendix on the Constitution. Writing about the nature of the federal judiciary, he observed that those powers "have been equally the subject of applause and censure; of confidence and jealousy." When he turned to an Anti-Federalist author for support, he did not cite the most elaborate analysis of the defects of the judiciary, framed by the two most philosophically sophisticated authors, New York's Federal Farmer and Brutus. The essayist he turned to was far less profound on this subject: Tucker cited the criticisms of Pennsylvania's Centinel, whose writings enjoyed a much wider distribution. Centinel had predicted that "the state judicatories will be wholly superceded; for in contests about jurisdictions, the federal court, as the most powerful, will ever prevail." Tucker owned a copy of Centinel's essays that had been included in an important pamphlet edition of Anti-Federalist writings published in Richmond during 1788. Centinel documented the concerns of the time about the dangers of judicial usurpation. Tucker noted that those fears had been well founded, but any cause for concern had been removed by the Bill of Rights. When Tucker read Centinel, he did not do so in the same manner as the Carlisle rioters had during ratification; Centinel reflected his own elite conception of constitutionalism. The antiaristocratic rhetoric of Centinel was interpreted by Tucker, not as an indictment of a wellborn class of natural aristocrats, but as a critique of oligarchy.[45]

44. Ibid., I, preface, vii.
45. Ibid., 351, quoting Centinel [Samuel Bryan], no. 1, "To the Freemen of Pennsylvania." Tucker's pamphlet collection included a number of the most widely distributed Anti-Federalist and Federalist essays. In addition to the early numbers of Centinel's essays, his collection of Anti-Federalist writings included "The Address and Dissent of the Minority of the Convention in Philadelphia to Their Constituents," "Copy of a Letter from Richard Henry Lee, Esq. . . . [to Edmund Randolph]", "Hon. Mr. Gerry's Objections to Signing the National Constitution," "A Letter of His Excellency Edmund Randolph, Esquire, on the

If there was an Anti-Federalist voice that Tucker was eager to recover, it was that of the debates in the Virginia ratification convention. When citing the concerns raised there, Tucker followed the common Democratic-Republican practice of according nearly equal weight to both the Anti-Federalist fears and the Federalist replies. For Tucker, it was the dialogue between Anti-Federalists and Federalists within the individual state ratification conventions that had fixed the meaning of the Constitution.[46]

The one published author appearing frequently in Tucker's commentary was Publius. Tucker refined the strategy that other opposition thinkers had developed in the 1790s of using *The Federalist* in preference to Anti-Federalist writers. His characterization of *The Federalist* reveals how this text was recycled and reinterpreted to suit the needs of Jeffersonian jurisprudence:

> The very elaborate and masterly discussion of the constitution, in the Federalist, to which I have repeatedly referred the student in the course of this essay, would probably have saved me the labour of this attempt, if the defects of the constitution had been treated with equal candour, as the authors have manifested abilities in the development of its eminent advantages.[47]

Although Tucker had been exposed to some of Publius's writings, perhaps through a subscription to the *American Museum,* during the debate over ratification, he did not purchase a copy of the full text of *The Federalist* until 1792, when he requested that his friend John Page send him a copy of it, Paine's *Rights of Man,* "and any other *good republican* tracts." Among the many roles played by Tucker's *Blackstone,* his reading of Publius provided the most elaborate Jeffersonian interpretation of the *Federalist,* an exegesis deeply informed by Anti-Federalist concerns.[48]

The Federalist, Tucker argued, identified the Constitution as a government of limited authority. To move beyond that line would, in his view, violate the implicit understanding that had made ratification possible. Tucker's own copy of *The Federalist* contained extensive underlining in *Federalist* No.

Federal Constitution," George Mason's "Objections to the Constitution," "Elbridge Gerry's Letter to the Massachusetts Legislature," Luther Martin's *Genuine Information.* Tucker Pamphlet Collection, Virginia Historical Society, Richmond.

46. Tucker, *Blackstone's Commentaries,* I, appendix, note D, "View of the Constitution," 351.

47. Ibid., 376.

48. St. George Tucker to John Page, Jan. 15, 1792, Tucker-Coleman Papers, Swem Library, College of William and Mary, Williamsburg, Va.

9, where Publius responded to the Anti-Federalist charge that the new government would create a single consolidated government.[49]

Tucker's hermeneutic strategy demonstrated the dangers of using constructive interpretation to expand federal power. Once again, Publius was cast as the first exponent of strict construction. To arrive at this interpretation of *The Federalist*, Tucker had to do more than invoke Publius as the author of a thoughtful explication of the republican principles embodied in the Constitution. Publius became the quasi-official Federalist response to Anti-Federalist objections. *The Federalist* had to be understood as one side in a dialogue over the meaning of the Constitution. Out of the dialectic, the amendments proposed by the state ratification conventions were born.[50]

Tucker's reading of *The Federalist* was part of a larger commitment to uniting the most important aspects of Madisonian constitutionalism with an older Anti-Federalist critique. Tucker clearly favored Madison's approach to the Alien and Sedition crisis, not the more radical response favored by Jefferson. Tucker elaborated the Madisonian synthesis of the ideas of 1798, a vision of constitutionalism that had been elaborated most fully in the "Report of 1800."

When the "federal government should exercise powers not warranted by the Constitution," appeals to the judiciary were the appropriate response in those cases affecting the rights of individuals. Incidents in which the aggrieved party was a state demanded that the "state legislature, whose rights will be invaded by every such act, will be ready to mark the innovation and sound the alarm to the people: and thereby either effect a change in the federal representation" or, ultimately, to begin the amendment process.[51]

One of the most interesting features of Tucker's discussion is the additional amendments he believed necessary to complete the process undertaken by Congress with the adoption of the Bill of Rights. To finish the task

49. Tucker's copy of *The Federalist* with his marginal notes is in the Tucker-Coleman Papers.

50. For an interesting analysis of the different uses to which *The Federalist* was put by southern and northern jurists, see Jack N. Rakove, "Early Uses of *The Federalist*," in Charles R. Kesler, ed., *Saving the Revolution: "The Federalist Papers" and the American Founding* (New York, 1987), 234–249. On the role of Anti-Federalist arguments in *The Federalist*, see Murray Dry, "Anti-Federalism in *The Federalist*: A Founding Dialogue on the Constitution, Republican Government, and Federalism," in Kesler, ed., *Saving the Revolution*, 40–60.

51. Tucker, *Blackstone's Commentaries*, I, appendix, note D, "View of the Constitution," 153.

of reform, he returned to the amendments first recommended by the state ratification conventions. Reviving those alternative amendments was an obvious effort to bring the future development of American constitutionalism closer to the original desires of Anti-Federalists.

1. Finding a body other than the Senate to try impeachments of Senators.
2. A reform of the method of electing the president in the case of a tie in the electoral college.
3. Congressional approval of treaties.
4. Limits on the jurisdiction of the federal courts, particularly an explicit acknowledgment that there was no federal common law of crimes.
5. Modification of federal powers of excises and direct taxes in accordance with the concerns of the state ratification conventions.
6. Limitation of congressional oversight over the District of Columbia.
7. Prohibition on congressional interference with state control of elections.
8. Prohibition of standing armies in times of peace.
9. Prohibition of granting monopolies.
10. Forbidding the president to command the army in person.
11. Forbidding Congress to declare war without two-thirds approval of both houses.
12. No laws regulating commerce or navigation without two-thirds approval of both houses.
13. Provision for states' recall of senators.
14. Ineligibility of senators and representatives for any office during the term for which they were elected. (Tucker wished to extend the ban for a year after.)[52]

The general pattern of these amendments fits with the original Anti-Federalist agenda: restrict the powers of the federal government, strengthen the powers of the state, and expand the power of the lower house of Congress. The proposed amendments also responded to the great constitutional controversies of the 1790s; they would have ensured that the controversies over the bank, the Whiskey Rebellion, the Jay Treaty, and the Alien and Sedition Acts would never occur again.

Tucker confessed that his primary goal was to strengthen the *federal union* and "the principles of a democratic government." To facilitate this end, he admitted that he "regarded with a jealous eye those parts of the

52. Ibid., 372–375

constitution which seem to savour of monarchy, or aristocracy, or tend to a consolidated, instead of a federal, union of the states." His statement reiterated many of the essential components of the Anti-Federalist critique of the Constitution, particularly the concerns about aristocracy, consolidation, and individual liberty. He shared the suspicion of power that was so central to the Anti-Federalist critique: "All governments have a natural tendency towards an increase, and assumption of power." The federal government provided the best example of this ineluctable tendency. "We have seen that parchment chains are not sufficient to correct this unhappy propensity." Still, he expressed his faith that "they are, nevertheless, capable of producing the most salutary effects; for, when broken, they warn the people to change those perfidious agents, who dare to violate them." Written constitutions and bills of rights, therefore, served multiple functions within a republican polity. These texts not only were "intended to give law, and assign limits to a government," but also instructed the people so that "by reducing speculative truths to fundamental laws, every man of the meanest capacity and understanding may learn his own rights, and know when they are violated." Tucker's constitutionalism reflected the faith in a constitutional plain style that characterized so much Anti-Federalist thought. Constitutional texts had to be crafted in clear, precise language. When properly drafted, written constitutions served as important checks and instilled republican values in the people. By linking a culture of constitutionalism to the public sphere itself, written constitutions provided a powerful check against government tyranny. A culture of constitutionalism would create an active citizenry who would sound the alarm at the first threat to their liberty.[53]

Federalism occupied a central place in Tucker's jurisprudence. He devoted eight pages to a detailed list of exactly which powers were reserved to the states, which delegated to the new government, and which enjoyed concurrently by both parties. The danger posed by consolidation remained a serious problem. Tucker accepted an essentially Anti-Federalist interpretation of American constitutional history: the Constitution drafted by the framers was severely flawed because it did not clarify enough the boundaries separating state from federal authority. The alarm sounded by Anti-Federalists resulted in a clarification of the fatal ambiguities in the Constitution, and the danger of consolidation had been addressed by the adoption of the Tenth Amendment. The threat to federalism would have been obviated had there not been a deliberate effort to expand the powers of the new government through constructive interpretation: "Notwithstanding this remarkable se-

53. Ibid., 289–290, 303, 308, 376.

curity against misconstruction, a design has been indicated to expound these phrases in the constitution, so as to destroy the effect of this particular enumeration of powers." Tucker cited the bank and the Alien and Sedition laws as glaring examples of the effort to destroy the original understanding of the limited scope of federal authority.[54]

Tucker's theory of strict construction reaffirmed the close connection between federalism and individual liberty that had defined dissenting constitutionalism throughout the 1790s. Strict construction was essential in cases where "the antecedent rights of a *state* may be drawn in question" and "wherever the right of personal liberty, of personal security, or of private property may become the subject of dispute." His jurisprudence espoused a moderate variant of an emerging states' rights theory closer in spirit to Madison's "Report of 1800" than Jefferson's Kentucky Resolutions. Tucker wove together a variety of different opposition discourses that had been central to dissenting constitutionalism in the postratification period and produced a coherent constitutional theory. Tucker's Blackstone was a landmark in the evolution of dissenting constitutionalism, the logical culmination of a decade of Democratic-Republican dissent. By elaborating a coherent theory of jurisprudence, Tucker provided an important foundation for subsequent efforts at dissent.[55]

The Alien and Sedition crisis prompted the most serious examination of the tenets of loyal opposition since ratification. The two most important efforts to take the diverse strains of opposition thought and formulate a systematic alternative to the Federalist vision were Tunis Wortman's *Treatise* and St. George Tucker's *Blackstone's Commentaries*. Wortman gave voice to the aspirations and ideals of the middling democrats who dominated the opposition in places like New York, Pennsylvania, and parts of New England. Tucker, the preeminent jurist within the opposition, spoke for the ideals of an elite opposition that was particularly strong in Virginia and parts of the South.[56]

54. Ibid., 287. On Anti-Federalist views of the Tenth Amendment, see Charles F. Hobson, "The Tenth Amendment and the New Federalism of 1789," in Jon Kukla, ed., *The Bill of Rights: A Lively Heritage* (Richmond, Va., 1987), 153–163.

55. Tucker, *Blackstone's Commentaries,* I, appendix, note D, "View of the Constitution," 146, 151.

56. For a brief but thoughtful discussion of other important voices within the Democratic-Republican coalition, see Robert E. Shalhope, *The Roots of Democracy: American Thought and Culture, 1760–1800* (Boston, 1990). Tucker and Wortman were not only influential figures within different wings of the Democratic-Republican movement, but each man was among the most intellectually sophisticated constitutional theorists of the opposition.

Tunis Wortman followed the lead of earlier authors who stressed the centrality of federalism to opposition political and constitutional thought. The division of power between the states and the federal government was essential for the preservation of liberty. In many respects, Wortman's conception of liberty went further than earlier theorists in attempting to circumscribe the sphere of political authority and carve a zone of individual liberty beyond the reach of government. In seeking to restrict government authority, Wortman argued for an expansion of the public sphere. Thus the variant of liberalism he championed was shaped, not by a commercial vision, but by his notion of the public sphere. Participation in the public sphere, not immersion in private life or the economy, was the most important interest and obligation of citizens. Wortman's theory of freedom of the press sought to guard the public sphere and free it of all encumbrances. This vision of the public sphere was shaped by his democratic ideals, particularly his belief that all men possessed a moral sense that would ultimately guide individuals to truth. His emphasis on the centrality of public opinion to free government also led him to embrace a democratic theory of representation. For Wortman the use of libel by government was destructive of liberty and undermined the effectiveness of representation. The danger posed by the licentiousness of the press was small when compared to the danger posed by government use of criminal libel prosecutions.

St. George Tucker's *Blackstone's Commentaries* brought together the diverse elements of opposition constitutional thought into a coherent theory of jurisprudence. Tucker gathered the texts and outlined the strategies to be used when interpreting them. His work was the most elaborate and detailed effort to demonstrate the dangers of consolidation. The protection of individual liberty, according to this view, could be accomplished only in a properly balanced federal system in which the federal government was limited to those powers expressly delegated by the Constitution. The only means for protecting the integrity of the federal system was to adhere to a philosophy of strict construction. By limiting the scope of federal authority to the narrow grant that the states had made during ratification, federalism and liberty would be preserved. Identifying the limits of federal power necessarily led Tucker to consider the original understanding of the Constitution, wherein he accorded the original concerns of Anti-Federalists a privileged place.

The election of Thomas Jefferson to the presidency in 1800 solved the most immediate and pressing concerns of Democratic-Republicans. The tensions within the Democratic-Republican coalition and the threat posed by the nationalist jurisprudence of John Marshall, however, guaranteed that the language of Anti-Federalism would continue to shape the terms of debate.

CHAPTER 10 :

THE DISSENTING TRADITION,

FROM THE REVOLUTION OF 1800

UNTIL NULLIFICATION

The various strains of Democratic-Republican thought during the conflicts of the 1790s culminated in the principles of '98, summarized by James Madison in his "Report of 1800" and elaborated by St. George Tucker in his *Blackstone's Commentaries*. The two pillars of dissenting constitutionalism were the critiques of consolidation and constructive interpretation. Opposition thought was not entirely negative. The decentralized vision of federalism of opposition theorists advocated an expanded public sphere of political debate as a means of cementing the union together without the coercive authority that Federalists had advocated during the 1790s.[1]

The Revolution of 1800, which swept the Federalists out of power and ushered in an era of Jeffersonian hegemony, presented a new set of problems for theorists who had spent much of the previous decade in opposition. With the ascendancy of Jefferson to the presidency in 1800, the tensions within the former opposition were exacerbated: ideological differences, regional conflicts, and class divisions deepened fault lines within the Jeffersonian movement.[2]

1. On the principles of '98, see H. Jefferson Powell, "The Principles of '98: An Essay in Historical Retrieval," *Virginia Law Review,* LXXX (1994), 689–743.

2. On Jefferson, see Merrill D. Peterson, *Thomas Jefferson and the New Nation: A Biography* (New York, 1970). On the tensions within the republican movement, see Marshall Smelser, *The Democratic Republic, 1801–1815* (New York, 1968). For specific studies of the fragmentation of the Jeffersonian coalition, see Norman K. Risjord, *The Old Republicans:*

The southern wing of the coalition continued to be dominated by conservative agrarians. For John Taylor and other Old Republicans within the Jeffersonian coalition, the election of 1800 promised a constitutional revolution, which would radically restructure the government, including amending the Constitution to restrict federal power. Old Republicans viewed the Madisonian synthesis as too accommodating. For those eager to assert a more aggressive anticonsolidationist stance, Anti-Federalist rhetoric would prove extremely useful. Most Jeffersonians, however, preferred Madison's reformulation of Anti-Federalist ideas in the "Report of 1800" as the appropriate response to consolidation and constructive interpretation. Jefferson steered a moderate course. Rather than radical constitutional reform, Jefferson opted for a political solution. His first administration did dismantle the legacies of Federalist rule. The size of government was reduced. Offensive legislation such as the Alien and Sedition Acts was not enforced, its victims were pardoned, and the laws were allowed to expire.[3]

Although they won a decisive political victory, Jeffersonians remained an opposition party with regard to the federal judiciary, which continued to be a Federalist stronghold. The most controversial move of Jefferson's first term was to seek impeachment of Supreme Court justice Samuel Chase, the former Anti-Federalist who had become a convert to Federalist ideas after the French Revolution. The impeachment proceeedings placed an enormous strain on the Jeffersonians. Chase was ultimately acquitted, and the Jeffersonian coalition emerged weakened but united. Although Chase's polemical style had earned him the enmity of Jeffersonians, a far greater threat was the more temperate but no less assertive agenda of Chief Justice John Marshall, who was a formidable opponent. Marshall's vision of the Constitution posed the most serious Federalist challenge to dissenting constitutional theory since Hamilton's effort to charter a national bank.

Clinton versus Madison

The political and constitutional conflicts of Jefferson's first term paled in comparison to the problems posed by his second. The political and military

Southern Conservatism in the Age of Jefferson (New York, 1965); Kim Tousley Phillips, William Duane, Radical Journalist in the Age of Jefferson (New York, 1989). For a later period, see Charles Sellers, The Market Revolution: Jacksonian America, 1815–1846 (New York, 1991).

3. On Jefferson's constitutionalism, see David N. Mayer, The Constitutional Thought of Thomas Jefferson (Charlottesville, Va., 1994). For a more general account, see Peterson, Thomas Jefferson and the New Nation.

struggles of Napoleonic Europe brought the more commercial wing of the Jeffersonians into direct conflict with its southern agrarian wing. Rather than embroil America in the political conflicts of Napoleonic Europe, Jefferson enacted an embargo in 1807 that sought to remove American trade from the zone of conflict. In the heavily Federalist New England states and the overwhelmingly Democratic-Republican Middle Atlantic states, the Embargo fell heavily on commercial interests. The politics of the Embargo aggravated the tension within the Democratic-Republican movement between its southern agrarian wing and its strong base of support in the more commercially oriented Middle Atlantic.[4]

The problem of identifying a successor to Jefferson was colored by the conflict over the Embargo. The two leading Democratic-Republican contenders were George Clinton and James Madison. Although allied during the 1790s, the two men had been on opposite sides of the debate over the Constitution in 1788. The struggle over the future direction of the Jeffersonian movement revived many of the rhetorical and ideological issues of 1787. Clinton's cause was championed by Edmond Genêt, the controversial French politician who had done so much to stir up political passions during the 1790s.[5]

At the root of the split between Clinton and Madison was the growing rift between the middling and more commercial democrats who dominated Democratic-Republicanism in the Middle Atlantic and its southern gentry wing. Genêt excoriated the Virginia dynasty and the congressional caucus system for stifling the will of the people and imposing single-state rule on the nation, fixing on the system of the caucuses that picked presidential electors. This system, Genêt argued, undermined the idea of federalism. In defending the right of the states to choose presidential electors, he reiterated a basic principle of opposition thought. The choice of presidential electors had been given to the states as a safeguard by those concerned about the danger of federal power. "That right is reserved to the states themselves, and the natural guardians of that inestimable right, the state legislatures, are answerable to their constituents and to posterity." The issue of federalism was grafted onto the economic tensions that now split the agrarian and commer-

---

4. Peterson, *Thomas Jefferson and the New Nation,* 805–921. For a less than sympathetic account of Jefferson's presidency, see Forrest McDonald, *The Presidency of Thomas Jefferson* (Lawrence, Kans., 1976).

5. On Genêt, see Stanley Elkins and Eric McKitrick, *The Age of Federalism* (New York, 1993), 330–336, 365–373.

cial wings of the Jeffersonian coalition. His piece was explicitly procommercial and attacked Madison's support for Jefferson's embargo. In contrast to Madison, whom he portrayed as a spokesman for the planter class, Genêt praised Clinton as a middling democrat, "a republican of the old school, and not a leveller." Clinton, not Madison, was the appropriate heir of the Revolutionary tradition. Clinton spoke for the point of view of middling democracy and would encourage economic growth by promoting commerce and agriculture. Clinton's democracy, Genêt pointed out, was, not the unruly mobocracy of plebeians, but the sober vision espoused by middling sorts.[6]

In an effort to discredit Madison, Genêt published a short selection from Anti-Federalist Robert Yates's notes taken during the federal convention. Genêt claimed to present "an incontestible historical document which unriddles the plots and the machinations which have from the beginning of our federal constitution threatened its existence." "The origin of the parties which have agitated our states is there unravelled, the leading characters unmasked, and their secret views exposed." Genêt edited Yates's manuscript, possibly rewriting large sections to suit his goal of discrediting Madison.[7]

Yates's writings touch on three plans of government discussed during the convention—a consolidated government proposed by Virginia, a federal system defended by New Jersey, and a monarchical system advocated by Hamilton. Genêt argued that Madison, one of the architects of the Virginia plan, had always been a supporter of consolidation. At the end of the essay, Genêt offered a paean to the virtuous actions of Anti-Federalists Yates, Lansing, and Clinton, who had helped bring into being the amended Constitution that was the only barrier against consolidation and the destruction of individual liberty. In Genêt's view the amended Constitution became the "palladium of our liberty, the safeguard of our state rights, and the foundation of true republican principles." His argument was the most forceful effort to recast politics in terms of the debates of 1788 and thereby discredit Madison's commitment to federalism. This strategy was quite daring, since

6. A Citizen of New-York [Edmond Genêt], *Communications on the Next Election for President*... ([New York?], 1808), 9, 26.

7. A Citizen of New-York [Edmond Genêt], *A Letter to the Electors of President and Vice-President of the United States, Accompanied with an Extract of the Secret Debates of the Federal Convention* (New York, 1808), 3–4. Genêt's questionable and politically motivated editorial practices are discussed by James H. Hutson: "Robert Yates's Notes on the Constitutional Convention of 1787: Citizen Genêt's Edition," *Quarterly Journal of the Library of Congress,* XXXV (1978), 173–182; "The Creation of the Constitution: The Integrity of the Documentary Record," *Texas Law Review,* LXV (1986), 1–39.

it required a direct assault on the author of Virginia's "Report of 1800." Although slightly tarnished, the Madisonian synthesis of dissenting constitutional ideas weathered the assault by Clintonians. In the end, Genêt's plan failed, and his effort to discredit Madison failed: Clinton's candidacy fizzled.[8]

The use of Anti-Federalism in this debate departed from the standard ideological and rhetorical strategies employed by opposition theorists since ratification. In the 1790s, the opposition to Hamilton and the Federalists had generally sought to minimize its own differences and emphasize that Anti-Federalists had been legitimate participants in the compromises that produced constitutional consensus. The effort by Clintonians to challenge Madison's leadership presented an entirely different political problem, which called for a different argument. Discrediting Madison required a more acerbic and confrontational style. Clinton's supporters stressed the profound differences in 1788 between Publius and his Anti-Federalist opponents. Genêt's strategy challenged the notion of a founding dialogue between Federalists and Anti-Federalists, making it more difficult to connect the principles of '98 to those of '88. Genêt's arguments did not carry the day. Although the Madisonian synthesis had been weakened, it survived Genêt's assault and continued to provide the foundation for opposition thought.

McCulloch v. Maryland *and the* Collapse of the Madisonian Synthesis

The Supreme Court's decision in *McCulloch v. Maryland* in 1819 marked a new phase in the history of dissenting constitutionalism. The case arose out of an effort by the state of Maryland to tax the Bank of the United States.

In many ways the facts of the case in *McCulloch* seemed to hark back to the same issues that divided the nation in 1790s during the controversy over Hamilton's proposal to charter a national bank. Marshall's decision seemed to assert an essentially Hamiltonian vision of federal power. Affirming the constitutionality of the Second Bank of the United States and the illegality of the state of Maryland's effort to tax the bank appeared to put the full weight and authority of the Supreme Court behind a Hamiltonian reading of the Constitution. Marshall's opinion in that case galvanized the public. Not since the crisis of the Sedition Act had public attention been so focused on a constitutional question. Indeed, no other Supreme Court decision in the

8. Hutson, "Creation of the Constitution," *Texas Law Review,* LXV (1986), 3, 21.

previous thirty years had produced as wide-ranging and spirited a response in the press.[9]

The connection between the case and earlier constitutional struggles was underscored by the fact that Luther Martin, one of the nonsigners of the Constitution, presented the argument for Maryland. Martin took advantage of his role as one of the participants in the Philadelphia Convention. In Martin's view the meaning of the Constitution had to be gleaned from the original Anti-Federalist critique and Federalist response. He relied on the contemporary expositions of the meaning of the Constitution, including the state conventions of Virginia and New York and *The Federalist*. He recalled that the "enemies of the Constitution" argued that "it contained a vast variety of powers, lurking under the generality of its phraseology, which would prove highly dangerous to the liberties of the people, and the rights of the States." For exactly this reason the Tenth Amendment had been adopted. Martin went on to assert the limited nature of federal authority and defended the nearly unlimited power of the states to tax except in those cases such as imposts and tonnage duties in which the Constitution explicitly forbade state action.[10]

In his decision Marshall attacked the notion of federalism that had defined opposition constitutionalism since ratification: "The powers of the general government, it has been said, are delegated by the states, who alone are truly sovereign, and must be exercised in subordination to the states, who alone possess supreme dominion." Marshall's response to this assertion of states' rights was unequivocal: "It would be difficult to sustain this proposition." The Constitution, he argued, emphatically, was a creature of the people, not the states: "The government proceeds directly from the people." From the point of view of those who continued to venerate the perspective of the Anti-Federalists, Marshall's claim echoed the consolidationist rhetoric of 1787–1788. To complicate matters, Marshall struck at another cherished states' rights principle. "Even the 10th amendment, which was framed for the purpose of quieting the excessive jealousies which had been excited, omits the word 'expressly.'" Marshall not only impugned the fears of Anti-

9. On the importance of *McCulloch*, see G. Edward White, *The Marshall Court and Cultural Change, 1815–1835*, History of the Supreme Court of the United States, III–IV (New York, 1988).

10. Martin's brief is reprinted in Philip B. Kurland and Gerhard Casper, eds., *Landmark Briefs and Arguments of the Supreme Court of the United States: Constitutional Law* (Washington, D.C., 1978), I, 158.

Federalists but pointed out that the effort to restrict the government to those powers expressly delegated had been suggested and rejected by Congress when it had drafted the Bill of Rights. The Jeffersonians were now faced with the most serious challenge to their constitutional vision since Hamilton. Marshall's jurisprudence seemed to embody the worst consolidationist tendencies of Federalist thought.[11]

Marshall's decision drew responses from two of the most important spokesmen for the dissenting tradition, Spencer Roane and John Taylor of Caroline. Both men had been Anti-Federalists in 1788 and leading spokesmen for the opposition tradition in the succeeding years. In formulating their replies, each drew upon the essential elements of opposition constitutionalism defined by the Madisonian synthesis. Faced with the threat posed by Marshall's nationalist jurisprudence, these Virginia Anti-Federalists once again returned to the notion that the ideals of 1798 were the true expression of the intent of those who adopted the Constitution in 1788.

Although both men had attacked the argument of *The Federalist* in other contexts, both used Publius as the primary text with which to challenge the Marshall Court's interpretation. Both men relied on the strict constructionist reading of *The Federalist* that opposition authors had used since the 1790s. The overarching framework that each used to interpret the Constitution was the notion of the founding dialogue between Anti-Federalist criticisms and Federalist assurances. The Anti-Federalist voice that counted most heavily in this account was that in the published proceedings of the state ratification conventions, particularly those of Virginia.[12]

Roane took up his pen and adopted the venerable Whig identity of

11. Marshall's 1819 opinion in *McCulloch v. Maryland,* in Herbert A. Johnson et al., eds., *The Papers of John Marshall* (Chapel Hill, N.C., 1974–), VIII, 259–280 (quotations on 261, 263); also reprinted in Gerald Gunther, ed., *John Marshall's Defense of McCulloch v. Maryland* (Stanford, Calif., 1969). On the evolution of a dissenting tradition in the South between the War of 1812 and the rise of Jackson, see Risjord, *The Old Republicans.* On the importance of *McCulloch v. Maryland* as a turning point in southern jurisprudence, see R. Kent Newmyer, "John Marshall and the Southern Constitutional Tradition," in Kermit Hall and John Ely, eds., *An Uncertain Tradition: Constitutionalism and the History of the South* (Athens, Ga., 1989), 105–124. On the emergence of a distinctive Virginia tradition of constitutionalism, see Richard E. Ellis, "The Path Not Taken: Virginia and the Supreme Court, 1789–1821," in A. E. Dick Howard and Melvin I. Urofsky, eds., *Virginia and the Constitution* (Charlottesville, Va., 1992), 24–52.

12. For Roane's attack on *The Federalist,* see his decision in *Hunter v. Martin,* 4 Munford 1 (1813). On Taylor's negative views of *The Federalist,* see Risjord, *Old Republicans,* 35. On Roane's use of *The Federalist* and the Virginia debates as Hampden, see Gunther, ed., *John Marshall's Defense,* 108, 115, 116, 124, 127, 129, 140–142, 144–148.

"Hampden" to attack Marshall. The polemical fervor of the assault on a decision of the Court by Roane and others led Marshall to take the unusual step of writing defenses of the Court's decision under the pen names A Friend to the Union and A Friend of the Constitution.[13]

Roane's Hampden essays reiterated the critique of Federalist constitutional theory that had become a standard part of the dissenting tradition. Hampden did, however, represent a significant increase in the rhetorical fervor with which that tradition was voiced. Roane viewed the actions of the Court as the latest and in many respects the most insidious effort on the part of Federalists to achieve their goal of consolidation. Working through the Supreme Court, the federal government was engaged in rearguard action against the rights of the people and the states—a war not conducted in the open, but covertly, not by amendment, but by construction.

Roane also made oblique references to Anti-Federalism, invoking the spirit of prominent opponents of the Constitution such as George Mason and Patrick Henry. He queried his audience: what would these venerable statesmen think if they "could lift their patriot heads from the grave, while they mourned the complete fulfilment of their prophecies!" Roane also praised "the venerable *Clinton*," recalling the actions of this prominent Anti-Federalist and Democratic-Republican who cast a decisive vote against the chartering of the Second Bank. Although Roane studiously avoided mentioning Anti-Federalism, he asserted that the meaning of the Constitution had to be interpreted according to the original understanding at the time of ratification. That understanding involved linking the original Anti-Federalist critique with the Federalist response: the Constitution thus had been brought into existence by a compromise between the contending parties in 1788.[14]

The opposition text that Roane did explicitly cite was Madison's "celebrated report to the legislature of Virginia," which, he noted, was "called by an eloquent statesman,—his political bible." "It was the *Magna Charta* on which the republicans settled down, after the great struggle in the year 1799."

13. "Roane's 'Hampden' Essays," *Richmond Enquirer*, June 11–22, 1819," in Gunther, ed., *John Marshall's Defense*, 106–154. Marshall's defenses: Johnson et al., eds., *Papers of Marshall*, VIII, 287–300, 318–314, 335–352, 353–363; and in Gunther, ed., *John Marshall's Defense*, 155–214. For a discussion of Roane's role in Virginia legal culture, see F. Thornton Miller, *Juries and Judges versus the Law: Virginia's Provincial Legal Perspective, 1783–1828* (Charlottesville, Va., 1994).

14. "Roane's '"Hampden' Essays," in Gunther, ed., *John Marshall's Defense*, 112–113, 118. On Clinton's veto of the bank, see John P. Kaminski, *George Clinton: Yeoman Politician of the New Republic* (Madison, Wis., 1993).

Madison's distillation of opposition ideas in the aftermath of the Alien and Sedition crisis had become the central text for most opposition thinkers. Roane also cited the appendixes to Tucker's edition of *Blackstone's Commentaries*. The principles that Roane extracted had defined the core of the opposition creed since the 1790s: liberty required the preservation of a federal system, but constructive interpretation threatened individual liberty and the ability of the states to protect the rights of their citizens. Only a restoration of the original understanding of the Constitution as interpreted by the original parties to the compact, the states, could prevent the destruction of republican liberty.[15]

One important part of Roane's interpretation of the states' rights position was his effort to reassert the restrictive reading of the Tenth Amendment that Anti-Federalists had demanded and Democratic-Republicans had asserted during the 1790s. "It has been our happiness to believe, that in the partition of powers between the general and state governments, the former possessed only such as were expressly granted, or passed therewith as necessary incidents, while all the residuary powers were retained by the latter." To clarify the division of power between the federal government and the states and to quiet "the natural fears and jealousies of our citizens, in relation to this all important subject," Congress, he noted, had passed the Tenth Amendment.[16]

The other important text that Roane devoted substantial energy to analyzing was *The Federalist*. Writing as Hampden, Roane quoted extensively from *The Federalist* and was forthright about this strategy: "I shall also resort to a book, written, at least in part, by one of the highest-toned statesmen in America. That book is 'The Federalist,' and the writer alluded to, is Mr. Hamilton. The authors of that book have been eulogised by the Chief Justice, in his life of Washington" and "in the opinion before us." In effect, Roane intended to cross-examine Publius to demonstrate that the Marshall Court had violated the promises of chief spokesmen for the Constitution. "If I have any adversaries in this discussion, these *advocates* and this book are *their* witnesses, and I shall take leave to cross-examine them." The advantage of this strategy was plain to any lawyer. "The witness is the best for the defendant, who is produced on the part of the plaintiff . . . and testifies against his interest or prejudices."[17]

Roane's polemic did more than merely restate the established principles

15. "Roane's 'Hampden' Essays," in Gunther, ed., *John Marshall's Defense*, 112, 113, 148.
16. Ibid., 108.
17. Ibid., 113.

of earlier dissenting constitutional theorists. Marshall's actions had raised the stakes for both sides in this controversy and made the scope of Supreme Court authority a central point of contention. As a result of Marshall's decision, the status of the Supreme Court as the final arbiter on questions of federalism was now subjected to the most intense scrutiny it had ever undergone. Roane argued that the Court could not be a judge in a matter affecting its jurisdiction. In Roane's view only the states could serve that function. He believed that, for the federal system to function, the state courts and legislatures had to be able to exercise this vital check on possible encroachments by the federal government, lest the Supreme Court and the federal government be the final judge of their own actions.[18]

Many of Roane's points were taken up more systematically by John Taylor in *Construction Construed*. Taylor had proved himself one of the more consistent spokesmen for the tradition of dissent that harked back to the original Anti-Federalist critique of the Constitution. His response to Marshall's decision in *McCulloch v. Maryland* reiterated and elaborated themes he had developed during the 1790s.[19]

Taylor railed at the effort of an insidious faction to promote its consolidationist agenda by means of constructive interpretation of the Constitution. The supporters of aristocracy dared not bring their case before the people but had resorted to the more nefarious means of deliberately misinterpreting the Constitution to further their goals. Constructive interpretation violated the intent of the parties to the Constitution, the people of the states. Taylor challenged Marshall and his allies' use of the old Federalist theory of popular sovereignty. The Constitution could not have been the product of the people's will, since it was impossible for the people to act in a general capacity. The only means by which the will of the people could be ascertained was in their corporate identity, that is, the political agencies of the various states who were the parties to the original contract that created the nation. The states were the only true guardians of the people's rights, and it was essential that they retain the ability to judge infractions that violated the Constitution. This linkage of states' rights and individual rights had been a

18. Ibid., 113, 138–154. See also F. Thornton Miller, "John Marshall versus Spencer Roane: A Reevaluation of *Martin v. Hunter's Lessee*," *VMHB*, XCVI (1988), 297–314. For a general discussion of Roane's relationship to earlier dissenting constitutional thought, see White, *The Marshall Court*, 541, 554, 558–567.

19. John Taylor, *Construction Construed and Constitutions Vindicated* (Richmond, Va., 1820).

cornerstone of Anti-Federalist constitutional thought and continued to be a cornerstone of dissenting constitutionalism. The effort of the Marshall Court to monopolize constitutional interpretation and be the exclusive and final judge of all constitutional issues threatened to destroy the states and lay the foundation for a consolidated national government. The Court's effort to aggrandize federal power at the expense of the states was especially odious, since it violated the compromise that had made ratification possible. Taylor followed the same rhetorical strategy of Roane and many other dissenting constitutional theorists, using a distinctive reading of *The Federalist* to anchor his critique of consolidation. "It was," he noted, "successfully urged by the warmest friends to the Constitution, and in particular by the authors of *The Federalist,* that the supposed inequality of power between the state and federal spheres did not exist." The Constitution recognized that the states were the true expressions of local interests and that only they could adequately represent the social, economic, and cultural diversity of American society.[20]

The rhetoric of the Virginia opponents of *McCulloch* was leavened with themes drawn from the potent tradition of country protest. Even more than Roane, Taylor had been the opposition thinker most identified with that tradition. Taylor believed that an unprincipled junto led by a paper interest had endeavored to create artificial privileges and a commercial aristocracy, and in creating such a system they had abandoned the principles of equality that were the bedrock of Revolutionary constitutionalism. Although Taylor drew on rhetoric deriving from the older tradition of country protest, it is important to recognize that he was not simply mouthing tired political platitudes. The agrarian vision he defended was not static, did not oppose economic expansion. Taylor clearly distinguished between speculation and the honest pursuit of wealth. His critique was directed, not at wealth procured by "honest industry," but only at that "fostered by partial laws for enriching corporations and individuals." It was the actions of government on behalf of special interests that Taylor railed against. In his view the states were less likely to be manipulated by factions. Although couched in the familiar idiom of country republicanism, his critique of national power derived from a localist, anticentralizing critique of federal authority. His political philosophy was not antigovernment. Although Taylor generally viewed state efforts to guide the economy as misguided, his opposition was a matter of specific policy, not principle. Taylor's assault on aristocracy also derived from his

20. Ibid., 107.

conservative, state-centered, localist vision. Hostility to aristocracy in this context was not support for democracy. Taylor's vision of politics was essentially elitist, promoting the cosmopolitan localism that had defined elite opposition to the Constitution and much Democratic-Republicanism.[21]

Taylor's work was enthusiastically endorsed by a wide array of Virginians, including Thomas Ritchie, publisher of the *Richmond Enquirer,* and Thomas Jefferson. With its publication, Taylor became the most influential spokesman for southern opposition to Federalist ideas.[22]

The opposition to *McCulloch* was also intense in the Middle Atlantic. In contrast to the writings of Roane and Taylor, dissent in this region was framed in more egalitarian terms, reflecting the importance of middling democrats to the movement there. While the Richmond junto assailed the Marshall Court in the *Enquirer,* another, equally vociferous set of attacks on the decision in *McCulloch* appeared in Philadelphia in the leading platform for middling democrats, the *Aurora,* edited by William Duane. The *Aurora* was the most influential paper of old school Democrats, the heirs to the ideological tradition of Pennsylvania's constitutionalists and New York's Old Clintonians.[23]

Even before the decision in *McCulloch,* the Second Bank had come under fire in the *Aurora,* where criticism took several different forms. A few authors used traditional republican attacks on stockjobbing and corruption that would have pleased agrarians such as John Taylor. One author took the traditional republican assault on banking a step further than even Taylor would have wished, calling for a national dress code to reinstill the values of republican simplicity. Those critiques were not, however, typical of the *Aurora's* point of view, which reflected middling democracy. The language of its authors was not agrarian, but evoked an ideal of middling democracy in which all small producers—farmers, artisans, and even small manufacturers—would work together. This particular economic vision opposed the bank because it fostered inequality, not because it promoted economic

21. Ibid., 11. In 1821 Taylor explored these issues in greater detail. For an interesting discussion of this aspect of Taylor's thought, see John Taylor, *Tyranny Unmasked,* ed. F. Thornton Miller (Indianapolis, Ind., 1992), 42, 86.

22. On the reception of Taylor's *Construction Construed,* see Robert E. Shalhope, *John Taylor of Caroline: Pastoral Republican* (Columbia, S.C., 1980), 193. For another reading of Taylor's constitutional thought, see Andrew C. Lenner, "John Taylor and the Origins of American Federalism," *Journal of the Early Republic,* XVII (1997), 399–423.

23. On Duane's sympathy with Anti-Federalism, see Phillips, *William Duane,* 187; *Aurora* (Philadelphia), Aug. 1, 1805.

growth. The attack on aristocracy that had defined middling democracy during ratification and the 1790s was again a potent weapon.[24]

The most important challenge to the bank was formulated by one Stephen Simpson, under the persona of Brutus, the leading essayist for the *Aurora*. In both tone and content, the writings of the latter-day Brutus resembled those of earlier Anti-Federalist authors, including Clintonians such as New York's Brutus and Federal Farmer and Pennsylvanians such as An Old Whig. Brutus carried forward the ideological tradition of middling Anti-Federalists, such as Melancton Smith and William Findley, couching his assault on the bank and the Marshall Court in the same egalitarian democratic terms those men had used in 1788. In contrast to the anti-aristocratic rhetoric of Old Republicans such as Taylor, which was not particularly democratic, Brutus's denunciations were far more class-conscious. The bank had created "an aristocracy of wealth." He challenged the "servile respect to the exterior appearances of *property* and *wealth*," which he believed had become "the bane of the republic."[25]

Once the Supreme Court's decision in *McCulloch* became public, Brutus turned to Marshall and attacked the Court's opinion, echoing other writers in the *Aurora* that a strong judiciary was a threat to popular liberty. That suspicion of judicial authority had been a watchword of middling democratic constitutionalism for decades. Brutus was unequivocal about the Marshall Court's decision: it struck a blow against the "RIGHTS OF THE PEOPLE, and against the LIBERTIES OF THE STATES." The decision was "the most stupendous and mortal usurpation" of power since the Revolution and was typical of a "high toned aristocracy."[26]

Although more egalitarian and democratic, Brutus shared a language of protest with southern agrarians. Each followed the essential outline established by the Madisonian synthesis of 1800. To support his argument, Brutus

24. "Anaxagoras," *Aurora*, Sept. 25, 1819.

25. Brutus [Stephen Simpson], *Aurora*, June 24, 1819. The spectrum of dissenting constitutionalism included both agrarian conservatives and middling democrats. On the *Aurora*'s campaign against the banks, see Phillips, *William Duane*, 458–483.

26. "Brutus" [Simpson], *Aurora*, Mar. 16, 18, 21, 26, 1819. A suspicion of the judiciary had been crucial to middling Anti-Federalism (see Chapter 4, above). In contrast to elite proponents of the dissenting tradition such as St. George Tucker, middling democratic spokesmen were suspicious of both the state judiciary and the Supreme Court. For concerns about the Supreme Court, see Lucius, *Aurora*, Mar, 22, 1808. On the threat posed by the state judiciary to democracy, see [William Duane], *Experience the Test of Government* . . . (Philadelphia, 1807).

turned to *The Federalist* as a way of reconstructing the principles of the founding dialogue and thereby resurrecting the original Anti-Federalist concerns about the dangers of consolidation. The threat to state authority posed by the federal government's power to tax had been widely recognized at the time of ratification. Anti-Federalists had noted then that this power might be used as a subtle means of reducing the states to political ciphers. These fears had been explicitly aired by many Anti-Federalists, and Federalists had gone to great lengths to assuage them. Brutus reminded his readers that Publius had to be read in the context of the larger dispute between Federalists and Anti-Federalists.

> It must be remembered too, that he [Publius] is combating the arguments and attempting to dispel the *fears* of those *opponents* of the Constitution, who *dreaded* that the *unlimited* power of taxation in the union, would absorb and destroy the power and liberty of the states.[27]

By the time Brutus wrote his critique of *McCulloch,* few, if any, Anti-Federalist texts were circulating in the public sphere of political debate. Although rhetorical themes first championed by Anti-Federalists had become integral to a tradition of dissent, explicit references to Anti-Federalist ideas and citations of Anti-Federalist texts had become relatively rare. The Madisonian synthesis had effectively incorporated Anti-Federalist ideas into the notion of a founding dialogue, and they were now part of a penumbra that surrounded the arguments of the one text from 1788 that remained in circulation, *The Federalist.*

The decision of the Court, while legally binding, did not mean that the people were powerless and ought to resign themselves to a consolidated national system. Brutus turned to the public sphere, particularly the press, to rally the people. Once awakened, public opinion could overturn the Marshall Court's decision, through the existing political system: state legislatures and the amendment process. Resistance would be organized through the states, most importantly the legislatures, who might draft amendments to undue the damage by the Court to the original understanding of the Constitution. The notion that public opinion, the press, and the state legislatures could serve as a final check on government tyranny harked back to ideas most forcefully expressed by thinkers like Madison and Tunis Wortman. One difference existed between Brutus and Taylor. Whereas conservative southerners were more apt to see the legislature as a means of refining

27. Brutus [Simpson], *Aurora,* Mar. 26, 1819.

and filtering public opinion, Brutus believed that public opinion could be brought to bear directly on politics.

Although the Madisonian synthesis provided a common framework for dissent, it did not impose uniformity on opposition thought. Dissenting theory continued to include some of the most conservative voices in American politics, and many of the most democratic voices as well. Differences between these two wings of dissent were subtle but important, reflecting the role the people would play in preserving the original understanding of the Constitution and, when necessary, instituting constitutional change. Although Brutus's constitutionalism shared much with Roane, Taylor, and other more conservative southern thinkers, his approach was the more democratic.[28]

The Revival of Anti-Federalism: Robert Yates's Secret Proceedings

One of the most important developments in the transformation of dissenting constitutionalism was the publication of Robert Yates's *Secret Proceedings and Debates of the Convention Assembled in Philadelphia*. A short excerpt had appeared in 1808 in the midst of the controversy between George Clinton and James Madison over who would succeed Jefferson. Yates's volume brought back into circulation a diversity of Anti-Federalist texts, including those of Luther Martin, Edmund Randolph, and Abraham Yates and John Lansing. Suddenly, a range of Anti-Federalist writings that had been largely unavailable for more than three decades was now readily accessible. The most important of those pieces was Luther Martin's *Genuine Information*. Not only had Martin been the most assertive spokesmen for states' rights among the original opposition to the Constitution, but his discussion of the dynamics of the Philadelphia Convention lent credence to the theory that consolidation had been the original goal of Federalists. When read in combination with Yates's *Secret Proceedings,* Martin's *Genuine Information* provided evidence of a deliberate movement, beginning with the Philadelphia Convention, to create a consolidated government. Nor was the struggle against consolidation new; it too was part of a much longer battle that could be traced back to the Philadelphia Convention itself. The recent decisions of the Marshall Court thus were, not anomalies, but part of that systematic

28. *Aurora,* Mar. 28, Apr. 2, Nov. 29, 1819. For a similar critique of the Marshall Court that invoked the power of public opinion as a means of restoring the proper balance within the federal system, see *Liberty Hall and Cincinnati Gazette,* Apr. 16, 1821. On Wortman, see the discussion above, Chapter 9.

effort to bring about a national government that would eventually sap all power from the states.[29]

The introduction to Yates's *Secret Proceedings* recognized that *The Federalist* provided "ample discussions and elaborate comments to assist public judgement in the investigation of the plan of constitution presented to the consideration of the States." In contrast to the writings of Publius, which provided "discussion and comments" on the philosophical issues debated at the time of ratification, Yates's *Secret Proceedings* provided an eyewitness to history who recorded the true events within the Philadelphia Convention.[30]

The first work to make extensive use of Yates's *Secret Proceedings* was John Taylor's *New Views of the Constitution,* published in 1823. Taylor treated Yates's account as a revelation.

> Had the journal of the convention which framed the constitution of the United States, though obscure and incomplete, been published immediately after its ratification, it would have furnished lights towards a true construction, sufficiently clear to have prevented several trespasses upon its principles, and tendencies towards its subversion.[31]

Taylor even offered a new assessment of *The Federalist,* based on information revealed by Yates. When read through that lens, it was clear that *The Federalist* had been tainted by its authors' consolidationist philosophies. Much as Genêt's earlier decision to publish a brief excerpt from Yates's *Secret Proceedings* had tarnished Madison's credentials as a proponent of true federalism, so too did the full text of Yates's work lead to a reevaluation of Madison. In particular, Taylor singled out Madison's support in the convention for a federal negative on the laws of the states and his support for a powerful federal judiciary. For Taylor, Madison's failed proposal was central to understanding the limited nature of federal authority contemplated by the convention. The negative on state laws had been proposed and rejected

---

29. *Aurora,* Mar. 28, Apr. 2, Nov. 29, 1819. For a discussion of the politics behind the publishing history of Yates's notes, see Hutson: "Robert Yates's Notes on the Constitutional Convention of 1787," *Quarterly Journal of the Library of Congress,* XXXV (1978), 173–182; "Creation of the Constitution," *Texas Law Review,* LXV (1986), 1–39. For an interesting discussion of Madison's reactions to the publication of Yates's notes, see Drew R. McCoy, *The Last of the Fathers: James Madison and the Republican Legacy* (New York, 1989), 85–88. Genêt clearly edited the notes to bring them into accord with a distinctly Anti-Federalist view of the history of the convention.

30. Robert Yates, *Secret Proceedings and Debates of the Convention Assembled in Philadelphia, in the Year 1787. . . .* (Albany, N.Y., 1821), vii.

31. John Taylor, *New Views of the Constitution of the United States* (Washington, D.C., 1823), 11.

when the Constitution was being drafted. Had Madison's proposal been accepted, the public outcry would have been so intense that the Constitution would never have been ratified. Nor had any similar power been granted subsequently by amendment. Indeed, Taylor argued that the Tenth Amendment had clearly been added to the Constitution to make clear that no such power had been delegated.[32]

Taylor's ideal of federalism rested on this assumption: "Co-ordinate and independent powers alone, can beget mutual moderation." In contrast to the spirit of true federalism, consolidation advocated "an unchecked supremacy," which inspires "arrogance, and causes oppression." The power of the Supreme Court as a final arbiter on all questions of constitutionality struck Taylor as one of the most insidious developments in American life. Once again, Taylor blamed Madison, whose writings as Publius demonstrated the inconsistency between asserting the "sovereignty of states, and the supremacy of a federal judiciary."[33]

The disagreement over who the original parties were to the compact that created the Constitution was also crucial to Taylor's argument. He contested the claim that the people had been the authors of the Constitution: he denied that an American people existed apart from their corporate embodiments in the individual states. The idea of an American people was, Taylor asserted, a fiction invented by Federalists to procure ratification. "There never was, nor yet is, such a people, able to make a national constitution." In particular, Taylor singled out Madison's argument in *The Federalist* as an especially disingenuous effort to use "a figurative expression" to transform "the state organ, called a convention," into "an American nation."[34]

Taylor asserted that the goal of his constitutionalism was to preserve the character of the federal system. He attacked consolidation with the same vigor with which he assailed disunionist sentiments. He showed equal con-

---

32. Taylor, *New Views*, 25–26, 43, 50–51, 63, 76. On the importance of this aspect of Madison's thought, see Charles F. Hobson, "The Negative on State Laws: James Madison, the Constitution, and the Crisis of Republican Government," *WMQ*, 3d Ser., XXXVI (1979), 215–235.

33. Taylor, *New Views*, 33–35, 115.

34. Ibid., 87–89. Taylor's negative critique of Madison anticipates Edmund S. Morgan's more positive assessment of Madison's effort to reconceptualize a basic problem in Anglo-American politics, in *Inventing the People: The Rise of Popular Sovereignty in England and America* (New York, 1988). Madison's move was not, in Morgan's view, duplicitous, but a brilliant example of his political creativity. For a different interpretation of Madison's position, see Lance Banning, *The Sacred Fire of Liberty: James Madison and the Founding of the Federal Republic* (Ithaca, N.Y., 1995), 533.

tempt for Marshall's nationalism and the sentiments of the Hartford convention. The problem for Taylor, as it had been for Anti-Federalists and Democratic-Republicans, was how to create a system in which the centrifugal and centripetal tendencies in American political life were balanced. The only system capable of maintaining this balance was a truly federal system in which the powers of the central government were restricted to those expressly delegated by the Constitution.[35]

John Taylor's *New Views of the Constitution* marked a turning point for the southern wing of the dissenting tradition. Distinguishing this new phase was a more overt identification with the original Anti-Federalist critique of the Constitution. The most important casualty of this shift was the Madisonian synthesis and the notion of a founding dialogue.

The man most responsible for the resuscitation of Anti-Federalist ideas was the outspoken Democratic-Republican Oxonian educator and scientist, Thomas Cooper, who had migrated from England to Pennsylvania to South Carolina and become a leading figure in the state's premier intellectual institution, South Carolina College. In 1820 he became acting president and a year later was officially elected president of the college. There he became the most influential theorist of South Carolina's distinctive brand of states' rights constitutionalism. As the dominant intellectual influence on the students during the period 1824–1834, Cooper became schoolmaster to a generation of political leaders, many of whom would later be prominent in that state's nullification movement.[36]

The most important statement of this new, more assertive and self-consciously Anti-Federalist credo was Cooper's *Consolidation: An Account of the Parties in the United States from the Convention of 1787.* Cooper asked his readers to consider the historical question: "What are the distinctive characters of the Federal and Anti-Federal Parties?" For Cooper the tensions in American politics that divided the nation in 1787–1788 were not merely a matter of historical interest. The gulf between these two opposing positions had not narrowed, but actually widened in the subsequent decades. Al-

35. Taylor, *New Views,* 216.
36. Thomas Cooper, *Consolidation: An Account of the Parties in the United States from the Convention of 1787,* 2 vols. (Columbia, S.C., 1824–1834), I, preface, 14. On Cooper, see Dumas Malone, *The Public Life of Thomas Cooper, 1783–1839* (New Haven, Conn., 1926). On the political culture of South Carolina during this period, see William W. Freehling, *Prelude to Civil War: The Nullification Controversy in South Carolina, 1816–1836* (New York, 1965); Freehling, *The Road to Disunion,* I, *The Secessionists at Bay* (New York, 1990); Drew Gilpin Faust, *James Henry Hammond and the Old South: A Design for Mastery* (Baton Rouge, La., 1982).

though the names of these two parties had shifted over time, the essential division in American politics remained unchanged. Cooper made clear his own sympathies when he boldly declared that his work was "the statement of an Anti-Federalist." In his view, "The dividing line of 1787, has continued to be the dividing line from thence forward."[37]

Cooper's *Consolidation* acknowledged an important debt to Taylor's *New Views of the Constitution*. Both works took as their starting point the account of the origins of the Constitution in Yates's *Secret Proceedings*. The struggle between the friends of true federalism and the forces bent on consolidation began in the Philadelphia Convention and continued to divide American politics. Cooper endorsed Taylor's judgment about *The Federalist*. "It was a conciliatory publication," Cooper wrote, "and the motives of its authors did them honor." At the same time, Cooper conceded, "As we might expect, the party distinctions that took place in the convention are rather concealed than brought into view in that work." The value of *The Federalist* was diminished because it was written with the avowed "purpose of reconciling the people to the new constitution" and hence did not represent the true intent of Federalists, who, Cooper argued, were interested in creating a consolidated government. Cooper acknowledged that "it did much good at the time" but insisted that it was equally true that "experience has shewn that they were bad prophets." Cooper also depicted Madison as a latecomer to true federal principles, who had "gradually changed his views of a national government, and came round to the sentiments of the majority of republican leaders of his own state."[38]

Cooper went further than any previous writer to rehabilitate Anti-Federalism. The supporters of true federal principles "have been at different times since, branded with the appellation of anti-federalists, Jacobins, republicans, democrats, and radicals." Cooper restated the credo of Anti-Federalists effectively. "They are of opinion, that the people and the state governments of this country never meant to institute a magnificent, imposing, expensive, *national* government, with extensive powers, and high prerogatives, calculated to control or prostrate the quiet, unpretending, cheap and salutary governments of the separate states."[39]

Cooper refined his constitutional ideas in the essay "On the Constitution of the United States," published in 1826. In that work he picked up a

37. Cooper, *Consolidation*, preface, 3, 7. 14.
38. Ibid., 4, 6.
39. Ibid., 4, 5.

theme central to Taylor's critique of Federalist constitutional theory, that the "United States Constitution, is the immediate work of the *People* of the United States." He rejected this view flatly: "It is not so." This nationalist interpretation of the origins of the Constitution had been erroneously propagated by Justice Joseph Story and Chief Justice John Marshall. It had been promulgated since the time of Alexander Hamilton to obscure the role of the sovereign states as the original parties to the compact that created the Constitution. The danger of this conception had been recognized at the time of ratification by Patrick Henry and had been reiterated time and again by proponents of a dissenting vision of American constitutionalism.[40]

As he had done in *Consolidation,* Cooper summarized the principles of the Anti-Federalists, or Republicans. The twin principles of Anti-Federalist constitutionalism were states' rights and strict construction. Cooper identified this constitutional philosophy also with a more general concept of political jealousy. Opposition theorists were concerned that all governments would invariably seek to expand their authority and "encroach on the rights of the people." As did the Anti-Federalists, Cooper believed in simple government: "The less government has to do, and the fewest temptations to interfere with what the people can do without them, the better."[41]

Cooper's solution to the growing threat of the Marshall Court was a return to the original understanding of 1788. He rejected the notion that the Court was the final arbiter of constitutional matters. The House of Representatives, he asserted, provided an appropriate check on the Court, and aggrieved citizens could use the right of petition to impel the House to check the Court.

> The right of entertaining Petitions for redress of grievances, implies as a matter of course the right of redressing them, else the right of petition is nugatory. Does the Constitution limit this right? Does it say you may petition against any grievances but those inflicted by the Judiciary?

To deny Congress this power, Cooper concluded, would be to create "a class of functionaries, unamenable, unassailable," an idea incompatible with the republican principles upon which the nation had been founded. In extreme cases, Cooper admitted that the right of impeachment might be used to bring the Court into line. Cooper's theory was essentially conservative; the

40. Thomas Cooper, *Two Essays: 1, On the Foundation of Civil Government; 2, On the Constitution of the United States* (Columbia, S.C., 1826), 21, 23.
41. Ibid., 29.

goal was to use the existing structures provided by the Constitution to restore the original understanding of 1788.[42]

Ultimately, Cooper's constitutional theory embraced a neo-Anti-Federalist solution to the dangers of the Marshall Court's nationalist jurisprudence. The Constitution ratified by the people had been of limited authority, and the original Anti-Federalist critique, Cooper concluded, had been prescient. Even *The Federalist* had been tainted by the consolidationist philosophy of its authors. The key to understanding that original grant of authority, therefore, lay in the original Anti-Federalist critique of the Constitution, through which it was possible to restore the Constitution to its original purity.

Cooper's constitutionalism drew on well-established dissenting principles. The Constitution was a compact that ceded limited authority to the federal government; its meaning was governed by the intent of the people acting in their corporate capacity as citizens of the states that had ratified that document. In one sense Cooper's constitutionalism broke with earlier dissent, adding an important revisionist element to this historical argument that drew upon Yates's *Proceedings*. Earlier dissenting theorists accepted the notion of a founding dialogue that indissolubly linked Anti-Federalist objections and Federalist assurances. Yates's evidence demonstrated that the goal of consolidation was first put forward in the Philadelphia Convention. With that in mind, all subsequent Federalist writing, including that of Publius, was rendered suspect. The only way to purge constitutional theory of consolidationist heresy was to recognize the legitimacy of the original Anti-Federalist critique and bring the Constitution into conformity with it.

Nullification and the Splintering of the Dissenting Tradition

The effort of South Carolinians in 1832 to nullify the tariffs of 1828 and 1832 prompted nationalists and constitutional theorists of states' rights to reexamine their most cherished assumptions. The main proponent of nullification, John C. Calhoun, was in many respects an unlikely choice to become the leading theorist of a new, more aggressive variant of states' rights federalism. In contrast to many of the most important voices of dissenting constitutionalism, Calhoun had not begun his career as an exponent of such doctrines and was a relative newcomer to them. Indeed, the intellectual roots of the constitutional philosophy of Calhoun, educated at Yale, were not in

42. Ibid., 57.

Thomas Cooper's classes at South Carolina College. Although Calhoun was familiar with Cooper's writings, particularly on political economy, the two men were vocal opponents. Cooper had even accused Calhoun of being a Federalist in sympathy.[43]

Calhoun expressed his variant of states' rights theory in the pamphlet *Exposition and Protest*, from the Special Committee on the Tariff, which provided the intellectual defense of the state's protest against the tariff of 1828. The document not only attacked the economic philosophy behind the tariff; it formulated a new theory of states' rights. Instead of appealing to the original fears of Anti-Federalists, Calhoun placed himself within a tradition rooted in the ideas of the Federalist framers, rejecting the notion of a founding dialogue between Federalists and Anti-Federalists. Calhoun applauded the framers, calling them "no ordinary men." Indeed, he went so far as to describe them as "wise, and practical statesmen, enlightened by history and their own enlarged experience." He eschewed the argument, developed after the publication of Yates's *Secret Proceedings*, that the original goals of the convention had been consolidation, and constructed a rather different sort of intellectual genealogy for his own constitutional theory.[44]

Calhoun cast his thinking as the logical culmination of a tradition begun with the framers, including Publius, and culminating in Madison's "Report

43. On nullification, see Major L. Wilson, " 'Liberty and Union': An Analysis of Three Concepts Involved in the Nullification Controversy," *Journal of Southern History*, XXXIII (1967), 73–93; Freehling, *Prelude to Civil War*; Richard E. Ellis, *The Union at Risk: Jacksonian Democracy, States' Rights, and the Nullification Crisis* (New York, 1987). On the complicated relationship between Calhoun and Jefferson, see Merrill D. Peterson, *The Jefferson Image in the American Mind* (New York, 1960), 51–67. In Peterson's view Calhoun was a late convert to states' rights who used Jefferson's ideas opportunistically. The figure within South Carolina who explicitly invoked Anti-Federalism was Thomas Cooper. On the tensions between Calhoun and Cooper, see John Niven, *John C. Calhoun and the Price of Union: A Biography* (Baton Rouge, La., 1988).

44. John C. Calhoun, *Exposition and Protest*, Dec. 19, 1828, in Ross M. Lence, ed., *Union and Liberty: The Political Philosophy of John C. Calhoun* (Indianapolis, Ind., 1992), 311–366; Jonathan Elliot, *The Debates, Resolutions, and Other Proceedings in Convention . . .* , 4 vols. (Washington, D.C., 1827–1830). In 1832 Elliot published an edition of *The Virginia and Kentucky Resolutions* (Washington, D.C., 1832) that included one of Calhoun's addresses. Elliot also gained Calhoun's endorsement for the first edition of the *Debates*; see John C. Calhoun to Jonathan Elliot, May 16, 1831, in Robert L. Meriwether et al., eds., *The Papers of John C. Calhoun* (Columbia, S.C., 1959–), XI, 381–382. Although Calhoun encouraged Elliot and publicly endorsed his enterprise, he himself adopted a different political strategy.

of 1800." At the same time that John Taylor and Thomas Cooper were abandoning Publius in favor of a revived version of Anti-Federalist ideas, Calhoun was creating a states' rights reading of him. While Taylor and Cooper each sought to expose the divisions among the framers, demonstrating the tension between the true federalists in the convention and those dedicated to consolidation, Calhoun praised the framers for their constitutional ideals.[45]

Calhoun's states' rights constitutionalism not only depended on a different historical foundation, but it envisioned a new means of checking the authority of the central government. His proposal for special state conventions to nullify unconstitutional laws abandoned the Madisonian synthesis developed in the "Report of 1800." Calhoun did not look to an invigorated public sphere of debate and the existing structures of government. Instead, he proposed a new legal and constitutional mechanism for resolving conflicts between the states and the federal government: special state conventions empowered to nullify federal laws. The onus would then be on the federal government to pass an amendment to overrule a state's act of nullification. If passed, the state could then either acquiesce or leave the Union. There was nothing conservative about this approach. In contrast to those theorists who sought to restore the original understanding of 1788, Calhoun proposed a radical revision of American constitutional theory.

Calhoun elaborated and refined his radical revisionist reformulation of Madisonian constitutionalism in two posthumously published treatises on American constitutional government, *A Disquisition on Government* and *A Discourse on the Constitution and Government of the United States*. The cornerstone of his mature theory was his belief that the only means of eliminating the danger of the tyranny of the majority was to recast American politics in terms of a new understanding of representative government. In contrast to a simple majority rule, Calhoun championed the notion of a concurrent majority, the consensus that emerged when all of society's distinctive interests were adequately represented and consulted on matters of

45. Calhoun, *Exposition and Protest*, in Lence, ed., *Union and Liberty*, 311–366. On Calhoun's view of the framers, see 315, 358; on the strict construction of the Tenth Amendment and compact theory, see 343–344; on consolidation, see 348, 363; on Jefferson and Madison's Virginia and Kentucky Resolutions and the Virginia "Report of 1800," see 349–350. Calhoun's use of Publius, rather than of Anti-Federalist ideas, aptly illustrates Quentin Skinner's point that it is often the arguments that a particular thinker chooses not to make that are as significant as those he did make. See Skinner, "Meaning and Understanding in the History of Ideas," in James Tully, ed., *Meaning and Context: Quentin Skinner and His Critics* (Princeton, N.J., 1988), 62.

public concern. In contrast to simple majority rule, the concurrent majority provided minority interests a check on the tyranny of the majority.[46]

Calhoun's concurrent majority was not grounded in an Anti-Federalist constitutionalism, but rather based on a self-conscious and idiosyncratic Publian vision of politics. While he praised the opponents of the Constitution for correctly identifying "the danger of consolidation from construction," he accorded Anti-Federalist insights but a modest place in his understanding of it. The bulk of his discussion was devoted to the arguments developed in *The Federalist*. Intellectually, his theory of the concurrent majority showed greater kinship with Madison's argument in *Federalist* No. 10 than it did with any of the essays of leading Anti-Federalist authors.[47]

At a time when Anti-Federalist ideas were receiving their most sympathetic hearing in forty years, Calhoun consciously framed his theory of nullification in terms that represented a radical revision of the principles of '98, not those of '88. He saw himself as the heir to Publius, not to the Anti-Federalists. Calhoun went further than any previous exponent of the dissenting tradition to recast the argument of *The Federalist* as a states' rights treatise. Although such a move would have been unexceptional before the publication of Yates's *Secret Proceedings,* Calhoun's decision clearly set him apart from the tradition of dissent embodied in the writings of Cooper and Taylor, each of whom recast opposition thought in terms derivative of the historical argument in Yates's *Secret Proceedings*.[48]

46. On Calhoun's political theory, see Daryl H. Rice, "John C. Calhoun," *History of Political Thought,* XII (1991), 317–328; Gillis J. Harp, "Taylor, Calhoun, and the Decline of a Theory of Political Disharmony," *Journal of the History of Ideas,* XLVI (1985), 107–120; Pauline Maier, "The Road Not Taken: Nullification, John C. Calhoun, and the Revolutionary Tradition in South Carolina," *South Carolina Historical Magazine,* LXXXII (1981), 1–19; C. William Hill, "Contrasting Themes in the Political Theories of Jefferson, Calhoun, and John Taylor of Caroline," *Publius,* VI, no. 3 (Summer 1976), 73–91; J. William Harris, "Last of the Classical Republicans: An Interpretation of John C. Calhoun," *Civil War History,* XXX (1984), 255–267.

47. John C. Calhoun, *A Discourse on the Constitution and Government of the United States,* in Lence, ed., *Union and Liberty,* 175.

48. A number of scholars have linked Calhoun's thought to a tradition of states' rights thought rooted in Anti-Federalism. See, for example, Murray Dry, "The Debate over Ratification of the Constitution," in Jack P. Greene and J. R. Pole, eds., *The Blackwell Encyclopedia of the American Revolution* (London, 1991), 471–486. A similar view informs David F. Ericson, *The Shaping of American Liberalism: The Debates over Ratification, Nullification, and Slavery* (Chicago, 1993); and Morton J. Frisch, "The Persistence of Antifederalism between the Ratification of the Constitution and the Nullification Crisis," in Josephine F. Pacheco, ed., *Antifederalism: The Legacy of George Mason* (Fairfax, Va., 1992), 79–90. A more

States' rights constitutionalism had never been an exclusively southern tradition. Indeed, the most sympathetic account of Anti-Federalism written during the Nullification Crisis was framed by New Yorkers, not South Carolinians. As in 1798, the idea of rallying the people through their state legislatures led other states to respond to South Carolina's *Exposition and Protest*. In the report on nullification that Martin Van Buren drafted for the New York legislature in response to South Carolina, the fears of Anti-Federalists were acknowledged as both legitimate and, in many respects, prescient. The opponents of the Constitution had "supposed, that the natural tendency of the new system would be towards consolidation." While the New York Committee rejected nullification, it firmly defended its own commitment to states' rights federalism grounded in the tradition of dissent that had evolved between 1788 and 1828. "Time, and the course of events," observed the report, proved that "the tendency of the system is to encroachments by the Federal Government upon the reserved rights of the States, rather than to an unwillingness on the part of the States to submit to a full exercise of the powers which were intended to be delegated to the General Government." The committee then went on to praise the elections of Thomas Jefferson and Andrew Jackson as examples of the people's resolve to stay the progress of consolidation and restore the true principles of federalism.[49]

---

compelling account of the origins of Calhoun's thought may be found in Lacy K. Ford, Jr., "Inventing the Concurrent Majority: Madison, Calhoun, and the Problem of Majoritarianism in American Political Thought," *Journal of Southern History*, LX (1994), 19–58; Ford, "Recovering the Republic: Calhoun, South Carolina, and the Concurrent Majority," *South Carolina Historical Magazine*, LXXXIX (1988), 146–159. On Madison's negative reaction to Calhoun's appropriation of *The Federalist*, see McCoy, *The Last of the Fathers*, 131–151.

49. "Resolves of the Legislature of New York: Report," in *State Papers on Nullification . . .* (Boston, 1834), 131–159 (quotations on 135, 136). For a more general treatment of states' rights in the North and South, see Paul Finkleman, "States' Rights North and South in Antebellum America," in Hall and Ely, eds., *An Uncertain Tradition*, 125–158. On Van Buren's approach to the question of states' rights, see Ellis, *The Union at Risk*, 151–156, and the debate in the New York legislature. Ellis treats Van Buren as an heir to the agrarian democratic tradition of Anti-Federalism. This view of Anti-Federalism collapses together several distinctive traditions, including an elite southern gentry tradition, a plebeian populist tradition, and a middling democratic tradition. Van Buren's ideology seems more closely to resemble the Old Clintonian ideals of middling democracy than it does an agrarian populist tradition. On Van Buren's political career, see Robert V. Remini, *Martin Van Buren and the Making of the Democratic Party* (New York, 1951); Donald B. Cole, *Martin Van Buren and the American Political System* (Princeton, N.J., 1984).

The report rejected Calhoun's radical revision of states' rights theory in forceful terms. After considerable debate, in which members of the legislature argued over the meaning of the principles of '98, the legislature approved the report. Van Buren was the heir to the old Clintonian branch of Anti-Federalism, which sought to bring together the yeomanry, artisans, and small merchants into an effective coalition committed to the ideals of middling democracy. This particular political philosophy was characterized by its support for the ideals of equality, democracy, economic growth, and federalism.

More than any other political figure of the Jacksonian period, Van Buren recognized the importance of Anti-Federalist ideas to American political culture. In his posthumously published *Inquiry into the Origin and Course of Political Parties in the United States,* Van Buren sought to account for the evolution of American politics from the Revolution up to the Dred Scott case. Throughout his discussion, Van Buren focused on the political beliefs, attitudes, and feelings that formed the core of something he described as the "Anti-Federalist Mind." Van Buren grappled with the same issue Alexis de Tocqueville did in *Democracy in America:* the democratic localism of American politics. The key to understanding American political culture for both Tocqueville and Van Buren was its decentralized, democratic character.[50]

Although the Anti-Federalists had lost the battle with Federalists in 1788, Van Buren believed that they had won the struggle for America's political soul. The constellation of beliefs that defined the Anti-Federalist mind continued to shape American political life even after the term ceased to have any political currency. The label "Anti-Federalist," he acknowledged, seemed ill suited to the opponents of the Constitution, who were fierce partisans of the traditional view of federalism at the core of Revolutionary constitutionalism. What made Anti-Federalism so potent and enduring in American politics was its resonance for the vast majority of the people. "The political feelings which lay nearest to the hearts of the great body of the people," he commented, were a "veneration and affection for their local governments as safeguards of their liberties." According to Van Buren, their support for a form of democratic localism grounded in the authority of the state governments made Anti-Federalists the true spokesmen for the spirit of American politics.[51]

50. Alexis de Tocqueville, *Democracy in America,* ed. J. P. Mayer and Max Lerner, trans. George Lawrence (New York, 1966), book I, chap. 5.

51. Martin Van Buren, *Inquiry into the Origin and Course of Political Parties, in the United States* (New York, 1867), 35.

In Van Buren's view the reconciliation of Anti-Federalists and those Federalists who were genuine republicans was the crucial development in American political history. As a result of their fusion, the Constitution was amended, and a genuinely republican and federal party emerged. Amendments, Van Buren noted approvingly,

> converted the residue of the Anti-Federal party which had not supported the Constitution, whose members, as well as their political predecessors in every stage of our history constituted a majority of the people, from opponents of that instrument into its warmest friends.[52]

With the Anti-Federalists in the role of a loyal opposition, a set of core beliefs helped shape a tradition of opposition that was vital to the preservation of democracy and state autonomy. Although Americans might temporarily drift away from those ideals, they would never long stray from them. The elections of Jefferson and Jackson demonstrated that those values could not remain marginal for very long before the people reasserted their will.

The political triumph of the Anti-Federalist mind, however, had not dispelled all of the dangers facing America. Even after the threat posed by Federalists had been banished from the political arena, the dangers of consolidation persisted. Federalist ideas had found a home among judges, in reaction to whom the tradition of dissent continued even after the triumph of Jefferson. Van Buren believed, "The organization of the Federal judiciary was the very first opportunity that was afforded after the adoption of the Constitution to make the States feel the power which their inveterate opponents had acquired." The culmination of this Federalist strategy was the effort by the Supreme Court to assume the right to be the final judge of all constitutional matters. Van Buren asserted that the Court was final judge only in those areas in which its jurisdiction had been defined by the Constitution. Both in regard to questions of federalism (that is, arguments that necessarily involved state courts) and questions pertaining to the separation of powers (that is, arguments between the different branches of the federal government), the Supreme Court could not assume the role of final arbiter without making itself superior to both the states and the other branches of the federal government. The view "which claims for the Supreme Court a controlling power over the other departments in respect to constitutional questions" was, Van Buren argued, fallacious. The struggle to define the nature of American constitutionalism was the last battle in an older struggle against consolidation. In the end, the principles of Hamiltonian federalism

52. Ibid., 201.

could not withstand the onslaught of Democratic-Republican ideals. The Anti-Federalist mind would continue to shape the contours of American politics, because it represented the core values of Revolutionary constitutionalism that defined the nation's political identity. Ultimately, the Federalist ascendancy was doomed. Although descendants of the Federalists might achieve momentary victories, it was the heirs of the Anti-Federalists who were the genuine spokesmen for American constitutionalism. The Anti-Federalist mind would continue to be the mind of America.[53]

The reformulation of Anti-Federalist ideas by James Madison in the "Report of 1800" created a synthesis that was a foundation for dissent between 1800 and 1828. There were, however, threats to that consensus. Following the election of Jefferson, latent tensions within the dissenting movement that had opposed the Federalist agenda throughout the 1790s were finally brought to the surface. Regional and class tensions were exacerbated by Jefferson's Embargo policy and the struggle over who would succeed him. When the supporters of George Clinton challenged Madison's leadership of the Jeffersonian coalition, they turned to an older Anti-Federalist language to frame their opposition.

The most serious challenge to the Madisonian synthesis emerged in the wake of the Supreme Court's decision in *McCulloch v. Maryland*. The earliest reactions to the Court's decision derived from the Madisonian synthesis. For spokesmen for the dissenting tradition, a common constitutional framework did not, however, imply a broad consensus on more basic questions about the nature of American politics. Public responses to the Court were couched in different idioms, the agrarian perspective of old republicanism in the South against the more democratic, commercial-mindedness that filled the pages of papers such as the *Aurora* in Philadelphia. Old Republicans such as Taylor were not especially democratic in outlook; Duane and his allies, by contrast, had inherited the mantle of middling democracy and continued to attack aristocracy in terms that echoed earlier, more popular rhetoric.

The tone and character of opposition shifted after the publication of Robert Yates's *Secret Proceedings*. Yates's work provided the historical foundation for the most serious reexamination of the Madisonian synthesis of dissenting constitutional theory. Reading American constitutional history through Yates's lens led thinkers such as John Taylor and Thomas Cooper explicitly to affirm a neo-Anti-Federalist ideology. Rather than build on the Madisonian revision of Anti-Federalist ideas of 1800, these theorists sug-

53. Ibid., 299, 335, 341–342.

gested that the original Anti-Federalist critique of the Constitution might have been more accurate about the consolidating tendencies of the new Constitution.

Yates's record of the Philadelphia Convention's deliberations seemed to justify the view that a systematic conspiracy to create a consolidated government could be traced back to that convention. The impact of Yates's work was evident in the transformation of John Taylor's critique of consolidation. Although Taylor had put forth a standard Old Republican view of the Constitution, drawing extensively on the Madisonian synthesis, the publication of Yates's work led Taylor to reformulate his vision of states' rights federalism in a more radical direction, which questioned the moderation of Madison's solution. Taylor's new position was taken up by Thomas Cooper, whose own critique of consolidation explicitly invoked the Anti-Federalist critique of the Constitution and praised the insights of its original opponents.

Ironically, this emerging neo-Anti-Federalist constitutional theory was effectively undermined by an even more radical variant of states' rights thought that traced its intellectual roots to Federalist, not Anti-Federalist, ideas. The theorist responsible for this radical shift in focus of dissenting constitutionalism was John C. Calhoun. The theory of nullification enunciated in South Carolina's *Exposition and Protest* fundamentally reconceptualized the Madisonian synthesis of 1800. Calhoun stressed the continuities between Madison's writings as Publius in 1788 and his role in the "Report of 1800." In this account, Anti-Federalist ideas were reduced to insignificance. Calhoun proposed a new structural solution to the problem of consolidation, which inaugurated a new phase in the history of constitutional dissent.

Although Calhoun changed the terms of political and constitutional debate, he did not eradicate all traces of Anti-Federalist dissenting constitutionalism. The most important political figure to champion those ideals was Martin Van Buren, who recognized that it was the Anti-Federalists, not the Federalists, who represented the spirit of American politics and constitutionalism. The "Anti-Federalist Mind," Van Buren concluded, was the mind of America.

It is impossible to understand the structure of dissenting thought in this period without an appreciation for the ways in which Anti-Federalist ideas were recycled and brought to bear on constitutional questions. Between Jefferson's election in 1800 and the Nullification controversy in 1828, Anti-Federalist ideas and texts not only became more widely available than at any previous time since ratification but were accorded more respect as well. Anti-Federalist ideas provided a historical grounding for an alternative constitutional theory that gained strength in this period.

EPILOGUE :

ANTI-FEDERALISM

AND THE AMERICAN

POLITICAL TRADITION

In his classic study *The American Political Tradition,* Richard Hofstadter described a political legacy that was essentially liberal and democratic. Rather than conceive of the American political tradition as consensus, it makes far more sense to recognize that tension and conflict were central to that tradition, and, most important, its evolution. The figures who dominated Hofstadter's story, including Thomas Jefferson, Andrew Jackson, and John C. Calhoun, can be understood only when they are set against the many dissenting voices who outflanked them at both ends of the political spectrum. Each of these figures was a participant in a open-ended conversation about the nature of American politics and constitutionalism. That conversation was shaped at least as much by the challenges posed by various dissenting voices as it was driven by the vision of the men at the center of *The American Political Tradition.* Those three figures who loomed so large in Hofstadter's account were themselves products of a continuing struggle whose roots were in the public debate begun by Federalists and Anti-Federalists over the meaning of the Constitution.[1]

Between the adoption of the Constitution and the Civil War, the Anti-Federalist legacy was consciously used by those Americans eager to resist the centralizing tendencies of American life. While the centralized national state in this period remained weak by modern standards, the perception that

---

1. Richard Hofstadter, *The American Political Tradition and the Men Who Made It* (New York, 1948).

the local character of American politics was being eroded prompted many to turn to their attention back to Anti-Federalist ideas to formulate an alternative vision of politics. This tendency was facilitated by the nature of American constitutionalism, which continued to emphasize preserving the original understanding of the Constitution. The logic of American constitutionalism inexorably drew Americans back to the argument between Federalists and Anti-Federalists.

After the Civil War, Anti-Federalist ideas seemed to fade from view. Although Populists might have been the spiritual heirs of Anti-Federalism, they were not consciously asserting an Anti-Federalist legacy. Indeed, for most of the next hundred years, the Anti-Federalist legacy seemed to be of more interest to scholars than to politicians. It was the Progressive historians Frederick Jackson Turner and Orin Grant Libby, not the Populists, who looked to Anti-Federalism for inspiration.[2]

The New Deal reconfigured the structure and ideology of American politics. In the context of the Great Depression and the New Deal, the localist politics of Anti-Federalism seemed antiquated at best and an obstacle to the changes necessary to lead the nation back to prosperity. The New Deal coalition, historians now recognize, was extremely fragile and began to unravel by the middle of the 1960s. In the post-Reagan era, many argue that the faith in centralized government associated with the New Deal legacy was a temporary anomaly in American politics, not a permanent realignment in attitudes. As for much of American history, the distinguishing characteristic of politics is the intensity of localism, not support for strong central government. Hostility to centralization was evident both in the rhetoric of Barry Goldwater's Republican Party and Tom Hayden's Students for a Democratic Society. Neither of those movements conceptualized its agenda in terms directly borrowed from Anti-Federalist writings. Yet, resonances of a distinctively Anti-Federalist vision of politics can be detected in both. Goldwater and SDS both grappled with the structure of power within an increasingly centralized federal system. Their rather different critiques of centralized authority seemed to capture the same disparate ideals that led elite and popular elements of the Anti-Federalist coalition to oppose the Constitution more than two hundred years ago.[3]

2. On Populist and Progressive constitutional thought, see Clyde W. Barrow, "Historical Criticism of the U.S. Constitution in Populist-Progressive Political Theory," *History of Political Thought*, IX (1988), 111–128. On the enduring legacy of Populist rhetoric, see Michael Kazin, *The Populist Persuasion: An American History* (New York, 1995).

3. On the impact of the New Deal on American political culture, see Alan Brinkley, *The*

The election of Ronald Reagan marked another watershed in American political life. Reagan set out to transform the rhetoric and reality of American political life. It is not surprising that the triumph of Reaganism also set the stage for a rediscovery of Anti-Federalism. Reagan's agenda was guided by a number of policy makers who were deeply influenced by Anti-Federalist ideas. A number of high-ranking officials within the Reagan administration had been influenced by the scholarship of Leo Strauss and his students, many of whom had studied and written about the debates between Federalists and Anti-Federalists. The most notable element of this neo-Anti-Federalist agenda was the call for a jurisprudence of original intent. The Anti-Federalist critique of strong central government, particularly of a powerful, unelected judiciary, seemed well suited to Reagan's agenda. The role of judges, Reaganites argued, was to seek the meaning of the Constitution following the ideas of the founders, who were now understood to include both the Federalists and their Anti-Federalist opponents. This approach had a profound impact on the character of law and jurisprudence. Reagan was even more successful at shifting the terms of popular political discourse. As a result of Reagan's influence, a new, right-wing variant of populist politics emerged that was decidedly hostile to centralized government.[4]

The Anti-Federalist legacy helps account for one of the most interesting characteristics of American politics. Right-wing politics in America, unlike comparable traditions in European thought, is distinguished by its hostility to a strong national state. Similarly, in contrast to European socialism, left-wing radicalism in America shows a similarly localistic streak. Radicalism at both ends of the spectrum, therefore, shows a remarkable affinity for an Anti-Federalist conception of politics. In America, it seems, all politics is local, and distant government is looked upon with a suspicious eye by individuals from across a wide range of ideological positions.

Anti-Federalist localism, it is worth stressing, need not always take the

End of Reform: New Deal Liberalism in Recession and War (New York, 1995); James T. Patterson, *Grand Expectations: The United States, 1945–1974* (New York, 1996).

4. On Straussians and the Constitution, see Gordon S. Wood, "The Fundamentalists and the Constitution," *New York Review of Books,* Feb. 18, 1988; Garry Wills, "Undemocratic Vistas," *New York Review of Books,* Nov. 19, 1992. Gary L. McDowell, a prominent figure in the Department of Justice in the Reagan administration, was a student of Herbert Storing and brought one variant of Straussian thought into the formulation of policy; see "Were the Anti-Federalists Right? Judicial Activism and the Problem of Consolidated Government," *Publius,* XII, no. 3 (Summer 1982), 99–108. Justice Rehnquist's jurisprudence has also been described as essentially Anti-Federalist–Jeffersonian; see Jeff Powell, "The Compleat Jeffersonian: Justice Rehnquist and Federalism," *Yale Law Journal,* XCI (1982), 1317–1370.

form of antistatism. In America, localism is capable of producing both libertarianism and consensual communitarianism. In many instances, localists have been eager to assert power as activists at the local level. Once again, Anti-Federalist ideas have proved remarkably ductile. Libertarians eager to prevent censorship and local school boards eager to ban books can both confidently assert their roots in a distinctly Anti-Federalist constitutionalist vision.

It is not surprising that the rediscovery of Anti-Federalism has prompted an explosion of interest among legal scholars who have combed the writings of Anti-Federalists to find a host of different original intents or meanings for particular provisions of the Constitution. Homosexual rights advocates have found new ways of grounding privacy while the National Rifle Association has found new justifications for its opposition to federal gun control laws.

One of the most interesting but least appreciated aspects of Anti-Federalist thought is its effort to grapple with the problem of the public sphere. A vital connection between constitutionalism and the public sphere has been asserted by philosopher Jürgen Habermas, one of the most important modern theorists of democracy. Habermas has turned his attention to this connection as a means of developing a postmetaphysical grounding for law, an antifoundationalism that can withstand the corrosive critiques of postmodernism. What Habermas seeks is a justification for the rule of law that can counter the argument that law is simply a mask to disguise the brute exercise of power. Although many legal theorists have turned to republicanism as a means of rediscovering an alternative constitutional discourse, Habermas recognizes that the ideal of civic virtue may itself lead to a different form of tyranny. In place of republicanism, Habermas has posited a new connection between the rule of law and the ideal of a public sphere of rational communication. Habermas's notion of rational communication and its centrality to democratic constitutionalism shows a remarkable affinity for the ideas championed by Anti-Federalists and, later, by Democratic-Republicans.[5]

Recasting Anti-Federalist political theory as Habermas suggests might help raise the level of public constitutional discourse. Such a theoretical project would not eliminate the opposite tendency that might just as easily follow from a revival of interest in Anti-Federalism. Indeed, the conspiratorial fears expressed about the federal government associated with some far-right groups, including the self-styled militia, are eerily reminiscent of some of the most paranoid rhetoric marshaled by Anti-Federalists during

5. Jürgen Habermas, *Between Fact and Norms: Contributions to a Discourse Theory of Law and Democracy*, trans. William Rehg (Cambridge, Mass., 1996).

the debate over ratification. Anti-Federalism, it seems, can just as easily provide a foundation for a deliberative democracy as a politics of paranoia. Both legacies can be traced to the original opposition to the Constitution. In some cases those opposing and seemingly contradictory tendencies can be found in the same authors.[6]

The ability of Anti-Federalist ideas to function in so many different contexts is one reason that Anti-Federalism has endured for so long. For much of American history Anti-Federalism has helped define the limits of legitimate dissent. No commentator was more insightful about the relevance of Anti-Federalism to the American political tradition than Martin Van Buren, who believed that Anti-Federalist ideas continued to shape American political culture long after there was an Anti-Federalist party. He conceded that America's institutions were crafted by Federalists. Yet, he believed, its spirit was shaped by Anti-Federalists. The defining feature of the Anti-Federalist mind, and therefore the apotheosis of American political culture, was its localism. For Van Buren, the "Anti-Federalist Mind" was the mind of America. Although Van Buren's brand of localism was democratic in spirit, there were others who gravitated toward Anti-Federalism because localism provided a means of protecting a distinctly elitist vision of politics.

Given the varied uses to which Anti-Federalist ideas have been put, it should come as little surprise, then, that Anti-Federalists texts would appear to be useful in contemporary constitutional debates. The recycling of Anti-Federalist texts in modern constitutional controversies has been driven by the same logic that motivated earlier generations to canvass the writings of the Founders and the Other Founders. The ideas of the Anti-Federalists, the Other Founders of the American constitutional tradition, continue to provoke, inspire, and complicate our understanding of what the Constitution means. The legacy of the Other Founders will likely continue to be a source of inspiration for individuals from across the political spectrum as long as the Constitution shapes the limits of legitimate dissent in American political life.

6. On privacy, see David A. J. Richards, "Constitutional Legitimacy and Constitutional Privacy," *New York University Law Review*, LXI (1986), 800–862. On uses of Anti-Federalism by National Rifle Association supporters, see "Second Amendment Symposium," *Tennessee Law Review*, LXII (1995), 443–821. For efforts to use Anti-Federalism to reconstruct a communitarian vision of the law, see Cass R. Sunstein, "The Enduring Legacy of Republicanism," in Stephen L. Elkin and Karol Edward Soltan, eds., *A New Constitutionalism: Designing Political Institutions for a Good Society* (Chicago, 1993), 174–206. For a good example of an Anti-Federalist author whose ideas could be used to justify an expanded public sphere or a new paranoid style, see my discussion of Centinel, Chapter 4, above.

Reprinting of Anti-Federalist Documents

Information on republication and authorship was obtained primarily from *DHRC*. The items in this list were all republished at least once as a pamphlet, broadside, or book. Some additional copies of particular items have been identified since the publication of the *DHRC* volumes, and more will probably be found in time. Thus, this listing is not intended to be authoritative, but, rather, to suggest the dispersal of Anti-Federalist writings and serve as a handlist of those documents.

46 REPRINTINGS

Amendments proposed by Wiliam Paca in the Maryland convention, *Maryland Journal* (Baltimore), Apr. 29, 1788 (*DHRC*, XVII, 240–246).

Elbridge Gerry, "Hon. Mr. Gerry's Objections to Signing the National Constitution," *Massachusetts Centinel* (Boston), Nov. 3, 1787 (*DHRC*, XIII, 548–550).

30 REPRINTINGS

An Address of the Subscribers, Members of the Late House of Representatives of the Commonwealth of Pennsylvania, to Their Constituents [Philadelphia, 1787] [address of the seceding assemblymen] (*DHRC*, II, 112–117).[1]

George Mason, "Objections to the Constitution of Government Formed by the Convention," *Massachusetts Centinel* (Boston), Nov. 21, 1787 (*CA-F*, II, 11– 13).

27 REPRINTINGS

Centinel [Samuel Bryan?], no. 1, "To the Freemen of Pennsylvania," *IG*, Oct. 5, 1787 (*CA-F*, II, 136–143).

22 REPRINTINGS

A Letter of His Excellency Edmund Randolph, Esquire, on the Federal Constitution [Richmond, Va., 1787] (*DHRC*, XV, 121–134).

20 REPRINTINGS

[Samuel Bryan], "The Address and Reasons of Dissent of the Minority of the Convention of Philadelphia to Their Constituents," *Pennsylvania Packet, and Daily Advertiser* (Philadelphia), Dec. 18, 1787 (*CA-F*, III, 145–166).[2]

"Copy of a Letter from Richard Henry Lee, Esq. . . . [to Edmund Randolph]," *Pennsylvania Packet, and Daily Advertiser* (Philadelphia), Dec. 20, 1787 (*DHRC*, XIV, 366–372).

Robert Yates and John Lansing, Jr., report of New York's delegates to the Constitutional Convention, *Daily Advertiser* (New York), Jan. 14, 1788 (*DHRC*, XV, 368–370).

14 REPRINTINGS

Correspondent, false report of John Jay's opposition to the Constitution, *IG*, Nov. 24, 1787 (*DHRC*, XIV, 208–209).

13 REPRINTINGS
Correspondent, blessings of the new government, *IG*, Oct. 6, 1787 (*DHRC*, XIII, 345–346).

12 REPRINTINGS
An Officer of the Late Continental Army [William Findley?], *IG*, Nov. 6, 1787 (*DHRC*, II, 211–216).

11 REPRINTINGS
Centinel [Samuel Bryan?], no. 2, "To the People of Pennsylvania," *FJ*, Oct. 24, 1787 (*CA-F*, II, 143–154).
Arthur Lee, report of Virginia Anti-Federalism, *IG*, Mar. 7, 1788 (*DHRC*, XVI, 340).

10 REPRINTINGS
Luther Martin, "Mr. Martin's Information to the House of Assembly" [*Genuine Information*], no. 6, *Maryland Gazette* (Baltimore), Jan. 15, 1788 (*DHRC*, XV, 374–379).
Luther Martin, "Mr. Martin's Information to the House of Assembly" [*Genuine Information*], no. 7, *Maryland Gazette* (Baltimore), Jan. 18, 1788 (*DHRC*, XV, 410–414).
William Paca et al., address of the minority of the Maryland convention, *Maryland Gazette* (Annapolis), May 1, 1788 (*DHRC*, XVII, 242–246).

8 REPRINTINGS
Luther Martin, "Mr. Martin's Information to the House of Assembly" [*Genuine Information*], no. 1, *Maryland Gazette* (Baltimore), Dec. 28, 1787 (*DHRC*, XV, 150–155).
Luther Martin, "Mr. Martin's Information to the House of Assembly" [*Genuine Information*], no. 2, *Maryland Gazette* (Baltimore), Jan. 1, 1788 (*DHRC*, XV, 204–210).
Luther Martin to the printer, *Maryland Journal* (Baltimore), Jan. 18, 1788 (*DHRC*, XV, 415–416).
Report from a gentleman from New York, *FJ*, Jan 2, 1788 (*DHRC*, XV, 230).
"Extract of a Letter from John Williams," *Federal Herald* (Albany), Feb. 25, 1788 (*DHRC*, XVI, 200–201).
On the Constitution and France, *FJ*, Mar. 5, 1788 (*DHRC*, XVI, 320).

7 REPRINTINGS
Centinel [Samuel Bryan?], no. 3, "To the People of Pennsylvania," *IG*, Nov. 8, 1787 (*CA-F*, II, 154–161).
Centinel [Samuel Bryan?], no. 7, "To the People of Pennsylvania," *IG*, Dec. 29, 1787 (*CA-F*, II, 174–175).
An Old Whig [George Bryan, John Smilie, and James Hutchinson?], no. 4, *IG*, Oct. 27, 1787 (*CA-F*, III, 30–34).[3]
James M'Cormick et al., "An Address to the Minority of the Pennsylvania Convention," *Carlisle Gazette* (Pa.), Jan. 2, 1788 (*DHRC*, XV, 228–230).[4]
Luther Martin, "Mr. Martin's Information to the House of Assembly" [*Genuine Information*], no. 3, *Maryland Gazette* (Baltimore), Jan. 4, 1788 (*DHRC*, XV, 249–256).
Luther Martin, "Mr. Martin's Information to the House of Assembly" [*Genuine Information*], no. 5, *Maryland Gazette* (Baltimore), Jan. 11, 1788 (*DHRC*, XV, 348–352).
Luther Martin, "Mr. Martin's Information to the House of Assembly" [*Genuine Information*], no. 9, *Maryland Gazette* (Baltimore), Jan. 29, 1788 (*DHRC*, XV, 494–497).

Philadelphiensis [Benjamin Workman?], no. 8, *FJ*, Jan. 23, 1788 (*CA-F*, III, 124–127).
"On the New Constitution," *State Gazette of South-Carolina* (Charleston), Jan. 28, 1788
(*DHRC*, XV, 486).

6 REPRINTINGS
Cato [George Clinton or Abraham Yates, Jr.?], no. 1, "To the Citizens of the State of New-
York," *New-York Journal*, Sept. 27, 1787 (*DHRC*, XIII, 255– 257).
Cincinnatus [Arthur Lee], no. 1, "To James Wilson, Esq.," *New-York Journal*, Nov. 1, 1787
(*DHRC*, XIII, 530–533).
"Extract of a Letter from Queen Anne's County," *FJ*, Nov. 21, 1787 (*DHRC*, XIV, 163).
Z, *Independent Chronicle* (Boston), Dec. 6, 1787 (*DHRC*, XIV, 358–360).
C. Brutus, *Independent Chronicle* (Boston), Jan. 24, 1788 (*DHRC*, XV, 137– 138).
Elbridge Gerry, defense of his conduct, *Massachusetts Centinel* (Boston), Jan. 5, 1788
(*DHRC*, XV, 273).
Centinel [Samuel Bryan?], no. 9, "To the People of Pennsylvania," *IG*, Jan. 8, 1788 (*CA-F*, II,
179–182).
Luther Martin, "Mr. Martin's Information to the House of Assembly" [*Genuine
Information*], no. 4, *Maryland Gazette* (Baltimore), Jan. 8, 1788 (*DHRC*, XV, 296–301).
Luther Martin, "Mr. Martin's Information to the House of Assembly" [*Genuine
Information*], no. 8, *Maryland Gazette* (Baltimore), Jan. 22, 1788 (*DHRC*, XV, 433–437).
Luther Martin, "Mr. Martin's Information to the House of Assembly" [*Genuine
Information*], no. 10, *Maryland Gazette* (Baltimore), Feb. 1, 1788 (*DHRC*, XVI, 8–11).
Luther Martin, "Mr. Martin's Information to the House of Assembly" [*Genuine
Information*], no. 12, *Maryland Gazette* (Baltimore), Feb. 8, 1788 (*DHRC*, XVI, 89–93).
Luther Martin, "To the Citizens of Maryland," no. 1, *Maryland Journal* (Baltimore), Mar.
18, 1788 (*DHRC*, XVI, 415–420).
"Extract of a Letter from Franklin County [Pa.], 24th April, 1788," *IG*, Apr. 30, 1788
(*DHRC*, XVII, 251–252).
Philadelphiensis [Benjamin Workman?], no. 6, *FJ*, Dec. 26, 1787 (*CA-F*, III, 119–122).

5 REPRINTINGS
A Republican, no. 1, "To James Wilson, Esquire," *New-York Journal*, Oct. 25, 1787 (*DHRC*,
XIII, 477–480).
A Son of Liberty, *New-York Journal*, Nov. 8, 1787 (*DHRC*, XIII, 481–483).
Correspondent, *IG*, Oct. 27, 1787 (*DHRC*, XIII, 503).
The new ship *Federal Constitution, Independent Chronicle; and the Universal Advertiser*
(Boston), Nov. 1, 1787 (*DHRC*, XIII, 522–523).
Extract of letter from New York, *FJ*, Nov. 7, 1787 (*DHRC*, XIII, 572–573).
Federal Farmer [Melancton Smith?], *Observations Leading to a Fair Examination of the
System of Government Proposed by the Late Convention . . . Letters from the Federal
Farmer to the Republican* (New York, 1787) (nos. 1–5) (*CA-F*, II, 214–256).[5]
"Extract of a Letter from a Gentleman in New-York," *Virginia Independent Chronicle*
(Richmond), Nov. 14, 1787 (*DHRC*, XIV, 103–105).
Centinel [Samuel Bryan?], no. 6, "To the People of Pennsylvania," *Pennsylvania Packet, and
Daily Advertiser* (Philadelphia), Dec. 25, 1787 (*CA-F*, II, 171–174).

Centinel [Samuel Bryan?], no. 8, "To the People of Pennsylvania," *IG*, Jan. 2, 1788 (*CA-F*, II, 176–179).

Centinel [Samuel Bryan?], no. 15, "To the People of Pennsylvania," *IG*, Feb. 22, 1788 (*CA-F*, II, 196–197).

Luther Martin, "Mr. Martin's Information to the House of Assembly" [*Genuine Information*], no. 11, *Maryland Gazette* (Baltimore), Feb. 5, 1788 (*DHRC*, XVI, 39–42).

"A Real State of the Proposed Constitution in the United States," *IG*, Mar. 7, 1788 (*DHRC*, XVI, 341–342).

4 REPRINTINGS

Cato [George Clinton or Abraham Yates, Jr.?], no. 2, "To the Citizens of the State of New-York," *New-York Journal*, Oct. 11, 1787 (*DHRC*, XIII, 369– 372).

A Democratic Federalist, *Pennsylvania Herald, and General Advertiser* (Philadelphia), Oct. 17, 1787 (*CA-F*, III, 58–63).

Brutus [Abraham Yates, Jr.?], no. 1, "To the Citizens of the State of New-York," *New-York Journal*, Oct. 18, 1787 (*DHRC*, XIII, 412–421).[6]

Brutus [Abraham Yates, Jr.?], no. 3, "To the Citizens of the State of New-York," *New-York Journal*, Nov. 15, 1787 (*DHRC*, XIV, 119–124).[6]

An Old Whig [George Bryan, John Smilie, and James Hutchinson?], no. 2, *IG*, Oct. 17, 1787 (*CA-F*, III, 22–26).[3]

An Old Whig [George Bryan, John Smilie, and James Hutchinson?], no. 5, *IG*, Nov. 1, 1787 (*CA-F*, III, 34–38).[3]

An Old Whig [George Bryan, John Smilie, and James Hutchinson?], no. 7, *IG*, Nov. 28, 1787 (*CA-F*, III, 43–46).[3]

Philadelphiensis [Benjamin Workman?], no. 3, *FJ*, Dec. 5, 1787 (*CA-F*, III, 109–112).

Alfred, "To the Real Patriots of America," *IG*, Dec. 13, 1787 (*DHRC*, XIV, 432–434).

Tamony, "To the Freeholders of America," *Virginia Independent Chronicle* (Richmond), Jan. 9, 1788 (*DHRC*, XV, 322–326).

Centinel [Samuel Bryan?], no. 5, "To the People of Pennsylvania," *IG*, Dec. 4, 1787 (*CA-F*, II, 166–171).

Centinel [Samuel Bryan?], no. 10, "To the People of Pennsylvania," *IG*, Jan. 12, 1788 (*CA-F*, II, 182–184).

Centinel [Samuel Bryan?], no. 13, "To the People of Pennsylvania," *IG*, Jan. 30, 1788 (*CA-F*, II, 190–193).

Centinel [Samuel Bryan?], no. 14, "To the People of Pennsylvania," *IG*, Feb. 5, 1788 (*CA-F*, II, 193–196).

"Extract of a Letter from the Eastern Shore of Maryland," *IG*, Feb. 8, 1788 (*DHRC*, XVI, 87–88).

James Bowdoin to James de Caledonia, *IG*, Feb. 27, 1788 (*DHRC*, XVI, 238–241) (spurious).

A Columbian Patriot [Mercy Otis Warren], *Observations on the New Constitution, and on the Federal and State Conventions* (Boston, 1788) (*CA-F*, IV, 270–286).

Luther Martin, "To the Citizens of Maryland," no. 2, *Maryland Journal* (Baltimore), Mar. 21, 1788 (*DHRC*, XVI, 452–460).

Luther Martin, "To the Citizens of Maryland," no. 4, *Maryland Journal* (Baltimore), Apr. 4, 1788 (*DHRC*, XVII, 18–22).

Elbridge Gerry, "To the Public," *American Herald* (Boston), Apr. 18, 1788 (*DHRC*, XVII, 173–176).

A Correspondent, *IG*, May 5, 1788 (*DHRC*, XVII, 385–386).

A Correspondent, *IG*, May 9, 1788 (*DHRC*, XVII, 398).

A Freeman, *IG*, May 13, 1788 (*DHRC*, XVIII, 13–14).

Cato Uticensis [George Mason?], "To the Freemen of Virginia," *Virginia Independent Chronicle* (Richmond), Oct. 17, 1787 (*DHRC*, VIII, 70–75).

3 REPRINTINGS

Remarks on the proposed Constitution, *FJ*, Sept. 26, 1787 (*DHRC*, XIII, 244– 245).

An Old Whig [George Bryan, John Smilie, and James Hutchinson?], no. 1, *IG*, Oct. 12, 1787 (*CA-F*, III, 18–21).

An Old Whig [George Bryan, John Smilie, and James Hutchinson?], no. 6, *IG*, Nov. 24, 1787 (*CA-F*, III, 39–43).[3]

Cato [George Clinton or Abraham Yates, Jr.?], no. 3, "To the Citizens of the State of New-York," *New-York Journal*, Oct. 25, 1787 (*DHRC*, XIII, 473– 477).

Cato [George Clinton or Abraham Yates, Jr.?], no. 4, "To the Citizens of the State of New-York," *New-York Journal*, Nov. 8, 1787 (*DHRC*, XIV, 7–11).

Cato [George Clinton or Abraham Yates, Jr.?], no. 5, "To the Citizens of the State of New-York," *New-York Journal*, Nov. 22, 1787 (*DHRC*, XIV, 182– 185).

Philadelphiensis [Benjamin Workman?], no. 1, *IG*, Nov. 7, 1787 (*CA-F*, III, 102–106).

Philadelphiensis [Benjamin Workman?], no. 2, *IG*, Nov. 28, 1787 (*CA-F*, III, 106–109).

Philadelphiensis [Benjamin Workman?], no. 4, *IG*, Dec. 12, 1787 (*CA-F*, III, 112–117).

Philadelphiensis [Benjamin Workman?], no. 5, *IG*, Dec. 19, 1787 (*CA-F*, III, 116–118).

Cincinnatus [Arthur Lee], no. 2, "To James Wilson, Esq.," *New-York Journal*, Nov. 8, 1787 (*DHRC*, XIV, 11–14).

Centinel [Samuel Bryan?], no. 4, "To the People of Pennsylvania," *IG*, Nov. 30, 1787 (*CA-F*, II, 161–166).

Centinel [Samuel Bryan?], no. 11, "To the People of Pennsylvania," *IG*, Jan. 16, 1788 (*CA-F*, II, 184–187).

Centinel [Samuel Bryan?], no. 12, "To the People of Pennsylvania," *IG*, Jan. 23, 1788 (*CA-F*, II, 187–190).

Centinel [Samuel Bryan?], no. 16, "To the People of Pennsylvania," *IG*, Feb. 27, 1788 (*CA-F*, II, 197–200).

Centinel [Samuel Bryan?], no. 18, "To the People of Pennsylvania," *IG*, Apr. 9, 1788 (*CA-F*, II, 202–207).

Brutus [Abraham Yates, Jr.?], no. 4, "To the People of the State of New-York," *New-York Journal*, Nov. 29, 1787 (*DHRC*, XIV, 297–303).[6]

Brutus [Abraham Yates, Jr.?], no. 5, "To the People of the State of New-York," *New-York Journal*, Dec. 13, 1787 (*DHRC*, XIV, 422–428).[6]

Brutus [Abraham Yates, Jr.?], no. 8, "To the People of the State of New-York," *New-York Journal*, Jan. 10, 1788 (*DHRC*, XV, 335–338).[6]

Brutus [Abraham Yates, Jr.?], no. 9, "To the People of the State of New-York," *New-York Journal*, Jan. 17, 1788 (*DHRC*, XV, 393–398).[6]

Brutus [Abraham Yates, Jr.?], no. 15, "To the People of the State of New-York," *New-York Journal*, Mar. 20, 1788 (*DHRC*, XVI, 431–435).[6]

Poplicola, *Boston Gazette,* Dec. 24, 1787 (*DHRC,* XV, 72–74).

Helvidius Priscus [Samuel Adams or James Warren?], "To the Public," no. 2, *Independent Chronicle; and the Universal Advertiser* (Boston), Jan. 10, 1788 (*DHRC,* XV, 332–334).

Luther Martin, reply to Maryland Landholder, *Maryland Journal* (Baltimore), Mar. 7, 1788 (*DHRC,* XVI, 343–348).

Correspondent, *FJ,* Mar. 12, 1788 (*DHRC,* XVI, 375).

A Plebeian [Melancton Smith or John Lamb?], *An Address to the People of the State of New-York . . .* (New York, 1788) (*DHRC,* XVII, 147–166).

None of the Well-Born Conspirators, *FJ,* Apr. 23, 1788 (*DHRC,* XVII, 205–206).

2 REPRINTINGS

An Old Whig [George Bryan, John Smilie, and James Hutchinson?], no. 3, *IG,* Oct. 20, 1787 (*CA-F,* III, 26–30).[3]

Brutus [Abraham Yates, Jr.?], no. 2, "To the Citizens of the State of New-York," *New-York Journal,* Nov. 1, 1787 (*DHRC,* XIII, 524–529).[6]

Brutus [Abraham Yates, Jr.?], no. 14, "To the Citizens of the State of New-York," *New-York Journal,* Feb. 28, 1788 (*DHRC,* XVI, 255–258).[6]

Timoleon, *New-York Journal,* Nov. 1, 1787, extraordinary (*DHRC,* XIII, 534–538).

Brutus, Junior, *New-York Journal,* Nov. 8, 1787 (*DHRC,* XIV, 3–7).[7]

Cincinnatus [Arthur Lee], no. 3, "To James Wilson, Esq.," *New-York Journal,* Nov. 15, 1787 (*DHRC,* XIV, 124–128).

Cincinnatus [Arthur Lee], no. 4, "To James Wilson, Esq.," *New-York Journal,* Nov. 22, 1787 (*DHRC,* XIV, 186–191).

Cincinnatus [Arthur Lee], no. 5, "To James Wilson, Esq.," *New-York Journal,* Nov. 29, 1787 (*DHRC,* XIV, 303–310).

Cincinnatus [Arthur Lee], no. 6, "To James Wilson, Esq.," *New-York Journal,* Dec. 6, 1787 (*DHRC,* XIV, 360–364).

Cato [George Clinton or Abraham Yates, Jr.?], no. 6, "To the People of the State of New-York," *New-York Journal,* Dec. 13, 1787 (*DHRC,* XIV, 428–432).

Cato [George Clinton or Abraham Yates, Jr.?], no. 7, "To the Citizens of the State of New-York," *New-York Journal,* Jan. 3, 1788 (*DHRC,* XV, 240–242).

An American, *American Herald* (Boston), Jan. 28, 1788 (*DHRC,* XV, 139–140).

Philadelphiensis [Benjamin Workman?], no. 9, *IG,* Feb. 7, 1788 (*CA-F,* III, 127–130).

Philadelphiensis [Benjamin Workman?], no. 10, *FJ,* Feb. 20, 1788 (*CA-F,* III, 130–133).

Philadelphiensis [Benjamin Workman?], no. 12, *FJ,* Apr. 9, 1788 (*CA-F,* III, 136–138).

Centinel [Samuel Bryan?], no. 17, "To the People of Pennsylvania," *IG,* Mar. 24, 1788 (*CA-F,* II, 200–202).

A Farmer, "The Fallacies of the Freeman Detected by a Farmer," *FJ,* Apr. 23, 1788 (*DHRC,* XVII, 135–145).

Honestus, *New-York Journal,* Apr. 26, 1788 (*DHRC,* XVII, 220–221).

The Federalist's political creed, *IG,* May 10, 1788 (*DHRC,* XVIII, 4–6).

1 REPRINTING

[John Nicholson], *A View of the Proposed Constitution . . .* (Philadelphia, 1787) (*DHRC,* microfiche: Pa. 141).

Observations on the Proposed Constitution . . . (New York, 1788).[8]

Luther Martin, *The Genuine Information Delivered to the Legislature of the State of Maryland*... (Philadelphia, 1788) (*CA-F,* II, 19–79) (pamphlet edition).

Aristocrotis [William Petrikin], *The Government of Nature Delineated*... (Carlisle, Pa., 1788) (*CA-F,* III, 196–212).

Federal Farmer [Melancton Smith?], *An Additional Number of Letters from the Federal Farmer to the Republican*... (New York, 1788) (nos. 6–18) (*CA-F,* II, 256–349).

NOTES

1. Signed by James M'Calmont, Robert Clark, Jacob Miley, Alexander Wright, John M'Dowell, John Flenniken, James Allison, Theophilus Philips, John Gilchrist, Abraham Smith, Robert Whitehill, David Mitchel, John Piper, Samuel Dale, William Findley, and James Barr. For information about publication and reception, see *DHRC,* XIII, 293–294.

2. Composed by Samuel Bryan and signed by the following members of the state ratification convention: Nathaniel Breading, John Smilie, Richard Baird, Adam Orth, John A. Hanna, John Whitehill, John Harris, Robert Whitehill, John Reynolds, Jonathan Hoge, Nicholas Lutz, John Ludwig, Abraham Lincoln, John Bishop, Joseph Heister, Joseph Powel, James Martin, William Findley, John Baird, James Edgar, William Todd. For information about authorship and reactions, see *DHRC,* XV, 7–13.

3. Probably the joint effort of George Bryan, John Smilie, and James Hutchinson, three influential members of Pennsylvania's Constitutionalist Party and leaders of the Anti-Federalist cause. For information on authorship, see *DHRC,* XIII, 376.

4. Signed by James M'Cormick, David Boyd, William Gelson, James Irvin, Andrew Irvin, William Carothers, Sr., William Addams, William Carothers, Jr., John Douglass, Arch. Hamilton, Joseph Junkin, John Clandinen, Thomas Henderson, Robert Bell, John Junkin, James Bell, Thomas Atchley, William Irvin, William Douglass, John Walker, William Greason, David Walker, Jonathan Walker, John Buchanan, Francis M'Guire, John Armstrong, Benj. Carothers, Jr., James Fleming, and Thomas Carothers (*DHRC,* XV, 230).

5. For a discussion of the circulation and reception of Federal Farmer, see *DHRC,* XIV, 14–18. The identity of Federal Farmer has been a subject of considerable controversy. In "The Authorship of the *Letters from the Federal Farmer,*" *WMQ,* 3d Ser., XXXI (1974), 299–308, Gordon S. Wood suggested that it was probably written by a New Yorker. In "Melancton Smith and the *Letters from the Federal Farmer,*" *WMQ,* 3d Ser., XLIV (1987), 510–528, Robert H. Webking provides compelling textual evidence that Smith was the author. Smith thus now seems the most likely author, although we still lack evidence to establish a final identification.

6. There has been considerable controversy over the identity of Brutus. Among the likely candidates are Abraham Yates, Jr., George Clinton, Thomas Tredwell, Robert Yates, and Melancton Smith. For discussion of the possibilities, see *DHRC,* XIII, 411–412.

7. Although the identity of Brutus, Junior, is not known, it seems likely that he was a prominent Clintonian. A number of passages and references in this essay are identical to ones found in Federal Farmer. The connection suggests the possibility that this essay also was written by Melancton Smith.

8. This anthology of previously published Anti-Federalist writings contained "Copy of a Letter from Richard Henry Lee, Esq. . . . [to Edmund Randolph]"; [Samuel Bryan], "The Address and Reasons of Dissent of the Minority of the Convention of Philadelphia to Their Constituents"; and Centinel [Samuel Bryan?], nos. 1–9, "To the People of Pennsylvania."

Pamphlet, Broadside, and Periodical Republication of Anti-Federalist Documents

Republication in Nationally Circulated Periodical, American Museum

An Address of the Subscribers, Members of the Late House of Representatives of the Commonwealth of Pennsylvania, to Their Constituents [Philadelphia, 1787] [address of the seceding assemblymen] (*DHRC*, II, 112–117).

Elbridge Gerry, "Hon. Mr. Gerry's Objections to Signing the National Constitution," *Massachusetts Centinel* (Boston), Nov. 3, 1787 (*DHRC*, XIII, 548–550).

An Officer of the Late Continental Army [William Findley?], *IG*, Nov. 6, 1787 (*DHRC*, II, 211–216).

"Copy of a Letter from Richard Henry Lee, Esq. . . . [to Edmund Randolph]," *Pennsylvania Packet, and Daily Advertiser* (Philadelphia), Dec. 20, 1787 (*DHRC*, XIV, 366–372).

[Samuel Bryan], "The Address and Reasons of Dissent of the Minority of the Convention of Philadelphia to Their Constituents," *Pennsylvania Packet, and Daily Advertiser* (Philadelphia), Dec. 18, 1787 (*CA-F*, III, 145–166).

Robert Yates and John Lansing, Jr., report of New York's delegates to the Constitutional Convention, *Daily Advertiser* (New York), Jan. 14, 1788 (*DHRC*, XV, 368–370).

William Paca et al., address of the minority of the Maryland convention, *Maryland Gazette* (Annapolis), May 1, 1788 (*DHRC*, XVII, 242–246).

George Mason, "Objections to the Constitution of Government Formed by the Convention," *Massachusetts Centinel* (Boston), Nov. 21, 1787 (*CA-F*, II, 11–13).

A Letter of His Excellency Edmund Randolph, Esquire, on the Federal Constitution [Richmond, Va., 1787] (*DHRC*, XV, 121–134).

Republication as Pamphlet, Broadside, or Book

5 REPRINTINGS

Centinel [Samuel Bryan?], no. 1, "To the Freemen of Pennsylvania," *IG*, Oct. 5, 1787 (*CA-F*, II, 136–143).

[Samuel Bryan], "The Address and Reasons of Dissent of the Minority of the Convention of Philadelphia to Their Constituents," *Pennsylvania Packet, and Daily Advertiser* (Philadelphia), Dec. 18, 1787 (*CA-F*, III, 145–166).

4 REPRINTINGS

Centinel [Samuel Bryan?], no. 2, "To the People of Pennsylvania," *FJ*, Oct. 24, 1787 (*CA-F*, II, 143–154).

Centinel [Samuel Bryan?], no. 5, "To the People of Pennsylvania," *IG*, Dec. 4, 1787 (*CA-F*, II, 166–171).

Federal Farmer [Melancton Smith?], *Observations Leading to a Fair Examination of the*

System of Government Proposed by the Late Convention . . . Letters from the Federal
Farmer to the Republican (New York, 1787) (nos. 1–5) (*CA-F,* II, 214–256).

*An Address of the Subscribers, Members of the Late House of Representatives of the
Commonwealth of Pennsylvania, to Their Constituents* [Philadelphia, 1787] [address of
the seceding assemblymen] (*DHRC,* II, 112–117).

Elbridge Gerry, "Hon. Mr. Gerry's Objections to Signing the National Constitution,"
Massachusetts Centinel (Boston), Nov. 3, 1787 (*DHRC,* XIII, 548–550).

An Officer of the Late Continental Army [William Findley?], *IG,* Nov. 6, 1787 (*DHRC,* II,
211–216).

"Copy of a Letter from Richard Henry Lee, Esq. . . . [to Edmund Randolph]," *Pennsylvania
Packet, and Daily Advertiser* (Philadelphia), Dec. 20, 1787 (*DHRC,* XIV, 366–372).

A Columbian Patriot [Mercy Otis Warren], *Observations on the New Constitution, and on
the Federal and State Conventions* (Boston, 1788) (*CA-F,* IV, 270–286).

A Letter of His Excellency Edmund Randolph, Esquire, on the Federal Constitution
[Richmond, Va., 1787] (*DHRC,* XV, 121–134).

1 REPRINTING

An Old Whig [George Bryan, John Smilie, and James Hutchinson?], no. 4, *IG,* Oct. 27, 1787
(*CA-F,* III, 30–34).

An Old Whig [George Bryan, John Smilie, and James Hutchinson?], no. 5, *IG,* Nov. 1, 1787
(*CA-F,* III, 34–38).

Timoleon, *New-York Journal,* Nov. 1, 1787, extraordinary (*DHRC,* XIII, 534–538).

Centinel [Samuel Bryan?], no. 3, "To the People of Pennsylvania," *IG,* Nov. 8, 1787 (*CA-F,*
II, 154–161).

Centinel [Samuel Bryan?], no. 4, "To the People of Pennsylvania," *IG,* Nov. 30, 1787 (*CA-F,*
II, 161–166).

Centinel [Samuel Bryan?], no. 6, "To the People of Pennsylvania," *Pennsylvania Packet, and
Daily Advertiser* (Philadelphia), Dec. 25, 1787 (*CA-F,* II, 171–174).

Centinel [Samuel Bryan?], no. 7, "To the People of Pennsylvania," *IG,* Dec. 29, 1787 (*CA-F,*
II, 174–175).

Centinel [Samuel Bryan?], no. 8, "To the People of Pennsylvania," *IG,* Jan. 2, 1788 (*CA-F,* II,
176–179).

Centinel [Samuel Bryan?], no. 9, "To the People of Pennsylvania," *IG,* Jan. 8, 1788 (*CA-F,* II,
179–182).

Luther Martin, *The Genuine Information Delivered to the Legislature of the State of
Maryland* . . . (Philadelphia, 1788) (*CA-F,* II, 19–79) (pamphlet edition).

A Plebeian [Melancton Smith or John Lamb?], *An Address to the People of the State of New-
York* . . . (New York, 1788) (*DHRC,* XVII, 147–166).

William Paca et al., address of the minority of the Maryland convention, *Maryland Gazette*
(Annapolis), May 1, 1788 (*DHRC,* XVII, 242–246).

Federal Farmer [Melancton Smith?], *An Additional Number of Letters from the Federal
Farmer to the Republican* . . . (New York, 1788) (nos. 6–18) (*CA-F,* II, 256–349).

[John Nicholson], *A View of the Proposed Constitution* . . . (Philadelphia, 1787) (*DHRC,*
microfiche: Pa. 141).

Aristocrotis [William Petrikin], *The Government of Nature Delineated* . . . (Carlisle, Pa.,
1788) (*CA-F,* III, 196–212).

Adams, John, 100, 168, 234–235
Adams, Samuel, 72, 74, 154–157
Adolphus (pseud.), 155–156
Agrarians: as Anti-Federalists, 83; and political economy, 175–178, 192; in the South, 178–179, 275–278, 280–286
Agrippa (pseud. of James Winthrop), 58, 64–65
Alien Act. *See* Alien and Sedition Acts
Alien and Sedition Acts, 13–14, 230–241, 246, 253–273
Amendments, constitutional, 31–32, 136, 138–139, 153–157, 198, 270. *See also* Bill of Rights; Constitution, U.S.
American Museum, 28, 316
Ames, Fisher, 197, 231
Amicus (pseud.), 131
Anonymous publication, 37–38, 76, 105–106
Anti-Federalism: Democratic-Republicans as successors to, 164–171; and Jeffersonianism, 172–173n
Anti-Federalists: and historiography, 2–8; writings of, 5–6, 9, 24; regional diversity of, 22; and constitutionalism, 24; as described by Federalists, 27; and agrarianism, 83; as procommerce, 83, 94, 102; and criticism of printers, 122–124; and seditious libel, 125–128; on elections, 148–153; on constitutional amendments, 153–157, 270; in the First Congress, 157–171; on political economy, 175–187, 192–193; and public debate with Federalists, 222–228; and revival of early ideas, 303–307. *See also* Elite Anti-Federalists; Middling Anti-Federalists; Plebeian Anti-Federalists
Appleton, Nathaniel W., 151
Aristocracy: and the Constitution, 30, 34, 52, 100; natural, 69–70, 72, 79–80, 96–97, 104–105, 107, 151–152, 205; and middling Anti-Fedralists, 286

Aristocrotis (pseud. of William Petrikin), 37, 47, 107–109
Armstrong, John, 140–141
Articles of Confederation, 60, 62–64
Aurora (Philadelphia), 285–286
Austin, Benjamin, 153
Authorship: and pseudonymous writings, 20, 37, 76, 105; and anonymous writings, 37–38, 76, 105–106; and audience, 42–50, 225–228

Backcountry: newspapers in, 45–46, 84. *See also* Plebeian Anti-Federalists
Bank of the United States, 174, 177, 179; constitutionality of, 189, 221–222; Second, 278–286
Bard, William, 115
Billerica, Mass., 176, 184
Bill of Rights, 3–4, 30–31, 58–59, 90, 158–164, 231. *See also* Constitution, U.S.
Blackstone, William: and common law, 38, 41, 132–134, 263–264; and natural rights, 55–57; and seditious libel, 125, 261
Blackstone's Commentaries (Tucker), 262–273, 282
Blyth, Benjamin, 115
Bowdoin, James, 41
Brackenridge, Hugh Henry, 205
Breckinridge, John, 239–240
Brent, William, 226–227
Brown, Andrew, 128
Brown, David, 185–186n, 236–237
Brutus (pseud. of Tobias Lear), 75
Brutus (pseud. of Stephen Simpson), 286–287
Brutus (pseud. of Abraham Yates, Jr.?), 25–26, 45, 95
Bryan, George, 82, 85–87, 124n, 128
Bryan, Samuel: as Centinel, 20–21, 25–26, 46, 99–105, 122, 135, 255, 267; "The Address and Reasons of Dissent of the

Minority," 25–26, 29, 32–34, 46, 116–117, 224, 228, 267n

Burke, Aedanus, 122, 161–162

Caledonia, James de (James Wilson), 41–42

Calhoun, John C., 14, 294–298, 302

Callender, James, 232–235

Carlisle, Pa.: Anti-Federalists in, 41–42, 45–47, 107n, 109–118, 137–138, 141; and Whiskey Rebellion, 208–209

Carlisle Gazette (Pa.), 45–46, 112–113

Carrington, Edward, 27

Cato (pseud. of George Clinton or Abraham Yates, Jr.?), 37, 45

Cato Uticensis (pseud. of George Mason?), 38

Centinel (pseud. of Samuel Bryan?): writings of, 20–21, 25–26, 46, 255, 267; as radical Anti-Federalist, 26, 40–41, 46–47, 99–105, 116; on Martin's *Genuine Information,* 52n; and criticism of printers, 122–123

Chase, Samuel: and Anti-Federalist writings, 44–45, 47–48; impeachment of, 235n, 275

Cincinnatus (pseud. of Arthur Lee), 37–38, 44, 57, 60, 69–70, 126

Class: and constitutionalism, 12; and yeomen, 37–39, 92–93; divisions of, 81–82n; and merchants, 102, 119. *See also* Elite Anti-Federalists; Middling Anti-Federalists; Plebeian Anti-Federalists

Classical antiquity, 37–38, 53, 56

Clinton, George, 82, 84, 88, 168, 276–278

Clymer, George, 149, 163

Coke, Edward, 38

Columbian Patriot, A (pseud. of Mercy Otis Warren), 37, 52n, 55–57, 59, 70–72

Commerce, 83, 94, 102, 276–277

Common law, 8, 41, 44, 133–134, 263–264

Confederation, 62, 64

Congress, First, 153, 155–171. *See also* House of Representatives, U.S.; Senate, U.S.

Connecticut, 29, 88

Consolidation: and Anti-Federalists, 29–30, 242–245, 300, 302; and Demo-cratic-Republicans, 249, 265, 270–272, 290–292; and *McCulloch v. Maryland,* 279–282

Constitution, U.S., 1–2; and original intent, 3–4, 89, 189, 194, 221–230, 266–267, 281–282; and Ninth Amendment, 4n, 244–245; and plain style, 7, 11, 134; and ratification debate, 7, 8n, 136–143, 147–153, 164–171, 268; language of, 35, 59, 77, 188n, 190, 248, 260–261, 271; Article 6, 60; and states' rights, 61–64; and Second Amendment, 93; and Tenth Amendment, 160, 193, 244–245, 260, 271–272, 279–280, 282, 290, 296n; strict construction of, 187–194, 244–245, 272; constructive interpretation of, 193, 195, 244, 269–273, 282–283; and treaty-making power, 222; and First Amendment, 232, 260

Constitutional Convention, 19–20, 109, 189, 229, 288–295, 302

Constitutionalism: and class, 12, 70, 101, 112–114, 120, 212; and Anti-Federalists, 24, 51, 54–61, 79; culture of, 184, 214, 270–271; and public opinion, 248–255; and states' rights, 294–302

Construction Construed (Taylor), 283

Constructive contempt, 131–132

Cooper, Thomas, 233–234, 291–295, 297, 301–302

Countryman (pseud.), 156

Coxe, Tench, 163

Customer, A (pseud.), 41

Dedham, Mass., 236

Democracy, 118–120, 140

Democratic Federalist, A (pseud.), 37, 124–125

Democratic ideals, 3, 37, 98–99

Democratic-Republicans, 7; as successors to Anti-Federalism, 13, 164–177; in Middle Atlantic, 179; and strict construction, 187–191, 193–194; societies of, 195–200, 217–218; and Jay Treaty, 222, 229; and dissenting constitutional theory, 231–232, 238–245; and Alien and Sedition Acts, 231–237; and federalism, 237–245

Despotism, 63, 69, 93, 107–108
DeWitt, John (pseud.), 58–59
Discourse on the Constitution (Calhoun), 296
Disquisition on Government (Calhoun), 296
Duane, William, 285

Elections, 30, 148, 161, 275–278. *See also individual states*
Electoral districts, 151n
Elite Anti-Federalists, 26, 43; rhetorical strategies of, 38, 155–156; and constitutionalism, 51, 54–61, 79; and political contacts, 52–53; and religion, 57; and federalism, 61–62; and the legislature, 69, 91; and localism, 72–74; and representation, 205, 213n, 215. *See also* Whigs
Elliot, Jonathan, 295n
Ellsworth, Oliver, 29
Embargo (1807), 276, 301
Equity, 66, 181–183, 185
Executive power, 31, 34

Federal Farmer (pseud. of Melancton Smith?): writings of, 25–26, 38–39, 88–94, 227–228; as moderate critic of Constitution, 45, 64; on natural aristocracy, 96–99; and notion of democracy, 119; on freedom of the press, 124; on political economy, 175
Federal Gazette (Washington, D.C.), 128
Federal government, 60–61
Federalism: and centralization, 11; compact theory of, 60–68, 237–245, 260–262, 271–272; and elite Anti-Federalists, 61–62, 79; and localism, 62, 64–67; and middling Anti-Federalists, 119–120; and states' rights, 178–181, 276–277; and Democratic-Republicans, 192–194, 201–218; and liberty, 265–266
Federalist, The [Jay, Hamilton, Madison]: and constitutional interpretation, 189, 227–228, 268–269; as critique of consolidation, 243–244, 279–280, 282–284, 287, 289–292, 294, 296–297

Federalists: and constitutionalism, 2; and the Constitution, 20, 167; and the public sphere, 21, 75, 104, 183–184, 260; and view of Anti-Federalists, 27, 89, 153–157, 168–169; and Anti-Federalist writings, 28–29; in agreement with Anti-Federalists, 32, 100; as aristocratic, 41, 107, 183; as correspondents with Anti-Federalists, 43–44; writings of, 46; on Anti-Federalist writing, 46–47, 81; and Bill of Rights, 58; and centralized government, 73, 106, 139–140, 217; class divisions among, 81–82; and Anti-Federalists, 109–114; and the press, 121–123; and seditious libel, 125; and Blackstonian doctrine, 132–133; and view of democracy, 140, 151; and elections, 148–153; as court party, 164–165; and Democratic-Republican Societies, 196–197, 200–201; and Whiskey Rebellion, 205; and founding dialogue with Anti-Federalists, 222–228, 269, 278, 280, 287–288; and Alien and Sedition Acts, 231, 253n
Findley, William: writings of, 26, 40–41, 99, 172, 176; as middling Anti-Federalist, 82, 168–171; and middling democracy, 117, 133–134, 215–216; on elections, 148–149, 168–171; on political economy, 175, 181–184, 192; and Whiskey Rebellion, 201, 203–207; and Anti-Federalist writings, 225–226
Freeman's Journal (Philadelphia), 123
French Revolution, 196
Friend to the People, A (pseud.), 123

Gallatin, Albert: political opinions of, 172, 176, 179–181; political economy of, 192; and Whiskey Rebellion, 201–204; and Anti-Federalist writings, 226; and strict construction, 231–232; correspondence of, with Wortman, 254–256, 258
Gates, Horatio, 141
Genêt, Edmond, 276–278, 289
Genuine Information, The (Martin), 37–38, 52, 57, 73–74, 254, 267–268n, 288
German religious sects, 102

Gerry, Elbridge: "Objections to Signing the National Constitution," 25, 28–30, 46, 52n, 267n; as elite Anti-Federalist, 26, 53; Federalist attacks on, 27; and plebeian radicalism, 117–118, 155; candidacy of, 154–157; on proposed amendments, 158, 161–162; on political economy, 175; on *The Federalist*, 189–190

Giles, William, 199

Goldwater, Barry, 304

"Good Old '75," 153

Gorham, Nathaniel, 29

Government of Nature Delineated, The (Aristocrotis [Petrikin]), 47, 107–109

Grayson, William: as elite Anti-Federalist, 53; on jury trials, 66–67; speech by, 76–77; on proposed amendments, 159; on court party, 164

Great Britain: and plebeian culture, 109n; and finance, 177; and Jay Treaty, 222

Greenleaf, Ann, 233

Greenleaf, Thomas, 37, 112, 172, 233

Habermas, Jürgen, 8n, 10n, 77–78n, 306

Hamilton, Alexander: economic agenda of, 174–187; and Anti-Federalist opposition, 177–187, 278; and broad construction, 187–194, 293; and whiskey tax, 200; and *The Federalist*, 282

Hamiltonianism, 7, 174–187, 278–288

Hampden (pseud. of Spencer Roane), 37, 280–283

Harrisburg, Pa.: convention at, 137–142, 224, 226, 228

Havens, Jonathan, 223

Hay, George, 235

Hayden, Tom, 304

Hazard, Ebenezer, 122–123

Henry, Patrick, 159, 164, 235, 281, 293

Honestus (pseud. of Benjamin Austin?), 153

Honorius (pseud.), 150–151

House of Representatives, U.S.: and the Constitution, 30; wealthy in, 45; Federalists in, 157; and Democratic-Republican Societies, 198–199; and treaty-making power, 222–229; as check on judiciary, 293

Hutchinson, James, 85–87, 124. *See also* Old Whig, An

Independent Gazetteer (Philadelphia), 84, 128, 135, 172

Individual rights, 257–258, 283–284

Innes, Harry, 212–214

Inquiry into the Origin and Course of Political Parties (Van Buren), 299

Jackson, Andrew, 2, 298–299

Jackson, Jonathan: *Thoughts upon the Political Situation*, 151–152

Jacksonianism, 2

Jacobinism, 196–197

Jay, John, 222

Jay Treaty (1795), 222, 229

Jefferson, Thomas: and constitutional theory, 13; and perception of Anti-Federalism, 166, 168, 173; and states' rights, 239; and Virginia and Kentucky Resolutions, 239–242; and Alien and Sedition Acts, 269; presidency of, 275–278; and John Taylor's constitutional writings, 285; and 1800 election, 298, 301–302. *See also* Jeffersonianism

Jeffersonianism, 2, 7, 68n, 166n, 172n, 268–269

Jeffersonian Republicans, 275–278

Jeremiad, 70–71

Judges: role of, 130–132

Judicial power: and Anti-Federalist opposition, 31, 33, 90–91, 108, 121, 130–131, 159–160, 267, 286; and Federalists, 131–134, 300

Judicial review, 242

Jurisprudence, 14, 38, 44, 263–273

Jury, 126–127, 134, 212–213, 252

Jury trial: threat to, by Constitution, 31–32, 59–60, 66–67; as judicial control, 87–88, 90–92, 108; and seditious libel, 125–126, 130–131, 262

Kent, James: *Commentaries on American Law*, 264
Kentucky, 212–214
Kentucky Resolutions, 13, 239–242, 245

Lamb, John, 39, 88, 136–137
Landholder, A (pseud.), 29
Lansing, John, 25, 277
Lear, Tobias, 75
Lee, Arthur: and Cincinnatus essays, 37–38, 44, 57, 60, 69–70, 126; and Anti-Federalist readings, 43–44
Lee, Richard Henry, 39, 88; letter of, to Edmund Randolph, 25, 66, 75–76, 267n; as elite Anti-Federalist, 26, 53; Federalist attacks on, 27; on James Wilson, 43; and Anti-Federalist readings, 43–44, 47–48; and role of judiciary, 67–68; on republican government, 68–69, 72; on the public sphere, 74, 78; on proposed amendments, 162; and court party, 164–165; on political economy, 175
Legislature, federal, 91, 99–100
Legislature, state, 178, 188, 248–249, 287
Lewis, William, 148
Libby, Orin Grant, 304
Libel, 125–126, 261, 265–266
Liberalism, 5–7, 54–55, 180
Libertarianism, 95–96, 263, 265
Liberty: and proposed Constitution, 54–58, 85–87, 89; and Democratic-Republicans, 257–258, 273, 283–284
Liberty poles, 208–209, 236
Literacy, 26n
Localism: and federalism, 62, 64–67; and small republic, 72–74, 79; and middling Anti-Federalists, 109–114, 299; and plebeian Anti-Federalists, 114–116; and elections, 148–153; and Federalists, 151–152; and Democratic-Republicans, 206, 209, 213–215, 249–253, 284–285; and Anti-Federalist legacy, 305–307
Locke, John, 55, 256
Logan, George, 172
Lyon, Matthew, 233

Mably, Gabriel Bonnet de, 55–56
Maclay, William, 164–165
Madison, James: and constitutional theory, 13; and "Report of 1800," 14, 241–245, 269, 275, 281–282, 295–296, 301; and view of Anti-Federalism, 27, 166–168, 171, 173; on proposed government, 63–64; and small republic, 73n; on elections, 149, 151–152; and amendments, 158, 160, 162–163; "A Candid State of Parties," 166–168; and strict construction, 188–191, 193, 199; and representation, 215; and Anti-Federalist writings, 227; and original intent, 228–229; and Virginia and Kentucky Resolutions, 239–241; *National Gazette* essays of, 247–253; presidential election of, 276–278; on states' laws, 289–290. *See also* Publius
Maine, 151n
Manning, William: on political economy, 176, 184–187, 193; and Whiskey Rebellion, 204n, 210–211; and localist government, 216; and original intent, 229; "Key of Libberty," 249–253
Marcellus (pseud.), 155
Marshall, John: and Marshall Court, 14, 280, 283–285, 293, 301; and *McCulloch v. Maryland*, 278–288
Martin, Luther: and the Constitution, 51–52; as elite Anti-Federalist, 53; and state interests, 59, 61–63, 188n; on jury trial, 59–61; and *McCulloch v. Maryland*, 279. See also *Genuine Information, The*
Maryland: amendments in, 32, 227; ratification convention of, 44; debate in, over elections, 148, 150; Federalists in, 150; and *McCulloch v. Maryland*, 278–288
Marylander, A (pseud.), 150
Mason, George: "Objections to the Constitution," 24n, 25, 29–30, 51–52, 74–75, 267–268n; as elite Anti-Federalist, 26, 53, 69, 281; and the public sphere, 78; on proposed amendments, 162–163
Massachusetts: Anti-Federalists in, 28, 78, 81; Federalists in, 29; ratifying convention of, 31–32; on proposed amend-

ments, 32, 136; Anti-Federalist pamphlets in, 88; debate in, over elections, 148, 150–157

Massachusetts Centinel (Boston), 28, 153

McCulloch v. Maryland, 14, 278–288, 301

McKean, Thomas, 110, 113, 127–133, 208

Mennonites, 102

Merchants, 102, 119

Middle Atlantic: Democratic-Republicans in, 179; commercial interests in, 276; and *McCulloch v. Maryland,* 285, 301

Middling Anti-Federalists: rhetorical strategies of, 38–39, 155–156; in New York and Pennsylvania, 82–96, 285–286; and constitutionalism, 83, 85–96; and natural aristocracy, 96–97, 258–259, 286; and plebeian radicalism, 116–119; and Harrisburg convention, 138–140, 142–143; and taxation, 175, 183; and Whiskey Rebellion, 201–207, 213–214. *See also* Brutus; Cato; Federal Farmer; Old Whig, An

Militia: state control of, 33–34, 60, 92–93, 108, 161; local control of, 114

Minot, George, 81

Mobocracy: and Anti-Federalists, 93, 116–117, 138, 153; and Federalists, 114; and Democratic-Republicans, 197, 236

Monarchy, 31

Monroe, James, 53

Montesquieu, Charles de Secondat, baron de: cited, 38, 44, 58, 62

Montgomery, John, 81

Muhlenberg, Frederick A., 158

National Gazette (Philadelphia), 173, 177, 247

Neville, John, 200

New Deal, 304

New England: Anti-Federalists in, 22, 53; literary culture of, 26n, 71n; and political economy, 176; Democratic-Republican Societies in, 198; and Virginia and Kentucky Resolutions, 240; and the Embargo, 276

New Hampshire, 32, 75, 88, 227

New Jersey, 277

Newspapers: and Anti-Federalism, 14; circulation of, 25–26, 129; as forum for Anti-Federalist writings, 37, 43–44, 84, 100, 105–106, 114–120, 122–124; in backcountry, 45–46, 84; and Federalist letters, 76; as forum for Democratic-Republicans, 173–174, 177; and public opinion, 247–253

Newton, Pa., 211

New York (city): Federalists in, 81–82n; newspapers in, 84; crowds in, 111–112; and Democratic-Republican Society, 196–197

New York (state): Anti-Federalists in, 22, 82, 119; and Anti-Federalists writings, 26, 44, 75, 81–82n, 88, 94–96; and constitutional amendments, 32, 227; constitutional convention of, 136; ratifying convention of, 279; and states' rights, 298–302. *See also* Brutus; Clinton, George; Federal Farmer

New-York Journal, 37, 84, 172

Nicholas, Philip Norborne, 235

Nicholson, John, 46–48, 83–84

North Carolina: Anti-Federalists in, 22, 115n; and amendments, 32, 227; Anti-Federalist pamphlets in, 88; ratifying convention of, 189

Northumberland Gazette (Pa.), 234

Nullification Crisis, 294–302

Numa (Federalist author), 148

Observations on the New Constitution (Warren), 37, 52n, 55–57, 59, 70–72

Officer of the Late Continental Army, An (pseud. of William Findley), 26, 40–41, 99

Old Man, An, 110

Old Patriots, 53, 55

Old Whig, An (pseud. of James Hutchinson): on uniformity of Anti-Federalism, 27–28; on the Constitution, 31–32, 37, 45; in backcountry, 46; on individual rights, 85–87, 90, 101, 119; on freedom of the press, 124

One of the Common People (pseud.), 37, 132

Originalism, 3–4

Osgood, Samuel, 155

Oswald, Eleazer, 127–136, 142, 172, 262

Page, John, 268

Paine, Thomas, 268

Pamphlets: and definition of Anti-Federalism, 14; circulation of, 25, 88, 267n; and Anti-Federalist satire, 47, 107–109

Patterson, William, 165

Pennsylvania: Anti-Federalists in, 22, 82, 115–116, 119; proposed amendments in, 32; and Anti-Federalist writings, 75, 88; and constitutionalism, 85–87; state constitution of, 100–101, 132–134; and seditious libel cases, 127; and second convention movement, 136–143; debate in, over elections, 148–150; and Bank of North America, 182n; ratifying convention of, 189–190, 225–226, 228; and Whiskey Rebellion, 200–213. See also Carlisle, Pa.; Centinel; Petrikin, William

Pennsylvania Mercury and Universal Advertiser (Philadelphia), 148

Pennsylvania Test Acts, 101–102

Peters, Richard, 141

Petrikin, William: radicalism of, 46–48, 107–109, 216–217; and Carlisle riot, 115; and second Pennsylvania convention, 137–140

Pettit, Charles, 138–140

Philadelphia: and Anti-Federalist writings, 44; newspapers in, 84; and Democratic-Republican Society, 197; and *McCulloch v. Maryland,* 285. See also Constitutional Convention

Philadelphiensis (pseud. of Benjamin Workman?), 40, 46, 99, 105–106, 125

Plebeian, A (pseud. of Melancton Smith?), 27, 37, 39

Plebeian Anti-Federalists: and identity, 41; and Centinel, 46–47; and politicians, 71–72; writings of, 84–85, 184–187; and Carlisle riot, 109–114; and direct democracy, 120; and individual liberty, 120; at Harrisburg convention, 137–139, 142–143; and radicalism, 141–142, 210–212; on political economy, 175, 192; and Democratic-Republican Societies, 196; and populism, 196, 201, 206–209, 213–214, 216–218, 251–253, 304–305; and constitutionalism, 251–253

Political economy, 175–187

Popular Anti-Federalists: on aristocracy, 40, 104–105, 107, 110–111, 119; rhetorical strategies of, 40; and plebeian Anti-Federalists, 40–41, 81–84, 99–106; and constitutionalism, 101, 112–114, 120, 212; and judicial power, 108; and religion, 109

Populist politics. *See* Plebeian Anti-Federalists: and populism

Post Office, U.S., 122–123

President, 33–34, 158

Presidential electors, 276

Press: and the public sphere, 21, 104–106, 115–117, 135–136; and support for the Constitution, 21. *See also* Newspapers

—freedom of: and Bill of Rights, 31; and proposed amendments, 32; importance of, in republic, 103–104, 112; and Federalists, 121–123, 135, 183–184, 186; and Constitution, 124–125, 242–243; and localism, 250–253; and Alien and Sedition Acts, 253–273

Progressive historians, 22n

Protestantism, 8, 57, 94

Pseudonymous writings, 20, 37, 76, 105. *See also individual authors and works*

Public opinion, 247–253

Public sphere, 10; and political discourse, 11, 19–50, 74–80, 186–187, 243–247, 306; and press, 104–106, 115–117, 135–136; and the crowd, 111–113, 115–117, 120, 217; and middling Anti-Federalists, 143; as focus of Democratic-Republicans, 173–174, 183, 196–199, 254–262, 273; and popular meetings, 201–204, 236–237

Publius (pseud.), 2, 243–244, 268–269, 280, 282, 287, 297

Quakers, 102

Randolph, Edmund, 30n, 43, 75–76, 288
Ratification: debate on, 7, 8n, 136–143,
    147–153, 164–171, 268; and state conven-
    tions, 9n, 14, 20, 21n, 31–42, 139, 187–190,
    225–230, 244, 264–268, 270, 279–280
Rawle, William, 207n
Reagan, Ronald, 305
Real Farmer (pseud.), 152–153
Rehnquist, William, 305n
Religion, 8, 57, 94, 101–102, 109
"Report of 1800" (Madison), 14, 241–245,
    269, 275, 281–282, 295–296, 301
Representation: and the Constitution, 31,
    33, 45, 69–70, 101, 119, 163; and congres-
    sional elections, 148–153
Republic: small, 68–74, 78–80, 106
Republican, A (pseud.), 154
Republican Federalist (pseud.), 78
Republicanism: and Anti-Federalism, 7–8,
    293; as classical, 37, 55–56; and wealth,
    102–104, 177, 179–187, 258
Revolutionary war: and rhetoric, 35n; and
    localism, 65; ideals of, 71, 85; and debt
    assumption, 174–175, 179, 181, 185–186
Rhetoric: and class, 11, 35, 38–42, 155–156;
    and paranoia, 123–125, 142
Rhode Island, 22, 115n
Richmond Enquirer (Va.), 285
Richmond Examiner (Va.), 234
Rights: and public good, 86–87, 89–90,
    112; and property, 112–113; of individual,
    257–258, 283–284. *See also* States' rights
Ritchie, Thomas, 285
Ritual: and Anti-Federalist protest, 41–42,
    110–111, 208–209, 236
Roane, Spencer, 37, 53, 280–283
Rodney, Thomas, 81

Satire, 41, 47
Scottish moral philosophy, 256–258
Sedgwick, Theodore, 224
Sedition Act. *See* Alien and Sedition Acts
Senate, U.S., 30–31, 157, 223–227
Separation of powers, 30–31, 33–34

Shaysism, 116–117, 153–156
Shays's Rebellion, 116, 210–211
Shippen, William, Jr., 68–69
Sidney (pseud.), 37
Simpson, Stephen, 286–287
*Sketch of the Finances of the United States,
    A* (Gallatin), 179
Smilie, John, 85–87, 117, 124, 126, 205
Smith, Melancton: as A Plebeian, 27, 37, 39;
    as Federal Farmer, 38–39, 88–94; as mid-
    dling Anti-Federalist, 83–84; on second
    convention, 136
Smith, William, 223
Son of Liberty, A (pseud.), 94–96
South: and role of honor, 77n; agrarians
    in, 175, 178–179, 275–278, 280, 285–286;
    and Whiskey Rebellion, 212; and Alien
    and Sedition laws, 235; jurisprudence
    in, 264n, 279–280; and election of 1800,
    275–278; and states' rights, 294–298
South Carolina, 22, 32, 115n, 291, 294–298,
    302
"Speech at a Public Meeting in Philadel-
    phia" (Wilson), 28, 38, 40–43
Stamp Act, 124
Standing army, 31–33
State: and control of militia, 33–34, 60,
    92–93, 108, 161; as model of small repub-
    lic, 73–74, 106; as representative of peo-
    ple, 99, 215–216; and jury trials, 125–127;
    and Constitution, 139; libel prosecutions
    in, 261, 265–266
State conventions: and ratification, 14, 20,
    21n, 34–42, 139, 187–190, 225–230, 244,
    266–267, 270; and amendments, 31–34,
    136, 158, 161–163
States' rights: and nullification, 14, 294–
    298, 302; and Bill of Rights, 33; and sov-
    ereignty, 61–63; and federalism, 178–181,
    276–277; compact theory of, 238–241,
    245, 282–284; and constitutionalism,
    294–302
Story, Joseph, 293
Supreme Court, U.S., 3n, 281–284, 290,
    300. *See also* Marshall, John

Taxation: direct, 31, 160; state power of, 33, 61; and individual freedom, 94–95, 121, 159, 185; and freedom of the press, 124; and middle class, 175, 183. *See also* Whiskey Rebellion

Taylor, John, of Caroline: and political opinions, 172, 176–177, 180–181; and strict construction, 187–188; on representation, 213n, 215; and compact theory of states' rights, 239, 296–297; and challenge to Marshall Court, 280, 283–285, 301; *New Views of the Constitution*, 289–292, 302

Thoughts upon the Political Situation (Native of Boston [Jackson]), 151–152

Tocqueville, Alexis de, 299

Treaties, 33, 223–227

"Treatise Concerning Political Enquiry" (Wortman), 255

Truth (pseud.), 154

Tucker, St. George, 262n, 263–273, 282

Tucker, Thomas Tudor, 158, 160–161

Turner, Frederick Jackson, 304

Tyler, John, 79

Valerius (pseud.), 76

Van Buren, Martin, 14, 298–302, 307

Vermont, 198

Virginia: Anti-Federalists in, 22, 53; and proposed amendments, 32, 227; and religious freedom, 57n; separation of law from equity in, 66; and jury trials, 66–68; and Anti-Federalist writings, 75, 88; Federalists in, 76; and public sphere, 76–77; ratifying convention of, 189, 264–265, 268, 279–280; and treaty-making power, 224n; and *McCulloch v. Maryland*, 280–288

Virginia Independent Chronicle (Richmond), 76

Virginia Resolutions, 13, 239–243, 245

Virtue, 86–87, 97–98, 103–104

Warren, James, 53

Warren, Mercy Otis, 37, 52n, 55–57, 59, 70–72

Washington, George: on the Constitution, 20; on Anti-Federalists, 123; as new president, 170; on Democratic-Republican Societies, 197–201

Wealth, 45, 102–104, 177, 179–187, 258

Westpensbro, Pa., 211

Whigs: and pen names, 37; and disinterested virtue, 44, 56, 71–72, 80; and Old Republicans, 53, 55; and despotism, 69, 93. *See also* Old Whig, An

Whiskey Rebellion, 200–213, 216–218

Whitehill, Robert, 32, 117, 124n, 138, 209–210

Wilson, James: "Speech at a Public Meeting in Philadelphia," 28, 38, 40–43; as James de Caledonia, 41–42; effigy of, 110; on seditious libel, 125; on elections, 151–152

Winthrop, James, 53; as Agrippa, 58, 64–65

Wirt, William, 235

Wood, Gordon S.: and Revolutionary rhetoric, 35n; on constitutionalism, 54n, 72–73n, 83n; on middle class, 82n; on identity of Federal Farmer, 88n; on conspiracy theory, 124n

Workman, Benjamin, 125. *See also* Philadelphiensis

Wortman, Tunis, 254–262, 272–273

"X to the Electors of Middlesex," 155

X. Z. (pseud.), 131–132

Yates, Abraham, 82, 95, 96n

Yates, Robert: "Reasons of Dissent," 25, 30n; *Secret Proceedings and Debates of the Federal Convention*, 255, 288–295, 297, 302

Yeomanry, 37–39, 92–93

Zenger, John Peter, 125–126, 130, 134